MW01285963

"Being and finality—these principles account for all of reality. Nothing is without them. Nothing makes sense without them. And this is why *The Order of Things* is so important: it introduces readers to the dynamics of real being. In this book, Father Garrigou-Lagrange teaches his readers how to think. Dr. Minerd's editorial notes reveal that he is not only a faithful translator of Garrigou's words but also an insightful expositor of Garrigou's thought. Thus, we rejoice in the fact that this 'handbook of wisdom' is once again available to a world that continues to search—rather desperately—for the order of things."

—CAJETAN CUDDY, O.P.
Dominican House of Studies

"Maritain described the conditions in which Garrigou-Lagrange wrote this work to Yves Simon as laboring 'without a secretary, crushed by courses to teach, in the *Collegio Angelico* in isolation from everyone, facing exhausting work all alone,' saying further, 'If we have understood something regarding Thomism, it is thanks to him . . .' In *The Order of Things*, Garrigou-Lagrange brought forth an uneven but illuminative and profound work, powerfully communicating the insights of the *philosophia perennis*. Matthew Minerd performs a very great service in rendering this work available to English readers. Those who see that *scientia* is not merely a source but a *habitus* will feel renewed gratitude to the old Dominican Master and to his insightful translator."

—STEVEN A. LONG
Ave Maria University

"An English translation of this neglected work of Garrigou-Lagrange's is long overdue. We are in Matthew Minerd's debt for bringing it off at last. The availability of *Le réalisme du principe de finalité* to English-speaking audiences is sure to further the current revival of interest in Scholastic thought and Aristotelian philosophy."

—EDWARD FESER
Pasadena City College

"This book should shed light on Thomas's understanding of the final cause even for those who are skeptical about Garrigou-Lagrange's approach to metaphysics. Furthermore, I know of no better instance of how a Thomist might argue for the existence of God on the basis of the natural desire for happiness."

—THOMAS M. OSBORNE, JR.
University of St. Thomas

THE ORDER
OF THINGS

THE ORDER
OF THINGS

THE REALISM OF THE
PRINCIPLE OF FINALITY

Fr. Réginald Garrigou-Lagrange, O.P.
Translated by Matthew K. Minerd

EMMAUS
ACADEMIC

Steubenville, Ohio
www.emmausacademic.com

EMMAUS
A C A D E M I C

Steubenville, Ohio
www.emmausacademic.com
A Division of The St. Paul Center for Biblical Theology
Editor-in-Chief: Scott Hahn
1468 Parkview Circle
Steubenville, Ohio 43952

The original French edition *Le realism du principe de finalité* was published in Paris in 1932 by Desclée de Brouwer.

Library of Congress Cataloging-in-Publication Data
Names: Garrigou-Lagrange, Réginald, 1877-1964, author. | Minerd, Matthew
   K., translator.
Title: The order of things : the realism of the principle of finality / Fr,
   Réginald Garrigou-Lagrange, O.P. ; translated by Matthew K. Minerd.
Other titles: Réalisme du principe de finalité. English
Description: Steubenville, Ohio : Emmaus Academic, 2020. | Includes index.
   | Summary: "This text is an exploration of the metaphysical principle,
   "Every agent acts for an end." It is split into two parts, the first
   being primarily pedagogical and general, the second topical. In the
   first part, Fr. Garrigou-Lagrange sets forth the basics of the
   Aristotelian metaphysics of teleology, defending its place as a central
   point of metaphysics. After defending its per se nota character, he
   summarizes a number of main corollaries to the principle, primarily
   within the perspective established by traditional Thomistic accounts of
   metaphysics, doing so in a way that is pedagogically sensitive yet
   speculatively profound. In the second half, he gathers together a number

of articles which he had written, each having some connection with themes concerning teleology. Thematically, the texts consider the finality and teleology of the human intellect and will, along with the way that the principle of finality sheds light on certain problems associated with the distinction between faith and reason. Finally, the text ends with an important essay on the principle of the mutual interdependence of causes, causae ad invicem sunt causae, sed in diverso genere"-- Provided by publisher.

Identifiers: LCCN 2020037839 (print) | LCCN 2020037840 (ebook) | ISBN 9781949013726 (hardcover) | ISBN 9781949013733 (paperback) | ISBN 9781949013740 (ebook)

Subjects: LCSH: Teleology.

Classification: LCC BD542 .G313 2020 (print) | LCC BD542 (ebook) | DDC

124--dc23

LC record available at https://lccn.loc.gov/2020037839

LC ebook record available at https://lccn.loc.gov/2020037840

Cover design and layout by Emily Demary

Cover image: *God creating Heaven and Earth*, The loggia of Raphael (1483–1520) Raffaello Sanzio da Urbino, Hermitage Museum, Villach, Austria

"Every being acts for an end, from the grain of sand all the way to God."

"Our intellect knows its own, proper finality: to judge in conformity to the nature and existence of things and to raise itself to their First Cause and Ultimate End."

TABLE OF CONTENTS

FOREWORD

Jon Kirwan, D.Phil. (Oxon.)
February 22, 2020
Chair of Saint Peter

In his celebrated 1998 encyclical *Fides et Ratio*, Pope St. John Paul II warned that certain modern rationalist and materialist philosophies pose an existential threat to Catholic theology and faith by denying the human person a "full metaphysical range" of knowing. He declared that the *sine qua non* condition for any authentic philosophy is an *implicit first philosophy*, having as its most fundamental constituents the first, universal principles of common-sense realism, such as the principles of non-contradiction, finality, and causality, on which all rational discourse depends, as well as any possible understanding of reality itself.

Just a decade earlier, then Cardinal Ratzinger, in his famous Erasmus Lecture, called for an "open philosophy" to combat the post-Kantian thought that had gravely wounded Scripture studies, there citing as an example the importance of the principle of finality operative in the very movement of salvation history. He declared that for Aquinas, drawing on fifteen hundred years of thought,

> it is the case that nature, the heavenly bodies, things in general, life, and time follow a course—that is, a movement directed toward a goal, then we can discover the true meaning that lay hidden, so to speak, within them. This meaning, which comes to light at the end of the movement, transcends whatever

meaning might be revealed in the individual sections of the course followed.[1]

The question then arises: why would two such renowned Catholic intellectuals (and popes no less!) stress the philosophical, theological, and exegetical importance of such a neglected philosophical concept, the principle of finality? This volume, written by the Catholic philosopher who labored to defend the notion of finality in the modern age more than any other, proposes to answer that question. Indeed, Reginald Garrigou-Lagrange was convinced that to concede the ground of this contested principle was to lose the very battle for Catholic intellectual thought itself, as reality itself depends upon this principle, so crisply and clearly summarized in the formula drawn from the common-sense philosophy of Aristotle: "*Omne agens agit propter finem*; every agent acts on account for an end."

Originally published in 1932, *The Order of Things* (in French, *Le réalisme du principe de finalité*) is a collection of articles dedicated to articulating the importance of the principle of finality, defending it from modern attacks, and exploring its implications for various aspects of Catholic philosophy and theology. Far from being a haphazard and incoherent collection of journal articles, this book represents the clear and cohesive continuation of a philosophical project that began during the Modernist crisis at the turn of the 20th century. Moreover, it brings to the Anglophone world Garrigou's oft-forgotten philosophical work from the 1920s and early 30s, a decade usually overshadowed by his much-celebrated work in Catholic spirituality, as exemplified in *Three Ages of the Interior Life*.[2] Those who are interested in Garrigou's larger project should recognize that this volume in many ways represents the philosophical bridge between his is early work during the Modernist crisis and his later exchanges with the *nouvelle théologie* in the late 1940s.

Thus, in this introduction, in order to highlight this volume's

---

[1] Benedict XVI, "Biblical Interpretation in Conflict," in *God's Word: Scripture—Tradition—Office*, ed. Peter Hünermann and Thomas Söding, trans. Henry Taylor (San Francisco: Ignatius Press, 2008), 119.

[2] Reginald Garrigou-Lagrange, *Three Ages of the Interior Life*, vols. 1 and 2, trans. Timothea Doyle (St. Louis: B. Herder, 1947–1948).

contextual importance, I shall first provide an overview of Garrigou's oeuvre, followed by brief sketches of the thirteen chapters, highlighting their central themes and overall continuity. However, before I begin, permit one brief note about the translator, Dr. Matthew Minerd.

Laboring in the well-worn hills of Appalachia, Minerd has devotedly worked to bring Garrigou-Lagrange's philosophical oeuvre to the English-speaking world. Already published or on the way are his translations of *Sens commun*, both volumes of *De revelatione*, *Le Sens du Mystère et le Clair-Obscur Intellectuel: Nature et Surnature*, a volume of Garrigou's *nouvelle théologie* writings, and an edited and translated volume of assorted philosophical writings, *Philosophizing in Faith: Essays on the Beginning and End of Wisdom*. All English-speaking readers who are lovers of wisdom should rejoice at such an ample harvesting of fruits drawn from one of the great modern sons of St. Dominic.

Four Phases

The expanse of Garrigou's bibliography is staggering.[3] Numbering almost eight hundred entries, its contours reflect precisely those of Catholic thought in the first half of the twentieth century. His years of intense production stretched from 1907 to 1951, a period that spans the Modernist crisis and St. Pius X's *Pascendi Dominici Gregis* (1907) and the *nouvelle théologie* affair along with Pius XII's *Humani Generis* (1942–1950). Moreover, his oeuvre is difficult to historically categorize, because his intellectual interests develop and flower from year to year, growing together here, and then apart there, only to converge and intertwine once again. When his thought sprouts new branches, he rarely leaves them unpruned for long, and his bibliography develops from philosophy to theology to spirituality, to mysticism and asceticism, to the theology of the priesthood and the nature of the sacrifice of the Mass, and on and on. Thus, periodization can be messy, not only on this account, but also because his books at times contain repeated

---

[3] See Benedetto Zorcolo, "Bibliografia del P. Garrigou-Lagrange," *Angelicum* 42(1965): 200–272.

themes, and even versions of earlier works. Sometimes books tell the real story, sometimes articles, and sometimes ecclesiastical and political events furnish the best historical boundaries. Nonetheless, a basic intellectual biography might settle on four productive phases in Garrigou's life, the first and the last being the most well-known.

The first period (1907-1919), characterized by his involvement in the Modernist crisis and work during the First World War, is foundational and directed much of his later work, especially the influential articles that emerged out of the *nouvelle théologie* affair in the 1940s. Three programmatic books emerged during these years: *Sens commun* (1909), *God, His Existence and His Nature* (1914), and *De revelatione* (1918), all books that would pass through a number of editions through the course of his lengthy career.

Sens commun was an influential response to the Modernist critique of knowledge, especially as expressed by the Bergsonian mathematician Édouard Le Roy. According to Garrigou-Lagrange, common sense lays at the foundation of all knowledge of the basic principles that then are scrutinized and defended by philosophical wisdom. Following the sober methodology of Aristotle and not that of philosophers such as Thomas Reid and Théodore Jouffroy, the Dominican theologian characterized common sense apprehension (through increasing abstraction, from empirical-experiential apprehension to fully philosophical abstraction) as providing the foundation for a realism which could readily connect the more abstruse reflection of philosophical meditation to the basic data of human experience. His teacher, Ambroise Gardeil, who adopted his common-sense philosophy, summarized this well in *Le Donné révélé et la théologie*:

> Spontaneously, the intellect sees in these notions something which is utterly universal, thereby touching the very structure of universal being. And likewise in a spontaneous manner, it also makes use of them to formulate principles which it conceives of as being self-evident...[Indeed,] the spontaneous datum of our awareness—made up of notions, principles, and inferences which are immediate and necessary—is itself also a datum of common sense, that is to say, of instinctive intui-

tion, which is not reasoned out and analyzed, bearing its proof within itself, and playing a role in the intellectual order akin to that which is played by the common sense faculty in the order of [sense] experience as the centralizing power bringing together everything perceived through the external senses. Indeed, this whole ensemble is ordinarily what is meant when one speaks of using the expression "Truths of common sense." Obviously, this common sense is both properly human and intellectual, since it forms and elaborates its notions in view of the idea of being, as is characteristic in human affirmations.

This real continuity and homogeneity between the data of common sense and metaphysical categories is of the utmost importance, since it manifests the possibility that, through the spontaneous movement of their intelligence, all men, without distinction, can attain those expressions of reality in which a rigorous analysis will come to manifest absolute and irreformable notions. We owe to this continuity and homogeneity the power that we all have to attain, through the terms of common sense, the meaning of dogmatic formulae which are expressed in metaphysical terms.[4]

With the absolute character of the metaphysical affirmation established, Garrigou treats of revelation, the truth of which is based on its homogeneity with the absolute character of the human affirmation. Through the inspiration given to the prophets, a supernaturalized human language of divine things is made possible. Gardeil continues:

Undoubtedly, Christian revelation is an interior grace, but it is one that is *social*, not individual. Consequently, what it communicates must be *infinitely transmissible*, in its original form, to humanity, to whom the Spirit of God *Qui locutus est per prophetas*, gives it, once and for all, using inspired men as

---

[4] Ambroise Gardeil, *Le Donné révélé et la théologie* (Paris: J. Gabalda, 1910), 33–34, my translation.

His instruments. Hence, inspiration must fall not on human sentiment, walled up within itself and forever equivocal in its expression, but rather, on *human affirmation, which alone is capable of being fixed and absolute.*[5]

With a certitude that is intrinsically divine, yet also extrinsically reasonable, faith adheres to such truths with a certitude greater even than what reason has in its knowledge of the first principles. And this body of doctrine—those truths held *de fide*—form the basis for what could be called "Christian common sense," the foundational truths of the supernatural order. *De revelatione* is devoted to spelling out the very character of such knowledge, carefully distinguishing what therein belongs to the supernatural light of faith and what is, at least objectively, of the order of reason. In this era, we see much that lies in line with the work of his great master, Gardeil, himself a master of theological methodology.

The second phase (1919-1932) begins to reveal Garrigou's creative breadth and pastoral sensitivity. He was deeply involved in the mysticism-contemplation-asceticism debates of the 1920s, writing extensively for the journal *La vie spirituelle*. During this era, we sense that he is beginning to work out his unified theory of spirituality, drawing extensively on St. John of the Cross, publishing *Christian Perfection and Contemplation, according to St. Thomas Aquinas and St. John of the Cross* (1923) and *The Love of God and the Cross of Jesus* (1929).[6] Also, during this decade, he wrote initial treatments of subjects to which he frequently returned: the Blessed Virgin Mary (1924), predestination (1924), the priesthood of Christ (1926), and ecclesiology (1928), as well scores of book reviews reflecting wide engagement, and the first articles of what would be the *Three Ages of the Interior Life*.[7] In

---

5 Gardeil, Le Donné, 74.

6 Réginald Garrigou-Lagrange, *Christian Perfection and Contemplation*, trans. Sr. M. Timothea Doyle, O.P. (St. Louis: B. Herder, 1937); Garrigou-Lagrange, *The Love of God and the Cross of Jesus Christ*, vols. 1 and 2, trans. Sr. Jeanne Maria, O.P. (St. Louis: B. Herder, 1947).

7 Réginald Garrigou-Lagrange, *Les Dominicaines de la Vierge: Discours prononcéper le Père Garrigou-Lagrange, OP pour l'affiliation de la Compagnie de la Vierge à l'Ordre*

addition to all of this, Garrigou wrote several important philosophical articles—precisely those contained in this volume, which substantially developed what he had already begun to formulate in *Sens commun* and *God: His Existence and His Nature*.

The third phase (1933–1937) was the shortest period. While continuing to publish in the above areas, Garrigou wrote a significant number of Christology articles, mostly in *La vie spirituelle*, as well in *The Sense of Mystery* (1934), which engaged in the influential Christian philosophy debate (1930-1936), which was in certain ways a philosophical precursor to the *nouvelle théologie* controversy.

The final phase (1938-1951) saw the publication of his commentaries on the *Summa Theologica*, beginning in 1938, as well as his involvement in the *nouvelle théologie* affair. His engagement was prompted by the debate surrounding Marie-Dominique Chenu's work in the 1930s on Revelation and dogma, especially his *Une école de théologie*, as well as the 1942 dissertation by Henri Bouillard, *Conversion et grâce chez St. Thomas d'Aquin*.[8] In the midst of discussing the particular problem indicated in the title of his work, Bouillard also ventured to make strong remarks concerning the historical character of dogma and theology, (in)famously insisting that "a theology that is not current is a false theology." In a famous article in the *Angelicum* ("La Nouvelle théologie où va-t-elle?"), followed by a series of subsequent articles in the same periodical, Garrigou-Lagrange claimed that the path recommended by Bouillard would lead back to Modernism. Although Bouillard claimed to preserve the absolute character of dogmatic assertions, he allowed for such conceptual relativization in their formulation that, to Garrigou's eyes, Bouillard was returning to position far too

---

de Saint-Dominique le 18 Janvers 1924 (Rome: Le Prieuré de la Vierge, 1924); Réginald Garrigou-Lagrange, "Un nouvel examen de la predestination physique. Peut-on trouver chez Saint Thomas de la germe du Molinisme?" *Revue Thomiste* 29, no. 7 (1924): 494–518; Réginald Garrigou-Lagrange, "La Sacerdoce de Christ," *La vie spirituelle* 14 (1926): 469–490; Réginald Garrigou-Lagrange, "L'Église corps mystique du Christ," *La vie spirituelle* 18 (1928): 6–23; Réginald Garrigou-Lagrange, "Les trois âges de la vie spirituelle," *La vie spirituelle* 23 (1930): 5–23.

8   M.-D. Chenu, *Une école de théologie: le Saulchoir* (Kain-lez-Tournai: Le Saulchoir, 1937); Henri Bouillard, *Conversion et grâce chez St. Thomas d'Aquin* (Paris: Aubier, 1944).

close to that of Le Roy, which he had fought so vigorously four decades earlier. This affair ignited several series of interchanges between the Dominicans and Jesuits in the *Revue Thomiste*, in which a number of Garrigou-Lagrange's own students defended a position which ultimately was his own, although argued in a way that attempted to be less combative. (Though, truth be told, while the elderly Dominican's prose might have been more insistent than that of his younger confreres, it was by far not as strong as the common lore of the so-called "sacred monster of Thomism" would lead one to think. Moreover, his students, including Michel Labourdette, were not afraid to be quite pointed, though charitable, in their critique of the claims made by the Fourvière Jesuits. That is, however, a matter to be adjudicated elsewhere.)

What is relevant to the current volume is the common aversion to Aristotle shared by Bouillard and Le Roy, the latter of whom famously claimed that scholasticism insisted on a double conversion, first to Aristotle and then to Christianity. Thus, at stake for Garrigou was the same fundamental issue: the reality of common sense language in philosophy as well as theology. It was not a question of imposing Aristotelianism; rather, Aristotle merely had articulated the structure of common-sense knowing better than anyone else. Indeed, from the beginning to the end of his career, Garrigou was careful even to qualify this claim: the common-sense foundations of supernatural knowledge are themselves free from the overall systematic connections involved in Aristotelianism *as a given philosophical system*. As Gardeil summed it up: "In order to accomplish this work, must the simple concepts of revelation embrace the modalities of Aristotelianism? *Yes* and *no*. No, if we are speaking of the systematic and personal mindset of the Philosopher. Yes, if we are speaking of the human mindset itself, provided that it is present in the Aristotelian mentality through the data of common sense."[9]

Thus, in the final major exchange of his career in the 1940s, he harnessed the concepts and arguments he first developed during the Modernist crisis, and in light of this, we can see quite clearly the unity

---

[9] Gardeil, *Le Donné*, 306–307. See Reginald Garrigou-Lagrange, *Sens commun: La philosophie de l'être et les formules dogmatiques*, 4th ed. (Paris: Desclée de Brouwer, 1936), 361–399.

of Garrigou-Lagrange's philosophical thought, though, between the first and last phases of his productivity, his philosophical thought was not stagnant. In *Sens commun*, he is concerned with addressing a question of fundamental importance, the solution to which will understandably permeate all of his later philosophical (and theological) work: how does the mind naturally seize on and articulate objective reality? There, he declares that the *first principles* (non-contradiction / identity, being, substance, causality, and finality) of common sense follow one after the other, even though they are not deduced from one another. An order exists among the first metaphysical principles, and the denial of one casts all the rest into danger. Thus, it is important for the philosopher to meditate upon the principle of finality, an important first principle of being itself. Although Garrigou discusses this topic briefly in his earlier works, he deepened his reflection on the importance of this vital concept in a number of important articles written in the 1920s and 1930s, collecting and publishing them in 1932 in this volume, originally titled *Le réalisme du principe de finalité*.[10]

The Order of Things

Far from lacking coherence and integration, Garrigou arranges the articles into two main parts. The first part, entitled "Being, Becoming, and Finality," consists of five articles The first two, written in the form of a dialogue, were both published in the *Revue Thomiste*, respectively in 1930 and 1931 and attempt to refute the "reappearance of the philosophy of becoming" and its attendant denial of the principle of non-contradiction, a philosophical notion essential to Garrigou's notion of common sense and in particular his argument for Realism. This was relevant, because French philosophy in the early 1930s had seen the emergence of Hegelianism, as well as a revival of ancient Greek thought and the continued importance of Henri Bergson's vitalist philosophy. The first article, "The Primacy of Being over Becoming," is

---

[10] Reginald Garrigou-Lagrange, *Le réalisme du principe de finalité* (Paris: Desclée de Brouwer, 1932).

a dialogue between Heraclitus, Parmenides, Plato, and Aristotle. Aristotle wins the day, arguing for being over becoming: "Thus, *becoming* is rendered *intelligible* by its relations to *being*, the first intelligible object, and these relations rest upon the division of being into potency and act."[11] This distinction is required in order to save both the principle of non-contradiction (Parmenides) and becoming (Heraclitus). Moreover, the principle of non-contradiction ultimately illuminates the path to affirming that the changing, bodily world is not Being itself but, instead, must have a Supreme Cause.

The second article pits Aristotle against a sophist in a wide-ranging dialogue. After successfully arguing for finality against the sophist's notion of chance, Garrigou continues his discussion, leading his interlocutor from the sensible *per accidens* to the aptitude or fitness of things: "The end is something determinate and fitting, to which that which is *fitted* to attain itself *tends*."[12] Moreover the dialogue makes clear a theme to which Garrigou-Lagrange returned many times throughout his career: a denial of the principle of non-contradiction (implied, for example, in the denial of the principle of finality) necessarily leads to nihilism.[13]

Following these dialogues is the article, also written in 1930, "The Philosophy of Becoming and Pseudo-Finality," in which Garrigou sees the return of Modernism reflected in the reissue of a well-known book by Édouard Le Roy, *Le problème de Dieu*, which renewed the latter's argument against the traditional proofs for the existence of God: "they rest on an unacceptable common-sense distinction, namely '[the distinction] of the mover and the mobile, of movement and its subject, of act and potency.'"[14] Thus, Le Roy concluded that "in the end, we must

---

[11] Reginald Garrigou-Lagrange, *The Order of Things*, (Steubenville, OH: Emmaus Academic, 2020), 26.

[12] Garrigou, *The Order of Things*, 53.

[13] This is the repeated theme in whole of the section "*Garrigou Pugnans*: Critical Philosophical Essays" in Reginald Garrigou-Lagrange, *Philosophizing in Faith: Essays on the Beginning and End of Wisdom*, ed. and trans. Matthew K. Minerd (Providence, RI: Cluny Media, 2019), 253–324. Also, see Reginald Garrigou-Lagrange, "Conclusion: the true God or radical absurdity," in *God: His Existence and His Nature*, trans. Bede Rose (St. Louis: B. Herder, 1949), 436–446.

[14] Garrigou, *The Order of Things*, 68.

always return to *religious experience.*"[15] Garrigou, however, argued that Le Roy's proofs constitute a "faux, imitation form" of Augustine and Pascal, ultimately relying for validity on the faith and common sense of those who read his arguments, not upon the arguments themselves. And where there seems to be a declaration of finality (in a vitalistic and Bergsonian sense), this is nothing more than an appearance: "Here we are faced only with a *pseudo-finality*: the attraction of a Sovereign Good that will never be constituted in itself, deserving only the name and not the reality of the 'Sovereign Good.'"[16]

While the first three articles function as a propaedeutic, the final two articles in this first section constitute a kind of formal introduction to the question of finality. In "The Principle of Finality," the oldest in the volume (*Revue Thomiste*, 1921), Garrigou reviews modern philosophy's rejection of the principle of finality, along with critiques which are more contemporary to his own day. Following this, he summarizes how a number of other thinkers defined the principle of finality, himself providing a precise formulation of it, along with an argument for its necessity, critiquing various materialist positions and concluding with a careful parsing of the various senses of the analogical notion of goodness.

The final article in Part I, "The Principles Subordinated to the Principle of Finality," examines the metaphysical principles which rely upon the principle of finality, at least implicitly, including, for example, the principle of induction, the principle of the mutual influence of causes upon each other, and the primacy of subordination over coordination in a series of related activities. According to Garrigou, the principles subordinated to that of finality also call for further elucidation given that the principle of finality grounds not only the proofs for the existence of God but also the *first principle of practical reason* (do good and avoid evil). Even in this brief form, the reader immediately perceives the manifold consequences that follow upon one's position concerning finality. This chapter should be read in conjunction with the final essay in the volume, devoted to the principle of the mutual influence of

---

[15] Garrigou, *The Order of Things*, 71.
[16] Garrigou, *The Order of Things*, 89.

causes (*causae sunt invicem causae sed in diverso genere*).

Part II is composed of eight articles that explore the primary applications of the principle of finality in relation to the intellect and the
will. The first article, "Realism and the Finality of Our Intellect," sets
out to show that, far from being naïve, Thomist realism in fact has a
coherent and sophisticated methodology confirmed with "unshakable
certitude" through the intellect's own self-reflection. In the first half
of this article, Garrigou provides a defense of common sense realism
and its principles, which seems to be an extension of the first part of
Sens commun, and in the second half, he enters into a fascinating debate
with Etienne Gilson on the question of critical realism. Garrigou gently
critiques Gilson's position (while affirming much that they have in
common), for the latter held that any form of "critical realism" would
ultimately find itself trapped, wandering far from reality upon Cartesian byways. For his own part, Fr. Garrigou-Lagrange offers a spirited
attack on idealism and Descartes's *Cogito*, drawing heavily on the principle of identity.[17]

In the following article, "The Mystery of Knowledge and its Finality," Garrigou attempts to show that far from suppressing the mystery of
critical realism, common sense realism in fact recognizes *mystery* much
more than do materialism, empiricism or idealism, which he argues all
suppress mystery by reducing either spirit to matter or matter to spirit.
Indeed, everyday experience makes it easy to miss a mystery that is
forever right before our eyes: "how can a wholly material thing impress
within our senses a representative likeness that is, in some manner,
spiritual, even under the influence of light, understood according to
the principle of the subordination of causes?"[18] To reduce this mystery
would be "to diminish the beauty of the chiaroscuro painted by God
himself." This article touches deeply on themes drawn out in *The Sense
of Mystery*, and was written during the same period and reflects the
early years of the 1930s, when Aristotelian Thomism was under attack
by some quarters for allegedly lacking an appreciation for mystery.

---

[17] For a summary of this debate see Jason West, "Gilson, Maritain, and Garrigou-Lagrange
on the Possibility of Critical Realism," *Maritain Studies/Etudes Maritainiennes* 17
(2001): 49–69.

[18] Garrigou, *The Order of Things*, 179.

Here, the very possibility of sensation, as well as intellection, provide the Dominican theologian with a profound domain for reflecting on the mystery of reality and of human experience.

Following this essay, Garrigou continues by discussing the finality of the intellect, which he takes up in the following article, "The First Datum of Our Intellect and the March from the Known to the Unknown." After passing through an extended critique of modern theories of knowing, he argues that the analogy of being alone can refute pantheism and agnosticism. The entire edifice of human intellectual knowledge is built upon the foundation of analogy. At once humble but also opening up to transcendent knowledge, it is only by understanding the analogical nature of the human intellect's finalization by being that one can avoid the pitfalls of other, deficient outlooks concerning these matters.

Building on this realism of the intellect's finality, in the following article, "The Proper Order for Teaching the Philosophical Sciences," Garrigou-Lagrange provides an extended critique of the influence of Christian Wolff, arguing that natural philosophy should be taught before metaphysics, as this traditional ordering corresponds to the nature of the intellect in its slow, analogical pathways toward knowledge of being as such. The influence of the Wolff-inspired curriculum of studies had left its marks on many of the ecclesiastical faculties (as is even evidenced in Garrigou's own language). It became commonplace, moreover, to accuse scholastics like Garrigou of being covert Wolffians.[19] Yet, as this article makes clear, the Dominican Theologian holds nothing of the sort. To teach ontology / metaphysics at the head of philosophy poses grave problems. Here his own words are worth citing in full:

> Were we to place ontology immediately after logic, we would risk *not perceiving* the profound meaning of the fundamental

---

[19] See Ralph McInerny, "Cry Wolff" in *Praeambula fidei: Thomism and the God of the Philosophers* (Washington, DC: Catholic University of America Press, 2006), 121ff. For Fr. Garrigou-Lagrange's response to Gilson during their lifetime see Reginald Garrigou-Lagrange, "L'immuntabilité du dogme selon le Concile du Vatican, et le relativisme," *Angelicum* 26, no. 4 (1949): 321–322.

theses of Aristotelian and Thomistic metaphysics, above all the *meaning and value of the division of being into potency and act...*

To present this doctrine concerning potency and act in another, *a priori* manner, as happens in many manuals, is to suggest that it has merely fallen from the sky or that it is only a simple, pseudo-philosophical translation of common language, whose worth still must be established, as has been said by Henri Bergson. In such an undertaking, there is no longer any profundity in analyzing matters. One is content with some quasi-nominal definitions of potency and act, and it is no longer clear how and why potency differs from the simply possible being, from privation, as well as from imperfect act or from the Leibnizian force / virtuality, which is only an impeded form of act . . .

We must admit this fact: this fundamental chapter of metaphysics, i.e. regarding act and potency, remains in a state of great intellectual poverty in many manuals when we compare them to the first two books of Aristotle's *Physics* and to the commentary that St. Thomas left us concerning it. The method of discovery has been too neglected in philosophy, a method which is founded on the very nature of our intellect, the very least among created intellects.[20]

In such comments, we see the profound insight of a mind well-attuned to the needs of philosophical intelligence—indeed, so clearly stated that accusations of him being prey to a kind of "manualist system"[21] should be put to rest.

The fifth article in Part II, "The Finality and Realism of the Will: Does the Natural Desire for Happiness Prove God's Existence," sees

---

[20] Garrigou, *The Order of Things*, 240.

[21] See, for example, Brian van Hove, "Looking Back at 'Humani Generis,'" *Homiletic and Pastoral Review*, https://www.hprweb.com/2013/12/looking-back-at-humani-generis/.

Garrigou enter the renewed debate over the natural desire for God, which had been resuscitated after the War by the Rousselot disciple Guy de Broglie. Writing in the *Angelicum* in 1931, Garrigou builds on the principle of finality to offer a proof for the existence of God from the innate desire for God impressed upon the will in its natural formal object (though without blurring the orders of nature and grace). Clearly, he believes that he is providing an argument akin to that made by his own teacher, Gardeil, in a series of articles written in the late 1800s and early 1900s, indeed, with Garrigou recommending that these be published in their own right (a recommendation that he reiterated in his *in memoriam* remarks written upon the death of Gardeil).[22] Moreover, although Garrigou does not name his interlocutors, the footnotes bear witness to the recent debates in his own days. That same year Henri de Lubac had contributed his first article on the subject, later included in his controversial *Surnaturel* (1946). As with all of Garrigou's proofs, he claims to chart a path between ontologism and nominalism, starting "with the existing facts and, by means of the metaphysical principles of efficient causality and finality, [leading] to God by legitimate paths."[23]

In "Moral Realism: Finality and the Formation of Conscience," Garrigou takes up the long-debated Scholastic issue of probabilism in the formation of conscience. The Thomistic position is connected to the principle of finality, here discussed in relation to the importance of the virtues in rectifying the will and sense appetites: "Qualis unusquisque est, talis finis videtur ei… As our will and our sensibility are well or poorly disposed, the true final end appears to us as being sovereignly befitting or not."[24] As regards the formation of conscience, Fr. Garrigou-Lagrange believes that this basic principle, applied to the central importance of prudence in the moral life,[25] can help solve many of the problems and confusions which emerged in the probabilism

---

[22] See Reginald Garrigou-Lagrange, "In memoriam: Le Père A. Gardeil," *Revue Thomiste* (1931): 797–808.

[23] Garrigou, *The Order of Things*, 271.

[24] Garrigou, *The Order of Things*, 285.

[25] A topic discussed also at greater length in Garrigou-Lagrange, "Prudence's Place in the Organism of the Virtues," in *Philosophizing in Faith*, 153–170; Garrigou-Lagrange, "Prudence and the Interior Life," in *The Three Ages of the Interior Life*, 77–89.

debates undertaken most vigorously between the 17th and 18th centuries. Without disdaining the "weighing of probabilities," what is needed above all is the virtue of *prudence*, by which one commands oneself to perform acts befitting of virtue. However, forever looking higher still, the theologian notes the full breadth of what is at stake: "This principle explains not only the certitude of the prudential judgment or of conscience, but also explains the Spirit's *gift of wisdom* which makes us judge concerning Divine things by means of a connaturality or sympathy founded on the love of God. He who loves God with all his strength is increasingly led to judge that God is truly the Sovereign Good for him."[26]

In "Realism and Our Knowledge of the Supernatural," Garrigou wades into an area of apologetics much contested since the Modernist crisis and explores the realism of the supernatural and its different forms. Here too, he insists that the principle of finality provides significant illumination for these contested questions. The questions thus answered are of great importance: "Are miracles knowable? If they are, what kind of knowledge absolutely requires the supernatural light of infused faith? How do we pass from the loftiest natural knowledge to that of the order of grace?"[27] Once more, we have themes that spanned his whole career, best attested to in *De revelatione*, which he edited on multiple occasions through many years of teaching. For Garrigou-Lagrange there is a danger here, on the one hand, of rationalism, which reduces faith to a form of knowledge discursively following from the evidence offered by rational credibility, and on the other, a kind of fideism which reduces the rational knowledge of credibility to the supernatural act of faith. He critiques both positions, the first being held by thinkers such as Scotus, Molina, and in the modern age, Billot, and the latter position, defended recently by Rousselot and his student Joseph Huby. Garrigou's position, the Thomist position, lies between these two extremes, preserving both the natural finality of miracles as well as the supernatural finality of infused faith:

---

[26] Garrigou, *The Order of Things*, 285–286.
[27] Garrigou, *The Order of Things*, 287.

If miracles, as signs of revelation, were not naturally knowable, they would not be as the Church says: '(They are) a sign that is well adapted to the understanding of all ages and of all men, even those of the present time.' In other words, they would lose their finality.—On the other hand, if the formal object of infused faith could be attained without infused faith, it would be *useless*. So too would infused hope and infused charity be useless if their formal objects were accessible to the *natural good will* of the man who historically knows the Gospels and the miracles that confirm it.[28]

The final article, "The Principle of Reciprocal Influence in Causes and its Main Applications," provides a fitting conclusion, wherein Garrigou defends the Thomistic principle concerning the reciprocal influences of the four causes on each other. Exposited by an author with excellent pedagogical skills, this article lays out the implications of this principle, one that is closely connected to that of finality. The contents of this chapter illuminate a number of great philosophical and theological issues, deepening the most foundational principles needed for discussing matters pertaining to knowledge, volition, and the infusion of grace. It deserves study in any course of Thomist metaphysics.

This valuable work is an enduring testimony to the philosophical achievement of Garrigou-Lagrange. By no means is it a loose and disconnected collection of scattered and unrelated articles. Nor should it be dismissed as being cluttered with facile redundancy. For Garrigou, in the principle of finality, reality itself is at stake, and an understanding of it is the door to wisdom:

If wisdom (i.e., the highest of sciences) is knowledge of things through their loftiest causes, and if the end is the first cause, the principle of finality is indeed one of the loftiest principles of the loftiest of the sciences. We now more clearly see the virtualities that it contains and the immense regions of the

---

[28] Garrigou, *The Order of Things*, 318.

intelligible world that it illuminates. They can all be embraced, by fixing our gaze upon its formula: "Every being acts for an end," from the grain of sand, which tends to the center of the earth for the cohesion of the universe, all the way to God, Who does all that He does for the manifestation of His Goodness.[29]

---

[29] Garrigou, *The Order of Things*, 347.

Translator's Introduction

Omne agens agit propter finem. Every agent acts for an end. It is a dictum well known among philosophers. While we live in an era that doubts the importance of formal and final causality, Thomists hold this principle as a self-evident, or *per se nota*, proposition. Indeed, the principle is somewhat taken for granted, and its profound analogical scope is easily placed in the background of our awareness. We all experience such "forgetfulness of finality" and therefore can benefit much from reading the sage reflections of Fr. Garrigou-Lagrange concerning the scope and importance of this metaphysical principle.

Le réalisme du principe de finalité is a wide-ranging text. It not only treats of finality from the classic Aristotelian and Thomistic perspectives of natural philosophy and metaphysics; it also includes discussions of the role of finality in matters concerning the realism of human knowledge, the nature of moral knowledge, and the distinction between the natural and supernatural orders. Significant portions of the text are based on articles previously published by Fr. Garrigou-Lagrange, articles which he brought together into this volume along with several important guiding chapters concerning the overall theme of this book.

Granted, one might find such a gathering of texts to be methodologically suspect. Indeed, in a letter to Jacques Maritain, a young Yves Simon accused Fr. Garrigou-Lagrange of composing a text that had only an accidental unity, stitched together by mere verbal artifices. He remarked, "An article concerning the physiology of the pancreas could have been connected to a theory of finality as readily as a work concerning [Édouard] Le Roy or one concerning the order of philosophical disciplines."[1] Then, later in the letter, Simon voices his frustration at what he takes to be Fr. Garrigou-Lagrange's repeated use of the same examples and themes in his various works: "When we (Jacques[2] and I) made our division of philosophical minds into *dialectical minds* and those that are *sickly and weak*, we hesitated for a moment about how we should classify Fr. Garrigou-Lagrange. Today, hesitation is no longer permitted."[3]

In response to this comment, Maritain scolded his young friend:

> I am not pleased by the qualifier that you applied to Fr. Garrigou's book in a preceding letter—no! Fortunately, there was a mitigating post-script—*secundum quid.*[4] Do not be inhumane. Give some small thought to the conditions in which Fr. Garrigou-Lagrange must work—without a secretary, crushed by courses to teach, in the *Collegio Angelico* in isolation from everyone, facing exhausting work all alone. Were you to recall this, you would reproach him less for repetitions and short-comings in composition. If we have understood something regarding Thomism, it is thanks to him—you know this to be true. We must not forget this fact, as well as the work of *mittentes in lacrymis semina sua* [those who are sowing their seeds in tears]. Ungrateful youth![5]

Simon responded in haste to Maritain's letter:

> I offer even more repentance regarding poor Fr. Garrigou. You know very well that I too share in your thoughts regarding his merit and the recognition that all of us owe him. I was wrong

---

[1] Jacques Maritain and Yves Simon, *Correspondance*, vol. 1 *Les années françaises (1927–1940)*, ed. Florian Michel (Tours: CLD, 2008), 105 (30 July 1932).

[2] He likely refers here to Jacques de Monélon.

[3] Maritain and Simon, *Correspondance*, 105.

[4] In the earlier letter, Simon remarks that the matter is to be personal between him and Maritain, especially given that Simon wrote to Garrigou a letter to congratulate him on his book quite warmly (calling it a "très beau livre").

[5] Maritain and Simon, *Correspondance*, 109 (28 August 1932).

to be so fixed upon defects that have such a glaring appearance because they are primarily surface-level. Let us say that Fr. Garrigou-Lagrange is the prince of the *dialectical minds*, but that the rigors of his destiny impose upon him the language of *sickly and weak minds* [*valétudinaires*].[6]

Simon and Maritain would have mixed relations with Fr. Garrigou-Lagrange in future years. Nonetheless, their exchange helps to provide a hermeneutic for understanding the nature of the text before us.

Just as some theologians are touched with a spirit for historical or philological criticism, Fr. Garrigou-Lagrange (being a rather characteristic Dominican) was touched with a philosophical and metaphysical spirit. Thus, he produced works such as *Le réalisme du principe de finalité*, existing on the borders of philosophy and theology. Certainly, there are chapters in this text that are purely philosophical. However, to various degrees, the reader will notice the presence of a higher light—the light of faith—strengthening the philosophy being treated and giving the Dominican a self-surety of gait that one does not find in a philosopher who strives to write in a manner congenial to those not sharing that same supernatural light. This does not undermine Fr. Garrigou-Lagrange's claims. However, it does implicitly structure his prose and make certain demands of the reader regarding the light under which the text should be read. We should always remember that it is a text of philosophy that is strengthened by light of faith.[7]

Fr. Garrigou-Lagrange's philosophy is the self-assured philosophy of a theologian. The impact of faith radiates throughout this book. One is reminded of a similar character that could be found in Jacques Maritain, who is sometimes critiqued for a tone that seems self-assured and strident, as well as too "theological" in its concerns. Simon was an explorer who thought like a more "purified" philosopher. He addressed issues in detail and with closer restrictions on the subjective presuppositions expected of his readers. I pray that the reader will excuse me

---

6 Maritain and Simon, *Correspondance*, 111 (30 August 1932).
7 Granted, at times, it is explicitly theological. The transition is a bit fluid, and the reader should keep this in mind as well.

for one more citation from Simon, a remark pertaining to Maritain but applicable to Fr. Garrigou-Lagrange's philosophical work in *Le réalisme du principe de finalité*:

> In the discussions which have been going on for over thirty years on the notion of "Christian philosophy," Maritain has never failed to recall, against any possible misunderstanding, that this expression designates a *state* of philosophy, not an essence. If it designated an essence, it would be granted that philosophy receives premises from revelation, and of the great statements of St. Thomas concerning philosophy, theology, and their relationship, nothing would be left.
>
> When these positions are clearly formulated, the question remains as to whether it is desirable that philosophical issues be treated in a state of abstraction or in a concrete condition of association with the problems of our supernatural destiny. I would not hesitate to say that it is, to a large extent, a question of calling. I am strongly attracted by the method of isolation because it furnishes special guaranties of epistemological purity and logical rigor. To be sure, Maritain will never be tempted to use a revealed premise in a philosophical treatment. But there can be no doubt that his calling is that of the Christian philosopher who generally treats philosophical issues in the particular *state* that they assume by reason of their relation to Christian faith and theology.[8]

In introducing this book, I have felt it necessary to belabor these points because they help us to situate Fr. Garrigou-Lagrange's work in its proper place. *Le réalisme du principe de finalité* resounds with the words of the self-assured lion of Roman Thomism. With clarity, they voice the thoughts and concerns of what we might call a theological philosopher (or a philosophical theologian—depending on the topic).

---

[8]   John Howard Griffin and Yves R. Simon, *Jacques Maritain: Homage in Words and Pictures* (Albany: Magi Books, 1974), 13–14.

His philosophical *habitus* are animated from the depths of his soul by a light that is loftier than that of "pure reason alone." Here, a theologian speaks to us with clarity about some important philosophical truths.[9] Living as we do in an era of cultural confusion, we would do well to heed the words of a priest who was a master of the three wisdoms that enable the human intellect to soar: metaphysical wisdom, theological wisdom, and the Spirit's quasi-experiential gift of wisdom.

On the whole, all lengthy citations from Scripture in this volume are taken from the Revised Standard Version of the Bible. On occasion, it made sense to translate directly from the text at hand, especially when the sense of the Vulgate's Latin was presupposed in an explanation being presented. All citations from Denzinger are amended to follow the numeration and translations from Ignatius Press's 43rd edition of the text. When Garrigou-Lagrange translates Latin texts into French, I have generally translated from the original Latin. Notes in the text address any minor concerns that arise occasionally in this regard. Throughout my translation, I have included some pedagogical footnotes. In these, I have tried to provide the reader with remarks concerning points that may well be opaque, often citing the works of Thomists in the same tradition as that of Fr. Garrigou-Lagrange.

Throughout the text, bibliographical references required expansion, as Fr. Garrigou-Lagrange often did not provide complete reference information in his citations. Unless otherwise noted, when possible, I have chosen to cite the relevant pages of the English translations of Garrigou-Lagrange's works, as this will be more useful for English readers than would be French citations. I have foregone citing Walshe's adaptation and abridgment of *De revelatione*, given that it is not a full translation of the work. Emmaus Academic is planning a translation of this text in the near future.

No work comes about without the involvement of many hands. Special thanks go to Andrew Jones and, especially, Chris Erickson for shepherding this project throughout its process of publication. I was in need of able guides and gladly had his kind help. Personal thanks go to David Capan for insightful copyediting remarks during the translation

---

9 And, on occasion, some important theological truths as well.

process. Likewise, I express particular thanks to Scott Hahn, Matthew Levering, and Fr. Thomas Joseph White, O.P. for their initial interest in this project. Also, I would be remiss were I not to thank my dear friends James Bryan and Thomas Howes for indulging in my ruminations on matters treated in this text, Gregory Doolan for helping to clarify several reference issues, Joan Grimbert for providing insight on some French turns of phrase, Fr. Maurus Mount, O.S.B. for help with several such Latin texts, and above all to Benjamin Heidgerken for his helpful reading and critique of the full text. And, of course, I owe great gratitude to the hardworking production staff involved in editing, layout, and the lovely cover design for this text: Chris Erickson, Julia Snyder, Alex Renn, and Emily Demary. Finally, special thanks go to my wife Courtney, who has listened at length to the ramblings of a translator. And let us, together, give thanks God Almighty for the grace to begin this project and bring it to completion—not only from my pen but in your souls as you read. This translation is dedicated to the memory and eternal rest of Dr. John N. Deely, who passed from this mortal vale as I was completing the first draft of this translation. *Eternal Memory! Vichnaya pamyat'!*

Author's Introduction

As a contemplative once said, life is far too short to read and meditate upon books that are not those of the saints and men of genius. From this perspective, these pages concerning finality would be useless if they did not have as their end highlighting a principle that is dear to the greatest philosophers and the greatest theologians, while also stressing the primary consequences that they have drawn from it.

We will quickly proceed to what is essential in these matters, leaving in oblivion that which has justly fallen there, and we will not bestow too great importance to this or that philosopher who might be in the vogue today but who will no longer be spoken of by anyone in perhaps fifty years' time.

If one devotes a year to reflection on the writings of someone like Descartes, Spinoza, or Kant, one should devote a quarter of a century to meditation upon the works of Plato and Aristotle, and it is fitting to devote all of one's life to reading St. Augustine and St. Thomas.

Many histories of philosophy present us with nearly all teachings as though they were situated at the same level. In them, the most foolish of such doctrines seem to have the same value as those that are the wisest, merely because such foolish thoughts are proposed in a somewhat original way. Francis Bacon or the odd George Berkeley are given as much space as is Thomas Aquinas, if not more. Likewise, in these histories, we are presented with Kant's unreasonable idea that our knowledge of things, far from depending upon them, is, instead, their measure, as though this were something brilliant. Similarly, we are presented with the idea that *the causality* by which heat expands iron (or that by which the murderer kills another person) is only a subjective category of our mind, of such a nature that outside of our thought there is perhaps neither expansion of iron nor a murderer who can be justly condemned.

Once the superiority of genius is confused with these extreme positions *extra rationis viam* [outside the way of reason], we are thereby reduced to a merely-horizontal view of things, making the loftiest truths descend to the same level as the most lamentable errors. It does not take long for God and matter to come together on the very same level in the domain of what is unknowable.

By contrast, when we receive the light of glory and see all things in God, we will have a vertical view of things according to the true scale of values—from the Supreme Truth and Sovereign Good all the way to the most distant ramblings of error and evil. We will then see the value of Divine Revelation and, below that, the value of the *first principles* of natural reason that, in their own order, come from God.

In this work, we wish to highlight certain principles that are of capital importance in traditional philosophy, especially in the Thomistic synthesis. Without them, this synthesis would be completely unintelligible, but under their light, all the parts of this synthesis are illuminated.

We are concerned here above all with the principle of finality, "Every agent acts for an end," from the lowliest stone, which tends toward the center of the earth for the sake of the universe's cohesion, all the way to God Who governs all worlds so as to manifest His Goodness. If it is the case that there is no efficient causality without finality and if the end is, as Aristotle himself says, the first of the causes, then this principle is no less important than is the principle of efficient causality,

Since the time of Hume and Kant, numerous works have been written about the value of the principle of efficient causality, which we have discussed at greater length elsewhere.[1] However, despite the importance of the principle of finality, it is often left in the shadows.

We will see that its twofold ontological and transcendent value presupposes the *primacy of being over becoming*, a primacy that is expressed

---

[1] See Réginald Garrigou-Lagrange, *God: His Existence and His Nature: A Thomistic Solution of Certain Agnostic Antinomies*, vol. 1, trans. Bede Rose (St. Louis: B. Herder, 1949).

with various nuances in the fundamental teachings of Plato and Aristotle, as well as in those of the great Christian Doctors.

We will insist upon two highly important applications of the principle of finality by discussing the finality of our intellect and that of our will. We will bring our work to a close by studying an often-forgotten corollary of the principle of finality, namely, "*causae ad invicem sunt causae, sed in diverso genere,* causes are causes of each other, though in different genera of causality." To express the classic formula another way: there is a reciprocal dependence between the end and the agent, as well as between matter and form. This often-neglected principle is, in fact, rather fruitful. It enables us to grasp the mystery of things, revealing the true scope of this mystery, placing us in the presence of one of the most captivating chiaroscuros, one that is found everywhere that we must pass from one order to another—from inanimate matter to plant life, from plant life to sense life, from sense life to intellectual life, and from intellectual life to the life of grace.

Above all, these pages aim to show that the principle of finality leads to God no less than does the principle of efficient causality. They are intimately united: *no efficient causality without finality.* Hence, as we will see, it follows that in every domain, *the order of agents* (i.e., their subordination) *corresponds to the order of ends.* Every coordination presupposes subordination, and one would commit a grave error by confusing them.

We will present the first two, fundamental chapters concerning *being, becoming, and finality* in the form of a dialogue. We have chosen this format in order to provide a livelier presentation of these topics and, in this way, to better manifest the unity of the teachings that are necessarily connected (according to Aristotle and his disciples) to the true formulation of the principle of finality, its universality, its absolute necessity, and to its double ontological and transcendent value.

Part I

BEING, BECOMING, AND FINALITY

IN ORDER TO KNOW whether there is finality in reality and to know what it is—i.e, in what way it differs from blind, materialistic fatalism, as well as from chance—we must first to ask ourselves what *reality* itself is. Is it constituted by *that which is* or by *that which becomes*? What is the relationship of becoming with being, and if it is not the primary reality, what are its causes?

Chapter One

THE PRIMACY OF BEING OVER BECOMING

The Origin of the Distinction Between Act and Potency, as well as the Origin of the Theory of the Four Causes

The reappearance of the philosophy of becoming, which denies the ontological value of the principle of contradiction[1] (or, of identity) and identifies being with becoming (as well as God with self-creative evolution[2]), invites us to take up a study of the problem of becoming in order to furnish ourselves with a better account of the true foundation of the traditional proofs of the existence of God.

In order to make our thought about these matters livelier, we will present the first two chapters of this work in the form of a dialogue, referring above all to the fragments of Heraclitus and Parmenides, to Plato's *Sophist*, and to the first book of Aristotle's *Physics*, as well as to the fourth, ninth, and twelfth books of his *Metaphysics*.[3]

---

[1] [Tr. note: On a few occasions, Fr. Garrigou-Lagrange refers to it as the principle of non-contradiction. I have opted to translate him directly in each case.]

[2] See Édouard Le Roy, *Le problème de dieu*, 5th ed. (Paris: L'artisan du livre, 1929). [Tr. note: Édouard Le Roy (1870–1954) was a French Catholic intellectual who had work concerning the development of dogma placed upon the Index. He was a vitalist of sorts, being associated with Henri Bergson, as well as Fr. Pierre Teilhard de Chardin.]

[3] [Tr. note: I generally maintain Fr. Garrigou-Lagrange's references to these books by their numbers. He is referring to *Metaphysics* Γ, Θ, and Λ. Since he does not engage in the historical-textual question about the unity of the *Metaphysics*, he

* * *

Heraclitus: *That which is, is not; and that which is not, is, for all things become and nothing is abiding,* nothing remains what it is. Perpetual change fills the sensible world. The fertile earth thrives upon the water that it absorbs, fire lives upon the death of air, the animal draws its life from the death of plants, man lives upon the death of animals, and then his body returns to the earth through decay—and so forth. Every being is made of transformed fire; air and water are made of fire on the way toward extinction or rebirth; earth is made of extinct fire, and it flares up anew at the hour marked out by Destiny. The soul is an emanation of celestial fire. The universe is a fire on the way of ceaseless transformation, an eternally living fire that periodically flares up and again is extinguished. It did not begin to exist; it will not come to an end. The world is eternally reborn from its ashes. Every day it dies so that it may live anew. It lives its death and it kills its life. In our body, there is constantly an assimilation of food and a perpetual deassimilation. We too kill our life and live our death, until we are replaced by others. One human generation lives upon the death of the one preceding it, as a wave upon the sea is formed from another one that has disappeared, and so on in endless undulation. Nothing comes to a halt. Doctrines are formed and decline; so too for peoples and races. Nothing abides, except for the law of eternal return.

That which is, is not, for before we are able to finish saying, "It is," it ceases to be—just as that which is lifted to the highest point on the wheel of fortune quickly descends therefrom, or as the pendulum in motion only appears to stop, in order that it may immediately swing back in the opposite direction.

understandably follows the numerical identification of books as they would have been followed by someone like Aquinas.]

That which is, already is no more, and *that which is not yet, already is something, for it becomes.* And therefore, the fundamental reality is becoming, the living fire that forever dies and blazes back to life. And therefore, *being* and *non-being* are only artificial abstractions, *words* needed for discourse, so that we can express the surface of things. The fundamental reality is becoming. Being and non-being are identical within it, for that which becomes in a certain manner *is*, and nonetheless, it *is not* yet. Likewise, that which is withering in a certain manner is not and yet still is. Truly—*it fades away*. Soon after having become, it disappears. *Becoming is the mobile identity of contraries.* In this way, we have an explanation for the *universal contradiction* that is found in all things: the conflict and war that exists everywhere between contraries. It must exist. It is not a disorder. Indeed, far from it: war is the mother of all things, for harmony is born of the violent reconciliation of contraries—of the high-pitched and the low-pitched, of the life and death of doctrines, of individuals, and of peoples.

Thus, the principle of contradiction which is supposedly the basis for *the identity* of each thing with itself—its permanence or subsistence, as though it were *one and the same* while being *distinct* from others—this principle of contradiction sinks down into becoming, which at one and the same time is and is not.

Parmenides: What you say is true only from the perspective of the senses, which perceive only the phenomena or appearances of reality. Your affirmations are therefore only hypotheses and opinions. It falls to the intellect, not to the senses, to know the truth, and the object of the intellect is intelligible being, not phenomena. Its object is not the colored, the sounding, the high-pitched or the low-pitched; nor is it water, air, or *fire*. No, it is *intelligi-*

ble being, which the animal's senses cannot perceive but which only man's intellect can perceive.

You say, "That which is, is not." I say that *being is* and cannot not be. Moreover, *non-being is not* and cannot be. Indeed, if non-being did exist, it would already be being, instead of being opposed to it.

Such is the truth for the intellect: *being is, non-being is not.* There is no way to part from this idea.

We cannot part from it. We know no way to affirm anything else in the order of truth, which is above opinions and appearances. The proof of this is the fact that all *multiplicity* and *change* is impossible.

Heraclitus: In order to prove the possibility and existence of movement, does it not suffice that I walk in front of you?

Parmenides: In that, there is only a sensible appearance. However, for the intellect, which is founded on intelligible being, its object, movement is impossible. Being does not become; it is. *Indeed, if being were to become, it would arise either from being or from non-being.* However, being cannot come from *being*, which already is, for that which comes into being, before becoming, is not. On the other hand, nothing can come from *non-being*, which is pure nothingness from which nothing can emerge without any cause. Why would it emerge at this moment rather than earlier or later?

And, therefore, nothing comes into being. Being exists eternally and does not change. This is what traditional religions affirm in their own manner concerning the Supreme God and is what was said by my master, Xenophanes.

Therefore, it is false to say that the principle of contradiction sinks down into becoming. Instead, causeless becoming is what comes to be broken against the principle of contradiction.

Heraclitus: Certainly, becoming would not occur if there were not some real or possible *multiplicity*. However, *the multiple exists in reality*. You and I are men and are quite distinct from one another, if only from each of our own perspectives. We are not [even] close to understanding each other. And if it is said that my doctrine is opposed to common sense, your doctrine is hardly more conformed to it. Multiplicity is a certain fact.

Parmenides: Multiplicity is only an appearance for the senses. It cannot exist for the intellect. Indeed, we cannot conceive of any diversity at the very heart of being. This *diversity* could arise only from *being* itself or from *non-being*. However, being is and contains *nothing other* than itself, for that which is *other* than being is non-being, which is opposed to being. On the other hand, non-being cannot provide a differentiation from outside of being, for non-being is nothing. Consequently, being remains one and that multiplicity is impossible for the intellect. Therefore, it is only an empty appearance of the senses.[4]

---

4 These arguments by Parmendies were taken up by Spinoza in his *Ethics* in order to establish that there is only one substance and that it is impossible for there to be a second. This outlook represents an *absolute intellectual realism* concerning what pertains to the notion of *substantial being*, holding that *universal being* exists outside the mind [*esprit*] with its universality in the same way as this is the case when it is conceived. Thus, it finds itself being confused with the Divine Being, giving rise to a form of pantheistic ontologism. Moreover, for inferior notions of being, this position leads to the opposite extreme, namely, to *nominalism* holding that the essences or natures of different things are mere *words*. Besides the one, single substance, there can be only phenomena which are more or less illusory. Plato will still follow Parmenides in the way of absolute intellectual realism, although he will attenuate the position. Aristotle will arrive at a moderate form of realism that will dominate, at once, the excesses of both absolute realism and of skeptical nominalism.

As I already said, "Being is; non-being is not. There is no way to part from this idea." This is the truth—indeed, the sole truth.

* * *

Plato:[5]   Venerable Parmenides, you certainly have a lofty doctrine. The intellect is incomparably superior to the senses, and if the senses were ever perfected in their own order—if our eyes were to be become more powerful than eagle eyes—they would never attain to the order of that which is intelligible. Obviously, the ability to know the truth, which is the conformity of our thought with true reality, belongs to the intellect.

You have very well said that the intellect's object is *intelligible being*. Nothing can be conceived without it or absolutely apart from it. Furthermore, if movement and multiplicity are opposed to being and to existence, it is manifestly the case that they are impossible. You have admirably posed the problem in all of its profundity, and your doctrine, according to Homer's expression, is venerable and redoubtable.

However, did Heraclitus not correctly observe that all things change in the order of sensible phenomena? The generation of one thing is the corruption of another; matter always receives new modifications; nothing is stable. The child, having become an adolescent, will reach maturity and soon thereafter will decline—and such is ever the case.

Did you not find yourself obliged to write two parts in your poem: τὰ πρὸς τὴν ἀλήθειαν, the doctrine of truth,

---

[5]   Here, we are summarizing Plato's dialogue *The Sophist*.

and τὰ πρὸς δόξαν, the opinions or hypotheses concerning appearances, otherwise called the noumenon (νοητόν) and phenomena?

If you permit it, let us examine your great principle: "Being is; non-being is not. There is no way to part from this idea."

I readily grant the first part of the formula: "being is." It is the object of our intellect's intuition,[6] above the senses, imagination, and opinions. Being is, and we owe you much, Parmenides, for so powerful an affirmation of this first truth. You are our intellectual father in that you have shown us the chief object that our intellects must contemplate, the object that distinguishes our intellects from the senses and from the kind of knowledge animals can have.

For that, I will always venerate you as a master; however, at the risk of being thought to be a patricide, I nonetheless do not fear to place my hand on the second part of your formula and affirm that, *in a sense, non-being is.*[7]

---

[6] [Tr. note: In the sense of "direct self-evident insight" and not one that is inferentially known through syllogistic reasoning. The language is being used loosely here and not in the developed sense of the contrast between intuitive and abstractive cognition taken up at length by members of all the major schools after the time of Scotus. On this theme, see R.M. Jolivet, "L'intuition intellectuelle," *Revue Thomiste* 15 (Jan. 1932): 52–71. Fr. Garrigou-Lagrange cites this text below.]

[7] See Plato, *Sophist*, 241d: "τό τε μὴ ὂν ὡς ἔστί." Likewise, Plato, *Sophist*, 257a, 259a. Also, see the dialogue *Parmenides*, 132d, 133a. In the aforementioned passages from the *Sophist*, we read:
"Visitor: I will make a second, more urgent, request of you.
Theaetetus: What?
Visitor: That you not consider me to be a kind of patricide.
Theaetetus: What do you mean?
Visitor: In order to defend ourselves, we find that we must submit Parmenides' doctrine to a severe examination and must prove, by doing violence to him, that it also is the case that *non-being in a certain respect is . . .*
. . . Must we not say that one soul is just and the other unjust, that this one is wise

This seems paradoxical, but we indeed must make this concession to Heraclitus.

In fact, in the intelligible order, far above the order of the senses, we must admit not only that *Intelligible Being* exists, but also *Truth* and *Wisdom*. Do you not speak of them, Parmenides, in the very title of the first part of your poem? We also must admit that *Justice* exists, and you certainly will not deny its existence. How would you contrast the just man with the criminal and the wise man with the fool? However, if Justice exists in the intelligible order, it is distinct in some way from Being,[8] which it presupposes without Being presupposing Justice. Therefore, it is *Other* than Being, and that which is *Other* than Being,

---

and that other one is unwise? . . .

Theaetetus: Without a doubt.

Visitor: . . . Is it not by the presence and possession of justice that the soul becomes just? . . . Therefore, if *justice* exists, as well as *wisdom*, what are they? . . . (Are they not something *other* than being? And, nevertheless, they participate in being? Must not the same also be said as regards movement?)

Theaetetus: Nothing could be clearer.

Visitor: Consequently, *non-being* is necessarily found both in movement and in all of the ideas [*genres*], for the nature of the *other,* which is present in all the ideas, makes each of them be *other* than being, thus making it be *non-being.*

. . . What we call *non-being* is not, it seems to me, the *contrary of being,* but rather, is only a thing that is *other* . . . As when we are speaking about something that is *not large,* does it seem to you that we use this word to express the small rather than the average-sized? . . . The nature of *the other* seems to me to be divided into a thousand parts, like knowledge. This is the source of the diversity found in the so-called arts and sciences."

Whence, Plato draws the conclusion: If non-being in some manner exists, error also exists. If we express that which is as not being or that which is not as being, that discourse is false. From this, he draws the definition of the sophist, who has only the appearance of wisdom.

[Tr. note: I have chosen to translate Fr. Garrigou-Lagrange's text in place of following a translation from the Greek. There are slight modifications to the text that make it difficult to match his French to a more direct reading of the original.]

[8] [Tr. note: He is not consistent in capitalizing various Platonic forms. One would expect him to capitalize Being and Other. I have interpretively done so on several occasions above.]

as such, is *non-being*. Therefore, that by which Justice is distinguished from Being must be non-being; and, yet, it must in some manner be. Therefore, we must admit that, in some way, non-being is.

Were this not the case, we could not explain the multiplicity of intelligible and immutable Ideas, nor could we explain their union, nor consequently, could we explain the possibility of the affirmative judgment that reunites them. We could not say, "Justice is," but, instead only, "Being is." And, you yourself, Parmenides, could not speak of wisdom, for wisdom is not absolutely identical with Being, its object. Wisdom presupposes Being, and being does not presuppose Wisdom. Also, there are different sciences: without being as lofty as wisdom, mathematics is a science.

Moreover, we must concede to Heraclitus that the sensible phenomena of which you yourself speak in the second part of your poem are not a kind of pure non-being. Our bodies are not entirely devoid of reality. Therefore, we must admit that, in this order of sensible things, everything moves; matter perpetually receives new modifications, which are like a participation (or, a reflection) of the Intelligible Ideas. This matter, which is *capable* of receiving this reflection, is a *non-being* which in a some way exists— τό τε μὴ ὂν ὡς ἔστι.

What remains absolutely true, Parmenides, is the first part of your formula: "Being is." Admirably, you have seen the existence of the intelligible world, νοητὸν γένος, the order of the Immutable Ideas, far above the sensible world, ὁρατὸν γένος. Certainly, we must admit the Idea of the Good,[9] the most brilliant and beautiful part of

---

[9] See Plato, *Republic* VI (508e, 509a).

Being,[10] then Truth in itself, Wisdom, and Justice. And why not also the eternal essences of things? If we have knowledge [*science*] of man, it must have an intelligible and immutable object beyond the sensible, individual, and ever-variable contingent world. Why should there not be an Eternal Idea of man and of the lion? Individual lions are born and die, but the essence of the lion remains ever the same, like that of the deer and those of the rose and the lily. Each of these essences participates in *Being* and the *Same* (for it is identical with itself), but they also participate in the *Other* (for it is *other* than Being) and in this sense is *non-being*.

And therefore, *being is*, but *non-being in a certain sense also is*. In this way, we can explain the multiplicity of the Ideas, their union, and the possibility of an affirmative judgment such as, "Justice is." Likewise, by means of matter (i.e. non-being, existing in a certain way), we can explain the multiplicity of individuals of one and the same species, as well as the undeniable, perpetual change of sensible things.

* * *

Aristotle: Noble master, I certainly owe much to the loftiness of your thought. The flight of your spirit is like that of an eagle, and when you speak of the Sovereign Good, one cannot help thinking that these words of yours are immortal. However, just as you did not fear to lay hands on Parmenides' formula and affirm that, in a sense, non-being is, allow me, in turn, to contradict you on a point in order to better preserve, perhaps, what gives your doctrine its value.

---

10 Plato, *Republic* VII (518d).

Plato: When on certain days I did not see you among my disciples, I would say, "The intellect is absent."[11] Therefore, speak, for this doubtlessly will help us better distinguish truth from the myths in which it is sometimes enrobed.

Aristotle: Certainly, we cannot deny the existence of the Supreme Being, Essential Truth, and Sovereign Good which you affirm so very strongly. However, does not your doctrine still impoverish, after the manner of Parmenides's doctrine, the existence of this sensible world, of this earth that carries us?[12]

Plato: Recall the Allegory of the Cave.

Aristotle: It was only an allegory. If the real idea of Man and the real idea of Lion are separated from the sensible individuals, as is the idea of Rose from the roses that we see and that of Lily from the lilies, what then are these sensible individuals? What then are these men, these lions, these roses, and these lilies? Are they only shadows of reality or are they true realities? Do they have *their essence in themselves* or *outside of themselves*? If they do not have their essence in themselves, these men that our senses perceive are only men by way of an extrinsic denomination. They are like the image of our features found in clear water that flows by. However, the reproduction of our features in this water is only an image, a reflection. And certainly, my Master, you are more than the image of Man. You are truly a man, just as individual lions are true lions and individual roses true roses.

        Moreover, the lion that is separated from all matter could

---

[11] [Tr. note: To see an account of this anecdote, see Anton-Hermann Chroust, *Aristotle: New Light on His Life and On Some of His Lost Works*, vol. 1 (London: Routledge, 2016), 104.]

[12] See Aristotle, *Metaphysics* 1.9 and 7.13–17.

not exist, for according to its definition (or, its essence), it includes matter, not individual matter but common matter: flesh and bones. And *flesh* and *bones* cannot exist without being *this* flesh and *these* bones. The essence of the lion, like that of flesh, can indeed be *conceived* abstractly, *separately* from matter; however, it cannot *exist* as *separated* from matter.

The only perfections that can exist separately from matter are those that do not include any matter or imperfection in their definition (or, essence). Thus, as you affirm, do the Sovereign Good, Truth Itself, and the Intellect that is Thought of Eternally Subsistent Thought exist. However, Man-in-Itself cannot exist, nor can Lion-in-Itself, nor Lily-in-Itself, nor Rose-in-Itself.

Nonetheless, I recognize that there is a *real idea, εἶδος,* corresponding to our concepts, but it is, so to speak, buried in things. It is their intelligible essence, hidden in the shadows of the sensible order. It is the intelligible essence which only an intellect can discover in these shadows. It is the directive idea of the development of an embryo, the specific form of a mineral, plant, or an animal. It is the specific form received in matter, as a circular figure really exists in the brass sphere and as that of our features really exists in our human flesh.

Against the second part of Parmenides's formula, you said with great profundity: *"non-being in a certain manner is."* This is the substance of your dialogue *The Sophist.* Thus, matter receives, you say, successive modifications. However, these modifications are more than a reflection of the Ideas. They are more than an image impressed upon the flowing water. They are that by which the lion is the lion and the rose a rose. And this matter, *this non-being* that in some way exists is the matter of *a being that is still undetermined.* It is a *real capacity for perfection.* It is that which *can* become a rose, a lily, a lion, and so forth. Matter is the rose *in potency,* the lily in potency, the lion in potency—but only in potency. It is not actually (i.e. *in act*) the rose or lily; it is not the lion in act. It can receive many determinations, many perfections. When it receives them, that matter is not the perfection that it has thus received; it is not the act that it has received. No, it limits that act. Thus do we have an explanation for how there are many roses of the same species, many lilies, and so forth. And therefore, *being,* affirmed by Parmenides in opposition to Heraclitus, not only leaves room for a kind of *non-being* that in some way is but also is divided into *potency* and *act* (or, undetermined being and determination). And every sensible being is composed of potency and act. Act determines potency, specifying it. Potency limits the act that it receives, threby participating in it.

Thus, we can resolve Parmenides' argument against the possibility of becoming. He says, "*Being cannot become*—neither, certainly, from non-being, *nor from being* (for being already is, and that which becomes still is not)." It is easy to respond: This is true. Nothing can arise *from being in act,* for it is already determined. Thus, we cannot make a statue of Apollo from a statue of Apollo—it already is. However, why not *from being in potency,* from undetermined being? We can make a statue out of wood that *can* be sculpted or from clay that *can* be shaped. The fully-grown ear of wheat comes from the seed contained the grain. The oak comes from the seed contained in the acorn.

Moreover, nothing is reduced from potency to act except by a being that is already in act, which is called *the agent.* There is no statue without a sculptor, nor a begotten being without one that begets it. The agent acts through an *active potency* that is *ordered* to produce the act, as the *passive potency* is ordered to receive it. Without this ordination, there would be no *reason* for the fact that the agent acts instead of not acting, nor for the fact that it acts in one way rather than in another, nor for the fact that it produces this determinate effect that is *suitable* to it rather than any other effect that would not be thus suitable. Without this ordination, there would be no reason that the eye sees instead of hearing or tasting. It is made to see color, and light is for the sake of seeing. *Active potency and passive potency are ordered to act as to their end.* Thus, the *specific form* of the begotten thing (for example, of the lion or of the deer) is at one and the same time *the end of passive generation* and *of active generation,* for the agent and the patient have the same end, although they are related to it in different ways—the agent leads to it (or, realizes it), and the patient is led to it.

Thus, *becoming* is explained in function of *intelligible being,* by the first division of being into *potency and act* and also by the *four causes,* for act (from different perspectives) is the principle of action, the form, and the end. It is the principle of action, for to act is to determine, and the agent is only determined through the determination that exists in it—thus the ox begets the ox, and the deer begets the deer. At the terminus of generation, in the begotten being, the specific act that determines the matter is at once the specific form and the end of generation.

In this way, *becoming* is rendered *intelligible* by its [various] relations to *being,* the first intelligible object, and these relations rest upon the division of being into potency and act.

* * *

Aristotle:[13]   This distinction is imposed of necessity in order to simultaneously maintain the *principle of contradiction* (or, of identity) affirmed so strongly by Parmenides and *becoming*, which Heraclitus affirmed. In other words, this distinction is necessary for reconciling the first principle of reason and being with the most certain fact of experience.

Certainly, the principle of contradiction remains [the] fundamental law of thought and reality, and the teaching concerning *becoming without a cause*, of self-creative evolution, is shattered against it.

This becoming, which would be its own *raison d'être*, would be a movement without a subject, without a movable thing, without an efficient cause, without an end, and without a determined goal. It would be, as Heraclitus admitted, the *violation of the principle of contradiction*. That is, from the intellect's perspective, it would be absurdity itself, placed at the foundation of all things. If it were an ascending evolution,[14] it would constantly be the case that *the greater would come from the less*, the more perfect from the less perfect. We are told that this becoming would be God; however, as an attentive intellect has noted [*sic*], it would be a God who would go from surprise to surprise in everything that He would become,

---

13   [Tr. note: This passage is not explicitly marked as continuing Aristotle's portion of the dialogue. However, it seems to be such, given the response of Diotima below. The original text does not employ indents to clarify the dialogue; hence, the section break merely implicitly continues Aristotle's speech in the French.]

14   [Tr. note: Fr. Garrigou-Lagrange is here referring solely to absolute, metaphysical *evolutionism* which would posit a self-sufficient, continuous flux in reality. He is clear in later works that room is left for moderate forms of evolutionary theory. See Réginald Garrigou-Lagrange, "Vérité et immutabilité du dogme," *Angelicum* 24 (1947): 136–137. See the translator comments in Réginald Garrigou-Lagrange, *Philosophizing in Faith: Essays on the Beginning and End of Wisdom*, trans. Matthew K. Minerd (Providence, RI: Cluny Media, 2019), 256–257n6.]

without having been able to foresee any of it.

Moreover, if the principle of contradiction were false, there would no longer be any difference between becoming and non-becoming. In such becoming, there would no longer be a difference between the *terminus from which* [*a quo*] it begins and the *terminus toward which* [*ad quem*] it proceeds. To go from Athens to Megara, one would arrive before even having left. *Becoming would be immobile*,[15] and it would be identical not with the immobility of being but, rather, with the immobility of non-being—and with that of a nothingness that would be a negation not only of all existence but of every possibility of existence. This would represent a form of absolute nihilism. Heraclitus himself would not have existed and could never have existed. Whatever he may say, he did not evade the law of non-contradiction, for he cannot at one and the same time be and not be Heraclitus.

The principle of contradiction abides.

However, becoming is also certain and now becomes intelligible through a reduction to being. Being cannot be identified with becoming. *Being* remains more perfect than that which *becomes* and does not yet exist. Act is more perfect than potency, and potency is ordered to act as to its end. Every agent acts for an end. For example, the animal acts for its own preservation and for the preservation of its species. It even happens that it may sacrifice its individual life to defend its little ones for the good of the species, which it does not know, though it instinctually tends toward it.

If the agent of which we are speaking *is not its action* (i.e.,

---

[15] See Aristotle, *Metaphysics* 4.5–8.

its acting), it needs to be premoved in order to act. It must be premoved by a superior agent, which actually has an influence upon it. We can go to infinity for a series of past causes that no longer have an influence today; however, we cannot do so for a series of causes which are necessarily and actually subordinated at the present hour. This is so because the inferior cause moves only if it is actually premoved by other, higher causes, and if a first source of action did not exist at the summit of this subordination, no subordinate causality would exist and neither would any effect. Therefore, there must be *a supreme agent* that has no need of being premoved and, *thus, is its own action.* Moreover, given that act presupposes being (and the mode of acting presupposes the mode of being), this supreme agent must be *Being Itself, Pure Act* without any admixture of potency or of imperfection.

If we are thinking beings (sometimes in potency, sometimes in act), in this Pure Act there must also be *Ever-Subsistent Thought, Thought of Thought,* νόησις νοήσεως νόησις.[16]

Such is the Supreme Being that Parmenides conceived of indistinctly, the Supreme Being that can be called the Sovereign Good. However, besides the *Supreme Being,* there also is the *multitude of limited beings and movement.* Likewise, Parmenides was wrong in thinking that being can be said only in a univocal sense. It is said in various, *analogical* senses of God (the First Being and Pure Act) and of limited beings that are composed of act and potency.[17] In this way, *potency* explains the multiplicity of beings that have all received existence in various degrees according to the perfection of their essence or nature. In like manner,

---

16 See Aristotle, *Metaphysics,* 12.9.
17 See Aristotle, *Metaphysics,* 4.1.

the multiplicity of individuals in one and the same species is explained by *matter* (i.e., the real capacity for successive perfections). Thus, becoming is explained in function of being without denying the principle of contradiction.

Only, we no longer need to formulate this principle in the way that Parmenides did, "Being is." This principle is not a judgment of existence. It does not yet affirm the existence of being—neither of limited being nor of the Supreme Being. Parmenides was deceived in thinking that we have an immediate intellectual intuition of the First Being. The first intelligible object that our intellect, united to the senses, knows is the intelligible being of sensible things. It knows their essence in a vague manner, and this only has an analogical likeness to the Supreme Being.

This is why the principle of contradiction cannot be formulated, "Being is," but, instead, either as, "Being is being, non-being is non-being," or, "Being is not non-being." Being is opposed to non-being, and in being, act is opposed to potency as to a kind of relative non-being (or, better yet, to a kind of non-act or still-undetermined being)—*a real capacity for perfection*, as regards an act to be produced or received. Therefore, against Heraclitus, we say, "That which is is, and that which is not is not."

All that Nominalists (the disciples of Heraclitus) may maintain as the principle of contradiction is this merely verbal, hypothetical principle: "If something is, something is."[18] However, from their perspective, it may be

---

18 Indeed, in the Middle Ages, among the 53 propositions of the nominalist Nicholas of Autrecourt (Nicolaus de Utricuria) condemned in 1348, we find this formulation of the principle of contradiction: "This is the first principle and no other: 'If something is, something is [lit. *si aliquid est, aliquid est*]'" (cf. Denzinger, no. 1048). This is certainly the antipode of absolute realism, which still is present in some way in St. Anselm's argument [for God's existence] and in the realism of Meister Eckhart,

the case that nothing is or could be; it may be the case that our idea of being is deprived of all value and that it expresses nothing pertaining to reality, which would thus be pure becoming. But, as we have seen, if the principle of contradiction (or, identity) no longer has any value, then *becoming is no longer becoming.* It is the same as *immobility,* the immobility of pure non-being, the denial of all existence and of all possibility of existence.

The principle of contradiction (or, identity) abides, and we have its formula, which is virtually presupposed by every judgment of existence. [19] In order to say, "This tree exists," it must not be able to be a tree and a non-tree at one and the same time and also must not be able to exist and not exist at one and the same time. Likewise, if I doubt the value of the principle of contradiction, I cannot say, "I think; therefore, I am," for it may be the case that thought is non-thought, and that at one and the same time I exist and do not exist. These judgments of existence pertain to the existence of a contingent being, though the principle of contradiction (or, identity) is a universal and necessary truth—the most universal and

---

a realism that tends to confuse universal being with God, subsequently leading to nominalism regarding the being of things, which becomes only an appearance and a mere word.—We can see the difference between these doctrines in the very ways that they formulate the principle of contradiction (or, identity).

Absolute realism says: "being is, non-being is not." It confuses being in general with the Divine Being. It admits St. Anselm's argument without difficulty, for it believes that we have a vague intuition of God.

Nominalism says: "if something is, something is." Furthermore, it adds: "however, perhaps nothing exists and nothing is even really possible. Our notion of being is perhaps deprived of all its value. It is not certain that becoming is impossible without a cause; indeed, perhaps it is the fundamental reality, self-creative evolution."

Moderate realism says: "being is being, non-being is non-being." To put it another way: "*being is not non-being; that which is is and cannot at the same time not be.* There is *more* in *that which is* than in *that which becomes* and does not yet exist." Becoming cannot be the first and fundamental reality, for it is not [related] to being as A is to A.

[19] [Tr. note: That is, present within the power of that judgment, though not formally expressed.]

31

most necessary of all truths, implied in our very first idea, the idea of intelligible being.

The light of this principle of identity, the fundamental law of thought and of reality, the law to which the principle of causality is subordinated, *shows us,* in our experience of the mirror of sensible things, *that becoming is not the fundamental reality,* that the sensible, *composed,* and *changing* world is not the first being, for it is not related to being as A is to A. It is not Being Itself, and therefore, it *has* existence instead of being existence. Hence, it is only explained by a supreme cause which must be [related] to being as A is to A, which must be Being Itself and Pure Act, in Which this principle which is the fundamental law of our thought and of reality is verified in the purest manner possible. Here, we find what Parmenides indistinctly saw. However, becoming also has its place, certainly a minute place, but still a real one, enabling us to elevate our thought with absolute certitude all the way to Pure Act, the Supreme Cause of all that is and of all that moves—the Cause of causes, Thought of Thought, and the Sovereign Good.

Pure Act, like the Sovereign Good, attracts all things to Itself. If the lioness and the hen sometimes sacrifice themselves for their little ones, thus showing us that they love the good of their species more than themselves, for all the more reason do they love even more, though without knowing it, the good of the universe, as well as the Supreme Good that attracts all things to Itself.

Diotima:[20] You have spoken very well, Aristotle. You have admirably demonstrated the finality that exists in nature, and you

---

[20] We recall here Diotima, the foreigner from Mantinea, who is the personification of Wisdom in Plato's *Symposium*.

have quite justly said that every natural agent acts for an end without knowing it. However, there is a very important point which you have touched upon only in a very obscure manner. Pure Act, Thought of Thought, and the Sovereign Good attracts all things to Itself—thus, you say—as the ultimate end. Is It not also *the Intellect that has ordered all things, the Providence* which directs all?

Save in several places, on this point you have often maintained a silence that I can hardly understand, given the great praise that you expressed concerning the wise Anaxagoras. Recall what you wrote at the beginning of the *Metaphysics*: "It is not likely that the order and beauty that exist in things or are produced in them has the earth or some other element of this kind as their cause. . . . To attribute these admirable effects to chance, to a fortuitous cause, was far too unreasonable. Therefore, when a man came to proclaim that *an Intellect is the cause of the order and regularity that erupts everywhere in nature,* in animate and inanimate beings, this man alone seemed to have his wits about him and to be sober after the extravagant drunkenness and ravings of his predecessors. Now, we have no doubt that Anaxagoras was connected to this doctrine."[21]

Anaxagoras was right. He said that this Supreme Intellect must "be separated from the world in order to govern it." You see better than he did what such an Intellect must be. You call it Pure Act, Thought of Thought, the Supreme Truth, always known, the Sovereign Good, always loved. Add, without timidity and more clearly, what you have not said thus far: It is the Cause of the order of the world, which It directs toward the ultimate end, and is the Cause of our immortal intellects, watching over our destinies.

---

[21] Aristotle, *Metaphysics*, 1.3.

Chapter Two

CHANCE OR FINALITY?

See Aristotle, *Physics*, 2.5–9 as well as St. Thomas's Commentary on the text (esp. lect. 7–14).

In order to give more vigor to the exposition of these ideas, we will once again present them in the form of a dialogue, here between Aristotle and a sophist.

Aristotle: One commonly speaks of the value, worth, and usefulness of the things of nature and of art. These expressions of value and utility are received even among Democritus's disciples—convinced mechanists and materialists though they be—who claim that their intellects and wills arise from blind matter and chance, from a nature without any finality. For them, the animal sees because it has eyes, but it does not have eyes for seeing. Should not these men be wine merchants rather than philosophers?

If they feel threatened with blindness, they go to see a doctor. They speak about the value of their two eyes, and they do not deny their finality.

They still use the notion of value. However, what can it mean for them?

What is the value of a thing—of pure air, of wheat, of the

art of medicine, or of our eyes—if not its usefulness or its worth, that for which this thing deserves more or less esteem in relation to an end? The notion of value itself loses all of its value if one no longer thinks that there is finality and if one no longer knows how to distinguish the [good inasmuch as it is] fitting [*honnête*], useful, and delightful.

Value judgments that would abstract from finality and would not be based on judgments of reality are themselves without any value, for action follows upon being, the mode of action follows upon the mode of being, and every agent (whether it knows it or not) acts for an end.

Sophist: Every agent acts for an end! Outside of our own human intentions of ever-questionable value, finality is only a word with no foundation in reality (if reality even exists).

The order of the world, whatever Anaxagoras, Socrates, and Plato might say about it, arises out of chance. If one throws three letters of a verse of the Illiad into the air, they sometimes fall in a way that forms an intelligible word. Why could it not be the case that the same thing might happen if one were to throw four, five, six, or more letters in this way? Who can set the limit in this matter? If a word can be formed by *chance*, why not a verse, a song, or an entire poem? There are men for whom all things go well, and we say, "*This is good fortune*, the superior form of chance." There are other men for whom nothing turns out well, and here, we say, "*This is bad fortune*—the painful form of chance." One says that rain is for the sake of the wheat's growth. It sometimes happens that wheat sprouts after the rain, but it also happens that the rain spoils the whole crop when the latter is already shocked but not yet gathered [into the barn].

At the beginning of the world, among the thousands of useless combinations of atoms, chance produced in them certain, particularly fortunate combinations, which, being found useful, were preserved. It is the survival of the fittest. In order to explain this, we have no need of recourse (as Anaxagoras, Socrates, and Plato wish) to a superior intellect; one might as well deny chance. I repeat it to you again: if chance brings about a word, why not a verse, a song, or a poem?

I. The Hunt for the Definition of Chance

Aristotle: Could you please *define* for me the meaning of the chance of which you speak so eloquently?

Sophist: Define! Define! What value do definitions have? If I ask you what a *heap* of wheat grains is or a *heap* of sand grains, will you tell me that it is the union of *two grains*? And if two are not sufficient for making a heap, why then would three, four, five, or more suffice?

Aristotle: A *heap* is not a natural whole. It is the accidental union of many things of an indeterminate number. However, if you claim that a certain definition cannot be provided for anything, then tell me in what *sense* you make use of the *words* that you employ? For example, what meaning do you give to the word "chance"?

Sophist: What meaning? I give the meaning that is usually given for it, as when one says, "This happed by chance; this is an effect of chance or an effect of good fortune," unless this is an ill effect.

Aristotle: Then, you already admit a kind of nominal definition for chance. Otherwise, you would not employ this word rather than some other. Otherwise, chance would not be distinct from a trireme, a wall, or a sword. On the basis of this nominal definition, which everyone thinks when they pronounce the word "chance," would you like for us to hunt together for the real definition which will reveal to us more precisely just what this famed "chance," to which you attribute such beautiful things, is? This hunt for definitions, which Socrates taught us, is no less engaging than the hunt for a boar or for a deer.

Sophist: A wild goose chase, you mean. Do you believe that you can understand the very essence of things and pass beyond merely verbal meanings?

Aristotle: The meaning of words is already something. Would this not be a point of departure? You said just now, "It is commonly said, 'This happened by chance; this is the effect of chance.'" Does not the meaning of this word require us to conceive of chance as though it were a cause and to conceive of that which fortuitously happens as though it were an effect? You yourself say, "The world's order is the effect of chance." Therefore, you at least admit that chance is a *cause*.

Sophist: Why not? And it is a cause whose existence is no less certain than is the existence of Anaxagoras's God or Plato's Ideas.

Aristotle: However, if chance is a cause, is it a cause that is *necessarily required* for its effect, as when one says, "Man begets man; ox begets ox; no begotten being without begetting being; no statue without a sculptor; no house without a builder or an architect"? Or, rather, is it an *accidental cause,* as when one says that an architect is the cause of the disruption occurring because of the construction of a house or that a musician is a builder of a palace because it accidentally happens to be the case that an architect was a musician? I beseech you, respond to me: since you concede that chance is a cause, is it *necessarily required* by its effect or, rather, is it an *accidental cause, per accidens*?

Sophist: *Per accidens*, for sure, for nothing is necessary.

Aristotle: You believe that it is not necessary that there be a begetting being in order for there to be a begotten being or a sculptor for there to be a beautiful statue; however, you do at least concede to me that chance is a cause, an accidental one in the domain of the *per accidens*, for which you have a particular affection.

Now, allow me to ask: does *the effect* of this accidental cause, chance, happen *always* or at least *frequently*, or on the contrary, *rarely*? One says, "It is by chance that the tripod, in falling, fell on its three feet and, likewise, that this man, while digging a grave, found a treasure." Each time that the tripod falls, does it fall the same way, as each time a rose bush sends forth its flowers they are roses and not lilies? Or, at least, is it the case that the tripod frequently falls this way? Likewise, does it frequently happen that one finds a treasure when digging a grave?

Sophist: Certain particularly striking effects of chance are rare, but very frequently, there are a number of accidental occurrences.

Aristotle: I concede that if I go out onto the road, it is accidental and very frequently the case that I meet such-and-such unknown people who are of no interest to me. However, do I *frequently* run into the very person who is indebted to me, encountering him at the moment when I absolutely need money, and then receive the sum that he owes me? Now, isn't this what one calls "chance"? An accidental meeting of no interest passes by unperceived and does not have a special name. However, is not a *fortunate, accidental meeting* attributed to good fortune (and an *accidental, unfortunate meeting* to bad fortune)? Finally, does not one speak of good and bad fortune, not in relation to things of *nature* but, rather, in relation to *human affairs*, while chance is spoken of in relation to both kinds of things? Have we not thus arrived at the goal of our search? Has our hunt remained fruitless? Do we not now have the definition for chance? Why would you not wish to admit that it is *the accidental cause of something that rarely occurs, not in an indifferent manner but, rather, in a fortunate or unfortunate manner, outside of the intention of nature or of man?*

II. The Value of Definitions

Sophist:　　On the whole, this definition expresses nothing more than what we started with, and indeed, doesn't express anything beyond the conventional language of men.

Aristotle:　In one respect, it does not express anything more, for it does not speak of something different from what we started with. However, does it not express the matter more precisely? The conventional language of men has, in one group of people this word, in another group, that word, for designating the same *vague [confus] concept* of chance, which all men use and without which the word "chance" (or whatever equivalent word one may find in another language) would no more designate what one wishes it to mean than it would designate a helmet or a breastplate. At the beginning of our investigation, did not you yourself admit this vague concept of chance under pain of not being able to make use of this word? Did you not do so under pain of not being able to express anything by the word "chance"? Do you not now find that our hunt has put us in possession of a more precise idea of the same thing? Do we not now know the genus and the difference of chance?

Sophist: Genus and difference have no more worth than do the artificial methods of your investigation. They have no more worth than your divisions of causality and no more worth than your comparative induction by which you seek to see how fortuitous effects resemble others and how they differ from them. Your definition of chance cannot be demonstrated by a major and minor premise that is absolutely certain. You yourself are forced to admit this of the second book of your *Posterior Analytics*. Therefore, what can be the value of an indemonstrable definition?

Aristotle: I agree, a definition is not demonstrated—neither in an *a posteriori* manner nor an *a priori*[1] manner—unless one were to deduce a definition through a formal cause from a definition through a final or efficient cause, as happens

---

[1]   [Tr. note: The senses of *a posteriori* and *a priori* here are not the same as what is received from Kant's *Critique of Pure Reason*. Although Kant is the inheritor of much medieval, renaissance, and baroque Scholasticism, his sense of the terms is quite different from the developed Scholastic position within the Thomist school. Although Fr. Garrigou-Lagrange may be using the terms a little bit loosely, he was well aware of how these terms were used by Thomist logicians in his day. Indeed, he approved of Édouard Hugon's *Cursus Philosophicus Thomisticae*, vol. 1: *Logica* (Paris: Lethielleux, 1927). In this text, see p. 384: "Demonstration *a priori* does not coincide with demonstration *propter quid*, nor does demonstration *a posteriori* coincide with demonstration *quia*. For demonstration *a priori* proceeds through causes of any sort, whether proximate or remote; however, demonstration *propter quid* . . .through proper, immediate, and adequate causes. Hence, every demonstration *propter quid* is *a priori*; however, not every demonstration *a priori* is *propter quid*. Demonstration *a posteriori* is only through an effect; however, demonstration *quia* is through an effect or [lit. *et*] through remote causes. Therefore, every *a posteriori* demonstration is *quia*, while it is not the case that every *quia* demonstration is *a posteriori*." Although the immediate context justifies reading "et" as "or," see also his remarks from p. 383: "Demonstration *quia*, taking the word 'quia' not as causal [i.e., meaning "because"] but meaning 'that the thing is,' proceeds either through a sign and effect or through remote, common, and inadequate causes."

above all in the case of artificial things. In artificial things, if a saw must cut through wood, it must be made of a metal that is sufficiently resistant and must have teeth. If the circumference is begotten by the revolution of a straight line around one of its extremities, all of its points must be equally distant from its center. Outside of these cases, I agree with you that the definition of a thing is not demonstrated, for one does not place a demonstrative middle term between two terms which are immediately adequate to each other, between the defined thing and the definition, for example, between *man* and *rational animal*. This definition is what provides the foundation for the demonstration of the properties of this thing.

Sophist: A shaky foundation, for the hunt for the definition does not have sure rules. You descend in dividing a genus when you can do so by *sic et non* [*yes and no*], by contradictories or contraries, and then you climb back upward by your comparative induction. However, you do not know if the descent or the ascent truly arrives at the same point, corresponding to the very nature of the thing to be defined. Your hunt is rather haphazard. It does not have a directive principle. When your hunt has come to an end, how do you know that you have found a good definition? If you have found it, it is by chance, and you are not certain of possessing it.

Aristotle: This hunt would not have a directive principle if we did not from the start have the *vague* [*confus*][2] *concept* or commonly received meaning of the thing's name. Does not this vague concept direct our investigation, the descend-

---

[2] [Tr. note: I am translating *confus* as *vague*, as I think that in standard English, "vague" is more understandable. However, the notion of confused and distinct concepts plays a pivotal role in scholastic logic and accounts of knowledge (such that Descartes's deployment of the terms merely shows his dependence on scholasticism, though he deploys all such notions somewhat recklessly).]

ing division of the genus and the comparative, ascending induction?[3] And is not this same vague concept *what, so to speak, recognizes itself* at the meeting of the descent and the ascent? Does not the vague concept resemble a man who is still half-asleep but then little by little wakes up, washes himself, combs his hair, and at last, looking at himself in the mirror, *recognizes himself?* Has our investigation only been a mechanical juxtaposition? Or, has it not, instead, been an organic development like that of a plant that grows, all the while remaining the same?

You say that I cannot know whether I have found a good definition, given that it is indemonstrable. I would not look for it if, in a sense, I had not already found it. Common sense, with its still-vague concepts, is richer than you think. We merely need to interrogate it in a suitable way. Thus, one obtains responses—not merely the responses of this or that individual human, but those of human nature, of the human intellect, which thus gradually passes from the vague to the distinct. Why won't you accept the definition of chance to which your own responses led us?

III. The Accidental and the Essential (or, Necessary)

Sophist: I tell you, this definition is only concerned with the

---

[3] [Tr. note: For a brief, accessible, explanation of logical division as a preparation for definition, see Vincent E. Smith, *The Elements of Logic* (Milwaukee: Bruce, 1957), 66–74. Division is the primary instrument used by the first act of the intellect in its search for definitions. The interested researcher should also consult the remarks on definition and division in the texts of Fr. Garrigou-Lagrange's student Austin Woodbury, *Logic*, The John N. Deely and Anthony F. Russell Collection, St. Vincent College, Latrobe, PA, n.160–194 (p.116–142). Also see Réginald Garrigou-Lagrange, "On the Search for Definitions According to Aristotle and St. Thomas," in *Philosophizing in Faith*, 21–34.]

current order of things and not with the world's beginnings. Today, particularly remarkable, fortuitous effects are rare. However, at the world's beginnings, when men and their languages did not yet exist, there very well could have been, among many useless meetings of elements, numerous happy, fortuitous combinations that were perpetuated on account of their usefulness. And then, none of the terms of your definition would be worthwhile as regards the question of the world's beginnings.

Aristotle: However, even at the beginning, is not the chance of which you yourself speak (in saying that the order of things is the effect of chance) at least an *accidental cause*? Have you not conceded that it belongs to the domain of the *per accidens*—and does that hold true only today or not also for the world's beginnings? During these first days, was chance a cause necessarily required for its effect, like the sculptor for the statue and the ox begetting for the ox begotten, or was it, like today, an accidental cause?

Sophist: Certainly, an accidental cause, and that is why nothing is necessary.

Aristotle: However, what therefore is the *accidental*? Do you want us to begin here another hunt for a definition? Does not the accidental presuppose something other than itself, to which it is added in a wholly contingent manner? Is it accidental that the musician be a musician and that the doctor be a doctor? Do we not find something here that is necessary? And must we not say that it is accidental that the musician be a doctor or that the good doctor knows how to play harmonious chords upon a lyre?

Sophist: What are you getting at?

Aristotle: If the accidental presupposes the necessary to which it is added, the accidental cause presupposes the necessarily required cause to which it also is added. The man who digs a grave accidentally finds a treasure—on the condition that he digs the grave, that he wishes to do something, and that he has an intention. And like this man, does not nature have its own natural intentions? Does it not here tend to form an ear of grain and there an oak tree?

You say that the constitution of an oak tree or, at least, of an acorn is accidental; so too with the constitution of the ant, the lion, or the elephant. However, surely you will at least admit that if some element existed at the origins of the universe, this element (no matter how simple it may be), this atom, would have had some law. If it had no law, it would not have been immobile any more than it would have been in motion, and when moving it would not have moved in one direction rather than in another. If there was only gravity, what was it that made this atom fall vertically and not in some other direction? And, if it fell in this vertical direction, what was it that made it fall instead of rising? Why this angle, and why this direction? If you then go back to the efficient cause of this movement, why does it move in this direction rather than in some other?

Sophist: I already told you why: chance.

Aristotle: However, as you yourself admit, chance is an accidental cause, and that which is accidental presupposes that to which it is added. *Therefore, if everything were accidental, nothing at all would exist any longer.* If it is accidental not only that the doctor be a musician but that the doctor be a doctor (or that a man be a man, or that a body be a body, or that being be being, or that the true be the true), well then, nothing exists any longer—neither you, nor me, who are together talking.

Chance can be only the accidental meeting of two agents, but each of these agents *tends* toward a thing that is fitting for it. The stone and all falling bodies *tend* toward the center of the earth for the cohesion of the universe. Otherwise, all the elements would scatter in every possible and imaginable direction, and no more in one direction rather than in another.

In order to deny *all finality* in nature, we would need to say that, at least at the world's very beginnings, there had been no law, that *everything—absolutely everything—was accidental; however, then, the accidental itself would vanish,* for it no longer would have anything on which to base itself. The accidental modification of a thing presupposes this very thing. Otherwise, we must speak as though there were a dream without a dreamer, flight without that which flies, a flow without the fluid that flows. And, in such a case, we cannot even speak about flow or flight rather than some other thing, for flow and flight have their own laws by which they are what they are. *Chance,* which you love to speak about so much, *itself vanishes,* for as we have said, it is the accidental cause of that which happens outside every natural or human intention. Additionally, if there were no longer any intention, tendency, or finality in nature, chance would no longer exist. There would no longer be the fortuitous effect that can happen outside of such intention, tendency, or finality—just as there would no longer be any exception to laws if there were no longer any laws.

IV. The Finality of Every Tendency, of Every Action or Realization

Aristotle: Therefore, if only to save the chance that you hold so dear, acknowledge at least the finality of the least of atoms or in the least of corpuscles—name it whatever you wish—that falls instead of rising, which falls in one direction rather than in some other, which *tends* toward this result rather than to some other. Otherwise, if it does not *tend* toward anything, nothing happens, and if you reduce everything essential to the accidental, you destroy every nature—that of water, air, and fire. All that then remains are *chance encounters and nothing which could undergo such encounters.* We must choose between radical absurdity and finality.

You make the greater come from the lesser, order from absence of order, and the intelligibility of things from an absence of intelligibility. You make being come from pure non-being, without telling us how this pure non-being can produce it.

And if, in order to save the existence of chance, which is ever-so-dear to you, if you admit at least the smallest amount of *order* in the least of bodies in the least of its natural movements, why would you not admit the incomparably more excellent order of the eye, which is made for seeing, or of the ear, which is made for hearing, or of the intellect, which is made for understanding, or of the will, which is made for loving and willing the good (and, indeed, the supreme good, most especially among all goods)?

Sophist: You will never succeed at *demonstrating* that the eye is *for* seeing or the ear for hearing. Because I have an eye, I see, but prove to me therefore that the eye is made *for* seeing.

Aristotle: No, I will not *prove* that the eye is made *for* seeing, but if you know the very meaning of your words, in speaking to me about the eye and, above all, about sight, you yourself see, before every demonstration, that *sight is for seeing,* hearing for listening, and wings for flying.

V. *Per Accidens* Sensibles: The First Intellectual Contact with Reality

Sophist: The finality that you speak of is not a thing that is seen, like color, nor is it something that is heard, like a sound.

Aristotle: Certainly, it is not grasped by the senses. However, like existence, substance, and life, it is immediately grasped by the intellect, prior to every demonstration. When we were speaking the other day, why did you mock this phrase: "the *per accidens* sensible"? Have you, who so love the *per accidens*, truly understood it? When you see Callias coming toward you, do you not perceive immediately, without any demonstration, that he is living? When we met earlier, you saw with your own eyes the color of my face, and did you need to perform a demonstration in order to establish that here, before your eyes, was an existing and living being who came toward you?

   Existence, substance, life—certainly, these are not sensible qualities like color or sound. Nor are they sensible objects that are common to several senses, like the extension or shape of bodies. However, immediately, as soon as the body of a man coming toward you is present, you perceive by your intellect something that will never be perceived by a dog, which cannot grasp the meaning of this little word, *is*. You perceive by your intellect that before you is not only something *colored* but a *being*, something *real*. With more attention, you perceive that there is a *being that is one and the same* under multiple, changing phenomena. That is, you perceive a substance. With more attention still, you perceive a *being that acts by itself*, which walks, breathes, and speaks—in a word, you perceive a being that *lives*.

You grasp all of this without needing to reason. It is more certain than your reasoning. Obviously, you do not doubt it. Otherwise, why would you speak to me if you were in doubt about my existence and my life?

Existence, substance, and life are not objects that are *sensible of themselves*. Instead, they are intelligible objects that are, however, called *sensibles per accidens*, for they accompany the sensible and are immediately grasped by the intellect at the presentation of the sensed objects. You who deny the objectivity of human knowledge do not seem to doubt that we have here *its first contact with reality* and the foundation of the value of knowledge [*science*], which you declare to be vain without knowing what it is.[4]

Ultimately, you deny efficient causality, just as you deny finality. You deny that the sun enlightens and heats us, that the nightingale sings, that the dog barks—and that it barks *for* something. You deny the efficient cause and the end, which are inseparable from one another, and you do not know what they are. You have taken care to note that they are *sensible per accidens*. The agent produces or *realizes* its effect. What faculty can grasp this *realization*—that which has color for its object or that which has being (or, *reality*) for its object?

When you strike a body, although your senses (like those of the animal) grasp its hardness, your intellect immediately grasps the impression passively received and the impression actively exercised upon you. Just as it grasps *reality* (or, being) without reasoning, it also grasps the active and passive *realization* of this sensed *reality*. Likewise, it sees that *every* active and passive *realization tends* toward *a goal*. Otherwise, the action of the agent would

---

[4] See Aristotle, *De anima*, 2.6.

lack a *raison d'être* for its action.[5] Without it, there would be no reason for acting rather than not acting, nor for acting in one way rather than in some other. Also, when you look upon my eyes with yours, your intellect immediately grasps that they are made for seeing and not for listening or tasting.

VI. Fitness [Aptitude] and Finality

Sophist: The eyes are made for seeing! The survival of the fittest suffices for explaining the eye's organization, without needing any recourse to finality. It suffices that chance would have produced an eye only one time and that this fortunate ability was preserved in the midst of a host of useless combinations that have disappeared.

Aristotle: You speak of the "fittest" and pronounce the word "fitness," a word providing matter for lengthy reflection, and you deny finality! Therefore, what do you mean by these words, "Fit for seeing," rather than for hearing, if not *made for seeing* rather than for hearing. And there is no need here for there to be constancy or frequency. If

---

[5]   [Tr. note: This phrase will occur throughout the translation. One could follow other translators and render it as "sufficient reason." (Indeed, Fr. Garrigou-Lagrange will occasionally speak literally of the "principle of sufficient reason.") Nonetheless, because of certain rationalist misunderstandings of the expression, I have chosen to leave it as *raison d'être* when that is what Fr. Garrigou-Lagrange uses. As will be seen by Fr. Garrigou-Lagrange's own use of the expression, the sense is that of the literal meaning. The *raison d'être* provides the reason explaining the being of the thing in question. Thus, the means, as means, has its *reason for being* in the end toward which it is directed. Indeed, in his own writing in Latin, he will come to translate it as *principium rationis essendi*. See Garrigou-Lagrange, "On the Search for Definitions According to Aristotle and St. Thomas," 25. Moreover, he very clearly states his reason for avoiding calling it the principle of sufficient reason in Réginald Garrigou-Lagrange, *De revelatione per ecclesiam catholicam proposita*, 5th ed. (Rome: Desclée de Socii, 1950), 238–239n2. Likewise, he defends himself against critiques coming from Gilson on this topic in Réginald Garrigou-Lagrange, "L'immutabilité du dogme selon le Concile du Vatican, et le relativisme," *Angelicum* 26 (1949): 321–322.]

there were only one eye in all the world, only your eye, and if there were only one act vision looking upon the starry sky, only your own act, it would already be obvious that this one, unique eye is made for seeing and by that very fact is a marvel superior to all the stars in the firmament above.

Sophist: This one, unique eye could perhaps be the fortuitous meeting of the various elements that constitute it.

Aristotle: An accidental meeting and nothing that can meet, once again, since, according to you, none of these elements would have a law, an essential structure, a nature, for all would be accidental and indeed the accidental itself would disappear.

However, above all, how can you think that through accident and chance multiple elements, indeed thousands, would concur with such good fortune in order to constitute a thing as *one, simple,* and *excellent* as *vision*? And if we consider in this eye, inasmuch as it is living and not dead, *the visual faculty,* how can you think that something *so one and simple* as this faculty can be the result of a fortuitous meeting of various elements?

Finally, tell me, is not your intellect for knowing? And would your *intellect,* in its unextended, spiritual simplicity, be the accidental meeting of some atoms without a nature or law, without any intelligibility? Would this be the case for the intellect, which seeks out *the intelligible* and finds it, as the hunt for our definitions has shown? What greater absurdity is there than to claim that the intellect comes from a blind, materialistic fatalism or that it comes from chance, from chance which itself disappears if there is no longer any intelligibility in the world, no natural intention, and no law! There are no exceptions to laws unless the laws themselves remain.

Sophist: Could you at least summarize all this discourse for me in a short form of reasoning since you claim to make me admit the finality of nature, that of my eyes and of yours?

Aristotle: This finality of your eyes and of mine is seen and does not need to be demonstrated, properly speaking. However, I will summarize what I have said to you in an explicative syllogism, rather than an illative one.[6] It is as follows.

---

[6]   [Tr. note: Properly speaking, a syllogism is objectively illative, inferring a truth (i.e. the conclusion) from two premises. As regards the distinction between an explicative and an illative syllogism, see the remarks of Fr. Garrigou-Lagrange's student, Fr. Austin Woodbury, S.M. in Woodbury, *Logic*, 239–241 (n.299–300, slightly edited.): "In every syllogism properly so-called, from one truth is inferred ANOTHER TRUTH. Therefore, whenever a NEW TRUTH is not inferred by a syllogism, this is a syllogism improperly so-called. The syllogism improperly so-called is twofold, to wit: the expository syllogism and the explicative syllogism. . . .

The explicative syllogism must be distinguished from the expository syllogism. The following is an example of the former: 'Man is mortal. But a rational animal is a man. Therefore, a rational animal is mortal.' Here, [the middle term] is universal, and therefore there is a true inference [or, illation]. Nevertheless, it is not a syllogism properly so-called, because it does NOT infer in the conclusion another truth, i.e. a judgment other than in the premises. For here, the conclusion expresses the same truth but explicates it BY OTHER CONCEPTS. For these two propositions, 'man is mortal,' and, 'rational animal is mortal,' express the same truth, but the latter expresses it by more distinct concepts than the former. Wherefore, this is rightly called an EXPLICATIVE syllogism.

In the explicative syllogism, the conclusion is IDENTICAL AS REGARDS ITSELF (*quoad se*) with the major but NOT AS REGARDS US (*non quoad nos*); and therefore, there is a formal illation, but not an objective illation. [He cites here R.-M. Schultes, *Introductio ad historiam dogmatum* (Paris: Lethielleux, 1922).]

OBSERVE that the major [premise] and the conclusion of an explicative syllogism are in THE SAME MODE OF SAYING 'PER SE'; otherwise, there would be had, not an explicative syllogism but a syllogism PROPERLY SO-CALLED. In the example given above, both these propositions are IN THE SECOND MODE of saying 'per se.' But the case is otherwise with this syllogism: 'A rational animal is capable of science. But man is a rational animal. Therefore, man is capable of science.' Here, the major [premise] is in the FOURTH mode of saying 'per se'; otherwise, the syllogism would be employed to no purpose. But the conclusion is in the SECOND manner of saying 'per se.' Wherefore this is a syllogism properly so-called."

Also, see Garrigou-Lagrange, "On the Search for Definitions According to Aristotle and St. Thomas," cited above.]

The end is something determinate and fitting, to which that which is *fitted* to attain it itself *tends*. Now, natural agents are *fitted* and *tend* to something determinate and befitting, even something excellent, like wings to flight, feet to walking, the ear to hearing, and the eye to vision. Therefore, natural agents tend toward an *end*.

In order to deny this, one must reject the notion of the end that all men have or must reject the notion of action. *Action* is necessarily *tendential*. That is, it always *tends* (whether naturally and unconsciously or with intelligence) to an end. The stone tends toward the center of the earth for the cohesion of the universe without being aware of this. The swallow tends toward her nest, which she knows only sensibly. She knows it thus as a sensible thing that is an end without knowing finality as such. Man, having an intellect, whose object is *being* (and not color or sound), tends intelligently towards an end by knowing that the end is the *raison d'être* of the means.[7]

VII. Art and Nature

Sophist: Your argument represents a vulgar kind of anthropomorphism. It comes down to saying, "There certainly is finality in human art. Now, an analogy exists between nature and art. Therefore, nature acts for an end."

You gratuitously project human finality onto nature, as others, through anthropomorphism, attribute our passions to God.

---

[7] A modern author recalls this when he writes, "Every movement is the product of a spontaneity that is directed towards an end; however, a spontaneity that is directed toward an end is a *tendency*, and a tendency that produces a movement is a force." See Jules Lachelier, *Du fondement de l'induction*, 3rd ed. (Paris: Ancienne Librarie Germer Bailliere, 1898), 87.

Aristotle: Far from projecting the finality of human art onto nature (as though I said that nature acts like art), I say on the contrary that *art imitates the finality that is found in nature.* It is not placed there by human art. Instead, it finds that finality there, and it existed before such art. I affirm this not by a conceptual reduction to our artistic human activity but, instead, through a conceptual reduction to *intelligible being,* for if the wings of the bird were not for flying, they would have no *raison d'être.*

I do not say to you that the fish moves itself in the water like the best swimmer, but, instead, that the swimmer moves in the water like the fish, which has nothing to learn from him. And if men wanted to travel in the air, they should *imitate* the bird's flight. Even when an art like medicine *aids* nature, *it still imitates it.* As you know well, it serves the vital principle as well as possible, a principle that already exists in the sick person. As the master proposes an argument to the disciple's natural intelligence, the doctor must place the natural properties of bodies, pure air, the salts of the earth, and above all those of plants all at the service of the vitality that still remains in the sick person. He utilizes the natural *capacities* [*aptitudes*] of these plants and does not succeed at completely imitating them when he wishes to make remedies himself.

Above all, human art cannot succeed at imitating the surety of the animal instinct of the spider, the ant, or the bee that so excellently constructs its hive and makes its honey. Is it not quite clear that this bee tends toward something *very determinate and excellent*? Why does it make honey and not something else? What is the *raison d'être* of this *tendency*? And if you deny the excellence of the honey that is thus made, attempt therefore to imitate its taste through all the resources of art.

VIII. Instinct

Sophist: Who knows if the bee is not endowed like us with a kind of intelligence that would explain the finality of its acts quite well without us needing to admit that there is finality in nature?

Aristotle: It is proper to the intellect to know not only color or sound but *being* and the *raisons d'être* of things, to see that the end is the reason for the being of the means and, consequently, to be able *to adapt* and *vary* these means according to the circumstances as does every artist who is not a slave to routine. All architects do not make houses according to the same plan, and all painters do not produce the same paintings. All musicians do not play the same tune, whereas, by contrast, all swallows make their nests the same, all spiders weave their webs alike, and all bees alike make their hives and their honey.

This is a sign that these animals, whose instinct is nonetheless so admirable, do not know finality. They do not see *in the thing, which is an end, the raison d'être* of the means. This is a sign that they do not have an intellect but, rather, are determined *ad unum* by their very nature. The bee only knows how to make honey, and indeed, it ever makes it in the same, excellent manner. If it had an intellect, its intellect would be determined, without a doubt, by its nature *ad unum*—but to *intelligible being* and not to honey. And, under the light of intelligible being, it would perceive the *raisons d'être* of things, efficient causality and finality and would also perceive the range of various means possible in view of the same end. It would make *judgments of value* (as say certain young people, who believe that they have discovered something new), that is, judgments of fittingness and finality as we have always spoken of.[8]

Sophist: Nature makes monstrosities in which there is no finality. How can you affirm that it acts for an end?

Aristotle: And does not the artist, who obviously acts for a determined end, at times deviate from the rules of his art and at times make eyesores? Likewise, do not moral monstrosities exist, even though man acts for an end. However, when the artist deviates, it is not his art that errs,[9] and no more is it prudence that is the principle of the imprudent act, nor justice that is the *source* of injustice. For the same reason, *nature* is not what produces monstrosities. It does not preserve them either. They are the result of an accidental cause on account of which matter escapes the domination of the form (or of the directive idea of the embryo's development). As it happens that a man may prefer the pleasing good to the fitting good, it sometimes happens that matter escapes the domination of form, above all when the form requires multiple, very complex dispositions into which deviations can slip.

These exceptions confirm the rule in the sense that without the rule they would not exist as exceptions and also in the sense that they arise from the accidental omission of a condition required by the rule. Although monstrosities may exist in nature, it remains the case that the seed contained in the grain of wheat is ordered to the formation of ear of grain and not an oak. Likewise, the

---

[8] [Tr. note: On the topic of animal intelligence, the reader would benefit from reading John Deely, "Animal Intelligence and Concept-Formation," *Thomist* 35, no.1 (January 1971), 43–93. This text can also be found in John Deely, *Realism for the 21st Century: A John Deely Reader*, ed. Paul Cobley (Scranton: University of Scranton Press, 2009), 91–139.]

[9] [Tr. note: Granted, a great artist can make a mistake to teach his student something, for in contrast to the virtue of prudence, art is more about *judgment* than it is about *execution* or *command*. See ST I-II q.56 a.3.]

seed contained in the acorn is ordered to the formation of an oak and not a cedar or a larch.

Finality is obvious. In departing from it, monstrosities confirm it rather than overturn it. This is why they are called monstrosities. They instruct us in their own way, as when one listens to a sophistical argument and thus sees how not to reason.

Sophist: To act for an end presupposes deliberation. Now, nature does not deliberate.

Aristotle: And does he who admirably plays the harp (and, thus, who obviously acts for an end) deliberate in order to know at each moment what string he must pluck, at what height, and in what way? He who is most truly an artist no longer deliberates. His art is rooted in him like a second nature. Thus, first nature, in the order of vegetative and animal life acts for an end without either deliberating or ever being aware of the fact. The eye is made for seeing; the ear is made for hearing. Otherwise, you explain order by disorder, what is most beautiful and lofty in nature by that which is lowliest—by this accidental cause, chance. Therefore, if the object of wisdom is being inasmuch as it is being and its ultimate principles, the formal object of sophistics is the *accidental*, the *per accidens*, which for lack of support vanishes. Why waste your intelligence in defending such paradoxes, which are absurdity itself?

Sophist: It seems so to you, and for you it is true. Did not my master, Protagoras of Abdera, when he debated with Socrates, say that the individual man is the measure of truth and falsity and that there are no universal truths? But, then again, since you claim that it exists, tell me how you yourself avoid the absurdity with which you reproach others.

Aristotle: In rejecting every universal truth that would be valid for all men, do you also reject not only the grammatical value of the principle of contradiction but also its real and extra-mental value? Could your master, at one and the same time, be from Abdera and not? Could he, at one and the same time, be and not be Protagoras?

It is said that a young man of late thought that he made a discovery by reversing the relations of knowledge and reality, saying that man's thought vainly insists upon revolving around things in order to know them and that, in truth, things revolve around us, obediently entering into thought's subjective categories. How obedient these things are! Will they be so for long? Why should they not go into categories other than our own?

Like you, this young man came to doubt the real value of the principle of contradiction and naturally came to doubt the other subordinate principles of causality and finality. However, how does he himself subsist and distinguish himself from those who do not think as he does? Can he, at one and the same time, be and not be the young Gorgias?

And your master, so ingenious though he was, can he, at one and the same time, be and not be Protagoras? Neither he, nor the young Gorgias, despite the grave and stuffy airs he puts on, can be taken seriously for a long time. They have become sick willingly. They have fallen into mental illness and would have us believe that it is wisdom. They suffer from an incurable lung disease while humble common sense breathes with full lungs like a man from Piraeus and like the ploughman in the fields.

Sophist: Nonetheless, along with Heraclitus, the same Protagoras said—and not without profundity—that the principle of contradiction itself, as well as all the others, sink down into becoming. That which is, is not, and that which is not, is—for all things become and becoming is self-sufficient, having need of neither efficient, nor final, causality.

Aristotle: Does the principle of contradiction sink down into becoming, or does "causeless becoming" come to be shattered on the rock of the principle of contradiction? If, as you say, this principle came to sink into oblivion, becoming itself would disappear. It would no longer be becoming rather than non-becoming, and the terminus *a quo* would no longer be distinct from the terminus *ad quem*. Travelling from Athens to Megara, one would arrive before departing. Moreover, becoming would just as well be immobile. It would be identical with the absolute immobility of Being (or, rather, with nothingness) which would need no *raison d'être*—neither formal, nor efficient, nor final.

This would represent a form of absolute nihilism. One could no longer say anything at all, nor have any determinate thought, nor desire anything, nor will anything, nor do anything. Cratylus had to admit this—he who no longer said a word but, instead, remained content with merely moving his finger. The role to be played by the skeptic is to be mute like a bump on a log.

Certainly, yes, Heraclitus denied the principle of contradiction and after him, so did certain young men who repeated his paradoxes without having his originality, which led Plato reflect upon these matters. Heraclitus denied the principle of contradiction, but one does not need to actually think everything that comes out of one's mouth. And Heraclitus himself would have been quite unsatisfied to see the ineptitude with which people repeat what he said. In his errors, he was profound in his own way, like the person who poses a problem well. His recent imitators no longer share in his profundity.

IX. Finality or Nihilism

Sophist: Since you boast of connecting everything to being, I would very much like to see how you connect finality to it. If all things are not, as Heraclitus claims, mixed together in a perpetual flux or perpetual becoming, into which the principle of contradiction sinks down, then *being is* and non-being is not, as Parmenides affirms. However, it then follows that nothing becomes. For if something *becomes* or *tends* toward an end, it would proceed either from being or from non-being, which itself is nothing. There is no middle path. Now, it is obvious that nothing can come from noth-ingness. However, no more can anything come from being, for being *already is* and that which becomes *does not yet exist*. Nothing can come from being, just as a statue is not made from a statue precisely because it already exists.

Aristotle: Certainly, one does not make a statue from a statue. However, a statue is indeed made out of marble (which *can* be sculpted) or out of clay (which *can* be fashioned), just as the oak comes into existence from the seed con-tained in the acorn and as the seed contained in the grain of wheat gives birth to the ear of grain.

That which becomes and tends toward a determinate end comes neither from nothingness, nor from already determined being, but rather, from undetermined being, capable of receiving a given determination or perfec-tion. Men call this real capacity for receiving a perfection "passive potency," just as they call the capacity for produc-ing this same perfection "active potency." The perfection itself is called "act."

Hence, you see that being is divided into potency and act, and do you not see at the same time, that *potency is essentially ordered to act,* passive potency to the act to be received, and active potency to the action to be produced (as the power of sight to the act of seeing or the power of hearing to the act of hearing)? Now, in response to your question, this is exactly where we see the finality that is connected to being by the division of being into potency and act. Do you wish to continue to use the word "can" and to say that the marble *can* be sculpted and clay molded?

Finality exists, and if it did not, all efficient causality and, indeed, even all material causality would disappear. In fact, chance itself would disappear along with them, for like every accidental cause, chance must itself be based upon something. If you do not grasp this, you resemble, as someone said, a person who visits a zoo and looks obliviously at an elephant, seeing only the tiny birds standing on its back. This is not the rarest of occurrences in the intellectual order.

At least for love of chance and for being able to continue to make use of this word, admit, in the most insignificant of actions in the smallest of bodies, that this action or *tendency* has a law and an *end*. This will lead us to Pure Act.

Chapter Three

THE PHILOSOPHY OF BECOMING AND PSEUDO-FINALITY

In order to form a correct idea of finality and to avoid confusing it with what merely has some kind of resemblance with it, we here should point out the kind of *pseudo-finality* to which the philosophy of becoming must lead, especially as it is conceived of by several contemporary philosophers.

First, we will recall their point of departure and will see how they are led to utterly alter the notion of finality and, especially, the notions of perfection and the ultimate end, changing them from how they are formulated by traditional philosophy, to the point of confusing the latter with "the vital impulse" and "infinite progress." From the perspective of traditional realism, this represents the very negation of the Sovereign Good and, consequently, of every end truly subordinated to the ultimate (or, supreme) end.

* * *

All those who paid attention to the modernist movement approximately twenty years ago recall the article published by Édouard Le Roy in the *Revue de métaphysique et de morale* in March 1907, entitled, "Comment se pose le problème de Dieu."[1] Recall that it was a critique

---

[1] Édouard Le Roy, "Comment se pose le problème de Dieu," *Revue de métaphysique et de morale* 15 (March and July, 1907): 129–170, 470–513.

of the traditional proofs of God's existence, such as they are presented by St. Thomas. This critique denied the real ontological and transcendent value of the first principles of reason that are the foundation of these proofs—the principle of contradiction (or, identity) and the principle of efficient causality. There, it was declared that "every form of ontological realism is absurd and ruinous."[2] In rejecting the ontological value of the principle of identity (or, contradiction), the author asked, "Why not identify being with becoming?"[3] From this perspective, God did not seem to be really and essentially distinct from the *vital impulse*, which is, according to the expression of Henri Bergson, "*A reality that makes itself through that which unmakes itself*,"[4] and it is henceforth no longer clear how God can be, as [First] Vatican Council declared Him to be, "distinct from the world in existence and essence . . . and ineffably exalted above all things that exist or can be conceived besides Him."[5]

It is also well known that soon thereafter, on July 3, 1907, the decree *Lamentabili* was promulgated by the Holy Office, condemning modernist errors, in particular its pragmatic conceptions of truth and of dogmas, matters that are quite familiar to the readers of Édouard Le Roy. In that decree, the Holy Office condemned these two propositions: "Truth is no more immutable than man himself, since it evolved with him, in him, and through him"[6] (a proposition that is the very consequence of the principle, "Being is identical to becoming") and "the dogmas of the faith are to be held only according to their practical sense, as a preceptive norm of conduct and not as norms of believing."[7] If the second of these condemned propositions were true, we would need to behave toward Jesus Christ as we would toward God, without however, needing to affirm that *He is* God, and similarly would need to behave toward God as we would toward a person.

---

2   Le Roy, "Comment se pose le problème de Dieu," 495.
3   Le Roy, "Comment se pose le problème de Dieu," 135.
4   Henri Bergson, *L'évolution créatrice*, 4th ed. (Paris: Félix Alcan, 1908), 269. [Tr. note: Fr. Garrigou-Lagrange does not mention the edition. The pagination appears to match this one.]
5   [First] Vatican Council, *De filius*, c.1. (Denzinger, no. 3001.)
6   Decree of the Holy Office (under Pius X), *Lamentabili*, no. 58. (Denzinger, no. 3459.)
7   *Lamentabili*, no. 26. (Denzinger, no. 3426.)

The encyclical *Pascendi dominici gregis* appeared two months later on September 8, 1907. It condemned modernism as representing the renewal of numerous heresies, in particular its agnosticism regarding proofs of God's existence and of the distinction between God and the world (i.e. the Uncreated One's distinction from the created order). It rejected modernism's conception of religious experience which modernism substituted for these proofs, a conception in which the orders of nature and grace are mixed together.[8]

Finally, the Antimodernist Oath, prescribed on the first of September, 1910, started with these words,

> I . . . firmly embrace and accept each and every thing that is defined, proposed, and declared by the infallible teaching authority of the Church and, in particular, those points of doctrine that are directly opposed to the errors of this time. First of all, I profess that God, the beginning and end of all things, can be known with certainty and, indeed, also demonstrated through the natural light of reason from "the things that have been made" (Rom. 1:20), namely, from the visible works of creation, as the cause from its effects.[9]

The words, "I profess," show that it is a question of making a profession of faith.

Following upon these declarations by the Church, calm was reestablished, calm again gradually returned, and many intellects that were at first troubled returned to the right path by recognizing the value of natural reason and of its most fundamental affirmations (i.e., its first principles).

* * *

Then, in 1929, we found ourselves faced with the great disappointment of seeing Édouard Le Roy publish anew the article that originally

---

[8] See Pius X, *Pascendi*, Denzinger, nos. 3475ff, 3482ff, 3484, 3493ff.

[9] *Sacorum antistitum*, Denzinger, nos. 3537 and 3538.

appeared in 1907.[10] In the forward, he tells us:

> This volume contains two quite distinct parts. The first is a
> philosophy article that first appeared in the *Revue de méta-*
> *physique et morale* in 1907 and cannot be found today. It is
> reproduced nearly in its entirety without being retouched,
> except in small details and to establish a reasonable connec-
> tion with the second part. In it, we wish to draw attention to
> certain difficulties. Next comes a series of heretofore unedited
> conferences. Their tone is completely different, taking the
> form of a spiritual meditation rather than scholarly dialectic,
> and the investigation strives to maintain its immediately pos-
> itive allure.

Accordingly, it is quite clear that the article from 1907 is repro-
duced here without any concern to respond to the numerous criticisms
and refutations that it raised when it was first published.

The second part is, as he himself said, "a spiritual meditation." It
makes much use of Pascal and is concerned with "human inquietude,
the problem of the will's profound desire, faith in God, the preliminary
affirmations, the affirmation of God, the idea of God, the conditions
of religious life, and remaining obstacles." It represents a march toward
God, which in certain respects calls to mind, mediated through Pas-

---

[10] Édouard Le Roy, *Le problème de Dieu*, 6th ed. (Paris: L'Artisan du livre, 1929). This
work and three others by M. Édouard Le Roy were condemned by the Holy Office
on July 24, 1931. While correcting the final proofs of this current text, we are happy
to read in *La Croix* on January 16, 1932 the submission of Le Roy, who, obedient to
his faith as a Christian and responding to the friendly invitation of His Eminence,
the Cardinal Archbishop of Paris, responded to the Archbishop, "Your Eminence, my
will, in accord with all my convictions and with the sentiments that have ever been
mine, is to live in the faith and in communion with the Church. Therefore, in a spirit
of Christian fidelity, I receive with respect the decree of the Holy Office that you have
communicated to me, accepting it with a simple, filial spirit."
  "Given certain commentaries in the press, permit me, your Eminence, to add that
I believe, in the same sense as does the Church, in the possibility of the objective
demonstration of the existence of God, in the distinction between the Creator and
creatures, in the creation of man in general and, especially, of the soul by God, and in
the objective value of human knowledge."
  "Please accept, etc. . . . Édouard Le Roy."

cal's thought, the treatises of the Doctors of the Church concerning the ultimate end, man's aspirations, and the perfect beatitude which can be found neither in pleasures, nor in honors, nor in power, nor in knowledge of the human sciences, but only in the Sovereign Good who is God. These pages, which recall many of the ideas dear to St. Augustine and St. Thomas, will make an impression on many readers, above all on those who are already at least vaguely convinced of God's existence.

However, the question immediately arises: if this doctrinal construction (for Le Roy still indeed believes himself to be expositing a doctrine, a pragmatist one no doubt, but a doctrine nonetheless) has some persuasive force, where does it come from—from the philosophical foundations that it presupposes (i.e., from the Bergsonian philosophy of becoming) or, rather, from what it still draws into its employ from common sense and from Christian faith? Is this edifice supported by its foundation? Is it not, rather, supported from on high by the reader's religious faith and by whatever undisfigured natural reason he retains? Does it not call to mind the statue spoken of by Daniel, having a head of fine gold, a chest and arms made of silver, legs of iron, and feet of clay?

Let us look into the foundations of the new construction. Why does one refuse to admit the traditional proofs of God's existence? With what are they replaced? We will see whether, on the basis of a *philosophy of becoming* (and not of being) one can avoid falling into a form of pantheism that looks upon God and sees, "A reality that makes itself" and "creative evolution." We will see whether this route can enable one to affirm that God is *He who is—Ego sum qui sum—* Self-Subsistent Existence, who by His simplicity and His absolute immutability (that is, His eternal identity) is really and essentially distinct from all that is essentially multiple or composite and mutable.

The Fundamental Criticism of the Principles of the Traditional Proofs

The principle objection that Édouard Le Roy registers against these proofs can be summarized quite directly: they rest on an unacceptable common-sense distinction, namely "[the distinction] between the mover and the mobile, between movement and its subject, and between act and potency."[11] The other objections derive from this first one: the traditional proofs, we are told, presuppose unconscious recourse to St. Anselm's argument and therefore have no more worth than does his argument. Finally, they would not establish the transcendence of the First Cause or Its Infinite Superiority over everything created.

If anyone compromises the Divine transcendence, it most certainly is Le Roy, as can be seen in his book.[12]

However, let us begin by considering the first of these objections, which is summarized in these words, "Why not identify being and becoming?"[13]

How is Le Roy led to hold that the distinction that common sense (or, natural reason) makes "between the mover and the mobile, between movement and its subject, and between act and potency" is inadmissible? As he himself tells us, he is led to this by the very principle of the philosophy of becoming, such as Bergson conceives of it. As Le Roy states:

> I will refer above all to this excellent *Introduction to Metaphysics* [by Bergson], which he published in the *Revue de métaphysique et morale* in January 1903. Common thought is established in the immobile and tries to capture mobile reality as it passes on its way. Therefore, in short, it implicitly posits as an undisputed postulate that immobility is what is intelligible and has primacy and that movement is what must be explained by reduction to

---

[11] This text was found in Le Roy's original article, published in 1907. It is found in an equivalent form in the passages that we have cited from the new book.

[12] See Édouard Le Roy, *Le problème de Dieu*, 91–95, 282–283.

[13] Le Roy, *Le problème de Dieu*, 45.

the immobile. In so doing, it manifests its utilitarian attitude, for it is only from the practical point of view that it can suffice to ask oneself *where is the thing* that one is studying, that which has *become*, in order to see what one can extract from it or what one must say about it. However, such an approach is no longer appropriate for the work of pure, disinterested knowledge. "No matter how many stopped moments we may have at our disposal, we will never produce mobility out of them; whereas, if we start with mobility, we can, by way of diminution, use thought to draw from it as many stopped moments as we may wish to draw."[14]

(Also, M. Édouard Le Roy concludes:) *The true philosophical method proceeds in a direction opposed to that of common thought. It envisions movement as the fundamental reality and, on the contrary, regards immobility as being a secondary, derivative reality.*[15]

Further on, Édouard Le Roy says,

One wishes that the cause would contain at least everything that is in the effect. Why? Because one divides and deduces. The evidence of the axiom is due, in short, to the fact that, on the one hand, *one imagines an external and separated cause* and, on the other hand, attributes an *ontological scope* to the processes of deductive analysis . . .

To affirm the primacy of act is still to imply the same postulates. If causality is only a kind of discharge from what is full into what is empty, a communication to a receptive terminus coming from what another terminus possesses—in a word, the anthropomorphic work of an agent—so be it! However, what

---

[14] [Tr. note: The quote is taken from Bergson, though Fr. Garrigou-Lagrange does not cite the page. The text is Henri Bergson, "Introduction a la métaphysique," *Revue de métaphysique et de morale* 11 (1903): 26–27.]

[15] Le Roy, *Le Problème de Dieu*, 21. We have added italic emphasis to the text, as we will in the following text as well.

are these idols of the practical imagination worth? *Why not simply identify being with becoming? . . . Perfection* would appear as being a direction orienting the generative activity, *not as a final point or a first source.*[16]

It becomes increasingly clearer that, from this perspective, God, the supreme perfection, will be evolution in perpetual progress and not Being Itself, Eternally Subsistent and forever sovereignly perfect.

Again, Le Roy says:

Thus, we are now in a position to order the dialectical series from which the affirmation of God will emerge . . .

1. *Reality is becoming*, a generative effort or, as Bergson says, a dynamic outpouring, an impulse of life, a surge of unceasing creation. Everything indicates this in nature and we feel it even more so in ourselves . . .

2. *Cosmic becoming is oriented in a definite direction* . . . an ascent toward what is more and what is better. . . . Everything indicates this in nature, notably in biological evolution. Everything indicates it also in us, and history and psychology equally testify to it. In short, existence itself is an effort of growth, a work of ascending realization. Thus, *morality* appears as the foundation of being.

3. *Spirit is liberty*, since it is at the root of being as *creative action* and even, in a certain sense, *self-generative action* . . . Thus we see, in short, what we call *moral reality* (a demand for ascent). This moral reality, spirit of our spirit, is radically irreducible to every other form of reality by its very place at the summit, or rather, at the source of existence. Therefore, we must affirm *its primacy*, and this affirmation is what constitutes *the affirmation of God.*[17]

---

[16] Le Roy, *Le Problème de Dieu*, 45.
[17] This emphasis is in the original.

Therefore, we see in what sense we can and should say that God exists and is real. . . . And this means . . . that *we must behave in relation to Him* as though we were relating to the source whence we draw (and [indeed] must draw) our own existence and our own reality.[18]

This Divine source, God Himself, thus appears more and more like creative evolution, like a universal process of becoming, on whose surface our existence seems like a mere fleeting moment. We come back, in the end, to Bergson's formula, according to which *the vital impulse*, which does not seem to be really and essentially distinct from God, is "A reality that makes itself through that which unmakes itself."[19]

Le Roy concludes, "In the end, we must always return to *religious experience*."[20] This experience seems natural, but given that it is essentially a demand for ascent, it could well be called "supernatural," without it having to change its nature. From the outset, is it not a participation in the Divine Nature, like the sanctifying grace spoken of by the theologians? Furthermore, it is no longer clear why the Semi-Pelagians were condemned for having said that "the beginning of faith (or of salvation) belongs to us by nature and not by grace."[21] What am I saying? Did not the Semi-Pelagians and the Pelagians themselves have a much more elevated conception of God than what is presented to us here?

Let us see what this new theory ultimately is based upon in the final analysis. Is it not the rejuvenation of an old error?

The Foundation of This New Conception

What worth can be assigned to this affirmation, which could already be found in days of yore under Heraclitus's stylus: *reality is becoming*?

---

[18] Le Roy, *Le Problème de Dieu*, 114–115.

[19] Bergson, *L'évolution créatrice*, 269.

[20] Le Roy, *Le Problème de Dieu*, 132.

[21] Council of Orange, can. 5 (Denzinger, no. 375). [Tr. note: Fr. Garrigou-Lagrange has paraphrased the text slightly.]

To our day, the greatest philosophers, in agreement with natural reason, have said, "*Becoming is not self-explanatory. It cannot exist by itself.* It is not related to *reality* or to *being* as A is to A, as white is to white, as light is to light, and as spirit is to spirit." First of all, it requires a subject. Movement is always the movement of something—of water, air, or the ether. Movement in general does not exist as such. Only *this* movement exists. It is only *this* movement or *this* becoming because it is the movement of *this* subject, of *this* mobile thing. No dream without a dreamer, no flight without that which flies, no outflow without a liquid, no flow without a fluid (no matter how subtle and small it might be). *No thought without a mind, and if a mind is not*, like God, *Thought Itself* and Truth Itself Ever Actually Known *ab aeterno*, it is distinct from its thinking and from its thoughts, which vary and are concerned with various objects while it remains *one and the same* (i.e., the same substantial being under the multiple and changing phenomena). And this imperfect mind cannot know without the concurrence of Him who is Thought Itself, Truth Itself, and Life Itself, He who is more intimately present to us than we ourselves are to ourselves, all the while being really and essentially distinct from us.

The greatest philosophers also have said (along with common sense) that *becoming*, whether it be of the bodily or spiritual order, is a *passage* from indetermination to determination (or *from potency to act*). For example, from the seed contained in the grain of wheat to the ripe ear, from the cell serving as the basis of the embryo to the begotten animal, or again, in the passage of the intellect that awakens to a thought that is increasingly distinct. In a word, it is the passage from a capacity for perfection to the act that is this very perfection. And just as there is *more* in the act or perfection than in the potency that is not yet actualized, there must be a *cause* in order to provide a reason for becoming. There must be an *agent*: no begetting without a begetter, no bodily or spiritual *determination produced* without an already-*determined* being capable of realizing it.

Finally, natural reason, along with the greatest thinkers, adds, "*Action presupposes being, and the mode of action follows on the mode of being.*" Only the adult begets, and in order to beget, it first must exist. It acts or determines in accord with the determination that exists in it. The bodily agent performs a bodily action, and the spiritual agent, precisely inasmuch as it is spiritual, performs an action of the spiritual order. However, in order to act, every agent that *is not its very action* must be premoved by Him who alone *is* His action and who for this reason is *Being Itself*—for action presupposes being, and the mode of action follows upon the mode of being.

Such is the language of common sense, as it was understood, deepened, and justified by Socrates, Plato, Aristotle, Augustine, and Thomas Aquinas—to speak only of these thinkers. All of them said, *"Becoming is an effect, which presupposes an action, and action itself presupposes being."* In the final analysis, every action depends on Him who alone is Eternally-Subsistent Being Itself.

Édouard Le Roy comes now to ask us, *"Why not simply identify being with becoming?"*[22] This word "simply" strikes one's ears with a startlingly simplistic tone. There are two species of simplicity: that of the Sovereign Wisdom and then another kind that is very different, about which St. Paul, St. Augustine, and St. Thomas on occasion spoke, namely, the simplicity that judges all things, even of the loftiest, not by the Supreme Cause but, instead, by that which is *lowliest* in all of reality. It is the simplicity that wishes to reduce Being to becoming and the unique instant of immobile eternity to this *nunc fluens*, this fleeting instant, which constitutes the reality of time and the duration that we experience.

"Why not simply identify being with becoming?"—Even Being by Its Essence, Le Roy, even He who Is and who said of Himself, "Ego sum qui sum; [I Am Who Am] . . . *Ego Dominus et non mutor*; [I am the Lord, and I do not change]"? Oh! Then quite certainly, if one so readily identifies being with becoming, one concludes without hesitation as does the present work, "Given that things *are* movement, we no longer need to ask how they *receive* movement." In other words, the proofs of the existence of God by movement and efficient causality cease to exist and fade away.

* * *

---

[22] Le Roy, *Le Problème de Dieu*, 45.

However, in the end, what is the basis for this assertion that *being is becoming* and that *becoming is self-explanatory*, indeed the fundamental reality: God Himself, identical with creative evolution?

In the final analysis, what is the basis for all of this? Le Roy has told us: this is based on Henri Bergson's remark: "No matter how many stopped moments we may have at our disposal, we will never produce mobility out of them, whereas, if we start with mobility, we can, by way of diminution, use thought to draw from it as many stopped moments as we may wish to draw."

Bergson explained this point at greater length in his *Creative Evolution* where he says:

> There is *more* in movement than in the successive positions attributed to that which is mobile, *more* in becoming than in the forms traversed in turn, *more* in the evolution of the form than in the forms realized one after another. Therefore, philosophy will be able to draw terms of the second kind from the first but not the first from the second. Speculation must take its point of departure from the first. *However, the intellect reverses the order of the two terms,* and on this point ancient philosophy proceeds along the path traveled by the intellect. It installs itself in the immutable. It gives itself Ideas and passes on to becoming by way of attenuation and diminution.[23]

Likewise, we read a little later in *Creative Evolution*:

> A perpetuity of mobility is possible only if it is appended to an eternity of immutability that it unrolls in a chain without beginning or end. Such is the final word of Greek philosophy. It is connected by invisible strands to all the fibers of the ancient soul. One would wish in vain to deduce it from a simple principle. However, if we eliminate from it everything that came from poetry, religion, social life, as well as from a still-rudimentary physics and biology, thus setting aside from

---

[23] Bergson, *L'évolution créatrice*, 341–342.

our gaze the friable materials entering into the construction of this immense edifice, *a solid frame remains, and this frame sketches out the broad lines of a metaphysics that is, we believe, the natural metaphysics of the human intellect.*[24]

Bergson and Édouard Le Roy accept a dynamist philosophy of becoming, which is exactly at the antipodes of this "natural metaphysics of the human intellect." Why? They do so because such a metaphysics represents nothing other than, "The systematization of the associations and fragmentation effected upon the universal flow by common thinking, i.e. by the practical imagination and language." Indeed, according to Bergson, the intellect is made only for thinking about "inert objects, most especially the solid bodies where our action finds its fulcrum point and our industry its instruments for work. Our concepts have been formed in the image of solids, and our logic predominately is a logic of solids."[25]

* * *

And behold the foundation of this new conception! Here we see the latest effort of modern thought! Le Roy evidently does not deign to read what was written in response to him twenty-five years ago. At that time, after having examined this nominalist theory of common sense at length, we said that it confuses *intelligible being* (in which our intellect perceives the first principles of identity, *raison d'être*,[26] causality, and finality) with *solid bodies* which represent only the *lowest degree* of substantial being.[27] We showed that *the distinction of potency from act*, as well as those of the mover from that which is mobile, of movement from

---

[24] Bergson, *L'évolution créatrice*, 354.

[25] Bergson, *L'évolution créatrice*, 1.

[26] [Tr. note: See note 5 in the previous chapter.]

[27] See Réginald Garrigou-Lagrange, *Le sens commun: la philosophie de l'être et les formules dogmatiques*, 3rd ed. (Paris: Desclée de Brouwer, 1933), 158–247 (2nd part—*Common sense and the Traditional Proofs of the Existence of God*). [Tr. note: A translation of the fourth edition of *Le sens commun* is scheduled for publication by Emmaus Academic in the near future.]

its subject, and of our successive thoughts from our mind, represent divisions of *intelligible being* and not the fragmentation of *the sensible continuum*. Above all, we showed that the distinction of potency from act is necessary in order to render *multiplicity and becoming intelligible in function of being,* and not in function of solid bodies.[28]

A little later, taking up again the study of the same problem, we wrote:

> The argument that has been opposed to us has not made much progress since the time of Heraclitus. We can see its sensualist origin with ever greater clarity. If the intellect has for its object only *solid bodies*, one must find some way to explain to us the verb *to be*, the soul of every judgment, and must show us how it is that men can differ from animals. If the object of the intellect is not *solid bodies* but, instead, *being* and everything which has a *raison d'être*, the Bergsonian proposition, "There is more in movement than in the immobile," is true only of immobilities grasped *by the senses* concerning becoming itself. But it is false if it is erected as an absolute principle, for then it means, "There is more in that which becomes and does not yet exist than in that which is." For the *senses*, the immobile is that which *is at rest* as regards its location; for the intellect, it is *that which is*, in opposition to that which becomes, as the immutable is that which is and cannot not be—Bergsonian sensualism confuses the immutability that is superior to movement with that which is inferior to it. . . . Thus, it debases the immobile life of the intellect, which contemplates the loftiest eternal laws, to the inertia of solid, inanimate bodies.—From this perspective, time is superior to eternity. It is life, whereas immobile eternity is death.[29]

---

[28] See Réginald Garrigou-Lagrange, *Le sens commun*, 205–214.

[29] Réginald Garrigou-Lagrange, *God: His Existence and His Nature: A Thomistic Solution of Certain Agnostic Antinomies,* vol. 1, trans. Bede Rose (St. Louis: B. Herder, 1949), 170–171. [Tr. note: As has been the custom, I have cited Fr. Garrigou-Lagrange's works in translation. The translation here is mine, though it is substantially the same as Dom Rose's.]

Émile Boutroux responded likewise to [Herbert] Spencer:

Evolutionism is true *from the perspective of the senses*. However, *from the perspective of the intellect*, it remains true that the imperfect exists and is determined *only in view* of the more perfect. . . . Moreover, the intellect continues saying with Aristotle: "Everything has its *raison d'être*, and the first principle must be the ultimate reason for things. Now, to explain is to determine, and the ultimate reason of things can only be *entirely determined* being."[30]

"Such is the final word of Greek philosophy," as Bergson himself confessed. However, it is not true, as he says, that "this philosophy is connected by invisible strands to all the fibers of the ancient soul," and to that which provides the foundation of the human intellect. It is an error to say that one "cannot deduce it from a simple principle." It is fixed to the intellect by the ultimate law of thought and of reality, by the *principle of identity* (the positive form of the principle of contradiction), implied in the very first idea, the idea of being: "*Being is being, non-being is non-being*" or more briefly, "*Being is not non-being*; they are opposed as contradictories."

Now, if *becoming* is the fundamental reality, as Bergson and Le Roy claim, thus returning to the position of Heraclitus, one must say with this old Ionian philosopher that the principle of contradiction has no real value, for *being* and *non-being*, far from being opposed as contradictories, *are identical* in *becoming, which is self-explanatory*. Aristotle made this clear with great profundity in the fourth book of his *Metaphysics*, where he shows the full meaning, absolute necessity, real value, and full scope of the principle of contradiction.

If the fundamental reality is becoming, the principle of contradiction vanishes, and along with it, the principle of identity, which positively expresses the same law: "Being is being; non-being is non-be-

---

[30] Émile Boutroux, *Études d'histoire de la philosophie*, 3rd ed. (Paris: Felix Alcan, 1908), 203 and 205. [Tr. note: Fr. Garrigou-Lagrange has cited page 202 without an edition. He has reversed the order of the passages. The portion before the first ellipse comes from 205, and the second half is taken from 203.]

ing." Then, we would no longer need to say, "Truth [*le vrai*] is truth [*le vrai*], falsity [*le faux*] is falsity [*le faux*], *est est, non non*," as is said in the Gospel. Likewise, what would remain of the principle, "Good is good, evil is evil, they cannot be confused"? Would spiritual writers still be able to affirm, "Flesh is flesh, spirit is spirit; God is God, the creature is the creature"? Ought we not say about this universal becoming (or, creative evolution) what Pius IX said in the first proposition of his *Syllabus of Errors*: "God is identical with the nature of things and therefore subject to change; *God actually becomes himself in man* and in the world; all things are God and have the very substance of God"?[31] If the principle of identity (or, of contradiction) vanishes, what disappears along with it is the principle of causality, applied, not only to phenomena, but moreover in the order of being. With being, it sinks down into becoming.

Is it not to this conclusion that Le Roy leads us, despite the spiritual meditation making up the second part of his book? On the whole, he maintains what he had written in 1905 in the *Revue de métaphysique et morale*:

> The principle of non-contradiction [*sic*] is not as universal and necessary as it is believed to be. It has its domain of application and has its restricted, limited meaning. *As the ultimate law of discourse and not of thought in general, it holds only for the static*, the fragmented, the immobile—in brief, it holds for things endowed with an *identity*. *However, there is contradiction in the world*, as there is identity. It is made up of fleeting mobilities—becoming, duration, life—which by themselves are not discursive and are transformed by discourse in order that they may be grapsed in contradictory schemata.[32]

This comes down to saying that, given that the fundamental reality is *becoming*, the principle of contradiction (or, of non-contradiction)

---

[31] Denzinger, no. 2901.

[32] Édouard Le Roy, "Sur la logique de l'invention," *Revue de métaphysique et morale* 13 (1905): 200–204.

is the fundamental error, unless we say with Aristotle and St. Thomas: this ultimately means that *radical absurdity is at the root of all things*.[33]

Le Roy absolutely maintains his position. This is what led him to write in his new book, "*Reality is becoming . . . a spiritual activity from which emanate the relative immobilities that one calls matter or pure reason*."[34] Also, "*The principle of causality can only render judgments about phenomena. Its connection with fragmentation is well known*."[35] Hence, the proofs of God's existence, founded on this principle, which is closely connected with the principle of contradiction, no longer have any value.

* * *

We must choose. Either we will have *becoming, creative evolution* wherein the real and essential distinction between the Immutable and Eternal Uncreated One and the ever-changing created order disappears, or we can instead have *the truth of the principle of contradiction* (*or, of identity*) as the fundamental law of thought and of reality. Thus, the position adopted by the philosophy of becoming appears as being a proof of the existence of God by way of absurdity, and if this position did not exist, we would need to invent it in order to provide the choice: the true God or radical absurdity.

The principle of contradiction affirms that a square-circle is not only *inconceivable* but, even more, is *unrealizable* outside our intellect, unrealizable by any power that may ever exist, whether finite or infinite. In affirming this, our intellect already *goes forth from itself*. It is to affirm a law of *possible reality* and of that which is *really impossible*. The same principle also affirms that *that which becomes does not yet exist*—i.e. that *becoming is not being*—and that there is *more in being than in becoming*, in the begotten animal than in the development of the embryo.

This principle of contradiction, whether it is expressed in its negative form (being is not non-being) or in its positive form (*est est, non*

---

[33] See St. Thomas Aquinas, *In IV Meta.*, chs. 3–8, lect. 5–17.

[34] Le Roy, *Le problème de Dieu*, 115.

[35] Le Roy, *Le problème de Dieu*, 92; also, see 35 and 45.

non), is incomparably more certain than everything that we are told about human anxiety and the profound desire of the will. And all such things can hold only if the principle of contradiction abides. Without the principle of contradiction, the *cogito ergo sum* would vanish as well. I could no longer say, "I think," but instead, impersonally, "There is thought," as one says, "It's raining"[36]—and not even that, for it could be the case that thought is identical with non-thought. This is the doctrinal nihilism that leads one to moral nihilism.

As we have shown at length elsewhere,[37] by radically distorting the notion of creation, the doctrine of Self-Creative Evolution clashes with all the first principles of reason. Indeed, it allows there to be a becoming *without a subject*, a movement without something mobile, a becoming *without an efficient cause* distinct from itself, a becoming *without a final cause* known by a perfect intellect from all eternity. It holds that this self-creative evolution is *ascending*, and then, in it, *the more comes from the less, the more perfect from the less perfect*. It rejects the mystery of creation, which is in harmony with the principles of efficient and final causality, in order to substitute *absurdity* for it, now placed at the root of all things: the more that comes from the less without an efficient cause and without finality, properly speaking. As it has been put, God, who is identical with this creative evolution, goes from surprise to surprise by seeing all that He becomes, without having foreseen any of this.

This doctrine admits that becoming, which provides its own self-explanation, is a *realized contradiction*. However, it forgets what Aristotle remarked at the end of the fourth book of his *Metaphysics*—namely, that if the principle of contradiction no longer has any value, *becoming itself is not distinct from non-becoming*. In it, the point of departure is not distinct from the point of arrival. Thus, one will find oneself at the end before having set out for it. Bodily and spiritual becoming thus become *immobile* and are confused, not with the immobility of Subsistent Being but, instead, with the immobility of nothingness—indeed, with absolute nothingness, which is not only the absence of

---

[36] [Tr. note: This is a play on the impersonal French expression, "il pleut," for "it is raining."]

[37] See Garrigou-Lagrange, *De revelatione*, 3rd ed., ch.8, a.2.

every form of existence but also of every possibility of existence.

The truth of the principle of contradiction (or, of identity) is more certain than the ground beneath our feet. It is a certitude that is not only physical but that is metaphysical and absolute, and without it, nothing is intelligible for us any longer. In other words, along with the notion of being, which founds this principle, those of the true and of the good vanish, along with their opposition to error and evil.

Behold the bond that affixes to the human intellect the affirmation of the *primacy of being over becoming*, which underlies traditional philosophy and, as Bergson admits: "If we thus set aside from our gaze the friable materials entering into the construction of this immense edifice, a solid frame remains, and this frame sketches out the broad lines of a metaphysics that is, we believe, the natural metaphysics of the human intellect."[38]

Is It True That St. Thomas Did Not Establish the Divine Transcendence?

In his latest book, Édouard Le Roy criticizes St. Thomas quite cavalierly for not having established God's transcendence, i.e. His infinite superiority above every creature.[39] After having related the definition of *person* that the Common Doctor of the Church applies analogically to God, Le Roy, who has in no way understood the [nature of] analogy, is content to write, "It is an expression borrowed from legal language. We need not insist upon it."[40] Without understanding St. Thomas, Le Roy is rough with the him, like a school master who, paying no heed to the wealth contained in natural reason, is rough with a child who responds to him with an answer in accord with common sense. He does not grasp that we are here concerned with three absolute (*simpliciter simplices*) perfections, which formally imply no imperfection—subsistent being, intelligence, and freedom—all of which

---

[38] Bergson, *L'évolution créatrice*, 354.
[39] See Le Roy, *Le problème de Dieu*, 30, 38–43, 118.
[40] Le Roy, *Le problème de Dieu*, 118.

consequently can be applied to God *analogically*, though according to their *proper* sense and without metaphor. We have explained this at length elsewhere[41] by examining the objections, which are reprinted here [in Le Roy's text] as though they had received no response.

We are told that the Thomist proofs of God's existence conclude at the Divine Transcendence only by unconsciously having recourse to St. Anselm's argument and therefore have no more value than does his.[42]

We already responded to Le Roy: St. Anselm should have said only, "The greatest being that can be conceived exists necessarily of itself and not from another, *if It exists*." Reciprocally, one can say, "*If It exists*, the Necessary Being must be Being Itself. It must be related to being as A is to A, in virtue of the principle of identity (or, contradiction). Otherwise we would still need to ascend higher all the way to the pure identity of *Ipsum Esse Subsistens*, which is limitless and infinitely perfect."[43] Therefore, no unconscious recourse is had to St. Anselm's argument, for it has first been established *a posteriori* that the Necessary Being is required as the Cause of that which becomes.

* * *

Le Roy states several times, in different ways, that God's transcendence is not established by the Thomist proofs.[44]

The proof of the Divine transcendence given by St. Thomas is, however, connected in a rigorous manner to the principle of contradiction (or, identity), the necessity of which has not been shown to be lacking. It comes down to this: neither multiplicity nor becoming can exist within the Absolute. Now, the world is essentially multiple

---

[41] See Garrigou-Lagrange, *God: His Existence and His Nature*, vol. 1, 213–223, 232–241; vol. 2, 205–221, 246–267. [Tr. note: I have had to alter Fr. Garrigou-Lagrange's citation slightly. I have cited the whole section pertinent to the last selection, for which he cites only the first page. Also, he cites page 780 of the original French, a page number exceeding the length of the text of earlier editions, though over the years he did augment the text throughout its eleven editions.]

[42] See Le Roy, *Le problème de Dieu*, 38, 46, 94.

[43] See Garrigou-Lagrange, *Le sens commun*, 3rd ed., 215–219.

[44] See Le Roy, *Le problème de Dieu*, 30, 38, 39, 41, 43.

and changing. Therefore, God is really and essentially distinct from the world. We can find a presentation of this proof in the first chapter of *Dei Filius* promulgated by [the First] Vatican Council.[45] In other words: if the principle of identity (or, contradiction) is the fundamental law of thought and of reality, the fundamental reality must be related to being as A is to A. In other words, it must be Eternally-Subsistent Being Itself, Truth Itself Ever-Known, the Good Itself Ever-Loved, Thought Itself, and Love in its pure form [*par essence*]—*Ipsum intelligere et Ipsum velle subsistens.*[46]

Le Roy reiterates with Kant, "Whence does one draw the conclusion that this intelligence and wisdom (called for by the proof taken from the order of the world) are *infinite* and *creative*"?

If he had understood St. Thomas, he would have grasped that every intellect that is not infinite and is not Thought Itself and Truth Itself is *ordered to Truth and to Being*, as the living eye is ordered to the colored. Thus, he would have grasped that one must ascend all the way to a Supreme, *Ordering* Intellect, which is *Ipsum intelligere subsistens*. It is here that we find the very elements of traditional philosophy.[47]

The Philosophy of Becoming Represents the Utter Denial of Divine Transcendence

If St. Thomas had not proven God's transcendence, would it fall to the philosophy of becoming (or the philosophy of creative evolution) to establish it? After having admitted that *becoming* is the fundamental reality and source of all things, how therefore can this philosophy establish that God is infinitely superior to every bodily and spiritual creature, infinitely superior to bodily or spiritual movement, and supe-

---

45 See Denzinger, no. 3001: "As [God] is one, unique, and spiritual substance, entirely simple and unchangeable, we must proclaim him distinct from the world in existence and essence [*re et essentia*] . . . and ineffably exalted above all things." [Tr. note: Fr. Garrigou-Lagrange refers to this literally as "the first chapter of the third session."]

46 See *Thomas Aquinas, Summa Theologiae* I, q. 3, aa. 4, 7, 8; q. 4, a. 2; q. 7, a. 1; q. 9, a. 1; q. 10, a. 2.

47 See *ST* I, q. 14, aa. 2, 3, 4.

rior to time, which is the measure of movement? If God is creative evolution, how can this philosophy establish that *He can exist without the world that evolves?* How does it respect the dogma of creation *ex nihilo et non ab aeterno?* It claims that the expression "creation *ex nihilo*" is unthinkable, for it does not understand that these words mean, "*Ex nullo praesupposito subiecto;* [from no presupposed subject]."[48]

How can a philosophy of becoming be reconciled with the revealed affirmation that God freely wished to create the world *non ab aeterno,* that everything that exists besides Him *had a beginning,* and that bodily and spiritual movement, as well as time, had a beginning?[49]

We can see well what remains of the Divine Transcendence and of the dogma of creation by reading what Le Roy says about them in his recent book.[50] For example, we read:

"Creation is inconceivable as an historical event having its own date, unknown to us no doubt, but assignable in itself.... *One is duped by one's imagination when one believes that we can think of a beginning of the universe as a whole* on the model of its temporal continuation. Precisely because the idea of non-being [*néant*] is only a pseudo-idea, ... we can in no way conceive of *a passage from non-being* [*néant*] into being.... The principle of causality can judge only phenomena," etc., etc.[51]

"In the end, the idea of the first cause is an idol of deduction."[52]

Obviously, if the fundamental reality is becoming, the notion of creation *ex nihilo* is absurd. However, if being is divided into act and potency, if becoming presupposes a passive potency and an active potency, when the passive potency is equal to zero, it is necessary that there be an active potency which alone is capable of producing something, even a grain of sand, *ex nihilo,* that is to say—and this is no

---

[48] See *ST* I, q. 45, a. 5c, ad 3.
[49] See *ST* I, q. 46, a. 2: "Whether it is an article of faith that the world began to exist."
[50] See Le Roy, *Le problème de Dieu,* 91–93, 95, 282–283.
[51] Le Roy, *Le problème de Dieu,* 91–92.
[52] Le Roy, *Le problème de Dieu,* 93.

pseudo idea—*ex nullo praesupposito subiecto.*[53]

In other words, if God is not really and essentially distinct from the *vital impulse*, which is "a reality that makes itself," "a continuous gushing-forth," and "creative evolution," He is not conceived without the evolving world and therefore cannot exist before it, before time, in the unique instant of immobile eternity. From this outlook, God is not conceived without the world.

Moreover, He could not be infinitely perfect, for He is an infinity of becoming. Le Roy writes in his recent book, concerning what he calls the *static theory of perfection,* "Nothing is more contestable. . . . *Why, I repeat, cannot perfection quite simply be infinite progress. . . ? Why can we not say that the perfect is an ascent and an increase rather than an immobile plenitude?*"[54] Why not? Because, in this ascending creative evolution, *the more would come from the less*, and that is something that "quite simply" cannot be admitted.

Again, consider his remarks:

> We do not have completed and closed "natures". . . . On the contrary, our life is incessant creation. . . . God is at one and the same time immanent and transcendent: immanent as regards His efficacious and intimate presence, and as regards His inspiring and creative [*réalisante*] activity in us; transcendent as regards the infinity of creation and of the ever-higher reality toward which, without limit, he attracts us and raises us, and likewise, as regards His character as an inexhaustible principle.[55]

In sum, Le Roy maintains what he said in years past in the *Revue de métaphysique et de morale* in July of 1907 when he characterized God's transcendence by saying:

---

[53] See *ST* I, q. 45, a. 5c, ad 3. When theologians say that created angels are "outside" of God, the term "outside" obviously does not mean "locally outside" but, rather, that the angels *are not* God.

[54] Le Roy, *Le problème de Dieu*, 95.

[55] Le Roy, *Le problème de Dieu*, 283.

If we declare God to be immanent, this is because we are considering Him from the perspective of *what has come into being in us and in the world*. However, for the world and for us, an *infinity of becoming* forever remains, an infinity that will be creation properly speaking, not a simple development, and from this perspective, *God* appears as being *transcendent*.[56]

This is the same as saying that God will never be infinitely perfect, and in the ascending creative evolution, grace (which one still wishes to speak about) does not constitute a new order, infinitely superior to that of nature. We are told, "We are not complete and closed natures." Grace is a moment of evolution, as is Christianity itself as well, the most elevated moment but nothing more. Thenceforth, where is its essential supernaturality? Here, as ever, we find ourselves faced with pure modernism, which has been condemned.[57]

It is clear that the pragmatic symbol of the Divine Personality that one wishes still to preserve here covers over a pantheistic metaphysics of *becoming*, which stands in radical opposition to what the [First] Vatican Council tells about the *real and essential* distinction between the Creator and the creature, just as much as it stands in opposition with the principle of identity (or, contradiction), the fundamental law of thought and of reality.[58]

The Proposed New Proof and Pseudo-Finality: The Way of Doctrinal Nihilism

And then, what worth may be ascribed to the proof of God's existence proposed by Le Roy under the titles: human anxiety; the problem of the will's profound desire; faith in God, etc.?

Certainly, here we have a commentary on Pascal which attempts to preserve the proof of God's existence by way of the desire for happiness

---

[56] Le Roy, "Comment se pose le problème de Dieu," 512.
[57] See Denzinger, nos. 3458, 3482ff, 3493ff.
[58] See Denzinger, nos. 3001 and 3024.

and the human soul's aspirations. In reading it, one is reminded of St. Augustine's expression, "Our heart is restless, O Lord, until it rests in thee," as well of the beginning of the *prima secundae* of St. Thomas's *Summa theologiae.* Certain elevations of the mystics come to mind as well. However, does not Le Roy unconsciously reproduce them *in a kind of faux, imitation form* [*en simili*]?

As we will see better below,[59] this proof by the natural desire for happiness is valid only if the principle of finality has an ontological and transcendent value. This principle tells us that every agent acts for an end, that a *natural* desire cannot be *vain.* Why? First of all, because *desire* and love tend, not toward the notion of the good that is in the intellect, but rather, toward the good, which is in things. Second, a desire that is *natural* or immediately founded, not upon the imagination or upon a more or less erroneous conception formed by reason in its reasoning activity but, instead, upon *the nature* of the intellect and of the will is no more vain than is this nature, above all if it is a desire that makes a demand, as is the desire spoken of here, or that is not concerned with our elevation to the supernatural order.[60] Our will, *by its very nature*, desires a limitless good, as much as it is naturally knowable. Why? Because it is naturally illuminated, not by the senses or by the imagination, but by the intellect, which conceives of the universal good.

Therefore, if the human will, specified by the universal good, existed and if the naturally knowable Sovereign Good did not exist, we would be faced here with a psychological contradiction. By its very nature, the will simultaneously would tend and not tend toward a good without limit. St. Thomas showed this quite well in *ST* I-II, q. 2, aa. 7 and 8.

All this holds if the soul has a nature, the intellect a nature specified by intelligible being, and the will a nature specified by the universal good. This holds, if action presupposes being and the mode of action presupposes the mode of being, if each being has its own proper nature, and above all *if being is being* and is opposed to non-being [*néant*], instead

---

[59] See chapter 5 of part 2 below.
[60] [Tr. note: Which, by contrast, is elicited, inefficacious, and conditioned.]

of being identified with a *becoming* that would be self-explanatory. In other words, this holds if the principle of contradiction has an ontological and transcendent value and, consequently, the principles of efficient and final causality as well, if the order of agents corresponds to the order of ends, if there is something beyond our thought, and if that which is represented corresponds to the representation.[61]

However, this proof of God's existence obviously no longer has any consistency if being and non-being are mixed together in a causeless form of becoming which, even if it is oriented toward perfection, never will arrive at the sovereign perfection of Being, Wisdom, and Love. Here, we are faced only with a *pseudo-finality*: the attraction of a Sovereign Good that will never be constituted in itself, deserving only the name and not the reality of the "Sovereign Good." Thus, we find ourselves brought back to absolute nominalism.

What then are we to conclude? In *Sacrorum Antistitum*, Pius X said, "Further, let professors remember that they cannot set St. Thomas aside, especially in metaphysical questions, without grave detriment. Just as is said in the words of St. Thomas himself: 'A small error in the beginning is great by the end.'"[62]

If a slight deviation at the beginning of an angle becomes enormous when the sides are prolonged to great lengths and if a railway switching error causes an appalling derailment, what will happen if one

---

[61] In a philosophy course, when a professor (in appearance a convinced idealist) said, "Something outside of thought is unthinkable," a student, who no longer had anything to lose, permitted himself to express all sorts of irreverences. The idealist professor did not fail to respond to him. The young rebel responded, "*Esse est percipi*, as Berkeley said, and *something outside of thought is unthinkable*. How do you know, good sir, that I exist outside of your thought and that I say or do this or that? How can you describe my comments and my acts as *things in themselves* if at one and the same time, from the same perspective, they can be both proper and improper, reasonable and unreasonable?" [The professor responded,] "Whatever may be the case, get out!" [To which the student replied,] "I am going out, good sir—indeed, outside of your thought (judgment of existence). I am going out, and all the while also not going out, since one can, it seems, at one and the same time go out and not go out. According to you, this is *inconceivable* but *perhaps is realizable*. For me, the *realizable and the real* are *something outside of thought*; they are its *extramental object*. *Obiectum intellectus est ens.*"

[62] [Tr. note: The first half of this text reproduces something found in *Pascendi*, from which I have drawn the official ecclesiastical translation.]

begins by placing dynamite as an explosive under the first principles, the fundamental laws of thought and of reality? Thus, how can we not arrive at the modernist definition of truth condemned by the decree *Lamentabili*: "Truth is no more immutable than man himself, since it evolved with him, in him, and through him."[63] There is no longer any immutable truth, and truth is no longer the conformity of our judgment with something immutable. Rather, it is the conformity of our thought with ever-changing life, as someone has said, without seeing all the repercussions of this formula, which is true in what it affirms and false in what it denies: *veritas est adaequatio mentis et vitae*.[64] And then, is the *false* still distinct from what is *less true* in the current state of our science? Is *evil* still essentially distinct from what is only *less good*? Is it evil to betray one's country or is it less good than serving it, less in conformity to current ideas which, despite the push of internationalist communism, give patriotism its place?

Where do we go by pushing forward in this direction? And, according to the principles of the philosophy of becoming, how do we avoid the first proposition of the *Syllabus of Errors* to which Jean Weber, a convinced Bergsonian, returned when he wrote,

By planting itself on the terrain where ceaseless invention

---

[63] Decree of the Holy Office, *Lamentabili*, no. 58 (Denzinger, no. 3458).

[64] [Tr. note: The expression is that of Blondel, long fought against by Fr. Garrigou-Lagrange. For an example of his critique of this formulation, see Réginald Garrigou-Lagrange, "Theology and the Life of Faith," *Philosophizing in Faith: Essays on the Beginning and End of Wisdom*, trans. Matthew K. Minerd (Providence, RI: Cluny Media, 2019), 421–427. The topic repeatedly came up throughout the course of the famed crisis giving rise to the "Dialogue théologique" in *Revue Thomiste* in the late 1940s (in which Fr. Garrigou-Lagrange was not directly involved) and in Fr. Garrigou-Lagrange's own articles in *Angelicum* during the same period.

It should be noted, however, that Fr. Garrigou-Lagrange took care not to vilify Blondel personally, for whom he attempted to express personal kindness, as one can see even in the midst of heated battles such as those witnessed in Réginald Garrigou-Lagrange, "Verité et immutabilité du dogme," *Angelicum*, 24 (1947): 124–39 (esp. 124–125, n. 1). Various correspondence between the two men is publically found in journals from during their lifetime. A recent work in Croatian gathers the correspondence and merits consideration for details concerning the relationship between the two men. See *U potrazi za istinom: korespondencija Blondel - Garrigou-Lagrange*, ed. Hrvoje Lasic (Zagreb: Demetra, 2016).]

gushes forth, immediately and full of life, by posing itself as the most insolent encroachment of the world of the *intellect* upon *spontaneity*, morality was destined to receive continual rejections from this undeniable *reality of dynamism and creation* that is our activity. . . . Faced with these moral ideas, we outline morality or, rather, the amoralism of the fact. . . . *We call "good" that which has triumphed.* . . . The man of genius is profoundly immoral, but it does not fall to just anyone to be immoral. . . . "Duty" is nowhere and is everywhere, for all actions are equal to each other in absolute value.[65]

This represents the radical denial of finality not only in nature but [even more so] in what is most intimate in human life.

Indeed, if nothing absolutely immutable exists any longer, if being is not opposed to non-being [*néant*] but, instead, is identical with it in a causeless becoming, then there is no longer *an absolute, necessary, and immutable distinction between good and evil.* As radical nominalism holds, there is no longer anything but a contingent, free, and ever-variable distinction between them. Evil becomes a lesser good, a moment in evolution that must be overcome. That must be overcome!—Provided that we establish against Jean Weber that evolution MUST be ascending, in the direction of the *relative morality* that remains after the disappearance of *absolute morality* (though how it remains, nobody knows), after the disappearance of the necessary, immutable, and eternal distinction between good and evil. Le Roy posits "the primacy of morality," but this vanishes if the metaphysical primacy of Being [*sic*] is denied.[66]

How then are we to avoid the first proposition of Pius IX's *Syllabus of Errors*? We cited only the beginning above, but the whole text reads as follows:

---

[65] Jean Weber, "Une étude réaliste de l'acte et ses conséquences morale," *Revue de métaphysique et de morale* 2 (1894): 549–560.

[66] [Tr. note: The text has l'Être; however, Fr. Garrigou-Lagrange normally does not capitalize "Being" when using it in a general sense.]

God is identical with the nature of things and therefore subject to change; *God actually becomes himself in man* and in the world; all things are God and have the very substance of God; *God is one with the world, and so is spirit with matter, necessity with freedom, truth with falsehood, good with evil, and justice with injustice.*[67]

Indeed, if one denies the value of the principle of contradiction as the fundamental law of thought and of reality, how can these consequences be avoided? For example, how do Le Roy and Bergson make an *essential* distinction between *spirit* and *matter*, as well as *the intellect* and *the senses*, if the object of the intellect is the *solid body* already grasped by the senses and not *intelligible being* along with its universal and necessary laws? How do they distinguish *necessity* and *freedom* when they reduce freedom to simple *spontaneity*?[68] Above all, how do they draw an *absolute* and *necessary* distinction between *truth* and *falsity* [*le vrai . . . faux*], *good* and *evil*, the *just* and the *unjust*? If Truth Itself and Wisdom Itself did not exist in sovereign perfection from all eternity, they will never exist, and Creative Evolution will never provide

---

[67] Denzinger, no. 2901.

[68] Cf. Jacques Maritain, *La philosophie bergsonienne*, new edition, part 1, chapters 5–6.

[Tr. note: After consultation with various French editions of Maritain's text, it seems that there is an error in this footnote. Part one of *La philosophie bergsonienne* ends on a fifth chapter entitled "Bergsonian Evolutionism and the Intellect." In part 2 of the text, chapters five and six are respectively titled "Man" and "Freedom." It is likely that Fr. Garrigou-Lagrange meant to cite these two chapters. Maritain cites Fr. Garrigou-Lagrange as an important source for what he discusses in the sixth chapter (and indeed throughout *La philosophie bergsonienne*). The text can be found in English as Jacques Maritain, *Bergsonian Philosophy and Thomism*, ed. Ralph McInerny, trans. Mabelle L Andison and J. Gordon Andison (Notre Dame, IN: University of Notre Dame Press, 2007).

As a point of reference, chapters five and six of a later work from 1944 (historically *after* Fr. Garrigou-Lagrange's current text), *De Bergson à Thomas d'Aquin*, are concerned with related matters. They are respectively entitled "The Thomist Idea of Liberty" and "Spontaneity and Independence." An English translation of an earlier version of "The Thomist Idea of Liberty" was published as the fifth chapter in Jacques Maritain, *Scholasticism and Politics*, trans. Mortimer Adler (Indianapolis: Liberty Fund, 2011), 118–143. The other chapter can be found in an earlier edition as Jacques Maritain, "Spontanéité et indépendance," *Mediaeval Studies* 4 (1942): 23–32.]

us with an absolute norm for distinguishing the just from the unjust and good from evil. Without the objectively-founded idea of the Sovereign Good, perfect by its essence and man's last end, morality will remain like Kantian morality, comparable to a sunless region, an arid and gloomy land, one that can bear no fruit. Above all, it will bear no fruit for eternity, for it ceases to see that *the incomparable richness of the present moment*, however dull it may appear, does not come from the fact that this moment finds itself placed between a past that has vanished and the uncertainties of the future but, instead, comes from the fact that it *coexists with the unique instant of immobile eternity*, as well as from the fact that it can be lived in a supernatural manner, so that the merit which it can contain not only is realized as a tendency in perpetual evolution but, instead, truly leads us to the last end and remains for eternity.

In short, the new proof of God's existence that is proposed to us loses all its force from the fact that it places in doubt the ontological and transcendent value of the principle of finality upon which such a proof rests. Let us now undertake a closer study of this principle, its true formulation, its necessity, and its universality.

Chapter Four

THE PRINCIPLE OF FINALITY

Its True Formulation and Value

For some years, we have had to defend against Kantians and positivists the necessity and value (at once ontological and transcendent) of the principle of efficient causality on which the traditional proofs of the existence of God rest. The principle of finality, which today is similarly exposed to lively attacks, is of no less importance. It has been formulated in various ways: "All that is done is done in view of an end," or, "Nature makes nothing in vain; every agent acts for its end; everything exists for its operation," or again, "A natural tendency cannot exist without an end or without an object," or, finally, "The imperfect exists for the sake of the perfect, as the relative exists for the absolute."

We can furnish the state of the question by laying forth the opinions that are opposed to the principle of finality.

Materialists and mechanists deny the existence of finality in things in addition to the principle itself. They want to hold that, in natural facts, there are only material and efficient causes, to the point of excluding all final causes. Against the common sense of all men, they do not hesitate to say things such as, "The eye is not made for seeing but, instead, man sees because he has two eyes. The bird does not have wings so that it may fly but, instead, flies because it has wings . . . and so forth." Similarly, in the order of human actions, materialism admits only the delightful or the useful good as though man and animal were only separated by a difference of degree. This system rejects the *bonum honestum*, the "fitting good" that is good in itself, independent of the pleasure or usefulness that may be derived from it, and indeed is the end that should direct our action. It goes without saying that materialism conceives of the *end* only in a material manner, as though the achievement of our end were like the point terminating a line and as though the end of study were not the goal of investigating the truth (as the industrious student supposes it to be) but, rather, the cessation of the course (as the lazy student holds). Likewise, our life would not have an ultimate *end* (i.e., God and eternal life) but only a necessary *outcome* (i.e. death and the dissolution of the body). In every order of ideas, materialism denies the finality that subordinates the imperfect to the perfect. It attempts to explain the world in this upside-down manner, and this reduction of the superior to the inferior (e.g., intellective life explained by that of sensation, sense life by vegetative life, which itself is reduced to physio-chemical forces) is the very essence of materialism.

Such a position, which utterly denies finality in nature, was prepared for by Descartes and Spinoza. These philosophers restored the mechanistic philosophy of Democritus and Epicurus by reducing physics to mathematics, which abstracts from finality.

Descartes argued principally against *external finality* according to which inferior beings are ordered to superior ones—inorganic bodies to plants, plants to animals, and these latter being for the sake of man. In his *Principles of Philosophy* 1.28, he allows for the *internal finality* that orders the living being's internal organization and activity to its own preservation—and this manifests the intention of God the Author of nature to the eyes of natural reason. Although the external finality of some creatures escapes our rudimentary science, their internal finality is, in fact, undeniable. For example, it is difficult to know how the viper is useful to us. However, it is obvious that its organs and their activities are ordered to its own preservation and reproduction. Descartes did not wish to deny this in any way. Nonetheless, in 3.47[1] of the very same work, he takes up the thesis of Democritus and Epicurus (a thesis that coincides with the position of contemporary mechanist evolutionists), namely: the whole of nature can be explained solely by efficient

---

[1] [Tr. note: Garrigou-Lagrange's original French reads 3.37.]

causes and the laws of local motion, making abstraction from all finality. According to him, "Even when we presuppose the chaos spoken of by the poets, we can always demonstrate, thanks to the laws of nature, that this confusion must gradually return to the current order of things. Indeed, the laws of nature are such that matter must *necessarily* take on all the forms of which it is capable" (emphasis added). This could be restated: the organs of sense were not formed in animals *in view* of sensation but, instead, the animal mechanistically senses because these organs have been mechanistically constituted by vital concurrence and natural selection. Thus, we have the same kind of thesis as that which will be held later on by Charles Darwin, Herbert Spencer, Ernst Haeckel, and William James.

By contrast, Leibniz showed the contingency of the order of nature by proving that the admirable disposition of various parts of organic bodies could not be deduced in a necessary manner from mechanistic laws. In our own time, Émile Boutroux asserted similar things in his *La contingence des lois de nature*.

More recently, Édouard Le Roy contested the value of the proof of God's existence by means of the order of the world such as it is set forth by St. Thomas. For Le Roy, the affirmation of natural finality, even internal finality, is only a form of anthropomorphism. It is a gratuitous likening of the action of natural agents to human action. According to him, only the latter can be affirmed with certitude as being done in view of an end. Like subjectivist rationalism, empiricism cannot conceive of finality in any other way. According to such thinkers, we only perceive it as a fact of internal experience or as an *a priori*, subjective form of reason. In that way, we do get a particular law: *man acts for an end*. However, an extension of this law to the order of inferior agents is said to be gratuitous. We are told that such an extension is performed in virtue of a superficial analogy arbitrarily established between their activity and ours. Finality is not imposed as a law of action inasmuch as it is action. It pertains only to man's action.

Thus, finality does not pertain to the intimate constitution of natural agents. Instead, it is seen as being an element that is super-added by our mind in order to make it easy to classify the phenomena that we experience.

Among the modern defenders of the principle of finality, many acknowledge neither its necessity nor its [self-]evidence. For example, in his book *Causes finales*,[2] Paul Janet does not manage to show this principle's fully [self-]evident character. Perhaps this is because he did not formulate it rigorously enough. He limits his attention only to a very general expression, "Everything has an end," and he observes, "Before someone demonstrates to me the existence of a universal Providence, I do not see *a priori* that all that exists and acts, without exception, is ordered to an end, just as it is produced by some efficient cause."[3]

Likewise, some contemporary scholastics have held that before God's providence has been demonstrated[4], it is not rigorously certain—neither for common sense, nor for philosophical reason—that an innate natural desire cannot be without an object or that a natural activity cannot exist without an end.

In this case, the existence of a supreme ordaining power would not be known "certainly" and "easily" by the order of the world. Whence, it would follow that, for want of a sound doctrine, many would be invincibly ignorant of God as the Author of nature. Also, it seems that this theory brings in its wake this further conclusion: before one demonstrates Divine Providence, common sense itself is not rigorously certain that our will is essentially ordered to seek out the fitting good and to flee from what is evil. Indeed, the first principle of practical reason, *bonum est faciendum et malum vitandum*, presupposes the speculative principle of finality.[5] If this latter principle is uncertain so long as one has not proven God's existence, the first principle of practical reasoning would not be immediately evident. Hence, invincible ignorance of this principle would be quite possible, meaning that even adults (indeed, a great number of them) would be deprived of all merit and responsibility.

Moreover, if the principle of finality is uncertain in general metaphysics before recourse is had to natural theology,[6] why would one be

---

2   [Tr. note: The text can be found in English translation as Paul Janet, *Final Causes*, trans. William Affleck (New York: Charles Scribner's Sons, 1884).]

3   [Tr. note: The text seems to be a paraphrase from Janet's original text.]

4   For example, see Fr. M. de Munnyck, *Praelectiones de Dei existentia* (Louvain: 1904).

5   See *ST* I-II, q. 94, a. 2.

6   [Tr. note: The French text literally refers to natural theology as "theodicy." This terminology, inherited from the late-German scholastic curriculum influenced by thinkers

more assured of a similar principle such as the fact that our intellect is ordered to being and the true or that the senses are ordered to sensible qualities? The only thing that would remain, then, would be to search alongside with Descartes for the supreme criterion of certitude in the veracity of God the Author of our intellect and senses. How are we to give a firm demonstration of God's existence before having attained this criterion? Therefore, the question concerning the value of the principle of finality is quite a grave matter: is it a self-evident principle?

Many ancient philosophers and some modern ones hold that this principle is [self-]evident and necessary before every proof of God's existence. This is the position held by St. Thomas and the majority of scholastic thinkers. Outside of the ranks of scholastic thinkers, Théodore Simon Jouffroy (1796–1842), Félix Ravaisson (1813–1900), Nicolai Hartmann (1882–1950), Jules Lachelier (1832–1918), and others all think that this is the case. At the beginning of his *Cours de droit naturel*, while seeking the foundation for the laws of the moral order, Jouffroy says, "The first of these truths is the principle that *every being has an end*. It has all the same evidence, universality, and necessity as the principle of causality, and our reason finds it equally inconceivable that there would be an exception to either one of them."[7] Likewise, Ravaisson says, "We conceive it to be necessary that, along with the reason for its beginning, the cause also contains the reason for the *end* toward which its direction tends."[8] For Lachelier, induction is founded

---

such as Leibniz and Wolff, is not strictly speaking that of Thomism. It had been used in ecclesiastical circles for pedagogical texts, so the *terms* have crept into even as astute of a Thomist as Fr. Garrigou-Lagrange. He is in no way *conceptually* bound to the errors expressed by many who use this kind of terminology. These matters will be discussed at greater length in the fourth chapter of the next section. Likewise, for Fr. Garrigou-Lagrange's self-defense against the unfair critiques on this head registered by Gilson, see Réginald Garrigou-Lagrange, "L'immuntabilité du dogme selon le Concile du Vatican, et le relativisme," *Angelicum* 26, no. 4 (1949): 321–322. Also as regards this general claim of Wolffian influence even on those who were not so influenced, see Ralph McInerny, "Cry Wolff" in *Praeambula fidei: Thomism and the God of the Philosophers* (Washington, DC: Catholic University of America Press, 2006), 121ff.]

7 Théodore Simon Jouffroy, *Cours de droit naturel* (Paris: L. Hachette, 1843), 390.

8 Félix Ravaisson, *La philosophie en France au XIXe siècle* (Paris, L. Hachette, 1868), 239.

as much upon final causality as it is upon efficient causality.[9]

We believe that the statement of these various opinions sufficiently illuminates the nature of the problem. In order to resolve it in light of Thomistic doctrine, we will discuss in sequence:

1. The best formulation of the principle of finality;
2. Its necessity and its evidence.

Following this, we will speak about its corollaries and its principal applications.

I. The Exact Formula of the Principle of Finality

Certain philosophers, like Paul Janet (1823–1899), have proposed a very general formula for the principle of finality: Everything is ordered to an end. In other words: Everything that is done is done in view of an end; nothing is done in vain.

However, the necessity of this principle is not completely clear, for we see in the world many things that happen accidentally or due to chance. The countless indentations found in a mountain range are accidentally produced, and their form does not seem to correspond to a determinate end. Therefore, this principle, "All that is done is ordered to an end," is neither necessary nor [self-]evident. Indeed, Janet acknowledged this and joined the empiricists on this point.

Now, how do we respond?

This formula is too general and too vague. First of all, we must envision the principle in the very nature of things and their natural activities. The principle must not be envisioned in that which happens accidentally, for the accidental always presupposes the essential and the necessary. Moreover, the end immediately exercises its causality upon

---

[9] In his *Le Fondement de l'Induction.* [Tr. note: See Jules Lachelier, *Du fondement de l'induction suivi de Psychologie et Métaphysique et de Notes sur le pari de Pascal* (Paris: Alcan, 1924).]

the agent that it moves (or, attracts), and it is only by the intermediacy of this [i.e., the end] that it influences the patient[10] so as to determine it. Therefore, the true formula of the principle of finality is not, "Every being is ordered to an end." Expressed in this way, the principle of finality is not applicable to every being. Indeed, God, who is the absolutely self-sufficient reason for Himself, is not ordered to an end any more than He is caused. He is independent of all extrinsic causes. No more does it suffice for one to say in an indeterminate manner, "Everything that is done is done in view of an end [sic]."

This matter must be spoken of with the same precision that Aristotle,[11] St. Thomas, and the scholastics[12] ever maintained: "Every agent acts in view of an end." As St. Thomas says in *De potentia* q. 5, a. 1: "The end is a cause only inasmuch as it moves the agent to act, for it is not first in existence but is first only in intention. Whence too, where there is no action, there is no final cause, as is said in the third book of the *Metaphysics*."[13] In the passage of the *Metaphysics* to which St. Thomas alludes, Aristotle notes that mathematics, which abstracts from efficient causality and from movement, by that very fact ignores final causality. Mathematics does not demonstrate in any way by relying upon the notion of the *good*.[14] Thus, as is commonly said, "Man has two hands because by means of them he can easily and *better* realize the conceptions of his intellect (e.g., by writing, which could not be performed if man only had feet); however, one does not demonstrate that a triangle has its three angles equal to two right ones because it is *better* that it be such." Thus, we see why Spinoza, in wishing to apply the mathematical

---

[10] [Tr. note: i.e. that which undergoes (*patior*) the activity of the agent.]

[11] See book two of the *Physics* in its entirety, though see especially chapters 6–9. See also lectures 13–15 of St. Thomas's commentary.

[12] [Tr. note: The reader should note, as always, that this is a bit of an historical simplification. The general sense that one gets when reading Fr. Garrigou-Lagrange saying something like this is that he is referring to the more famed Dominican Thomistic commentators as well as the Salamanca Carmelites and (sometimes) thinkers like Suárez, along with certain later-day 19th- and 20th-century thinkers.]

[13] See St. Thomas Aquinas, *In III Meta.*, ch. 2, lect. 3, no. 375.

[14] [Tr. note: The reader would benefit much from reading Yves R. Simon, "Nature and the Process of Mathematical Abstraction" in *Philosopher at Work*, ed. Anthony O. Simon (Lanham, MD: Rowman and Littlefield Publishers, 1999), 113–133.]

method to physics and ontology, by this very fact rejected finality, not by demonstrating that it does not exist but, instead, by neglecting it in practice due to his exclusive use of the methods of mathematics, which he wrongly thought had a universal application, thereby abusing them in practice.

Therefore, the end is a cause in relation to the agent inasmuch as it is first in the order of intention, though it is last in the order of execution.[15] Thus, the true formulation for our principle is the classical one: "*Omne agens agit propter finem*; every agent acts for an end."

Below, we will comment on the necessity of understanding it in various ways, depending on whether it is a question of an intellectual agent or of a natural agent deprived of reason.

This Formulation Illuminates All the Others

Indeed, having presupposed its truth, we can thus understand why *everything that is done in a non-accidental* (i.e. *per se*) *fashion is done in view of an end*, whether it is an effect of nature or one of the will. Why is this so? St. Thomas responds in *ST* I q. 44, a. 4: "The agent as such and the patient as such have only one and the same end, though considered from different perspectives. The agent tends toward communicating the very same thing that the patient tends toward receiving." Also, as soon as we admit the *internal* finality of natural agents, we can prove the *external* finality of beings of an inferior order that are *used* by superior beings for their own preservation. Indeed, the superior cannot use the inferior if the latter were not apt to be used in such a manner. The animal can only nourish itself on the plant if the plant is made in view of such use. The end of the agent and the patient is one and the same. In this way, this other formulation of the principle is understandable: "the inferior is for the superior, the imperfect for the perfect."

In this way, we equally illuminate the adage, "A natural desire cannot be vain," whether it is a question of a natural desire for acting (e.g., all men desire by nature to know; therefore scientific knowledge cannot be impossible) or a natural desire for receiving something that

---

[15] See *ST* I-II, q. 1, a. 1, ad 1.

is essentially suitable for the nature of that which desires (e.g. as the ruminant has an appetite for grass or man desires beatitude, at least the natural beatitude that is the sovereign good in the natural order). This fundamental tendency cannot exist without an object, and this is because of the principle of finality. If this were not the case, every agent would not act in view of an end.

Likewise, it is said that *everything exists for its activity*, not as though substance could be subordinated to an accident but, as Cajetan noted, *everything is, of itself, something operative, propter semetipsam operantem.*

We can thus formulate the same principle more briefly: *potency is for act*; active potency for act, passive potency for receiving. . . . Likewise, *matter is for form*, and given that, according to St. Thomas, every substantial form is entirely in the whole and entirely in each part of the whole,[16] it follows that finality thus understood is not an entity arbitrarily superadded by the mind and, hence, posterior to being (as Édouard Le Roy would have it). Instead, it pertains to the intrinsic constitution of being.

These various formulations of the principle of finality mutually illuminate each other, depending on whether one considers things *a priori* or *a posteriori*, from on high or from below. However, the best of all of them is the classical adage: "omne agens agit propter finem." In this form, it holds even for the Divine Agent. Without a doubt, He does not act for the sake of a good to be acquired. However, He intends to communicate a participation in His Goodness[17]—and this is to act for an end. On the contrary, speaking of God, we cannot say, *potentia dicitur ad actum.* He is Pure Act. His Power (or, "Potency," *potentia*) is not a principle of action in Himself but, rather, is only a principle of His effects *ad extra.*[18]

The Analogical Meaning of This Formulation

In what way must we understand the principle thus formulated in

---

[16] See *ST* III, q. 76, a. 3.

[17] *ST* I, q. 44, a. 4.

[18] *ST* I, q. 25, a. 1, ad 3.

this manner? Obviously, it has an analogical signification, given that it applies to God, created intellectual agents, and to natural agents that lack reason.

In fact, the terms *agent, to act,* and *action* are said analogically of the First Cause and of secondary causes. Likewise, among created causes, they are said analogically of a principal cause and an instrumental cause. Consequently, *finality* is applied only in an analogical manner to the supreme end and to subordinate ends. Therefore, the principle, "Every agent acts in view of an end [sic]," must be understood analogically inasmuch as there is a proportionality (or, proportional similitude) between various agents and their correlative ends.

The general term "end," like that of *action*, does not always have the same meaning. According to Aristotle's expression, it is neither univocal nor, however, equivocal. It is an analogue according to the analogy of proper proportionality.[19] Now the analogue in an analogy of proper

---

[19] [Tr. note: Technically, this gives a bit too much to Aristotle, crediting him with the position that would be famously (or infamously) enunciated by Cardinal Thomas de Vio Cajetan in his *De nominum analogia*. Nonetheless, one should heed well the proportional structure that Aristotle *does* in fact use to explain analogical terms in *Metaphysics* 9.6 and *Nicomachean Ethics* 1.6. The reader would benefit immensely from considering the reflections on analogy undertaken in Yves R. Simon, "On Order in Analogical Sets" in *Philosopher at Work*, ed. Anthony O. Simon (Lanham: Roman & Littlefield, 1999), 135–171. Also, see Réginald Garrigou-Lagrange, *God: His Existence and His Nature*, vol. 2, 203–225.

As regards Cajetan himself, see Tommaso de Vio Cajetan, *The Analogy of Names, and the Concept of Being*, trans. Edward A. Bushinski and Henry J. Koren (Eugene, OR: Wipf and Stock, 2009), 46–51. As the reader likely knows, there are great controversies regarding Cajetan's work on analogy. Although we could cite a number of positions, on the negative register, a forceful account is that found in Bernard Montagnes, *The Doctrine of the Analogy of Being According to Thomas Aquinas*, trans. E.M. Macierowski and Pol Vandevelde, ed. Andrew Tallon (Milwaukee: Marquette University Press, 2008). For a general defense of Cajetan's position, one should consider together the work of Long and Hochschild, who respectively plumb the metaphysical and logical / semantic issues at play here. See Joshua P. Hochschild, *The Semantics of Analogy: Rereading Cajetan's De Nominum Analogia* (Notre Dame, IN: University of Notre Dame Press, 2010). Steven A. Long, *Analogia Entis: On the Analogy of Being, Metaphysics, and the Act of Faith* (Notre Dame, IN: University of Notre Dame Press, 2011). Likewise, see James Anderson, *The Bond of Being: An Essay on Analogy and Existence* (St. Louis: B. Herder, 1954). For a recent study of this matter in a number of thinkers up to the time of Cajetan, see Dominic D'Ettore, *Analogy after Aquinas: Logical Problems, Thomistic Answers* (Washington, DC: Catholic University of

proportionality implicitly and actually contains all of the analogates from which it cannot be perfectly separated by means of abstraction. Such a proportionality cannot be known distinctly without its other members being considered at the same time. So too, in order to fully understand this very principle, which is understood in different manners in different orders, we must quickly note its analogates, namely, their various modes which are, in truth, strictly speaking, different, though they are the same in some manner (i.e. proportionally): *simpliciter diversa, secundum quid eadem.*

1) *Agents endowed with intelligence or reason* act in view of an end directively, formally speaking (*directive formaliter*)—i.e. knowing finality itself (*ipsam rationem finis*, the very notion of the end [as an end]) and, under this light, disposing and orienting the means toward the end known as such. As St. Thomas says in *ST* I, q. 18, a. 3: "Indeed, this happens only by way of reasoning and intellect, to which it belongs to know the proportion between the end and that which is directed toward the end, as well as to order one to the other." One of the wise man's properties is the fact that he *orders* things. The intellect—which has as its object neither color nor sound but, instead, *being*—is able to perceive the reason for the end and to grasp, in this end, *the raison d'être* for the means that lead to it.

2) Animals lacking in reason act for an end, directively but only materially speaking and not formally (*directive non formaliter sed materialiter tantum*), i.e. knowing the thing that is their end. Thus, the animal that has seen its prey at a given distance is not only passive in the movement by which it is driven along. In some way, it actively moves itself toward its prey. So too does the swallow as it gathers twigs for making its nest.[20]

America Press, 2019).]

[20] *ST* I-II, q. 6, a. 2: "There are two kinds of knowledge of the end, namely a perfect one and an imperfect one. Indeed, perfect knowledge of the end is had when not only the thing that is the end is grasped but when the notion of the end [as such] and the proportion of that which is ordered to the end itself are also known. Only rational creatures have such knowledge of the end. However, imperfect knowledge of the end is that which consists in only knowing the end without knowing what the notion of the end as such is, as well as the proportion of an act [i.e., the means] to the end. And such [imperfect] knowledge of the end is had by brute animals by their senses and their natural estimation." See *ST* I-II, q. 1, a. 2; q. 11, a. 2 and *ST* I, q. 18, a. 3. Also, see

This material knowledge of the end is already something admirable, and Scripture proposes it as an example for sinners who are cupably unaware of their end: "The ox knows its owner, and the ass its master's crib; but Israel does not know, my people does not understand" (Isa 1:3, RSV); "Even the stork in the heavens knows her times; and the turtledove, swallow, and crane keep the time of their coming; but my people know not the ordinance of the LORD" (Jer 8:7, RSV).

Moreover, on account of this rudimentary knowledge of their end, certain animals (e.g., dogs) are fit to have a certain kind of training. We can hold that they have a kind of material *discursus* consisting in the association of images and empirical associations of facts [*consécutions*].[21]

3 *Natural agents* wholly lacking in knowledge, even sense knowledge, act in view of an end *only executively* (*executive tantum*).[22] These are plants and inorganic beings, which obey finality only in the level of execution, though according to an admirable and preestablished order. Thus, the stone tends toward the center of the earth, and all bodies are attracted to each other for the cohesion of the universe, instead of dispersing in every direction.

It is therefore quite clear that the principle of finality, "Omne agens agit propter finem," can only be understood analogically, in accord with the very nature of the agent in question. The rational being acts for an end *directive formaliter*, the animal *directive materialiter*, and the plant and inanimate body *executive tantum*.

As regards the problem of the universal value and evidence of the principle of finality, prior to the proof of God's existence, a difficulty presents itself above all in the case of natural agents deprived of every form of knowledge. This is the question that we must address now.

---

the entry for *finis*, 39 in the *Tabula aurea* of Peter of Bergamo (d. 1482).

[21] See John Syri Uvadano, *Universa Philosophia Aristotelico Thomistca*, vol. 2 (Venice: 1719), 128–130, especially nos. 7–9, 17, and all of page 130.

[22] See *ST* I, q. 18, a. 3: "There are some things that move themselves . . . only with regard to the execution of motion . . . The form by which they act and the end for which they act is determined in them by nature."

II. What Is the Value of This Principle?

Before the demonstration of God's existence and His Providence, do we know that it is obviously true that every agent (even those deprived of knowledge) acts in view of an end? Is it obviously true that natural beings and their faculties are ordered to something so that we would be able prove the existence of a universal "Orderer" on the basis the evident character of this ordination?

St. Thomas's response is clear: 1° *a posteriori*, the examination of nature enables us to affirm finality with certitude; 2° *a priori*, the principle of finality is self-evidently necessary.[23]

What Does the Examination of Nature Say? Is There Finality in it?

The first point is demonstrated by Aristotle in the second book of his *Physics* where he discusses both chance and fortune. His argumentation is summarized by St. Thomas as follows in the so-called fifth way among his proofs for God's existence:

> Certain beings lacking knowledge, namely inorganic bodies, act in view of an end. This is obvious from the fact that they always (or nearly always) act in the same way, so as to obtain what is *best* for them. Whence, it is obvious that they do not act by chance but achieve their end by way of intention.[24]

In this text, St. Thomas speaks first of the internal finality that makes the natural agent act for its own end. This internal finality is manifested by the fact that natural agents act so as to attain what is *best* for them. The terminus of their action is not only that which they achieve (like a point terminating a line or like death which is the terminus of life). It is also *an end*, that is, something *final* and *best* in which

---

[23] [Tr. note: Recall what was said in note 1 of chapter two above about Fr. Garrigou-Lagrange's meaning in using the terms *a priori* and *a posteriori*.]

[24] *ST* I, q. 2, a. 3.

the appetite comes to rest as Aristotle noted, following Socrates and Plato. And, this final and excellent something attained by this action does indeed deserve to be called "the end"—that in view of which the agent acts, *ultimum et optimum, cuius gratia aliquid fit,* τὸ οὗ ἕνεκα. And all this is evident, not for the senses or the imagination, but rather for reason—whether it be the spontaneous reason of common sense or the reflexive reason of philosophy. Do children not ceaselessly ask about the "why" of things, about their end? How could they do this if they did not vaguely catch a glimpse of the principle of finality?

And one cannot say that the order of nature (i.e., the adaptation of means to the end) is accidental, unplanned, and fortuitous. The "happy meetings" of chance happen only rarely, whereas in nature agents *constantly* and *habitually* to tend toward the *best* [i.e., what is best for them].[25] This *fixity* of tendency would be something without a *raison d'être*, that is, unintelligible, if it were only the outcome of chance.

Placed before the striking order of the universe, spontaneous reason (or, common sense) grasps finality in natural activity as in a work of art, which imitates nature. If we examine a watch not only with our eyes but also with our reason, we will realize that all the gears and all its movement are determined in function of an end to be attained (*ultimum et optimum*): the indication of the hour. Therefore, final causality by rights has just as important a role to play as does efficient causality. Similarly, the spectacle of nature, the harmonious disposition of the cosmic elements, their ordered inter-connection, and their mutual relations all obviously reveal in them the existence of means and ends, i.e. the existence of finality. The eye is for seeing, the ear for hearing, feet for walking, and wings for flying. Therefore, it is not by a kind of superficial analogy between artificial machinery and the activity of nature that we affirm finality in nature. Instead, as much in nature as in art, the intellect perceives the notion of *end* in that which is *final and best*: the work of art brought to completion or the terminus of natural activity.

Mechanists will object, "All of this can be explained apart from all finality, solely by the interplay of material and efficient causes. Thus, in a pot of boiling water, there is the same quantity of matter, heat, and

---

[25] See Thomas Aquinas, *Summa contra gentiles* III, ch. 3.

movement as in the eagle in full flight."

To this, one might respond that it is perhaps true that the same quantity of physical energy is required for water to boil and for the eagle to fly. However, there are differences as well: the pot only has a lid upon it, whereas the eagle has upon its back powerful wings disposed for flight; the pot remains tranquil at the fireside, whereas the eagle takes to flight, lifting itself upward and soaring high in the air. . . . In truth, such differences do not deserve to be ignored. Behold how common sense (or, spontaneous reason) expresses itself in seeing the striking order of the universe. Under their deceptive appearance of profundity, Descartes's aforementioned words seem unintellible to common sense: "Even when we presuppose the chaos spoken of by the poets, we can always demonstrate, thanks to the laws of nature, that this confusion ought to gradually return to the current order of things," solely by the mechanical interplay of cosmic laws without the influence of God who orders all things, in other words, without finality. . . . In truth, this affirmation befits someone like David of Dinant, "Who most foolishly [*stultissime*] held that God is prime matter,"[26] as St. Thomas said. Indeed, foolishness is opposed to wisdom. It wishes to explain everything not by the highest cause but, rather, by the most trifling cause: matter and its blind activity. In all honesty, nothing is more absurd than the mechanistic outlook that claims to explain the superior by the inferior by rejecting finality: intellection by sensation, sensation by vegetative life, vegetative life, at last, solely by physio-chemical laws. Behold what common sense (which, in fact, is nothing other than spontaneous reason) thinks of mechanism.

* * *

Philosophical reflection confirms this common-sense attitude by methodically showing the insufficiencies of anti-finalist explanations.

Recourse to efficient causality alone does not suffice, for what we precisely want to know is that for the sake of which the agent acts instead of being at rest, as well as that for the sake of which it acts in one given

---

[26] *ST* I, q. 3, a. 8.

way rather than in another. Furthermore, we ask this question not only about this agent actually existing now but also about all agents that have existed in the past and about every agent in general: why, for example, does the eye see rather than hear or perceive odors?

Moreover, recourse to the material organization of the agent does not suffice, as though we were to say, "The eye is not made for seeing but, instead, sees because it has this given material disposition." Indeed, *why* this very disposition? Mechanistic philosophy has no response, and the question, which is not vain, remains to be asked. This disposition of the organ is not self-explanatory. It is not necessary with an absolute necessity, independent of every extrinsic consideration. This is quite the opposite of what holds, for example, in the case of a triangle, which has three sides and three angles in an absolutely necessary manner, indeed with an intrinsic necessity. Likewise, it is absolutely necessary that the sum of its angles be equal to two right angles. We do not ask ourselves why the triangle is a triangle. The question would be meaningless if it were asked. However, we can ask why this portion of matter is triangular instead of being round, why it has received the shape of an eye instead of becoming an ear. Indeed, that is contingent, just as it is contingent (as Leibniz said) that the sun seems to move from the east to the west rather than from the west to the east. Here, we are faced with only a *hypothetical necessity,* that which comes from the agent (if it acts) or from the end (if the agent must attain it). For example, *in order for* vision to be able to be produced, the eye must have the shape that we find it having. St. Thomas responds in these terms to the materialist objection: "The determination by which a natural thing is determined *ad unum* does not belong to it because of itself but, instead, is from another. Therefore, the very determination to a bring about a suitable effect demonstrates Providence."[27]

Moreover, it cannot be said that the first disposition of things was, at the beginning of things, the effect of chance and that the beings that were best armed for life persisted. This is a self-contradictory statement. Indeed, as Aristotle showed in the second book of his *Physics,* chance is an accidental cause of rare meetings—and not any such meetings, but

---

27 *De veritate,* q. 5, a. 2, ad 5.

happy and unhappy ones, outside of the intention of both nature and the human will. Granted, such meetings sometimes occur as though they were intentional: a man digs a hole and finds a treasure by happy chance; or, again, by an unhappy chance, a tile happens to strike a child who is thus killed by it. Here, everything happens outside the intention of the agent, and yet it is as though the intention had preexisted.

Chance cannot be the first cause of order in the world. This is so not merely because it would be improbable but, rather, because it would involve an obvious impossibility: in the end, an accidental cause presupposes a non-accidental cause to which it is added. The discovery of treasure presupposes the digging of a hole. And if the tile did not fall in virtue of gravity, it would not have harmed anyone. If the accidental were logically prior to the essential, if the order of things resulted from order's own privation, the *intelligibility* of the universe—which is not constituted by science but, instead, is discovered by it—would result from the *unintelligible*. The *more* would result from the less, and the perfect from the imperfect. The substantial foundation of being would thus vanish. There would no longer be any essence, nor any substance, nor any nature, nor any law. Reality would no longer be intelligible. Moreover, there would no longer be any reality or any being. All that would remain would be simple fortuitous meetings without anything that would meet. The contradiction involved in such a state of affairs is flagrant. Therefore, it is impossible that chance would be the first cause of the order of the universe.

For the same reasons, it is obvious—prior to any demonstration of God's existence—that numerous causes cannot be brought together *accidentally* in a way that produces an action which is *one of itself* and excellent, as are the various conditions necessary for vision brought together in a normal eye. This position would lead us to the same impossibilities as the previous: the more would come from the less, and the perfect would have its *raison d'être* in the imperfect.

Finally, a number of effects that are essentially connected to each other cannot be derived from *an essentially unified principle* in a merely *fortuitous manner*. The various parts of the oak do not come from the seed in an accidental manner. Chance (i.e., the accidental union of various things) is excluded by the very fact of the *simplicity of the seed* from which these multiple but essentially connected effects arise. For all the more reason, we cannot use chance to explain an *essentially unified* effect's dependence upon its equally *unified* principle. Chance is excluded as much by the simplicity of the principle as it is by the simplicity of the terminus produced. Obviously, it is not a chance affair that intellection proceeds from the intellect, volition from the will, and the activity of sight from the faculty of sight.

Therefore, we can find the existence of finality in nature *a posteriori*. Experience shows us natural agents *always (or for the most part) acting in the same manner*, in a way that is suitable for obtaining what is *best* for them. It is obvious that they TEND toward it. This fixity and this fittingness are inexplicable if we limit ourselves to material and efficient causes alone or to chance, which is an accidental cause.

Is the Principle of Finality Evident with an
a priori *Necessity?*

We now must examine whether the principle of finality is evident *a priori*[28] like the principle of efficient causality.

St. Thomas expressly taught that the principle of finality is self-evident. To prove this fact, we need only cite *ST* I-II, q. 2, where he explains Aristotle's own words—*not only the intellect but nature as well acts for an end*:

> It is necessary that every agent act for an end, for when causes
> are ordered to one another, if the first is removed, all the others

---

[28] [Tr. note: As has been noted before, by *a priori*, Fr. Garrigou-Lagrange does not mean to use the term in the same sense as many popularly understand, for instance, Kant. Here, as we will see, Fr. Garrigou-Lagrange holds that the principle of causality is a self-evident (i.e., *per se nota*) proposition. Such are primary, complex enunciations that are judged as being true or false, based upon the relation of the terms to each other. The terms themselves may require a good bit of work to understand them. As Thomists often say, some things are *per se nota* to the wise only. When one knows something *per se*, one grasps that the predicate must be related to the subject in the proposition, needing no syllogistic inference to justify this by way of a middle term. Such things are not proven but are only shown to be necessary through arguments like those in the form of *reductio ad absurdum*.]

must be removed as well. Now, the first among all the causes is the final cause. The reason for this is that matter only receives form if it is moved by an agent. Now, nothing reduces itself from potency to act. *However, the agent does not move except out of an intention for the end, for if the agent were not determined to a given effect, it would no more do one thing than another.* Therefore, in order for it to produce a determinate effect, it must be determined to some given thing, which has the character of an end. However, just as in the rational nature this determination is brought about by the rational appetite (i.e. the will), so too in other things this determination is brought about by a natural inclination which is called a "natural appetite" . . .

Therefore, those things that lack reason *tend toward* the end on account of a natural inclination, as being moved by another and not by themselves, given that they do not know the nature of the end [as such].

Let us summarize this as follows. Among all the causes, the end is the first. The reason for this is that matter does not receive a given form unless it is so determined by an agent. Now, no agent moves unless it *tends* toward an end. Indeed, if it were not determined to produce a given effect, it would not produce this particular effect any more than it would produce some other. . . . If natural agents were not *naturally inclined* by a spontaneous tendency to this rather than to that, they would produce no determinate effect whatsoever.

Elsewhere,[29] St. Thomas presents the absolute necessity and *a priori* self-evidence of our principle by means of the same reason: "Every agent acts for an end, otherwise one thing would not follow from an agent's action rather than some other thing, except by chance."[30]

There can be no doubt in this matter. Therefore, for St. Thomas, the principle of finality is not an anthropomorphic extension that illegitimately transfers our internal experience to the external things.

---

[29] See *ST* I, q. 44, a. 4.
[30] Likewise, see *SCG* III, chs. 2 and 3.

It is not perceived by sense experience, which attains only particular objects. Rather, it is perceived by the intellect, which alone is capable of grasping the objective and universal notion of *finality*, just as it alone is capable of grasping the objective concepts of efficiency, substance, and being.

Properly speaking, natural finality (e.g., in a living organism) is not something sensible like heat or color. It is an object that is intelligible in itself and only sensible *per accidens* as Aristotle said. In other words, finality is accessible to the intellect alone, which perceives it immediately and without *discursus* at the presentation of the sensible object. Thus, it is evident to our intellect that wings are for flying and the eye for seeing.

Thus, the principle of finality is self-evident. It requires only the enunciation of the subject and the predicate that compose it, on the condition that that they are understood aright.

If we attentively examine the meaning of the subject and the predicate, their necessary relationship is clear. Indeed, every agent produces not any effect whatsoever, but instead, a determinate effect that is proportioned to its nature, although it can produce an accidental effect as well. By sight, we see and do not hear. Sight obviously exists *for seeing*.

This effect proportioned to the agent rightly receives the name *end*, for it is the perfection of the agent that tends toward it and is the *raison d'être* for its activity. Indeed "end" expresses a final and excellent reality, and every agent tends toward that. The principle, *omne agens agit propter finem*, is therefore analytical [*per se nota*],[31] and this is best

---

[31] [Tr. note: Again, I feel the need to alert the reader to the language. Given Fr. Garrigou-Lagrange's training and the general character of his writings, he does not mean the expression "analytical" in the sense used by many authors today. It is evident that he only means that the proposition, "Every agent acts for an end," is *per se nota*—known of itself without objective inference through a middle term. He would most certainly agree with the summary notes made by Jacques Maritain in his unfinished text in material logic: "There are neither *analytic* judgments nor *a priori* judgments in the Kantian sense. Every judgment is a synthesis. [That is, inasmuch as the enunciation formed by the intellect's second operation involves the formation of a complex of two notions.] The authentic *a priori* is born of the evidence of the object." Jacques Maritain, *Grand Logique ou Logique de la raison vraie (Logica major)* in *Oevres Complètes*, vol. 2, ed. Jean-Marie Allion et al. (Fribourg, Switzerland: Éditions Universitaires, 1987), 758.

made evident in Aristotle's simple formula: *Potentia dicitur ad actum,* potency is *for* act. It is of the very nature of active potency that it is ordered to its act, just as passive potency, which is an essentially receptive capacity, is essentially ordered to receive something.

Can the Principle of Finality Be Demonstrated by a Reductio ad absurdum?

The texts from St. Thomas discussed above show us that this self-evident principle cannot be demonstrated in a direct manner (i.e., by means of a middle term) but, instead, is susceptible to in an *indirect* demonstration (or, by a *reductio ad absurdum*) by reducing it to the principle of *raison d'être* and, thereby, to the principle of non-contradiction. As St. Thomas states in *ST* I, q. 44, a. 1, "Every agent acts for an end, otherwise one thing would not follow from an agent's action rather than some another thing." Indeed, if, in producing a determinate effect proportioned to its nature, the agent did not have a foundational *tendency* to this effect, it would follow that this proportion (i.e., this suitability between the cause and its effect) would be *without a raison d'être*. In reality, the actual determination of the produced effect would not exist if it did not preexist in some way in the productive action. Now, it is not found there in a formal and actual state (as it is in the effect) but, instead, is there only in a virtual state (i.e., inasmuch as the action *tends* toward its effect and is ordered to it). If this is denied, we thereby suppress every *raison d'être* for the action, for its meaning, and for the suitability of the effect produced. Everything that exists must have its *raison d'être*, either in itself or outside itself; otherwise it would be pure non-being.

This appeal to the principle of *raison d'être* does not prevent the principle of finality from being self-evident.[32] In speaking in this way,

---

One can, however, speak of *analysis* as pertaining to syllogistic analysis (whence, one speaks of the "Analytics" of Aristotle). On the distinction between assent and analytical resolution, see John of St. Thomas, *The Gifts of the Holy Spirit,* trans. Dominic Hughes (London: Sheed and Ward, 1950), 132–134 (*Cursus theologicus,* I-II, q. 70, disp. 18, nos. 21–25).]

[32] [Tr. note: This point is discussed at length in Réginald Garrigou-Lagrange, *Sens*

we do not *directly demonstrate* it but, instead, *explain* the notion of end, which presupposes the more general notion of *raison d'être*. Indeed, the notion of *raison d'être* is analogical. It can designate an intrinsic *raison d'être*, as when we say that God alone has the reason for His existence in Himself —*Deus solus est ratio sui*. However, it can also designate an extrinsic *raison d'être*, as when we say that the means have their *raison d'être* in the end in view of which they are employed.

This *reductio ad absurdum* can be reduced to the following argument. Every action is essentially *intentional*, at least in the broad sense of tendency and natural inclination. In other words, by its very nature, every action *tends* toward a goal, whether consciously or unconsciously. Were this not so, *it would not emerge from the state of indetermination*; it would have no direction and no meaning. It would no more be an attraction than it would be a repulsion, no more an assimilation than a disassimilation, no more vision than hearing, etc.

This Thomist defense of the principle of finality is found almost in literally the same terms in Hartmann, who doubtlessly did not know of St. Thomas's thought but probably had read Aristotle. In his work, *The Philosophy of the Unconscious*, he manifests natural finality in the following way by using the very simple example of the attraction of one atom by another:

> The attracting atomic force strives to bring every other atom nearer to it; the result of this endeavor is the completion or realization of the approach. We have thus in Force to distinguish *the effort* itself as pure act, and that which is aimed at as the goal, content, or object of the endeavor. . . . *Were this, however, not at all contained in the endeavor, there would be no reason why the latter should produce attraction, and not something else, e.g. repulsion*; why it varies according to this and not according to that law with the distance. It would then be empty, purely formal endeavor, without definite goal or content; it must thus remain

---

commun, 4th ed. (Paris: Desclee de Brouwer, 1936), pt. 2, ch. 1. Emmaus Academic plans to publish this text in the near future.]

aimless and without content, and accordingly resultless [sic].[33]

This text has the appearance of being a literal translation of a passage from *Summa contra* gentiles, III, ch. 2:

If the agent DID NOT TEND to a given determinate effect, *every effect would be indifferent to it*. However, that which is *indifferently* oriented to many things, *no more does one* of them *than another*. Whence, from an agent that is contingently indifferent to both effects, a given effect does not follow unless it is *determined* to one effect by something. Therefore, it would be impossible for it to act. Thus, every agent TENDS to a given determinate effect that is called its end.

It might be objected, "There are actions that seem to exist without an end, such as games or actions that are done mechanically without the mind paying attention in the midst of performing them." To this, St. Thomas responds that they have either a conscious or an unconscious end:

Play activities sometimes are ends in themselves, as when someone plays solely for the pleasure that is found in the very activity of playing. However, at other times they are done for an end, as when we play so that we can work with greater strength later. However, actions that are done without attention do not arise from the intellect but, instead, from something suddenly arising from the imagination or a natural principle, as when an indisposition of the bodily humors excite the need to itch, thus causing one to itch one's beard without the intellect attending to the action. However, these do tend to other ends, though they are outside the order of the intellect.[34]

---

[33] [Tr. note: Instead of translating from the French edition cited by Fr. Garrigou-Lagrange, I have taken this from Eduard von Hartmann, *Philosophy of the Unconscious*, vol. 2, trans. William Chatterton Coupland (London: Kegan Paul, 1893), 177–178. Italics are based upon Fr. Garrigou-Lagrange's emphasis in his French.]

[34] *SCG*, III, ch. 2.

Taken in its full universality, the principle of finality (as formulated by Aristotle, "every agent acts for an end") is therefore necessary and self-evident. It is also indirectly demonstrated (i.e., by way of *reductio ad absurdum*). We cannot place it in doubt without thus also doubting the truth of the principle of *raison d'être* and, in the final analysis, the principle of contradiction.

The Division of the Good and That of Ends

The sense and scope of the principle of finality will stand forth with even greater clarity if we recall the division of goods and of ends. These divisions can be drawn from a number of well-known texts of Aristotle and St. Thomas.

The good can be considered *materially* in relation to the *being* in which it is found. From this perspective, it is divided according to the categories of being. For example: a good substance (a good stone for building,[35] a good fruit, a good horse), a good quantity, a good quality, a good action, a good relation, etc. By this, we can see that the good is analogous like being and is found proportionally in all the categories. It dominates them all and is thus called a transcendental property of being.[36]

The good can be considered *formally as good*. Thus, it is understood as a *perfection* or, more precisely, as a *desirable* reality or, finally, in relation *to the rules* of morality. As a perfection, we distinguish 1° the *bonum simpliciter, that which is good purely and simply speaking* (i.e., that which has all the perfection that it should have, for example as a good wine is a full-bodied and excellent wine), from a 2° *bonum secundum quid*, that which is good only from a given perspective (i.e., that which does not have all the perfection and integrity that it should have but at least has that which it should essentially have). In this latter sense, we say that a wine that is neither bitter nor spoiled, "is good." That is, it is

---

[35] [Tr. note: This example is a bit loose. The fitness of a stone for building is actually said in relation to the art of building (e.g. a house). In beings that lack significant internal complexity, intrinsic ontological goodness is difficult to explain.]

[36] See *ST* I, q. 5, a. 6, ad 1.

still truly wine and not vinegar.[37]

As desirable, the good can be desirable in itself, independent of every subsequent enjoyment or use. In this case, we call it *a fitting good*, and the action specified by it is deserving of praise and honor (e.g., to speak the truth and avoid lying, even if it means that one should die for doing so). By contrast, a good can lack this property of being desirable in itself but, instead, be desirable only because of the delight that can be found in it (*the pleasing good*) or because of its use (*the useful good*) like a bitter remedy.[38]

In relation to the laws or rules of morality (i.e., in relation to the eternal law and to right reason), the good is divided depending on whether it is conformed to these rules (*the moral good*) or opposed to them (an apparent good that specifies the *immoral* or *non-fitting* act), or it may be *indifferent* in its species (i.e. neither morally good nor morally bad) as is the case in activities like strolling, teaching mathematics or chemistry, and so forth. In this last case, we abstract from consideration of the moral end for which one teaches such subjects, whether it be good (e.g., to make a living to support one's children) or evil (e.g., to make explosives for an attack).

Finally, as St. Thomas notes,[39] the fitting good can be suitable to man inasmuch as he is a substance (e.g., to preserve his existence and not commit suicide), inasmuch as he is an animal (e.g., to follow the order indicated by nature for what pertains to the preservation of the species and to avoid vices that are against nature), or inasmuch as he is a man (e.g., to observe justice in relation to other men, to seek to know and love the truth and, above all, to know God, who is the Supreme Truth, to love Him above all things and to serve Him).

This division of the *good* lies at the foundation of the various systems of morality, inasmuch as these consider, above all, either the fitting, useful, or pleasing good—so long as they do not make abstraction from the objective notion of the good, as did Kant and, before him, the radical nominalists.

---

[37] See *ST* I, q. 5, a. 1, ad 1.

[38] See *ST* I, q. 5, a. 6.

[39] See *ST* I-II, q. 94, a. 2.

Thus, we have this division:

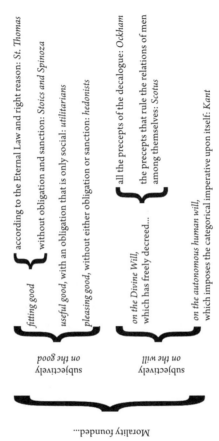

In light of what we have said, we see that a moral philosophy that makes abstraction from the objective notion of the good (as Kantian ethics does) loses all contact with reality and resembles, to the eyes of a realist philosopher, an arid world without the light of the sun. The objective notion of the good manifestly should illuminate the entire moral domain, just as being should illuminate all of metaphysics.

Ends are divided up in like manner. As the end is that for the sake of which the agent acts, ends can be divided up either from the perspective of *the object and the way* it attracts (i.e., finalizes) the agent or from the perspective of the subject (i.e., the perspective of the *agent's intention*). Thus, we have the following subdivisions to which St. Thomas often makes allusion:

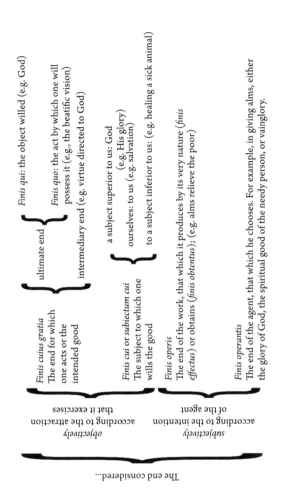

The end considered...

- **objectively** — according to the attraction that it exercises
  - *Finis cuius gratia* — The end for which one acts or the intended good
    - ultimate end — *Finis qui*: the object willed (e.g. God)
    - *Finis quo*: the act by which one will possess it (e.g., the beatific vision)
    - intermediary end (e.g. virtue directed to God)
  - *Finis cui* or *subiectum cui* — The subject to which one wills the good
    - a subject superior to us: God (e.g. His glory)
    - ourselves: to us (e.g. salvation)
    - to a subject inferior to us: (e.g. healing a sick animal)

- **subjectively** — according to the intention of the agent
  - *Finis operis* — The end of the work, that which it produces by its very nature (*finis effectus*) or obtains (*finis obtentus*); (e.g. alms relieve the poor)
  - *Finis operantis* — The end of the agent, that which he chooses. For example, in giving alms, either the glory of God, the spiritual good of the needy person, or vainglory.

Having thus determined the sense and scope of the principle of finality, as well as the various meanings of the word "end," it is fitting to briefly examine the principles that are subordinated to it.

Chapter Five

THE PRINCIPLES SUBORDINATED TO THE PRINCIPLE OF FINALITY

Among these subordinate principles, we will indicate the following six in particular:

1. The principle of *induction*;
2. The principle of *the interdependence of the agent and the end* (from various perspectives) and, consequently, the interdependence of matter and form;
3. The principle of *the subordination of agents and of ends*;
4. The principle of the relations between *coordination* and subordination;
5. The principle of the dependence of every order of means and end upon an *ordering intelligence*;
6. Finally, the first principle of the natural law: *the good must be done and evil avoided.*

The Principle of Induction

The problem concerning the foundation for the induction of the laws of nature consists in asking oneself, after the experience of many similar facts, "How can we affirm *with physical certitude* that in similar circumstances this is how things always will happen (e.g., that always, in the same circumstances, heat will make iron expand, the rosebush will bear roses and not lilies, and the lion will always beget a lion and not a tiger)?"

Empiricism holds that there is only a strong presumption that this will always be so, a presumption confirmed by many other similar cases. However, it cannot be elevated to a *truly universal law*. The empiricist notes the particular, observed facts and draws from them a probable presumption about what will happen in the future. Thus, positivism is unable to explain positive science and to provide a foundation for induction.

Kantian subjectivism cannot provide it with an *objective* foundation. It only affirms: according to the category of causality, heat seems to be the cause of the expansion of iron, and we will always think thus; however, outside of our minds, there cannot be any causality of this kind.

For Aristotelian realism, the foundation for induction is found in the universal notion of *nature* and of *a natural cause, of itself determined ad unum* [*to one*]. For Aristotle,[1] if, as experience shows, heat truly is the *cause* of the expansion of iron, if the begetting lion is the natural cause of the begotten lion, this will always be the case in the same circumstances. Why? Because the natural cause acts in virtue of its own, proper determination. It is determined *ad unum* and cannot alter its own, proper determination as human freedom can alter its own. In this sense, Jules Lachelier was quite correct in saying that induction is founded as much on final causality as it is upon efficient causality.[2] St. Thomas wrote with great precision on this matter in *ST* I, q. 19, a. 4c:

---

[1] It has sometimes been thought that Aristotle only spoke of induction by way of complete enumeration, which he discusses in *Prior Analytics* 1.25, where he shows that all animals without gall live for a long time. However, it is clear that complete enumeration cannot hold for the future. In reality, Aristotle provided the true foundation for induction when he explained the passage from knowledge of the singular to knowledge of the universal and also where he defined nature as well as natural causality, which is determined *ad unum*. Cf. *Posterior Analytics*, 1.4–5; 2.15 and 25 [sic]. *Physics*, 2.1. *Metaphysics*, 5.4 and 7.7.

[2] See Jules Lachelier, *Du fondement de l'induction*, §2, 21–22: "How are we to cross the infinite distance that separates probability from certitude" and pass from the present to the future?

It pertains to a *natural agent* that it produces *one effect*, for nature acts in one and the same manner so long as it is not impeded, for according to the fact that it is *such* does it act. Whence, so long as it is *such*, it does not act except in *such a way*. This is so because every agent by nature has a determinate kind of being [*esse*].

Simultaneously expressing the notions of efficiency and finality, Aristotle often expressed the matter, "Nature is determined *ad unum*."[3] Therefore, the principle of induction should be formulated: in the same circumstances, every *natural cause* always produces the same effect. Were this not the case, if the effect were to change without there being a prior variation in the cause or in the circumstances, such a change would lack a *raison d'être*. By this, we can see that this principle is connected to the principle of *raison d'être*, which dominates the principles of efficient causality and of finality.

The Interdependence of Causes

The agent and the end exercise reciprocal causality upon one another from different perspectives, as form and matter consequently do as well. This is the Aristotelian principle often invoked by St. Thomas: *Causae ad invicem sunt causae sed in diverso genere*—causes are causes of each other, though in different genera of causality.[4] Indeed, the end, which is first in the order of intention, attracts the agent, and in turn, the agent realizes or obtains the end in the order of execution.[5] It follows that the form in view of which the matter is disposed determines this matter, though it is also received and limited by it. Thus, the sculptor who desires to make a statue gradually gives it its form. So too, the seed contained in the grain of wheat and ordered to the production of the

---

[3] See the entry for *agens*, 14 in the *Tabula aurea* of Peter of Bergamo (d. 1482).

[4] See Aristotle, *Metaphysics*, 5.2. Also, the commentary of St. Thomas, lect. 2.

[5] Furthermore, the end would not *actually* attract the agent, if the agent had not already begun *to tend actually* to it, at least by an initial desire.

fully developed plant develops in this direction up to its full development. An attentive intellect can grasp the mutual dependence of causes at play in this process of development, the mutual dependence of the agent and the end, as well as that of matter and form.

At length at the end of this work, we will insist on the importance of this principle concerning the mutual relation of causes and will see that it explains innumerable difficulties by showing the profound harmony existing among the four causes, precisely where some believe that they initially see a contradiction in terms or a vicious circle.

This principle is one of the great leitmotivs of Thomism. It alone resolves difficulties pertaining to the mutual relations of the intellect and the senses that furnish the matter for the intellect's consideration while, nonetheless, being judged on high by the intellect. Likewise, it illuminates the no-less-mysterious relations between the intellect and the will in free choice at the terminus of our moral deliberation,[6] or again in the act of faith. Likewise, this principle explains the mutual relations existing between our deliverance from sin and our justification, as well as, conversely, the mutual relations between an initial sin and the loss of grace. Many other problems would remain absolutely insoluble without this principle concerning the mutual priority of the causes from different perspectives.

The Subordination of Agents and Ends

The order of agents corresponds to the order of ends. This represents a corollary of the principle, "Every agent acts for an end that is proportioned to it." Thus, the action of a soldier is subordinated to that of the leader of his battalion and the latter to that of the leader of the army, for the particular end of the former is subordinated to the ends that his superiors pursue. Likewise, as St. Thomas says, it is impossible for man

---

[6] We have explained this at greater length elsewhere. See Réginald Garrigou-Lagrange, *God: His Existence and His Nature: A Thomistic Solution of Certain Agnostic Antinomies*, vol. 2, trans. Bede Rose (St. Louis: B. Herder, 1949), 306–338 and 370–372.

to be oriented to the ultimate end of his entire life without the motion of the Supreme Agent to which this end corresponds. For the same reason, the sinner cannot be disposed to receive the sanctifying grace that justifies without an actual grace of the same order. In other words, one cannot tend to an end that is essentially supernatural without the gratuitous help of a supernatural agent (i.e., God the Author of grace). The order of agents corresponds to the order of ends.[7] In this way, we have an explanation for the expression, "You would not seek me, if you had not already found me"; you would not aspire to conversion if I had not already preveniently come to you through my actual grace.

St. Thomas vigorously insisted upon this subordination of agents and ends. According to him,[8] every creature, by the very fact that it is necessarily subordinated to God, is *naturally inclined* to love God, its Author, more than it loves itself. It is more *of Him* and *for Him* than it is of itself and for itself, just as the part exists more for the whole than for itself. Just as the hand sacrifices itself in order to save the body, above all to save the head, so too does the stone tend toward the center of the earth for the cohesion and good of the universe, and so too does the hen sacrifice herself for her chicks for the good of the species, which is a manifestation of the goodness of the Creator.

Every Coordination Presupposes a Subordination

Often, modern authors write "coordination" where St. Thomas would write "subordination." Coordination is one form of order established among various elements ordered to the same end. However, it presupposes the superior form of ordering which is called subordination. Why is this the case? Because, in general, order is the disposition of several realities according to before and after, in relation to a *principle* to which these various realities are subordinated. Thus, says St.

---

7   See *ST* I-II, q. 109, a. 6.

8   See *ST* I, q. 60, a. 5.

Thomas,[9] the coordination of two or more soldiers presupposes their subordination to the same leader. Many people who more or less theoretically confuse subordination and coordination with each other nonetheless continue to complain (without confusion) about their subordinates' insubordination. It never dawns upon them to speak here of a mere lack of coordination [*incoordination*].

The confusion between coordination and subordination that we find in many modern thinkers predates them.

While the doctrine of St. Thomas can be called a doctrine of the *subordination of causes*, we could call Suarez's doctrine one of the *coordination of causes*.

For St. Thomas, just as *the creature is not its own existence* (*non est suum esse*) but only receives it (so much so that in the creature essence and existence are distinct prior to our intellect's consideration), *so too is the creature not its action* (*non est suum agere*) but, instead, in order to act, must be *premoved* by God through a motion conformed to its nature. They are two total, subordinated causes.[10]

By contrast, for Suarez, these are two *partial, coordinated causes*. The creature, whose essence (according to Suarez) is not really distinct from its existence, acts without being premoved by God. Its active power is a "virtual act" that is reduced to second act (or, to the action itself) with the *simultaneous concurrence of God*. It is a somewhat like two men pulling a ship mutually aiding each other without the first influencing the second.[11] Here, in place of two total causes that are subordinated in such a way that the second cause acts only inasmuch as it is premoved by God, we have two partial, coordinated causes.[12] To this, the Thomists respond: Every coordination presupposes a subordination, as much in the order of action as in the order of being. Therefore, above all in relation to God, the First Cause, we cannot hold that it is a question of created activity being a kind of activity coordinated with

---

9   See *ST* I-II, q. 109, a. 6.

10 *ST* I, q. 105, aa. 4 and 5. Also, *ST* I, q. 23, a. 5.

11 See Suarez, *Disp. Met.*, disp. 29, sect. 1, no. 7.

12 See Suarez, *Disp. Met.*, disp. 22, sect. 2. Also, Suarez, *De auxiliis gratiae* III, ch. 38. Also, Molina, *Concordia*, q. 14, a. 13, disp. 26 and q. 23, aa. 4 and 5, disp. 1, membr. 7, ad 6.

God's. Instead, created activity is a subordinate form of activity.

Likewise, for St. Thomas, the knowing faculty and the represent-ative likeness of the object (i.e., the *species impressa*) are two total subordinated causes in such a manner that the entire vitality of the act of knowledge comes from the faculty and its determination from the likeness of the object impressed in it.[13] For Suarez, they are, instead, two partial, coordinated causes.

We find ourselves faced with this same opposition again at the ter-minus of moral deliberation in relation to the last practical judgment and the will's act of choice. According to St. Thomas, choice is always conformed to the last practical judgment, and by accepting its direction makes it be the last judgment.[14] By contrast, for Suarez, choice is not always conformed to the last practical judgment.[15] The Thomists say that this is irreconcilable with the principle, "Nothing is willed unless it is first known as something fitting." Now, this represents a problem of great importance. It is raised not only in the cases of man and the angels but also in that of God when, according to our analogical mannner of knowing, we come to discuss the relations between the Divine Intel-lect and Will as regards, for example, the ultimate foundation of moral obligation.

We find the same difference between the Thomists and the Suarezians in many other important theses, notably when in discus-sions concerning the relations between our faculties and grace (e.g., the intellect and the light of glory).[16] For St. Thomas, these are two total, subordinated causes. For Suarez they are two partial, coordinated causes. This is why Suarez holds that there is an "active obediential potency" in our faculties. To the eyes of the Thomists,[17] this represents a contradiction, for it would be, at one and the same time, essentially natural (as a property of our nature) and essentially supernatural (as being specified by a supernatural object). It would simultaneously

---

[13] [Tr. note: See note 24 in the fourth chapter of the next section.]

[14] *ST* I-II, q. 13, a. 1 and a. 6, ad 3.

[15] See Suarez, *Disp. Meta.*, disp. 19, sect. 6.

[16] [Tr. note: that is, the subjective disposition by which the finite intellect will be ele-vated to receive the Beatific Vision.]

[17] See John of St. Thomas, *Cursus theologicus*, in *ST* I, q. 12, disp. 14, a. 2.

violate the principle of contradiction and the principle of finality.

By substituting coordination for subordination, Suarez often sought after a golden mean between St. Thomas and Scotus. For example, in the question concerning what is formally constitutive of beatitude, instead of choosing between the primacy of the intellect (as St. Thomas held) and the primacy of the will (as Scotus held), Suarez preferred to say that beatitude is found formally in the two faculties *ex aequo*. This expression *ex aequo* is synonymous with coordination. Thomists can respond to him: coordination is never something primary; it always presupposes a subordination, for order is conceived only in relation to a first principle.

In virtue of this law, "Every coordination presupposes subordination," every *nature* as such is determined *to one*: the nature of man, that of sight, hearing, the intellect, the will, and so forth. In other words, one faculty cannot bear upon *two primary objects ex aequo*. These objects would be coordinated without being subordinated, something that is impossible. For the same reason, our intellect cannot have two first principles *ex aequo* (e.g., that of contradiction and that of sufficient reason [*raison suffisante*]).[18] With Aristotle and St. Thomas, we must acknowledge the priority of the principle of contradiction, which is immediately founded on being, the first object of the intellect.

A Means Can Be Ordered to an End Only by an Ordering Intellect

In *ST* I, q. 2, a. 3, St. Thomas thus enunciates this principle:

Things that do not have cognition do not tend to an end unless

---

18 [Tr. note: It is precisely because of passages like this that I have hesitated to follow other translators in rendering every instance of Fr. Garrigou-Lagrange's "*principe de raison d'être*" as "principle of sufficient reason." He certainly appears to have that in mind in passages where he uses the expression. However, at other times (such as here), he explicitly states "*principe de raison suffisante*." In an effort to save him from being *wrongly* misinterpreted as a wrong-headed follower in the tradition of Leibnizian-Wolffian scholasticism, I have chosen to maintain ambiguity in the English by rendering *principe de raison d'être* literally when encountered. See my comments above in note 5 of chapter 2 above.]

they are directed by some knowing and intelligent being, as an arrow is directed by an archer. Now, certain bèings lacking knowledge, namely, inorganic bodies, act in view of an end. This is obvious from the fact that they always (or nearly always) act in the same manner in order to obtain that which is *best* for them (for example, their preservation by eating and breathing, and their reproduction). Therefore, an Intelligent Being exists, by Which all natural things are ordered to an end, and we call this Being God.[19]

This conclusion is rigorously certain, for *the intellect* alone knows the end as such, the notion of the end, and the arrangement of means to that for which they are done [i.e. to the end]. In other words, *the intellect alone* knows the *raison d'être* of the means. This *raison d'être* can be perceived only by a faculty whose formal object is *being*—and not color, sound, or any inner fact [of consciousness] whatsoever. Likewise, as it is said, "*Sapientis est ordinare*": the wise man, not the impulsive or impassioned man, has the property of ordering things, of finding the order according to which things should be disposed. Moreover, this principle does not only require us to trace our reasoning back to a finite intellect, as Kant held, but moreover, requires us to trace back to Intelligence Itself, to Self-Subsistent Intellection or Thought. This is so because every finite intellect that is not its own act (i.e., which is not Thought Itself and Truth Itself, as well as Being Itself) is *ordered* to its act, as to its perfection, and likewise ordered to truth or to the being to be known, and this realized order presupposes a supreme Orderer, who is related to Thought, Truth, and Being, as A is related to A, *Ipsum intelligere subsitens.*

How is the principle, "Every ordination presupposes an ordering intelligence," related to the principle of finality, "Every agent acts for an end"?

We can say that here we have a corollary to the principle of finality,

---

[19] [Tr. note: The parenthetical notes are Fr. Garrigou-Lagrange's remarks. The passage is slightly reordered by him into a clearer syllogistic form. I have followed his order, translating from the Latin, though keeping an eye to his French. The sense of the passage remains the same as St. Thomas's in *ST* I, q. 2, a. 3.]

on the condition that we note well that the principle of finality, as we discussed earlier, is *analogical* (i.e., is applied in different ways to natural agents that are not endowed with knowledge, to animals endowed with sense knowledge, and to intellectual agents).

The corollary of which we are speaking precisely determines the relationship between the *inferior analogates* of the principle of finality and its *superior analogates*. And this relationship is already clear with certitude before one has proven the existence of God, the supreme analogate.[20] Indeed, as we just said, it suffices that one note that finality would not exist in nature if a *natural tendency* did not have *its raison d'être* in an end and that only an *intellect* can know the *raison d'être* of things, means having their *raison d'être* in the ends to which they are essentially related as means.

Therefore, if there is an *order* that is made, that *becomes*, and that therefore requires a cause (e.g., as in the development of an embryo), this cause must be an intelligent cause, and as every intellect that is not Being Itself and Truth Itself *is ordered* to Being and to Truth, we must arrive, at last, at the Supreme Intellect that is Truth Itself Ever Actually Known.[21]

It follows that the proof of God's existence drawn from the order of the world is very easy to understand, so much so that one could call it a natural kind of knowledge. This is what St. Thomas himself thought:

> There is a kind of common and vague knowledge of God, which is in a manner found among all men. . . , for by natural reason, man can immediately arrive at some knowledge of God. In fact, seeing natural things run along according to a certain course *and knowing that an order cannot occur without someone who orders it thus*, men perceive that in most cases there is some orderer of the things that we see. However, they do not immediately, by way of this ordinary consideration of the matter,

---

[20] [Tr. note: That is, of this particular set of analogates, namely those pertaining to the imperfect abstraction involved in the principle of finality, which is analogical in a properly proportional manner.]

[21] We have explicated this proof at greater length elsewhere. See Garrigou-Lagrange, *God: His Existence and His Nature*, vol. 1, 345–372.

know who or what sort of being this might be, or if there is only one orderer of nature.[22]

There cannot be an ordination without an ordering intellect.

Even though it held that there are multiple gods, polytheism also acknowledged a supreme one (e.g. Zeus or Jupiter).

The easiness of this proof is proclaimed in many passages of Sacred Scripture. For example, consider Wisdom 13:1–9 (RSV):

> For all men who were ignorant of God were *foolish* by nature; and they were unable from the good things that are seen to know him who exists, nor did they recognize the craftsman while paying heed to his works. . . . For from the greatness and beauty of created things comes a corresponding perception of their Creator. . . . (Not even they who have ignored God) *are to be excused;* for if they had the power to know so much that they could investigate the world, *how did they fail to find sooner the Lord of these things?*

Commenting on the words of Psalm 19:1, "The heavens proclaim the glory of God," St. John Chrysostom writes in the same sense, "The Scythian and the barbarian, the Jew and the Egyptian, and every man on the earth hears this voice. Both the simple and the learned man can equally read from this book (i.e., the book of nature)."[23]

By means of this common insight, one at least grasps the *probability* of the existence of a Supreme Ruler of the earth. Having posited this, man is *bound* to strive after greater enlightenment concerning the existence and nature of this Supreme Orderer. And if he neglects this duty, he is culpable: from that point on, *his ignorance is no longer invincible (i.e. absolutely involuntary).*

This knowledge of God, by way of the vague and rudimentary knowledge that we just explained, can be acquired, on account of its

---

[22] *SCG*, III, ch, 38.
[23] See St. John Chrysostom, *Hom. IX ad popul. Antioch.*

easiness, *without any particular teaching.* Also, we cannot admit that, having arrived at natural knowledge of the first rational principles (i.e., by common sense), man can be *invincibly ignorant* concerning the existence of God, the Author of nature. In virtue of the naturally known first principles of efficient causality and of finality, each person can and ought easily to arrive at not only an *implicit* knowledge of God (i.e., of God implicitly known in the notion of the fitting good, the good-for-itself) but also at an *explicit,* though *vague,* knowledge of Him. God is thus known from the general perspective of being the Supreme Principle and Governor without His various naturally knowable attributes being yet determined.

Now, by contrast, when it comes to knowledge that is not only *explicit* but also *distinct,* invincible ignorance can exist, as the history of polytheism bears witness.

Here, as is clear, it is important not to forget the classical distinction between the *obscure* (or, *implicit*) idea and the *clear* (or, *explicit*) idea expressed by common sense. The latter already enables one not to confuse what one is speaking about with other things (e.g., not to confuse animal with plant, nor God with the stars or evil spirits). This *explicit but still-vague* [*confus*] idea expressed by common sense is still far removed from the *explicit and distinct* idea that scientific knowledge expresses when it exactly determines the genus and specific difference of the thing or, if it is a question of God, when it analogically determines what His nature is and what are the attributes that can be derived from it.[24]

---

[24] Cf. Billuart, *De Deo,* diss. 1 a. 4: "This demonstration is so easy and so obvious, that no one with mental abilities (even though he be a peasant or even a barbarian) is unable to achieve it, such that there does not light upon him (either on the basis of some inspection of the world or of himself) some suspicion or conjectural opinion concerning the existence of some supreme divinity or ruler. Once this state of affairs is posited, such a person is bound to inquire into what it is. If he neglects this, he is *vincibly ignorant.*" St. Augustine, says, concerning Psalm 74: "God, everywhere secret, everywhere public, whom no one is allowed to know *as He is* and *whom nobody is permitted* not to know." Also, St. Gregory the Great, *Moralia in Job,* bk. 27, ch. 3: "Every man, from the very fact that he has been created as a rational being, must gather from reason that he who created him is God." Also see Zigliara, *Summa philosophica,* vol. 2, 398.

It has been objected, "Once the social system wherein the teaching concerning

This vague notion of a Supreme Orderer of the universe is found in all primitive religions, as also is the moral sense founded on the distinction between the obligatory good and evil.[25] The barbarian tribes of certain American islands who venerate, using the name "Mahoya," the principle of evil, which we call the devil, also call upon a supreme divinity to restrict the power of the evil principle.—Everyone who has arrived at the full use of reason is not slow to grasp that the order of the world presupposes an Ordering Intelligence.

---

the truth of God disappears entirely has been established and consolidated, the great mass of people no longer will find there to be any possibility of coming to know the true God and His law. Therefore, they experience *invincible ignorance along with all the consequences that follow from the perspective of moral responsibility and the sanctions of the future life.* . . . The common and easy means of initiation prepared and disposed for the general run of men by nature itself is instruction (and not personal research). . . . However, the implementation of this economy is placed in the hands of man; therefore, for the general run of people in the world, it can corrupt and destroy the natural order on which the coming to *adult maturity* depends, along with the development of *superior reason*. . . . Theologians have always neglected this question, . . . and they have not applied themselves to seeking the degree of precision to which the notion of God must arrive so that, beginning to penetrate the sanctuary of conscience, it can pose to conscience the first foundations for moral responsibility and the true conditions of spiritual adulthood. Here, we are faced with a considerable *lacuna* . . . one that motivates us anew to desire there to be a revision concerning a case that has been judged too superficially in the past." [Tr. note: The parenthesis are in the text as presented by Fr. Garrigou-Lagrange and, therefore, are likely something he has added.]

If this were the case, there would be a considerable number of men outside the normal way of salvation, many people lacking faith, adults (as regards their age though not as regards their reason or conscience), who would go neither to heaven nor to hell but to an intermediate place, the limbo of those who are adults with regard to age. They would have been able to commit, materially speaking, the greatest crimes without, formally speaking, sinning. And, if they would have been baptized before having committed them, they would go, by rights, to heaven. All of this seems inadmissible to us, for it inordinately enlarges the number of idiots, insane, and deeply disturbed. This is not what Scripture means when it says, "*Stultorum infinitus est numerus* [The number of fools is infinite]" (Eccl 1:15). This would represent the destruction of common sense (or, natural reason).

25 On this subject, one can consult Alexander le Roy, *The Religion of the Primitives*, trans. Newton Thompson (New York: Macmillan, 1922), 282ff.

The First Principle of Morality: "The Good Must Be Done and Evil Avoided." Can One Prove the Existence of God from This?

The principle of finality also founds the *first principle of practical reason,* as well as the *proof of the existence of God drawn,* properly speaking, not from moral obligation but, rather, *from the ordering of our will to the doing of good and to the need to flee from evil.* Once more, invincible ignorance is impossible here. On this subject, St. Thomas said:

> Just as *being* is the first thing that falls into apprehension, simply speaking, so too is *good* the first thing that falls into the apprehension of practical reason, which is ordered to a given work. For every agent acts according to the end, which has the nature of the good. Therefore, THE FIRST PRINCIPLE *in practical reason* is that which is founded on the *nature of the good,* namely *the good is that which all things seek.* Therefore, this is the first precept of the law: that *good is to be done and sought after, and evil avoided.* And, all the other precepts of the natural law [*legis naturae*] are founded on this first precept, so that all other things to be done or avoided, which practical reason *naturally grasps* as being human goods, pertain to the natural law [*legis naturae*]. However, because the good has the nature of being an end, whereas evil has the nature of being its contrary, reason therefore naturally apprehends as being good (and, consequently, as being things to be pursued) all those things to which man *has a natural inclination,* while their contraries are known as being evil and to be avoided. Therefore, the order of the precepts of the natural law [*legis naturae*] is in accord with the order *of natural inclinations.*[26]

For example, in accord with the inclination that man has (like every substance) to maintain himself in existence, we have the natural law requirement of preserving one's life. Likewise, in accordance with

---

[26] *ST* I-II, q. 94, a. 2.

the natural inclination of animal life, the law that nature itself teaches the animals (i.e., the union of the sexes and the education of children) thus enters into the natural law. Finally, in conformity with the tendency of rational nature, man must recognize God's existence and live in society.[27]

In sum, man (like every agent) works in view of an end (or, in view of a good). However, he does not know only the sensible good (whether it be *pleasing or useful*) but also knows the *fitting* good, which is *good in itself*, independent of every form of utility or of all the pleasure that might accompany it. For example, it is good to tell the truth and avoid lying. Our reason easily perceives the relationship (or, ordination) of our rational nature to the fitting (or, moral) good. Now, as the relation (or, ordination) of natural agents to their proportionate end obviously presupposes a Supreme *Orderer*, so too (and for all the more reason) does the natural relation of our rational nature to the doing of good and flight from evil manifest the existence of the Supreme Legislator or, *God the Author of the natural law*.

Thus, we can see that the *proximate foundation* for natural moral obligation is found in the fitting good itself, to which (as reason sees and notes) the inclinations of our nature tend (i.e., those to which they are *essentially* ordered). In other words, this proximate foundation presupposes the essential order of things, known and proclaimed by our reason, and it consists in this principle: "*The rational good*, to which our faculties are ordered, MUST *be done by the rational agent*; the rational agent MUST act reasonably." Here, reason not only sees but also *orders* like a second cause. The *ultimate foundation* for our natural moral obligation is found in the final, natural, objective end, namely in the Supreme Good and more formally in the Eternal Law of God who has ordered our nature to this end.[28] In order for the Eternal Law to obligate, it suffices that there be in God a creative will and the creative act: "*The promulgation* of the natural law [*legis naturae*] exists from the very fact that God placed it into the minds of men so that it may be

---

[27] See *ST* I-II, 94, a. 2; q. 100, a. 1.

[28] See *ST* I-II, q. 19, aa. 1–4; q. 71, a. 6, ad 4: "The natural law [*ius naturale*] is indeed first contained in the Eternal Law, but secondarily in the natural judgment [*in naturali iudicatorio*] of human reason."

known naturally."²⁹ Elsewhere, the holy Doctor says, "*First principles of acting must also be bestowed on us by nature,* as are the first speculative principles. . . . *Unchangeable notions* of this sort (i.e., as Augustine notes in the objection) are the first principles of things to be done, *concerning which one does not err.*"³⁰

The first principle of the practical intellect (or, synderesis), "*The good must be done and evil avoided,*" is not a conclusion but, instead, a true first principle, a self-evident axiom.³¹

---

²⁹ See *ST* I-II, q. 90, a. 4, ad 1.

³⁰ *ST* I, q. 79, a. 12c and also ad 3.

³¹ [Tr. note: Often, with regard to first principles in practical reason, one tends to forget the role of subordinate principles that would be known in the same way by *synderesis*. Synderesis is involved in all non-discursive practical knowledge and without it the virtues themselves would not have their own ends, formally specified by this non-discursive, practical, intellectual apprehension. See Lehu, *La raison: règle de la moralité d'après Saint Thomas,* 135–152. Also, see Yves Simon, *A Critique of Moral Knowledge,* trans. Ralph McInerny (New York: Fordham University Press, 2002), 28n2: "The object of moral sense is not only the first principle of the practical order ('Good should be done and evil avoided'), but any self-evident practical principle; if by preference we speak of the first practical principle, this is because it is the object par excellence of moral sense, as the principle of identity is the object par excellence of the *intellectus principiorum.*" Indeed, although Simon wrote his text around the same time that he privately made this semi-critical remark noted in the introduction to this translation, he does cite Fr. Garrigou-Lagrange's *Le principe de finalité* in a positive manner on two important issues in 13n8 and 48n8. On synderesis, also see Ryan J. Brady, "Aquinas on the Respective Roles of Prudence and Synderesis vis-à-vis the Ends of the Moral Virtues" (Ph.D. Diss., Ave Maria University, 2017). Also see Reinhard Hütter, "To Be Good Is to Do the Truth: Being, Truth, the Good, and the Primordial Conscience in a Thomist Perspective," *Nova et Vetera* 15, No. 1 (2017): 53–73.

For one possible interpretation of how synderesis would be super-elevated in the supernatural order, so as to enunciate first principles for ordering divinized human agency (thus providing the formality for the various infused *habitus*), see B.-H. Merkelbach, *Summa theologiae moralis,* 5th ed., vol. 2 (Paris: Desclée de Brouwer, 1947), no. 218: "Faith informs and elevates reason and synderesis, subordinating them to itself. Consequently, under the light of faith, synderesis is able to enunciate the first supernatural practical principles. And reasonably so, for supposing that faith teaches that God has elevated us to a supernatural end and that our ultimate good is only found in the beatific vision of God Himself, *reason* sees already that we must tend toward that end and that the ultimate good to be possessed in this manner must be loved in all of our acts. And do not say that synderesis does not have an idea of the supernatural end, for synderesis does not exist for conceiving ideas but, supposing these ideas, it sees and with ease enunciates their befittingness or unbefittingness.—

Our reason (or, better yet, our understanding of the first practical principles) is therefore not content with *showing* that good is to be done. Instead, it *rules by commanding: the good must be done and evil avoided.* It does not only say that good is doable (i.e., that it *can* be done). Not only is it *fitting* to do it. Instead, it *must* be done, *faciendum*. Practical reason thus gives the will a rule that is *imperative* and not only speculative, and it does this *like a secondary cause*, under the influence of the First Cause (or, the Eternal Law).[32] It exercises this action in dependence on the First Cause (i.e., *in actu exercito*) without determinately considering the Eternal Law (i.e., *in actu signato*), that is, by considering that the natural relation of our will to the obligatory moral good presupposes an Orderer who established it. Reason sees quite well that it did not itself create this relationship.

Consequently, just as invincible ignorance of the first, unchanging principles of the natural law (principles that cannot be erased from man's heart) is impossible, so too is this true regarding the existence of the Supreme Legislator. Obviously, there is no law without a Legislator.[33]

And in order for one to sin against the eternal law, it is not necessary that *superior reason actually* think about God's law. It suffices that it can and ought to think upon it before deciding anything. For, as St. Thomas says, when it thinks of it at the moment of sin, it despises this Divine Law. If it does not think of it, it neglects it by way of omission: "cum ratio superior *cogitate de lege Dei*, actu eam *contemnit*; cum vero *non cogitate* eam *negligit* per modum omissionis cuiusdam."[34] From whatever angle we consider it, the consent to the act of sin thus arises from superior reason, which considers the eternal reasons of things and not only their contingent aspects.[35]

St. Thomas does not expressly speak about supernatural conscience but everywhere says that the major premise is placed in conscience by synderesis; however, he is not speaking only about the conscience of philosophers but also is speaking of the conscience of believers; [therefore, supernatural conscience enunciates its major premise by means of synderesis]" (my translation).]

[32] See *ST* I-II, q. 19, aa. 3 and 4.

[33] See *ST* I-II, q. 94, aa. 4–6.

[34] See *ST* I-II, q. 74, a. 7, ad 2.

[35] See *ST* I-II, q. 74, aa. 6–9.

The End, Which Is Willed before the Means, Is Only Attained Last

This common-sense principle is philosophically formulated, "The end, which is first in the order of intention, is last in the order of execution." In order to build a wall, the mason must first will to do so. We can derive a number of consequences from this, as much in moral philosophy as in moral theology when it deals with Providence, as well as to the subordination of means to ends in God's providential plan for His creatures.

In moral philosophy, a particular consequence of this principle is the fact that the habitual rectification of the will in relation to the means presupposes habitual rectification in relation to the end. Hence, he who, through mortal sin, turns away from God (the ultimate natural and supernatural end[36]) cannot have, in relation to the means, the acquired cardinal virtues of prudence, justice, fortitude, and temperance, at least in the state of virtues (i.e. *in statu virutis difficile mobilis*) and in the state of *connected virtues*. Such a person can only have them in the state of disposition, *facile mobilis*. The radical disorder from which he suffers in relation to the final end does not permit him to be firmly rectified in relation to the means.[37]

When Providence is considered in theology, in virtue of the principle of finality and the corollary we are discussing here, it follows that *God* (like every intelligent agent) *for all eternity wills the end before the*

---

[36] [Tr. note: Regarding the aversion from our natural end included in our aversion from our supernatural end, see the text cited above in note 36 in the fifth chapter of part one.]

[37] See *ST* II-II, q. 23, a. 7. Also, this explains the fact that when one loses charity through any mortal sin, such a person also loses the infused moral virtues that pertain to the means [in the supernatural order], even though one does keep faith and hope, which do not presuppose charity but, rather, are presupposed by it. One only loses infused faith and hope through mortal sins that are directly opposed to them.

[Tr. note: On the topic of the state of the virtues in a mortal sinner, the reader can consult with great profit, Garrigou-Lagrange, "The Instability of the Acquired Moral Virtues in the State of Mortal Sin," *Philosophizing in Faith: Essays on the Beginning and End of Wisdom*, trans. Matthew K. Minerd (Providence, RI: Cluny Media, 2019), 171–182. Furthermore, see the admirably balanced article by Thomas M. Osborne, "Perfect and Imperfect Virtues in Aquinas," *The Thomist* 71 (2007): 39–64.]

means since He only wills the means for the sake of the end, *vult hoc esse propter hoc.*[38] According to the Thomists and a number of other theologians, this means that Predestination to glory precedes Predestination to grace. For example, from all eternity, God willed to give the grace of a happy death to one of the two thieves crucified alongside Jesus, rather than to the other, because He had the efficacious will to save him. Likewise, in accord with the same principle, God willed the predestination of Christ the Redeemer before our own. This is called for by the subordination of ends, and dogma itself requires it.[39]

Quite clearly, the principle of finality and its corollaries have countless consequences in natural philosophy, [philosophical] psychology, moral philosophy [*morale*], and theology. Here, it sufficed to note several principal ones. We will note others below in speaking about another corollary, namely the principle of the reciprocal influences of causes.[40]

Such are the principal corollaries of the principle of finality. In the second part of this work, we will consider its primary applications in relation to our intellect and our will.

---

[38] *ST* I, q. 19, a. 5.

[39] Regarding salvation, St. Paul says in Eph 1:3 (DR), "predestinated us unto the adoption of children through Jesus Christ unto himself," and in Rom 8:29 (DR), "[Those] whom he foreknew, he also predestinated to be made conformable to the image of his Son: that he might be the Firstborn amongst many brethren." See *ST* III, q. 24, aa. 3 and 4. These articles must always be kept in mind in order to understand aright St. Thomas's doctrine concerning the motive of the Incarnation. Also, see *ST* III, q. 1, a. 3. Also, see the end of the eighth chapter of next section below.

[40] See the eighth chapter of the next section.

Part II

PRIMARY APPLICATIONS OF THE PRINCIPLE OF FINALITY

FOR TRADITIONAL REALISM, above all as it was conceived of by Aristotle and St. Thomas, the primary applications of the principle of finality are twofold. First, there are those concerning the *finality of the intellect*, which by its very nature is ordered to knowledge of reality (i.e., to intelligible being) and, through that, to natural knowledge of God, the Ultimate Truth. Second, there are those concerning the *finality of the will*, which is essentially ordered to love and will the good in all of its universality and, above all, the Sovereign Good. In this second part, our attention will above all be devoted to speaking about these two applications of the principle of finality.

Chapter One

Realism and the Finality
of Our Intellect

Everyone who is interested in the study of the various sciences realizes
that all the particular sciences (e.g., physics, mathematics, biology, psychology, as well as individual and social morality) presuppose *general
principles* whose *real value* and *necessity* is recognized by common sense.
Such principles are denied by subjectivist, empiricist, and evolutionist forms of philosophy. However, they are defended by traditional
philosophy.

Physics, which studies the world of bodies and their movements,
mathematics, which treats of continuous or discrete quantity, psychology (which considers our soul, its functions, and its acts), moral
philosophy, which studies the laws of human action in relation to the
end that human acts must follow, and sociology, which seeks to understand what society is in its origins, constitution, various functions, and
its end—indeed, all these sciences that are concerned with a particular
aspect of reality or being (whether sensible and mobile being as such,
bodily being as quantitative, living being, or thinking, reasoning, and
sociable being) presuppose *the most universal laws of reality as real, or of
being as being*. In other words, they presuppose *the most general principles of the intellect and of the intelligible*. What are these principles from
the perspective of natural reason (or, the realism of common sense)?
And can this natural reason be justified by a critical realism?

The First Principles of Natural Reason

As Aristotle shows in the fourth book (γ) of his *Metaphysics*, it falls to first philosophy (i.e., metaphysics) to treat of these most universal principles of reality, for first philosophy's specific character consists in treating of the highest generalities that all the other sciences presuppose without being able to speak of them *ex professo*, given the too-restricted character of their own particular objects.

Already in the works of Aristotle, we find traditional metaphysics reducing these most general laws of the reality to the following principles.

First, there is the principle of contradiction: "*Being is opposed to non-being*, and no reality can at one and the same time both exist and not exist." In a positive form, this principle is enunciated as: Being is being, non-being is non-being; yes, yes; no, no—as the Gospel says. Therefore, we must not confuse being with non-being, yes with no, truth with falsity, good with evil, or again, spirit with flesh. Spirit is spirit, and flesh is flesh. In this positive form, this first principle is called the principle of identity instead of the principle of contradiction.

It has as its corollary the principle of substance: "*Every being is one and the same under its multiple and successive phenomena*; or, every being *which exists* as a first subject of attribution is *substance*; or, it exists *in itself* like the stone, plant, or animal, without it being necessary, however, that it exist *through itself* (or, necessarily)."[1]

To these first principles are subordinated the principle of *raison d'être*, the principle of efficient causality, the principle of finality, and the principle of change. *Every being has its raison d'être either in itself* (if it exists through and for itself) *or in another* (if it does not exist through and for itself). *Everything that happens (or, more generally, all that does not exist through itself) has an efficient cause. Every agent acts for an end,*

---

[1] [Tr. note: Strictly speaking, Aristotle's text in the fourth book of the *Metaphysics* provides for the principle of non-contradiction and, by that, a distinction between the *per se* and the *per accidens*. While this distinction is initially applicable to the case of substance (*in se*) and accidents (*in alio*), it is applicable more broadly to any cases where one contrasts what is *essential* and what is *accidental* (e.g. the case of moral acts, which have their object *per se* and their circumstances *per accidens*).]

without which it would not tend to some determinate thing that is suitable for it; likewise, there would not be a reason for which it acts and for which it acts in a given fashion. Thus, the wings of the bird are for flying, the ear for hearing, and the eye for seeing. Finally, *every transformation or change* (whether it be material or spiritual) *presupposes a subject* that receives a new modification. There is no flow without fluid, no flight without something that flies, no dream without a dreamer, no thought without a thinking subject.

Many other principles are derived from these first principles. For example, as we have seen, the principle of induction, "one and the same natural cause in the same circumstances always produces the same effect," is derived from the principles of efficient causality and final causality. Thus, if in a given set of circumstances, heat expands iron, it will always do likewise, otherwise, the change in the effect without prior change in the cause and in the circumstances would lack a *raison d'être*, whether efficient or final. In this way, the laws of nature are discovered by means of induction.

Likewise, from the principle of finality, "Every agent acts for a proportionate end," is derived the corollary, "*The order of agents corresponds to the order of ends* (or, *the subordination of the order of agents to that of the ends*)." For example, in society, the individual agent who pursues his own good is subordinated to the civil authority, which pursues the common good of the city, and this authority is necessarily subordinated to God who orders all things to the supreme end of the universe, i.e. to the manifestation of His Goodness.[2]

---

[2] Without the principle of finality, nothing is intelligible in nature, as well as in individual and collective moral life.

For example, in the case of animal life, why does the hen gather her little chicks under her wings and defend them against a hawk, to the point of sacrificing herself if it be necessary? This is because, as St. Thomas says, she instinctively loves the good of her species more than she loves herself. See *ST* I, q. 60, a. 5, ad 3.

Without the principle of finality and that of the subordination of agents and of ends, one cannot have any adequate [*juste*] idea of moral and social life. In particular, one can have no adequate [*juste*] idea of the subordination of the four species of justice that we must practice: (1) the commutative justice that rules exchanges in particular; (2) distributive justice, which proportionally distributes to individuals things of common usefulness, expenses, and obligations; (3) legal (or, social) justice, which must promote the common good through just laws and by making them be

As Aristotle says in the third chapter of book four of the *Metaphysics*, the first of all these principles is the *principle of contradiction*, for it is immediately founded on the first notion presupposed by all others, the *notion of being* (or, *of reality*), and on its contradictory opposition to non-being. Thus, this [self-]evident principle is absolutely indemonstrable. It does not rest on another principle. Moreover, if it is denied, the other principles no longer have any truth, but on the other hand, if it is admitted, the others can be defended or demonstrated *indirectly* (i.e., by a *reductio ad absurdum*), *though not directly* (i.e., through a middle term), for they are immediately self-evident.[3] For example, a being that would come into existence without any cause is as *absurd* as is a square circle. Similarly, a tendency that in no way tends toward an end is absurd.

The Problem Concerning the Value of Common Sense's Realism

These principles are admitted by natural reason (that is, by common sense) as being *necessary* and as having an *objective value*. In other words, they are recognized as *necessary laws of reality* and not only as directive, subjective laws of our thought.

By contrast, subjectivism like that of Kant, sees in them only subjective and necessary laws of our thought (or, being inasmuch as it is *thought by us*), not laws of *things in themselves* (which remain unknowable from this subjectivist perspective).

Empiricism holds that these principles express laws of reality but claims that their *necessity* cannot be established. It says that it may well be the case that beyond the limits of our experience, beings come into existence without any cause and that there are tendencies that do not tend toward any end.

Absolute, pantheistic evolutionism, represented in antiquity by

---

observed; (4) equity, which, above legality (or, the letter of the laws), ensures the spirit of the laws by interpreting them in accord with the intention that a wise legislator ought to have.

[3] [Tr. note: See note 32 in ch. 4 of part 1 above.]

Heraclitus and among modern philosophers by those who hold a philosophy of *becoming* instead of one of *being*, also reduces these principles, as it were, to merely grammatical laws of discourse, of language (i.e., absolute nominalism), or of discursive reason [*raison raisonnante*] that speculates about innumerable abstractions. Indeed, reality would be a *perpetual becoming* without extrinsic causes, whether efficient or final, without a subject that is distinct from that *perpetual becoming* (like a flow without fluid), in which being and non-being are identical. This is why Heraclitus is held to have denied the real value of the principle of contradiction (or, of identity) long before Hegel and his disciples. From this perspective, God is absorbed into the world and is identified with becoming and creative evolution. Renan was once asked, "Does God exist?" He responded, from the perspective of the philosophy of becoming, "Not yet."

If, on the contrary, *the principle of contradiction (or, of identity)* is the fundamental law of reality, the First Reality (the source of all other realities) must exist of Itself, and from all eternity must be *absolutely self-identical* and, therefore, be really and essentially distinct from the composite and changing world: *Ego sum qui sum*; I am He who is.

Traditional philosophy, above all the Aristotelian realism that was deepened by St. Thomas, defends the real value and necessity of these principles, holding that they are necessary laws of reality (or, of being) as it is in itself and not only laws of our mind.

What is the value of this traditional realism? Is it only, as William James has said, "Common sense's college-trained younger sister"?[4]

Subjectivists have long said: Its doctrine is only the naïve common-sense realism, prior to critical reflection.

It is recognized today that Aristotelian and Thomistic realism is not a merely naïve common-sense realism, for it methodically examines the objections raised by skeptics and subjectivist idealists, showing that this idealism is sterilely locked up within itself and cannot arrive at any knowledge of reality. Common sense does not undertake this kind of methodical examination.

---

4   William James, *Pragmatism and Four Essays from The Meaning of Truth*, ed. Ralph Barton Perry (New York: Meridian, 1958), 124.

Indeed, as Aristotle showed, against Heraclitus and the sophists (in the fourth chapter of the fourth book of the *Metaphysics*), if one doubts the real value and necessity of the principle of contradiction to which all the others are subordinated, the following consequences will follow:

1. *Words and discourse would no longer have any determinate meaning.* Such a denial reduces one to the most absolute kind of silence, as Socrates showed the sophists.

2. *There would no longer be any essence, nature, or determinate substance.* Gold would no longer be distinct from copper, nor plants, from inorganic beings, nor animals from plants, and all essences or natures would be confused in becoming, in a universal flux, indeed a flux that is without a subject, without that which flows, as though there would be a flow without liquid, flight without that which flies, and a dream without a dreamer—all in a flux without an efficient or final cause, in which the more perfect would come from the less perfect, despite the manifest absurdity of such a process.

3. *There would no longer be any diversity of things* if the principle of contradiction were not true. There would no longer be a distinction between a wall, a trireme, and a man.

4. *There would no longer be any truth* if the principle of non-contradiction were false, and if our first notion of being (or of reality) were deceitful.

5. *Even every merely probable opinion would disappear.* Skepticism itself could only affirm that it is probably true.

6. *Every form of desire and hatred would disappear as well,* for if there were no longer any opposition between being and non-being, there would no longer be any opposition between good and evil. Therefore, there would not be any reason to desire a piece of fruit or to refuse to drink a poison.

7. *Finally, there would no longer be degrees among errors.* They would all be equally as meaningless as each other—the smallest like the greatest, for every norm would disappear.

Aristotle adds, "Some say that Heraclitus denied the principle of contradiction (or, of identity) because, according to him, everything is moved and everything changes, whether in us or outside of us. However, one need not think everything that comes out of one's mouth."[5] If the principle of contradiction were false, movement itself would be impossible, for it would no longer be true to say that the point of departure *is not* the point of arrival and, thus, one would have arrived before having left.[6]

In other words, to deny the necessity and real value of the principle of contradiction (or even to doubt it) condemns one to the most absolute form of nihilism. One could no longer say anything, think anything, desire anything, will anything, or do anything.

This critique of skepticism was supplemented by the critique of modern subjectivist idealism.[7] Such a critique shows that it cannot lead to any knowledge of reality and that it cannot pass beyond the subjective representation in which it remains enclosed. Consequently, it cannot constitute any kind of livable philosophy, i.e. a philosophy that conforms to the first evidences of natural reason and of external

---

[5] [Tr. note: The text from *Metaphysics* 4.3 (1005b24–26) more literally reads, "For it is impossible for anyone to believe the same thing to be and not to be, as some think Heraclitus says; for what a man says he does not necessarily believe." The point is generally the same, though. See Aristotle, *Metaphysics* in *Complete Works*, ed. Jonathan Barnes, trans. W.D. Ross (Princeton: Princeton University Press, 1995), 1005b24–26.]

[6] See Aristotle, *Metaphysics*, 4.8.

[7] [Tr. note: For an excellent overview of how Maritain critiques idealism by way of the distinction between thing and object, see John C. Cahalan, "The Problem of Thing and Object in Maritain," *The Thomist* 59, no. 1 (Jan. 1995): 21–46. This criticism is also very important for understanding Fr. Garrigou-Lagrange. In almost all ways, Maritain's Thomism is far closer to Fr. Garrigou-Lagrange than is Gilson's, in spite of the significant agreement among the parties. One senses this fact in the combined usage made of Fr. Garrigou-Lagrange and Maritain by Austin M. Woodbury. On this matter, the researcher can consult with great benefit the index of Austin Woodbury, *Defensive Metaphysics*, The John N. Deely and Anthony Russell Collection, St. Vincent College, Latrobe, PA.]

and internal experience. Indeed, idealism not only cannot lead to any metaphysics or knowledge of being and of reality as such above the particular sciences. It also cannot objectively ground any individual or social morality truly worthy of the name. Indeed, the first principle of morality, "The good must be done and evil avoided," presupposes the real value and necessity of the principle of finality and that of contradiction.[8]

Can Methodical Realism Be Critical?

Therefore, Aristotelian and Thomistic realism far exceeds the realism of common sense, at least inasmuch as it is a methodical knowledge [*science*] of the first principles of natural reason, formulating them in the most universal way, explaining them, showing their subordination, and defending their real value against the objections of the ancient skeptics and modern idealists who cannot escape their subjectivism or solipsism so as to say anything about extramental reality.

However, is Thomistic realism only that, or is it also a *critical realism* founded not only on the critique of idealism but also upon a critique of the value of knowledge? Can this critique of knowledge be conceived of only from the ruinous perspective of idealism that sets forth from our subjective thought without being able to pass beyond it? Why could it not be conceived of from the perspective of the natural requirements of our intellect and of the knowledge that it can have of its own finality?

This is the question we asked ourselves while reading a very inter-

---

[8] Cf. *ST* I-II, q. 94, a. 2 (Whether the natural law contains many precepts or only one): "In this way, the precepts of the natural law pertain to practical reason just as the first principles of demonstration pertain to speculative reason; for both are principles that are *per se nota*." [Tr. note: This is why a discussion of *synderesis* is of such importance in explaining the natural law. See note 31 in the previous chapter. One should note as well that one must explain how synderesis is somehow super-elevated to be used in the supernatural order in the enunciation of moral truths ruling our action as subjects of grace. On this, see B.-H. Merkelbach, *Summa theologiae moralis*, 5th ed., vol. 2 (Paris: Desclée de Brouwer, 1947), no. 218. This latter topic is one that is not always acknowledged, even though it is of pivotal importance for explaining the full organism of the life of the child of God.]

esting article by Étienne Gilson, "Le réalisme méthodique," from which we will cite a rather long extract that poses the problem well.

On the subject of the realist philosophy of the scholastics (and above all of St. Thomas and his disciples), Gilson writes:

> We do not believe that it is a *naïve realism,* for it is clearly aware of the existence of idealism and the nature of the problem posed by it. . . . Scholasticism is a *conscious, reflective, and willed realism,* but it is not founded on the solution to the problem posed by idealism, for the data of this problem necessarily imply the same idealism as a solution. In other words, however surprising such a thesis may appear at first, scholastic realism does not exist in function of the problem of knowledge—rather the opposite is the case indeed—but, instead, reality is posited by it as something distinct from thought, *esse* is posited by it as being distinct from *percipi* on account of a *particular idea of what philosophy is* and as a condition of its very possibility. *It is a methodical realism . . .*

> Scholasticism is a philosophy, i.e., a study of wisdom, which is itself the science of first principles and first causes. The truth of its conclusions, whatever they may be, will be marked principally by *the evidence of these principles,* their simplicity, and their fecundity. *Therefore, its task is to find a set of evident principles such that they all agree with each other and with experience.* If idealism had succeeded in establishing one of them and in proving its explanatory fecundity, scholasticism would have nothing to object to in such idealism. Sadly, exactly the opposite is the case, and this is why *Thomist realism,* although it is not founded on a critique of knowledge, is not reduced to a naïve realism. *It is founded on a critique of idealism and on the demonstration of its inability to construct a viable philosophy . . .*

> First of all, every idealism of the Cartesian type, precisely because it *a priori* identifies philosophical methodology with the methodology of a given science (mathematics), necessar-

ily leads to the *emptying of philosophy of all of its own, proper content* and *is condemned to scientism.*[9]

A second consideration of the results acquired from history shows, we believe, that if the idealist method represents the suicide of philosophy as a distinct form of knowledge, this is because it engages philosophy in a series of internal contradictions that ultimately lead it to a form of skepticism. . . . This is why modern philosophy, to the degree that it does not abdicate its rights in favor of science, has the appearance of a battle-field where irreconcilable shadows ceaselessly battle: thought against extension, the subject against the object, the individual against society—all so many fragments of reality, disintegrated by the dissolving analysis of thought and all attempting in vain to be reintegrated by it.

Therefore, we first and foremost must be freed from the obsession with having epistemology be the preliminary condition for philosophy. . . . *With a sure instinct for the right path, the Greeks resolutely entered into the ways of realism,* and the scholastics remained there because it led somewhere. *Descartes tried the other path* and when he entered it, he had no evident reason for not doing so. *However, we know today that it leads nowhere,* and that is why we have the duty to get off this path. Thus, the realism of scholasticism was in no way naïve. It was the realism of the hiker who is directed toward a goal and, seeing that he is approaching it, has confidence that his route is good. . . . In the end, it is necessary that, instead of being a condition for ontology, epistemology instead grows with it, being at once the source of explanations and itself explained.[10]

---

[9] [Tr. note: On this ineluctable pull of metaphysics by falsely-placed methodologies, see the excellent text, Étienne Gilson, *The Unity of Philosophical Experience* (San Francisco: Ignatius Press, 1999).]

[10] Étienne Gilson, "Le réalisme méthodique" in *Philosophia perennis, Abhandlungen zu ihrer Vergangenheit und Gegenwart. Festgabe Joseph Geyser zum 60. Geburtstag,* vol. 2 (Regensburg: Mélange Geyser, 1930), 745–755, esp. 752 as discussed below.

What Is the Critical Value of Thomistic Realism?

Although they are contestable on one point, these lines written by Étienne Gilson contain many remarks that seem quite accurate to our eyes, and this is why we cited them at such length.[11] He recognizes

---

[Tr. note: A fuller treatment by Gilson can be found in Étienne Gilson, *Methodical Realism: A Handbook for Beginners*, trans. Philp Trower (San Francisco: Ignatius Press, 2011). Also, Étienne Gilson, *Thomist Realism and the Critique of Knowledge*, trans. Mark A. Wauck (San Francisco: Ignatius Press, 2012). Prudently, one should recall Gilson's less than warm consideration of Fr. Garrigou-Lagrange. In particular, see his remarks in *Thomist Realism and the Critique of Knowledge*, 41n22. The two Thomists were quite different in their approaches to St. Thomas. In their devotion to the classic Dominican commentators, Garrigou-Lagrange and Maritain are closer to each other than to Gilson. Indeed, Maritain himself cites Garrigou-Lagrange on the very topic facing us, for the former also believed that there could be a critical Thomistic realism, so long as one understands "critique" correctly. See Jacques Maritain, *The Degrees of Knowledge*, ed. Ralph McInerny et al., trans. Gerald B. Phelan et al. (Notre Dame, IN: University of Notre Dame Press, 1995), 75–144.]

[11] Let us note some important points on which there already seems to be fundamental agreement between him and many Thomists. We believe that according to Aristotle and St. Thomas, *the critique* of knowledge is not a science that would be distinct from metaphysics, as is made clear in the fourth book of the *Metaphysics*, which Aristotle devotes to the defense of the real value of the principle of contradiction and of reason itself.

On this subject, we must not forget what St. Thomas says in *ST* I, q. 1, a. 8: "It must be considered that, in the philosophical sciences, the inferior sciences do not prove their principles nor dispute against those who deny their principles. Rather, these inferior sciences relinquish this to a superior science. *Now, the science that is supreme among them, namely metaphysics, disputes against those who deny its principles, if their adversaries will concede something. However, if they do not concede anything, it is not possible to dispute with them, though the metaphysician can answer the objections presented to him.*"

In light of these principles, one can show that the critical problem was *poorly posed* by Descartes. In order to judge the value of our intellect, we must not begin by denying its essential finality, nor by saying that the square-circle is perhaps *realizable* even though it is *inconceivable*. Before seeking to resolve the problem of knowledge, we must methodically establish what this finality exactly is. Many insoluble problems are only problems that have been poorly posed, ones that misplace the mystery of things.

Fr. M.-D. Roland-Gosselin seeks this correct position of the problem in his "Projet d'introduction à une étude critique de la connaissance," *Revue des sciences philosophiques et théologiques* 20 (1931): 673–698. On page 692 of this article, he notes that "the thought of being dominates every step, punctuating the questions and the responses with its mark."

Moreover, according to the true thought of Aristotle and St. Thomas, we have that Thomist realism is not a naïve realism but, instead, a methodical realism founded on the critique of idealism. Nonetheless, for Gilson, it is not a critical realism, founded upon the critique of knowledge. In this, he disagrees with many contemporary Thomists, such as Msgr. Léon Noël.[12] Gilson even says:

> Léon Noël seeks out a point where things and the mind join back together in an indivisible unity, thus giving support to this realist epistemology, which modern thought has sought out and which scholasticism did not leave behind for us.

> However, if this point exists, it is still, indeed first of all, something belonging to the domain of thought. Hence, whether or not one so wishes, *every epistemology*, even one that is immediatist, *will be based upon a datum of thought*, wherein, by an effort of internal discrimination, it will attempt to grasp the object. However, how can we believe that this situation is entirely different from that of the *cogito ergo sum*? It is obvious that it is because I am that I think, but *it is in no way evident that I think about things because they exist*; the absolute being that the *cogito* immediately gives me can be mine and no other. ... On the basis of a *percipi*, one never will reach any *esse* other than that of the *percipi*.[13]

---

shown elsewhere that the *critique of knowledge* ought to come at the beginning of metaphysics (or, if one wishes, at the end by way of reflection) *only after natural philosophy and psychology*. This is so because in order to undertake the criticism of the value of knowledge, we must first psychologically know what it is and must distinguish the intellect's formal object (i.e., being and the *raisons d'être* of things) from the formal object[s] of the senses (i.e., the [various] sensible phenomena). We will discuss this matter in greater detail below in chapter 4.

    [Tr. note: Fr. Garrigou-Lagrange seems to accidentally cite Fr. Bernard Roland-Gosselin, though it was M.-D. Roland-Gosselin who wrote the aforementioned article.]

12 [Tr. note: Léon Noël (1878–1955) was the head of the Catholic University of Louvain's *Institut Supérieur de Philosophie* after Cardinal Mercier. He and Gilson had back-and-forth arguments on these topics, as is evidenced in the texts of Gilson cited above in note 10.]

13 Gilson, "Le réalisme méthodique," 750ff.

As he says a little later in the same article, Gilson even believes that "the problem of finding a critical realism is self-contradictory, like the notion of a square circle. . . . That which is outside of thought is not thinkable; it is not only the perfect formulation of idealism; it is also its condemnation."[14]

* * *

If one wishes to remain within Descartes's subjectivist perspective, and base oneself solely upon the *cogito*, after having affirmed that a square circle is perhaps realizable even if it is inconceivable, then, yes, critical realism is indeed an inconceivable idea.[15] On this subject, we completely accept what Gilson says about the method followed by Fr. Picard, who in his book, *Le Problème critique fondamental*,[16] "constantly returns to an attitude quite similar to that of Descartes." We also subscribe to Noël's own statement, which Gilson makes his own: if we base ourselves on subjective immanence, "the principle of causality will change it in no way. If you have a hook painted on the wall, you will only be able to hang upon it a chain that is painted on the wall."[17] Even if the intellect has a real, objective value, this method will not enable us to be assured of it.

In order for the principle of causality to be of use here, enabling us to exit from immanence and find extra-mental being, we would already need to know the ontological value of this principle.

However, if the direction taken by Descartes offers no way of escape, the meaning given to the expression, "critique of knowledge," by Cartesian idealism is not true. Strictly speaking, to critique means to judge in accordance with the object being examined. In this sense, St. Thomas, turned in the direction of realism, established the foundations for a *critique of knowledge* (i.e., an *epistemology*) that does not base itself

---

[14] Gilson, "Le réalisme méthodique," 751.

[15] See Léon Noël, "La méthode du réalisme," *Revue Néo-scholastique* 33 (Nov. 1931): 438ff, 442, 446.

[16] Gabriel Picard, *Le Problème critique fondamental* (Paris: Beauchesne, 1923).

[17] Léon Noël, *Notes d'épistémologie thomiste* (Louvain: Bibliotèque de l'Institut supérieur de Philosophie, 1925), 73.

on the mental being of our thought, nor *upon our thought of extramental being*, nor upon our idea of being in general (where *esse* and *percipi* would be difficult to distinguish). Critical realism, conceived from the perspective of Aristotle and St. Thomas, bases itself on this *primordial evidence* (whose value is increasingly imposed by the intellect's reflection[18] upon itself), namely, *that a given reality cannot at one and the same time exist and not exist—and that this is not only* INCONCEIVABLE FOR US *but, indeed, is* REALLY IMPOSSIBLE IN ITSELF. Here, we find a necessary law of being (or, of reality in itself) and not only a law of the intellect (or, of reality inasmuch as it is conceived). *This real impossibility* opposed to *esse in se* [existing in oneself] (*impossibilitas est repugnantia ad esse*) is necessarily conceived as being distinct from the *inconceivability* opposed to *intelligi* [being understood] (or, to the *percipi* spoken of by Berkeley).[19]

Intelligible being, the first object known by our intellect[20] (it will later on be verified that it is abstracted from sensible things) is not only that which the nominalist Berkeley called the *perceived* (*esse est percipi*). We do not base ourselves upon *our idea* of reality to say (by recurring surreptitiously to the principle of causality, whose real value would still be in question), "I think of extramental being, therefore it exists outside of my mind and is as I think it to be."—No, but our intellect's utterly first and indestructible evidence is that a being that at one and the same time exists and does not exist is not only *inconceivable for us* but is *really impossible in itself*. Here, we find the first and ineluctable distinction of reality inasmuch as it is conceived from reality in itself, of *percipi* from of *esse*, of the thing as conceivable from of the thing in itself.

This primordial and irrefutable evidence, the utterly primordial

---

[18] This *critical reflection* will show us precisely the *finality of the intellect*, as we will discuss below, something that L. Noël recognized in "La méthode du réalisme," 438–446.

[19] [Tr. note: Fr. Garrigou-Lagrange refers to George Berkeley (1685–1753), whose opposition to Locke's distinction between primary and secondary qualities led to a form of complete idealism, equating *being* with *being perceived*. He used this dictum *esse est percipi* above on several occasions.]

[20] See *ST* I, q. 5, a. 2; I-II, q. 94, a. 2; *De veritate*, q. 1, a. 1.

evidence for our intellect, is already concerned with *extramental being*, even though we do not conceive it yet positively as *extramental* (for we have not yet reflected upon our thought—the reflexive act is possible only after the direct act of intellection that has the real intelligible for its object) and even though we do not yet conceive of extramental being as *existing* in fact, for we speak here only of its *fundamental, essential law* confusedly understood: "If it exists, it certainly cannot at one and the same time exist and not exist." This is not only unthinkable. It is *really* impossible.

This is what Descartes, the founder of modern idealism, did not see when he wrote that if God had so wished He could have created square circles and mountains without valleys. Descartes did not understand that he was committing, in the philosophical order, an unpardonable sin as grave as that which, in the spiritual order, is called the sin against the Holy Spirit (or, the sin against the liberating light). From the dawning of our intellectual life, we have this absolute certitude that neither God (if He exists and however powerful He may be) nor any evil genius (however perverse and cunning as one may suppose him to be) can make a square circle, for this is not only *inconceivable for us* but is *really impossible in itself*.

* * *

This is grasped in a vague manner from the dawning of our intellectual life. When the child's intellect for the first time apprehends or grasps *being* (i.e., the *intelligible reality* of anything, for example, of milk, which sight attains as being colored and taste as being sweet and tasty), he does not yet affirm either the existence of the thinking subject or that of the milk. To speak in the language of the scholastics: "While taste grasps a sweet being inasmuch as it is sweet, the intellect grasps the sweet being *as being*, but it does not yet judge concerning its existence; nor does it judge concerning its properties." The intellect grasps *being*, making abstraction from the state of possibility and that of actual existence. And, immediately, its opposition to non-being is self-evident. This opposition is not evident only as a form of *logical opposition*, as saying, "It is impossible to affirm and deny the same predicate of the same subject in the same respect." Rather, it is evident as an *onto-logical opposition*, "Something cannot at one and the same time exist and not exist." In other words, "The absurd is not only inconceivable; it is *unrealizable*"; and he who says "unrealizable" or "really impossible" already affirms a law that has a real value outside of our intellect, without affirming any existing reality.

Such is the primordial evidence of immediate realism in virtue of which the intellect, before knowing itself through reflection (i.e., before saying *cogito*, "I think"), affirms (certainly not without having some direct knowledge of it), the real value of the principle of non-contradiction.[21]

* * *

It is only afterwards that, by way of reflection, we say, "*Cogito*," and if we doubt the real value of the principle of contradiction, we cannot have true certitude when we say, "I think," but can only say, "Perhaps it is the case that at one and the same time I think and do not think. Where does consciousness begin and where does the unconscious begin? And, likewise, perhaps it is possible that at one and the same time I am and am not. Who knows if I have the right to say, 'I'? Perhaps I must be content with impersonally saying, '*There is thought*,' as one says, '*It's raining*.'"[22] On the contrary, following upon the primordial evidence of the fundamental law of reality, which excludes contradiction, we can say with firmness, "I think."

And not only does the intellect know, through reflection, *the very existence* of its act. Moreover, it knows *the nature* of its act, whereas the senses and imagination cannot know the nature of their own activities. The intellect knows also by reflection *its own nature* as an intellectual faculty, as well as *its own essential finality* of being conformed to things in knowing them. As the intellect knows that the essential finality of the

---

[21] We have repeatedly insisted on this for over twenty years. See Garrigou-Lagrange, *Le sens commun*, 134–143. Also, see 100–106 of the first and second editions of the text. Garrigou-Lagrange, *God: His Existence and His Nature*, vol. 1, 111ff.

[22] [Tr. note: Again, this is a play on the impersonal French expression, "il pleut," for "it is raining."]

wings of the bird are made for flight, feet for walking, ears for hearing, and the eyes for seeing, so too does it know its nature as something essentially relative to intelligible extramental being.

This is what St. Thomas explains in a classic article in *De veritate*, namely q. 1, a. 9, where he shows the critical value of traditional realism founded on the knowledge of the nature of intellection and of the intellect. Consider now the translation of this well-known text:

> Truth exists in the intellect and in the senses, though not in the same manner. Now, it exists in the intellect as a consequence of an act of the intellect, and as known by the intellect. It follows upon the act of the intellect inasmuch as the judgment of the intellect is made concerning reality in accord with what it is. However, it is known by the intellect inasmuch as the intellect reflects back upon its own act, not only inasmuch as it knows its act, but also inasmuch as it knows its *proportion* (or, conformity) *to reality*.[23] Now, indeed, the intellect can know this proportion only if it knows *the nature of its act*; and it can know the nature of its act only if the nature of its active principle, namely, the intellect, *whose nature is to be conformed to reality*—IN CUIUS NATURA EST UT REBUS CONFORMETUR—is known. . . .
>
> [Now, truth exists in the senses as a consequence of its act, namely, when the judgment of the senses is concerned with a thing according to what it is. However, it does not exist in the senses as *known* by them, for even if a sense judges truly concerning things, it does not, however, know the truth by which it truly judges:][24] for although a sense knows that it senses, it

---

[23] [Tr. note: I often translate "res" (or, even "chose" in French) as "reality" in passages like this in order to accommodate for the role of synderesis *conformitas (adaequatio) ad rem*. Most choose a slightly more literal "thing," but it is arguable that this reduces such *adaequatio* solely to speculative cognition and not the speculatively-practical cognition attained by synderesis (and, by extension, "moral science," that is, the objectively inferential knowledge known in the conclusions in moral philosophy and, in a loftier manner, in moral theology.]

[24] [Tr. note: Fr. Garrigou-Lagrange has shortened this portion of the text. Although his

does not, however, know its *nature* and, consequently, does not know the nature of its act, nor its proportion to reality. Thus, it does not know its truth either.[25]

This reflection by the intellect upon its act and upon itself can take place in two ways: 1° as ordinary men reflect when they assure themselves that they are not dreaming and verify what they affirm; 2° as the philosopher does by studying the nature of intellectual and sense knowledge according to the various theories that are given for them and in themselves. In this way, reflective knowledge is constituted, not in an abusive sense but, instead, in its exact sense, like what we find in the fourth book of Aristotle's *Metaphysics* and in St. Thomas's *De veritate.*

Thus, the intellect appears to itself as being essentially relative to *intelligible, extramental being* whose fundamental law, which excludes contradiction, has been affirmed from the first moment of intellect knowing intelligible being (before knowing itself as being essentially relative to it). The *primum cognitum ab intellectu nostro*, that which is first known by our intellect, cannot be a relation, for a relation is inconceivable without a foundation and a terminus. No more can it be the intellectual faculty relative to being.[26] Instead, it is *intelligible being,* without which nothing would be intelligible, as sight first knows the

---

French does not distort its sense, I think it better to cite a translation of this section as a whole.]

[25] [Tr. note: A correct understanding of the nature of truth according to Thomistic doctrine is difficult but necessary. It certainly should not be seen as a kind of comparison of the intramental to the extramental. This has been justly critiqued, but it is not the full doctrine on truth according to the Thomistic school. For an excellent defense of the notion of truth as pertaining to a judgment in which two objects are affirmed as being united in a given thing (whether actual or possible), see the text of Cahalan cited above in note 7 and the text of Maritain cited in note 10 above. The interested researcher would benefit much from the detailed and lucid discussions in the works of Woodbury cited in the former note as well. Likewise, see Yves R. Simon, *Introduction to the Metaphysics of Knowledge*, trans. Vukan Kuic and Richard J. Thompson (New York: Fordham University Press, 1990), 136–149. Also, see Garrigou-Lagrange, *Le sens commun*, 4th ed., 41–42.]

[26] The faculty is only intelligible for itself if it is *actualized* (*nihil est intelligibile, nisi in quantum est in actu*), and its first act bears on intelligible being.

colored before the sensation of color is known, and as the will wills *the good* before willing to will (or willing to act), for it cannot will in an utter vacuum.[27] In his nominalism,[28] the idealist Berkeley says, "*Esse est percipi*: to be is to be perceived." To this, traditional realism responds, "*Something existing and not existing at the same time* most evidently is perceived *not only as unthinkable, but* as something that, in reality, is impossible. And *it would not be perceived thus in a most evident manner if it were not really impossible, for the objective evidence of being is nothing other than being in its evidence* [*nihil aliud est quam ens evidens*]."

Here we are confronted with the primordial evidence, prior to that of the *cogito* and without which the *cogito* would not hold, for "thought" could perhaps be "non-thought," "I" be "non-I", and "I am" be "I am not."[29]

This primary evidence belongs to the *first intellectual apprehension* of being (or, of reality) and to the *necessary and universal judgment* that immediately follows it. These direct acts necessarily precede any reflection upon them. Then, this primary and indestructible evidence is confirmed by the intellect's reflection upon its act, upon the nature of its act, and upon its own nature, whose *essential finality* it sees (as it sees the finality of the eye or the ear). Hence, the intellect itself sees that the idea of being, impressed upon it and then expressed by it is also essentially relative to *extramental being* (whether actual or possible), something altogether different from *being of reason*,[30] which is defined, *not as that which is or can be,* but instead, as *that which is conceived or can be conceived,* like a predicate and its universality, which can only exist in the intellect. Berkeley was condemned by his nominalism not to see the value of this distinction.[31]

---

27 See *ST* I-II, q. 8, a. 1.

28 [Tr. note: Reading *nominalisme* for *mominalisme* in the original.]

29 Some doubts could be raised: Where does consciousness stop and unconsciousness start? How can we distinguish personal thought from impersonal thought? How can we distinguish thought from the act of imagination, sense life, and even vegetative life?

30 [Tr. note: In some cases below, I will choose to translate this strictly as *ens rationis*.]

31 In Berkeley's proposition, *esse est percipi*, Thomistic realism sees a kind of twofold error, at once opposed to "realism" in both its modern and ancient senses.

The expression *esse est percipi aut intelligi* only holds true for beings of reason [i.e., *entia rationis*]. Real being is that which exists (or can exist) outside of the intellect, and its existence (*esse*) is that by which it is posited *outside of non-being and outside of its causes*. Thus, it can *exist* before being known by us, like the bodies that exist in nebulas outside of our experience or like the unknown gold deposits on a continent that has not yet been explored. This likewise holds true for evolutionist philosophers who hold that knowing beings appeared upon our world only long after inferior beings.[32]

Thus, the being that is first grasped by our intellect, *ens quod primo cadit in intellectu nostro*, is not only the idea of being but, instead, is *intelligible being*, which is expressed in it and is quite distinct from *being of reason*. This is why we see immediately that it is not only inconceivable but, indeed, *really impossible*[33] that a thing both be and not be at the same time. And we thus already affirm the objective and ontological value of the principle of contradiction *before every judgment of exist-*

Through his idealism (or, better, his immaterialism), Berkeley stands in opposition *to realism in the modern sense* of this word inasmuch as he denies the real value of our perception of the exterior world.

Through his nominalism, Berkeley stands in opposition *to the older sense of realism*, for he denies that the universal exists or that it even has a foundation in things outside of our mind.

In his nominalism, Berkeley went much further than William of Ockham, writing in the introduction to his *Treatise Concerning the Principles of Human Knowledge*, "Likewise the idea of man that I frame to myself must be either of a white, or a black, or a tawny, a straight, or a crooked, a tall, or a low, or a middle-sized man. *I cannot by any effort of thought conceive the abstract idea above described.*" Thenceforth, Berkeley could not see the sense or scope of the laws of being in general. And yet, many have considered Berkeley to be a sage and have held that every history of philosophy ought to cite his name, while often failing to cite the names of intellects that are incomparably superior to his, such as those of the great commentators on St. Thomas!

Berkeley is a striking case, showing us that the greatest errors (those most opposed to common sense and, for this reason, the most foolish) have been expressed by so-called philosophers who, wishing to treat not of commerce or agriculture, but of being, knowledge, and God, have made errors proportioned to the scope of the subject treated.

[Tr. note: Text of Berkeley taken from George Berkeley, *Principles of Human Knowledge* in *Principles of Human Knowledge and Three Dialogues*, ed. Howard Robinson (Oxford: Oxford University Press, 1999), intro. n.10 (p.11).]

[32] [Tr. note: See note 14 in pt. 1, ch. 1 above.]

[33] [Tr. note: Reading *impossible* for *possible*, which almost certainly is a mistake.]

ence, before reflecting that this first affirmation presupposes ideas, and before *verifying* that these ideas come to us, through abstraction, from sensible things, grasped by our senses.[34]

* * *

Furthermore, the intellect not only sees that idealism has not, in fact, found *other evident principles* that are in agreement with it and with experience but, indeed, also sees that it cannot find other such principles. Why? Because the principle of contradiction is immediately founded on our very first notion of being and of reality. It is presupposed by all other notions and is founded on the absolutely primary opposition of being and non-being. As regards the principles of efficient causality, finality, and change [*mutation*], they are all absolutely necessary for explaining (in function of being and of the principle of contradiction, or, of identity) the principal fact of experience that was so striking to Heraclitus: movement, the succession of phenomena, *becoming,* which can become *intelligible* only in terms of *being* (the first object of the intellect) and through the division of being into *potency and act*[35] (i.e., through the distinction of being that is still undetermined, like a seed, and the determination that it is apt to receive). The distinction of the four causes of becoming (i.e., material, formal, efficient, and final) is immediately derived from this, as well as the principles that are relative to these four causes.

---

[34] On this point, refer to what Cajetan writes at the beginning of his commentary on St. Thomas's *De ente et essentia* (prol., q. 1). There, he treats of the *primum cognitum ab intellectu nostro*. Likewise, see his remarks concerning the same topic in his Commentary on *ST* I, q. 17, a. 2 (Whether there is falsity in the senses); a. 3 (Whether there is falsity in the intellect); q. 85, a. 2 (Whether the intellect can be false); q. 88, a. 3 (Whether God is the first thing that is known by the human mind). When the reader attentively compares these articles by St. Thomas, in conjunction with Cajetan's explanation of them, to the Introduction to Berkeley's *Treatise Concerning the Principles of Human Knowledge*, he will see what an abyss separates the two works. It will be clear which of the two conceptions is more conformed to the very notion of wisdom (i.e., to knowledge of things through their first principles).

[35] [Tr. note: On this topic, the reader would benefit much from the reflections found in Yves Simon, "The Philosophy of Change" in *The Great Dialogue of Nature and Space,* ed. Gerald J. Dalcourt (Albany, NY: Magi Books, 1970), 59–86.]

These principles subordinated to the principle of contradiction cannot be denied or placed in doubt without also placing in doubt the real value of the principle of contradiction. For example, an UNCAUSED *contingent being* is absurd. It is not only *inconceivable* but also is *really impossible*, if the principle of contradiction is itself not only a law of the intellect but also of being or of the thing in itself.

And thus, the ontological value of the first principles can be expressed in function of this traditional division of being:

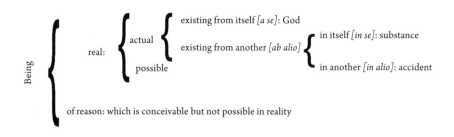

For idealists, these principles are only the principles of reason or of *being of reason* (*ens rationis*), not of *real being* (whether really possible or actual). And even some contemporary scholastics have not been careful enough in distinguishing *ens rationis* (like a predicate or its universality) from *being that is really possible* (i.e., from *real possibility*), which is still very different from real potency or the real capacity for perfection that we find either in matter in relation to the specific form of bodies or in the created essence in relation to existence.

Berkeley's formula, *esse est percipi aut intelligi*, "to be is to be perceived or to be known,"[36] is true of *being of reason*, like a predicate and its universality. Yes, this is true for that which can exist only inasmuch as it is conceived. It is proper to being of reason, as opposed to real being (whether possible or actual).

Already, as regards *possible reality* (or, that which is *really possible* or *realizable*), we cannot in truth say, "*esse est percipi aut intelligi*," for when

---

[36] [Tr. note: Fr. Garrigou-Lagrange is extending the sense beyond the classic formulation of Berkeley's position in order to show what it would mean for a philosophical position that distinguished clearly between the order of sensation (both external and internal) and that of intellection.]

individuals in a group of men each conceives and judges that a square circle is not only inconceivable for us but is *unrealizable in itself*, each one crosses from the *percipi* (i.e., from the thing in us) so as to enter into the order of the thing in itself. And each such person, in a mental (or, interior) world that is personal to him, reaches this *law of reality in itself* with evidence as something that is *necessarily* the same for all people.

And therefore, it is not merely the case that idealism has only *de facto* failed to find other evident principles that are in agreement with themselves and with experience, thus finding a foundation differing from the principle of contradiction and those subordinated to it. Rather, it is evident that it absolutely cannot find other principles than these.

Finally, in light of the first principles of the intellect and of reality, Thomist realism establishes a critique of the value of sense knowledge, showing that a *sensation without a real sensed object* is not only, *de facto*, contrary to sensible evidence but is necessarily (or, *de iure*) a contradiction like a square circle. Moreover, it shows that a sensation without an objective efficient cause and without finality is a violation of the principles of causality and of finality.[37]

---

[37] Cf. *ST* I, q. 17, a. 2 (Whether there is falsity in the senses): "*Concerning properly sensible things*, sense does not have false cognition except accidentally and in few cases, *namely because an unsound organ does not suitably receive the sensible form.*" *ST* I, q. 17, a. 3: "*Just as* a thing *has existence through its own proper form, so too*, does a knowing power *have* knowledge *through a likeness of the thing known. Whence*, just as a natural thing cannot fall short of the being [*esse*] that belongs to it according to its form (man, inasmuch as he remains man, retains a body and a rational soul in virtue of the principle of identity) but *can, however, fall short concerning certain accidental (or consequent) things, as a man can lack* two feet, *though he cannot be lacking in regard to being human*, so too a knowing power cannot fall short in knowledge with regard to that thing by whose likeness it is informed; *however, it can fall short concerning something following upon that or something accidental to it, just as it is said that sight is not deceived* (*except, accidentally*) *concerning its proper sensible* (e.g., *the colored*) *but can be deceived concerning common sensibles* (e.g. *magnitude and distance*) *and concerning that which is sensible per accidens* (e.g. *a seen living body*)."

Likewise, see Cajetan's commentary on *ST* I, q. 85, a. 6: "Every power by its very nature is essentially ordered to its proper object. However, things of this sort always always have such a relationship. Whence, as long as it remains a power, it does not fall short in its judgment concerning its proper object."

This reasoning is founded on the principle of contradiction (or, identity), applied

Thomist realism likewise *verifies* that intelligible being, which is the object of the first intellectual apprehension, is the intelligible being of sensible things and that the idea that exists in us was drawn from sensible things by way of abstraction.

Hence, this doctrine affirms that our metaphysical certitude of the real value of the first principles is based (or IS MATERIALLY RESOLVED) in sensible evidence, which was presupposed, and that it is FORMALLY RESOLVED in the objective intellectual evidence of the necessary and universal real value of these principles—a necessity and universality that the senses in no way can perceive. This objective evidence is evident being. Thus, the real value of the *material resolution* of our intellectual certitude into sensible evidence is *formally judged* under the superior light of the intellectual evidence into which this very certitude *is resolved* and *formally based*. This represents an application of the famed principle, which is a corollary to the fourfold division of causes, *causae ad invicem sunt causae, sed in diverso genere, absque circulo vitioso*; there is, without a vicious circle, a *mutual relation of causality*, from different perspectives, *between matter and form, as well as between agent and end*. Matter limits the specific form (e.g., the form of the lion) that it individualizes (e.g., this lion), and it is determined by the form that specifies it. Likewise, the agent is attracted by the end, which it obtains (or, which it realizes).[38]

In the case that now occupies us, the senses furnish the *matter* for intellectual knowledge, and their value is *formally judged* in light of the principles of intellectual knowledge.[39]

---

to things first, then to the knowing faculty. It is also founded on the principle of finality, applied to this faculty which is *essentially ordered* to its proper object.

[Tr. note: On this, see the lucid remarks in Simon, *Introduction to the Metaphysics of Knowledge*, 89–91n9. The topic of precisely understanding the nature of sensation has been repeatedly emphasized by John Deely. See John Deely, *Intentionality and Semiotics: A Story of Mutual Fecundation* (Scranton: University of Scranton Press, 2007), 159–163. One should also see Réginald Garrigou-Lagrange, "There Cannot Be Genuine Sensation Without a Real Sensed Thing," *Philosophizing in Faith: Essays on the Beginning and End of Wisdom*, trans. Thomas DePauw and Edward M. Macierowski, ed. Matthew K. Minerd (Providence, RI: Cluny Media, 2019), 101–119.]

[38] See Aristotle, *Metaphysics*, 5.2. Also, see lect. 2 of St. Thomas's commentary on this.

[39] See *ST* I, q. 84, a. 6: "Sense knowledge cannot be the total and perfect cause of intellectual knowledge, *sed magis quoddammodo est MATERIA CAUSAE*—it is rather

In this way, Thomist realism presents itself not only as a naïve, common-sense realism, but as a realism at once methodical and *critical*—so long as we understand this latter word not in the abusive sense given it by Cartesian idealism, but rather, in the exact sense of a critique or examination of the value of knowledge, which respects the essential and realistic nature, finality, and requirements of knowledge.

Now, is this the same as saying that critical realism dispels all obscurity in these matters? Oh, most certainly not! And while certain manuals of Thomistic philosophy speak little about the mystery of knowledge (because their primary end is to insist on what is clear and absolutely certain about knowledge), if true Thomists were asked to write *expressly* about the mystery of sense knowledge, or about the mystery of intellectual knowledge, and about their relations to one another, they could easily show that we find here a marvelous chiaroscuro, more beautiful than all of those painted by Rembrandt. And as, in this chiaroscuro, the two elements that compose it *mutually buttress each other*, the true Thomist does not wish to suppress the mystery but, rather, to set it forth in its true place. He has as much sense of mystery as does anyone else—certainly much more than the Cartesian idealist as well as the materialist—for, not wishing to deny *any* of the elements of the problem, *no matter how distant they may be from one another* (i.e., matter and spirit, as well as the sensible and the intelligible), he knows that the intimate mode of their union remains (and forever will remain) profoundly mysterious. This is what we still must show, though without in any way diminishing the first, unshakable certitude which we have discussed in this chapter.

---

something like the matter of the cause." Also, see Aquinas, *In Boetium de Trinitate*, q. 3, a. 1, ad 4: "Just as knowledge of principles is taken from the senses and, nevertheless, the light by which the principles are known is innate, so too faith is from what is heard and, nevertheless, the *habitus* of faith is infused."

Chapter Two

THE MYSTERY OF KNOWLEDGE AND ITS FINALITY

In the preceding chapter, we saw why and how Thomist realism is not a form of naïve, common-sense realism but, indeed, is a methodical realism in its own critical manner, founded not only on the critique of skepticism and of idealism but also on the examination of the value of knowledge, not basing itself upon the *cogito* but instead upon the primordial and indestructible evidence that *it is really impossible* (and, *not only inconceivable for us*) *that any reality at one and the same time both be and not be.*[1] This unshakable certitude is confirmed by the intellect's

---

[1] This is why we think that, according to Aristotle and St. Thomas, *the critique of knowledge* is not part of logic, which has *ens rationis* as its object. The critique of knowledge is not a distinct science but, instead, is *connected to Metaphysics* as is shown in the fourth book of the *Metaphysics*, dedicated to the defense of the real value of the principle of contradiction and of reason itself.

This is why St. Thomas says in *ST* I, q. 1, a. 8: "It must be considered that, in the philosophical sciences, the inferior sciences do not prove their principles nor dispute against those who deny them. Instead, these inferior sciences relinquish this to a superior science; however, the science that is supreme among them, namely metaphysics, disputes against those who deny its principles, if their adversaries will concede something; however, if they do not concede anything, they cannot be disputed with, though the metaphysician can answer the objections presented to him."

In light of these principles, one can show that the critical problem was poorly posed by Descartes. In order to judge the value of our intellect, the source of every judgment, we cannot begin by denying its essential finality, nor by saying that a square-circle is perhaps *realizable* even though it is *inconceivable*. Rather, we must begin by examining what this finality exactly is. Before seeking to resolve the problem of knowledge, we must methodically establish what its true position is. When this problem is posed poorly, one will render the problem insoluble by displacing the mystery that it contains.

own self-reflection, a reflection by which it knows not only its existence but also *the nature of its act*, its own *proper nature* as an intellectual
faculty, and its *essential finality* for being conformed to reality. This
reflection also verifies that intelligible being, the first object known by
the intellect, has been abstracted from sensible things. In this way, our
certitude concerning the real value of the principle of contradiction
and of the principles that are necessarily subordinated to it *is formally
founded (resolvitur formaliter)* upon the intellectual evidence of these
principles as laws of being (or, upon evident being) and is *materially
founded (resolvitur materialiter)* upon the sensible object of knowledge,
in such a way that the value of this latter foundation (i.e., *resolutio materialis*) is judged in the intellectual light of the superior foundation (i.e.,
resolutio formalis) in conformity with the general law of the mutual relation of causes: *causae ad invicem sunt causae, sed in diverso genere*, causes
are causes of each other, though in different genera of causality.[2] The
senses furnish *the matter* for our intellectual knowledge and their value
is *formally judged* in light of this same intellectual knowledge (as in a
body, matter receives and limits form and is determined by it).[3]

However, this methodical (and, in its own manner, critical) realism
does not intend to suppress the mystery of either sense or intellectual
knowledge in any way. Furthermore, we must insist on this point in
epistemology in order to indicate whatever remains (and will forever
remain) obscure in the intimate process of these two kinds of knowledge and in their mutual relations with each other.

The traditional realism of which we are speaking, all the while
remaining in agreement with common sense, recognizes the *mystery* of
knowledge much more than, on the one hand, materialism and empiricism and, on the other, idealism, both of which break with common
sense. These systems of thought *suppress the mystery* of knowledge (as
well as the very knowledge of reality) by denying one of its essential
elements—wishing either to reduce spirit to matter or matter to spirit.
Then, they come up against real impossibilities and *lead to absurdities*
which they call "the enigmas of the universe."

---

[2] See Aristotle, *Metaphysics* 5.2, as well as Aquinas's commentary, lect. 2.
[3] See *ST* I, q. 84, a. 6. [Tr. note: See note 24 in chapter four below.]

Traditional realism, remaining in agreement with natural reason (i.e., common sense), preserves all of the elements of the problem to be resolved here, maintaining everything that is required—as much from the perspective of the intellect as from the perspective of the object—in order for there to be "knowledge of reality" [*sic*]. It does not seek to reduce intellection to sensation and sensation to physico-chemical laws. Nor, conversely, does it seek to reduce inferior phenomena to the representation the intellect makes of them. Traditional realism even recognizes, with great clarity, *the immeasurable distance* that separates the different orders of inanimate matter, vegetative life, sense life, and intellectual life from each other. Consequently, it admits that there is always a natural mystery found in the passage from one of these orders to an order that is superior to it, as well as in their intimate relations. St. Thomas quite often cites this principle, formulated by [Pseudo] Dionysius: *supremum infimi attingit infimum supremi*, the supreme degree of an inferior order in a certain manner (*secundum quid*) reaches the lowest degree of the order that is immediately superior to it—although there is purely and simply (*simpliciter*) an immense distance (indeed, an immeasurable distance) between these two orders.[4]

At the summit of the mineral kingdom, a broken crystal reconstitutes itself when it is placed in the mother liquor [i.e. the leftover liquid from the crystallization process], and this phenomenon resembles, in a certain manner, the vital phenomenon by which the plant cell nourishes itself. However, an abyss separates these two cases. In the case of the crystal that reconstitutes itself, we have a juxtaposition of new parts with old parts, not a nutritive assimilation (i.e., intussusception), and the intimate mode of this assimilation of non-living food by the living being will always remain mysterious. It will always be difficult to say where physio-chemical phenomena end and where the most elementary vital phenomena begin. Likewise, we experience the same difficulty in every substantial change, with regard to the relationship between the final dispositions received in the compound that disappears and the specific form of the new compound.[5] At the very moment

---

[4] See *ST* I-II, q. 2, a. 8, ad 1.

[5] Another mystery: That of the *ultimate*, concomitant *disposition* produced at the same

that it disappears forever, the former admirably serves in the generation of the latter. *Corruptio unius est generatio alterius.* The death of one
serves in the production of the other for the preservation of the species
or the genus. It is a symbol of the loftiest and most luminous of things:
the bugle still sounds the charge when it dies off. In every death followed by a birth there is verified again, in a mysterious manner, the
axiom concerning the mutual relation of causes that concur in the production of anything new: *causae sunt invicem causae sed in diverso genere.*
Here we see something remarkable that we cannot grasp fully, and we
find a similar difficulty in the intimate process of sense knowledge, in
the much superior order of intellectual knowledge, and in their mutual
relations with each other.

The Mystery of Sense Knowledge

If it is quite difficult to explain the passage from the highest degree
of vegetative life to the lowest degree of sense life, it is also quite difficult to understand how a *material thing* can impress a quasi-spiritual

---

indivisible instant as the [substantial] form, contributing after the manner of a property, to the preservation of the form in the new subject. The antecedent (*praeviae*)
dispositions disappear at the precise moment when the ultimate, concomitant disposition and form are produced. Cf. St. Thomas *In IV Sent.*, d. 17, q. 1, a. 5, qu. 3:
"The ultimate disposition is the effect of the form in the genus of formal cause while,
however, preceding in the genus of material cause."

Theologians know the admirable application of this principle at the instant of the
justification of the ungodly [*impie*] (cf. *ST* I-II, q. 113, a. 8, ad 1) and also at the
moment of the entrance into glory. However, the very same principle already has
an application in the least case of substantial change, like in the case of the nutritive assimilation in our own organic life. Likewise, there is something similar in the
production of the image in our senses and in that of the idea formed in our intellect.

[Tr. note: Fr. Garrigou-Lagrange has "l'idée," which is terminologically inexact.
However, given his own strict adherence to the Dominican commentators' terminology elsewhere (including that of John of St. Thomas) concerning the question
of knowledge, it is almost certain that he is referring here to the *species impressa* that
provides the formal specification in first act that will then blossom, in second act,
into intellection, which although not, as such, formally productive of the concept is,
in the case of finite knowers, virtually productive of it. In strict Thomistic terminology, an *idea* is the exemplar cause formed by the artisan as providing the formal unity
in a work of art.]

likeness of itself within our senses of sight or hearing.

This problem would be insoluble if sensation were an action of the soul alone, as Descartes believed it to be, for the cause would be inferior to its effect and, in contrast to the principle of causality, the more would proceed from the less, the more perfect from the less perfect.

The problem can be resolved if sensation is an act of an animated organ, for example, of the living eye. Nevertheless, a difficulty still remains and must be explained: how can a *material thing* produce within an animated organ not only a material and physical impression (e.g., that of heat) but also a *psychological impression* received within the sense faculty united to the material organ (e.g., in a visual or hearing faculty). How can a material thing (e.g., sea water) impress in our senses this likeness of itself, which the scholastics called "intentional" or representative?

The difficulty arises from the fact that *the knower* differs from the non-knower inasmuch as the knower must have *some kind of spirituality* in order to receive within itself *the form of other beings—ut quodammodo fiat aliud a se*—in order to become, in a certain manner, *the other being* that it knows. Under the influence of the sun, the plant passes from being cold to being hot. However, it remains enclosed within itself. It receives another form, *alteram formam*, but it does not receive the form of another being, *formam rei alterius*. By contrast, the dog sees the sun. Not only does its eye receive the ray of solar heat (as does the plant); it also sees the sun. Its sensate soul, through its visual faculty, *in some manner becomes*, as Aristotle says, *all the sensible things that it sees*;[6] and, therefore, it receives the representation in a non-material way. As Averroes remarked, *"The knower and the known are more united than are matter and form."*[7] This is so because *matter does not become form* but, instead, receives it, individualizes it,

---

[6] Cf. Aristotle, *De anima*, 3.8.

[7] Averroes, *In III De anima*, comm. V, digressionis parte ultima, q.2. We have studied this problem at greater length elsewhere. See Réginald Garrigou-Lagrange, "Cognoscens quodammodo fit vel est aliud a se (On the Nature of Knowledge as Union with the Other as Other)," in *Philosophizing in Faith: Essays on the Beginning and End of Wisdom*, trans. Matthew K. Minerd (Providence, RI: Cluny Media, 2019), 63–78.

and appropriates it. By contrast, the *knower becomes, in some way, the known reality* and receives the form of the known without appropriating it, without making the other's form its own. It receives it *as the form of the other.* An abyss separates material reception, which appropriates the received form, from nonmaterial reception, which does not appropriate it.

St. Thomas admirably expressed this in a well-known text from the *Summa theologiae* (*ST* I, q. 14, a. 1):

> *Knowers are distinguished from non-knowing beings* because non-knowing beings only have their own form, while it is of the nature of knowers *also to have the form of another*, for the *species* of the known exists in the knower. Whence, it is manifest that the nature of a non-knowing thing is greatly contracted and limited [in comparison with that of knowers]. However, the nature of knowers has *a greater amplitude* and extension, for which reason Aristotle says in *De anima* 3.8 that *the soul is in a certain sense all things.* Now, the *limitation* of form occurs *by means of matter.* Whence, as we said earlier in *ST* I, q. 7, a. 1, the more immaterial that forms are, the more they approach to a kind of infinity. Therefore, it is obvious that *the immateriality of a thing is the reason that it is cognitive*, and the mode of knowledge is according to the mode of immateriality. Whence, in *De anima* 2.12, it is said that, *on account of their immateriality, plants do not know.* However, a sense is cognitive because *it is receptive of species without matter*, and the intellect is even more cognitive because it is more separate from matter and is unmixed, as is said in *De anima* 3.4. Whence, since God is of the highest degree of immateriality, it follows that the highest degree of knowledge exists in Him.[8]

Therefore, the knower must have some kind of spirituality in order to receive the form of a thing that is different from it, which it knows,

---

[8] Likewise, see *ST* I, q. 80, a. 1 and *De veritate*, q. 2, a. 2.

so that it may *become*, in some manner, *the other—ut intentionaliter fiat aliud a se.*[9]

Also, St. Thomas distinguished quite well the double *immutatio* (alteration) needed for sensation: the *material* (or, *physical*) alteration of the organ and the somehow-*spiritual* and psychological *alteration* likewise needed.[10] Indeed, he says in *ST* I, q. 78, a. 3:

> There are two kinds of alteration, one *natural* and the other *spiritual*. It is, indeed, *natural* inasmuch as the form of the altering being is received in the altered being according to *esse naturale*, as heat is in the heated. However, it is *spiritual* inasmuch as the form of the altering being is received in the altered being according to *esse spirituale—as the form of color exists in the pupil which does not thereby become colored*. However, a spiritual alteration is required for the activity of the sense. Through an alteration of this kind, *the intention* of the sensible form comes into being in the sense organ. Otherwise, if a natural alteration sufficed for sensation, every natural being would sense when it underwent an alteration.

Thus, we can see the mysterious character of sense knowledge: even if sensation is not an act of the soul alone but, instead, of an animated organ (e.g., the eye), it remains very difficult to explain how a *material thing* can impress its representative likeness in the living eye, for such a representative likeness is in some way *spiritual*, even though it is intrinsically dependent upon the organ where it is found. Thus, the sense soul of brute animals is simple and is not a body even though it is

---

[9] See Cajetan, *In ST* I, q. 14, a. 1. Also, see John of St. Thomas, *Cursus philosophicus*, p. 4 (*De anima*), q. 4, a. 1.

[10] [Tr. note: These topics are sounded to great depths in Simon, *Introduction to the Metaphysics of Knowledge*, 85–112; "To Be and To Know," in *Philosopher at Work*, ed. Anthony O. Simon (Lanham, MD: Rowman & Littlefield Publishers, 1999), 173–193. Also, the researcher would do well to consult the notes on "Knowledge in Common" by Fr. Austin Woodbury, S.M., a student of Fr. Garrigou-Lagrange. See Austin Woodbury, *Natural Philosophy, Treatise Three: Psychology*, The John N. Deely and Anthony Russell Collection, St. Vincent College, Latrobe, PA, n.614–713 (p.473–578).]

intrinsically dependent upon the matter that it informs and animates. In this sense, it is corruptible—not of itself but due to the composite of which it is the form and without which it cannot exist.[11]

St. Thomas, who had a profound sense for mystery, saw the difficulty. He expressed it in many places when he noted that *the agent as such is always nobler than the patient*.[12]

To this difficulty, St. Thomas gives two responses that are not opposed but, instead, complement each other. The first is of a wholly metaphysical order and is not interested in experimental psychology. We will recall it in order to show that the difficulty of the problem did not escape the philosophers of the 13th century. The second is easily harmonized with the data of experimental psychology and with the principle of the mutual influence of causes, which, as we have seen, is a corollary to the principle of finality.

* * *

The first response is given in *De potentia* q. 5, a. 8, where St. Thomas asks himself what kind of action will remain in the glorious bodies of the elect after the end of the world, when there will no longer be alteration (i.e., assimilation accompanied by disassimilation and corruption). He responds by making a distinction between *action that is, properly speaking, bodily*, like that required for the generation of plants and animals and for their corruption (this will no longer exist), and the *influence of visible bodies necessary for sensation*, in particular vision (this will remain for the glorious bodies). He then asks himself how a wholly

---

[11] In order to understand in what way the representation of the sensible order found in the sensitive soul of brute animals is *aliqualiter* (or, in a qualified sense, *secundum quid*) *spiritual*, even though it is *simpliciter* material, it is necessary to recall that for Aristotle and St. Thomas *that which is material* is defined, "That which is either composed of matter and form (e.g., bodies) or what which is intrinsically dependent on matter (like the sensitive soul of brute animals and its faculties). The word "material" is thus said *analogically* according to these two acceptations. Hence, one grasps that the sensible representation, while remaining in the material order and thus very inferior to the intellect is nevertheless called *aliqualiter* (or *secundum quid*) *spiritualis*. [Tr. note: See also the text of Woodbury cited above.]

[12] See *ST* I, q. 79, a. 2, ad 3; a. 3, ad 1. Above all, see *De potentia*, q. 5, a. 8c. See the general index of his works concerning the word *agens*, no. 36.

material thing can exercise such an influence, which is in some way spiritual, upon the organ of senses. He explains it by light inasmuch as this itself depends upon superior causes according to *the principle of the subordination of causes* which is applied no less in the order of objective influence[13] as it is in the physical motion subordinated to Divine pre-motion. Consider the text of St. Thomas in *De potentia*, q. 5, a. 8:

> It must be known that *a body has a twofold action.* One action is *according to the property of a body,* namely as it acts through motion (for it is proper to being a body that it moves and acts by itself being moved). It has *another action* inasmuch as it attains to the order of separate substances and *participates in something pertaining to their mode of activity,* just as inferior natures are accustomed to sharing in a given property of a superior nature. For example, this appears in certain animals which participate in a kind of likeness of prudence, which itself is proper to man. *However, this is an action of the body which does not pertain to the transmutation of matter* but, instead, *to a certain kind of diffusion of the likeness of a form in the "medium,"* in a similar way to the *spiritual intention* that is received from the thing *in the sense* or in the intellect. In this way does the sun illuminate the air and does color multiply its *species* in the "medium."

> Now, both of these modes of action in these inferior bodies are caused by the heavenly bodies. Thus, on the one hand, fire through its heat *transforms matter* by the power of a heavenly body (we would say today, instead, that earthly heat depends upon rays of solar heat); and, on the other hand, visible bodies *multiply their species* in the "medium" *by the power of light, which has its source in a heavenly body.* . . . Now, when the motion of the heavens ceases, the first action will cease but not the second. Therefore, when the motion of the heavens ceases, there will indeed be an action in these inferior bodies *by illu-*

---

[13] [Tr. note: That is, in the order of influence in objective-specificative extrinsic-formal causality.]

minating and altering the "medium" by sensible things. However, it will not be the action through which matter is transformed, resulting in generation and corruption.[14]

As John of St. Thomas remarks in commenting on this text,[15] St. Thomas is here explaining the impression of the representative likeness of bodies in our senses by the *subordination of causes* inasmuch as *light*, which is the least material of things and is the subtlest of things in the order of inanimate bodies, depends upon superior causes and, in the final analysis, on God its Author, who conserves it. This subordination of causes is admitted here by St. Thomas for the case of the objective influence of bodies upon our senses, as he admits that the activity of every created agent depends on superior causes (and, above all, on God, who is the First Mover). See his remarks in *ST* I, q. 105, a. 5:

> God acts in three different ways in any particular agent: first as end, . . . second as agent, . . . third as conserving the forms and powers of things, as the sun is said to cause the manifestation of colors inasmuch as it gives and conserves the light by which the colors are manifested.

This is not the occasionalism of Malebranche, for we are not saying here that God impresses the likeness of bodies in our senses on the occasion of the bodies' presence. Instead, we are here admitting the subordination of causes and the mysterious influence of God, the First, Universal Mover—an influence presupposed by every created influence, whether objective or physical.

It is no more accurate to say that this immaterialism is something akin to that held by Berkeley or Leibniz. Here, [for Aristotle and St.

---

[14] St. Thomas speaks in the same way in *ST* I, q. 67, a. 3, ad 1 and ad 3. [Tr. note: This issue is enshrouded in many mysteries and difficulties, and St. Thomas's own examples make it difficult. Penetrating remarks can be found in the lengthy footnote in Simon, *Introduction to the Metaphysics of Knowledge*, 104–106n23. There is not universal agreement on this topic, as can be seen in a dissenting voice like that found in George P. Klubertanz, "*De Potentia*, 5.8. A Note on the Thomist Theory of Sensation," *Modern Schoolman* 26, no. 4 (1949): 323–331.]

[15] See John of St. Thomas, *Cursus philosophicus*, p. 4 (*De anima*), q. 8, a. 4.

Thomas], matter has its place and plays its role. However, it is subordinated to the formal, efficient, and final causes.

Malebranche and Leibniz would have easily heard the sense of St. Thomas's response, which would correct that which is manifestly excessive in their immaterialism. However, if one were to explain this wholly metaphysical (and truly, very mysterious) response to those who study sensation only from the experimental point of view, they would probably respond to us as the Athenians responded to St. Paul on the Areopagus, "*Audiemus te de hoc iterum*. We will listen to you about this again" (Acts 17:32).

*   *   *

The principles formulated by Aristotle and St. Thomas concerning the mutual relations of causes enable us to give another response that is harmonized easily enough with the data of experimental psychology without misunderstanding the depths of the problem and its difficulty, which escapes many people.

Here, we are confronted with a mystery of the natural order, which common sense does not note, though it catches the attention of every philosophical mind: how can a wholly material thing impress within our senses a representative likeness that is, in some manner, spiritual, even under the influence of light, understood according to the principle of the subordination of causes? As is said in Shakespeare's *Hamlet*, "There are more things in heaven and earth, Horatio, than are dreamt of in your philosophy." Even here, far below the mysteries pertaining to the order of grace, there are mysteries of nature, splendid mysteries that cannot be denied by suppressing one of the extremes that constitute them: matter and an immaterial principle. Nor can we attenuate these mysteries, for this would be to diminish the beauty of the chiaroscuro painted by God himself.[16] To deny that which is clear on account of that which is obscure—as do materialism and idealism, though in opposite

---

[16] [Tr. note: This theme of the "chiaroscuro" is the leading theme of Fr. Garrigou-Lagrange's *Le sens du mystère*. See Réginald Garrigou-Lagrange, *The Sense of Mystery*, trans. Matthew K. Minerd (Steubenville, OH: Emmaus Academic, 2017), 103–120.]

ways—would lead one to break with common sense and to replace mystery with absurdity. Whatever some philosophers may think about it, common sense is useful not only for farmers and tradesmen. Socrates and Aristotle thought that it is useful for philosophers themselves and that to break with common sense is to break with the first principles of natural reason.

These principles remind us that the two elements of a chiaroscuro buttress each other. Likewise, they show us that the mystery in question is completely different from incoherence and absurdity.

Indeed, what is clear is the *fact* of the influence exerted upon our senses by the bodies that we see and touch. We cannot doubt the existence of the earth which carries us and that of the persons with whom we speak. What is obscure is the *intimate mode* of the influence of external bodies upon our senses.

Likewise, there is something clear and something obscure in the case of the application of the principle, "The agent as such is nobler than the patient, and the cause cannot be inferior to its effect." The material thing, inasmuch as it already has a *determinate form* (e.g., the form of the mountains or that of the ocean) is *superior* to our senses, which have not yet received the likeness of this form, even though the senses are superior to it inasmuch as they are faculties that are living, knowing, and in some manner, immaterial. This is what St. Thomas says in *ST* I, q. 79, a. 3, ad 1: "Sensible things are found *in act* outside the soul and, therefore, it is not necessary for us to hold that there is an agent sense [i.e., akin to the agent intellect]."

Moreover, the great principle concerning the mutual relation of causes (i.e. their interaction) is applied here in a mysterious manner: *causa sunt invicem causae, sed in diverso genere.*[17] In one respect, the senses *are assimilated* to their object and, in another respect, *they assimilate it.* The sense of vision, according to one order of causality, is *impressed or determined* by the colored object and, from another perspective, the representative likeness of this object is *vital and psychological in dependence upon the sense faculty,* which then reacts by the very act of sensation. In this way, from different perspectives (and without

---

[17] See Aristotle, *Metaphysics* 5.2.

contradiction), the sense is *assimilated* to the object and *assimilates* the form of the object, which becomes vital and, in some way, spiritual.[18]

As we have seen, the principle of the mutual interdependence of causes is a corollary to the principle of finality.[19]

Such is the response, one in harmony with the data of experimental psychology, furnished by the Aristotelian distinction of act and potency, as well as the distinction of the four causes. This response in no way misunderstands the depths of the problem and differs greatly from the simple realism of common sense, which it explains, all the while surpassing it.

* * *

John of St. Thomas excellently expresses the mystery that we are faced with here when he writes in his *Cursus philosophicus, Philosophia naturalis, De anima,* q. 8, a. 4:

> There is a difficulty involved in how such coarse and material objects can produce those *species* that are *more immaterial and perfect* than the material accidents that they represent. And yet, we say that they are emitted by the objects because they are *sensible by their own nature* and, particularly, because, with regard to this action of emitting intentional species, *they are subordinated* to a heavenly power, which has excellence for intentional actions. Likewise, in the same manner, we say that

---

[18] What we say here provides an explanation for the principle *quidquid recipitur ad modum recipientis recipitur,* generally invoked in the theory of sensation current among the Thomists—a theory that we admit, all the while insisting on the mystery that it seeks to explain. In the case that occupies us here, the principle of the reciprocal dependency of causes is applied. It intervenes everywhere where the four causes are at play—that is, in every form of *becoming.* It intervenes here in the form expressed by St. Thomas in *In IV Sent.* d. 17, q. 1, a. 5, qu. 3: "The ultimate disposition is the effect of the form in the genus of formal cause while, however, preceding in the genus of material cause." The psychological impression received by the senses is the *ultimate disposition* to their immanent, vital, assimilative action. It is an effect in the order of formal causality, although it precedes it in the order of material causality. See the final chapter of this text concerning the mutual dependence of causes.

[19] See the second section of the fifth chapter in the first part of this text.

species at one time received in the senses have the power of moving the same creature's *estimative sense* in which they are found, and consequently, have the power of emitting unsensed species that are more perfect but nevertheless contained in these sensed objects; and they do this both by the power of the soul and by a heavenly power (i.e., through the subordination of causes)[20] which are superior powers.

Indeed, the natural mystery that we are here discussing increases when we look to explain the acts of the superior internal senses, above all the act of the *estimative* sense (or, of instinct) by which, for example, the sheep flees from the wolf that it sees, however, for the first time, before having experienced its ferocity. It does not flee from it because of its color, which often differs very little from the color of a sheepdog. Instead, it flees because it experientially grasps that the wolf is its *natural enemy*. On this topic, St. Thomas says in *De veritate*, q. 25, a. 2:

> It must be known that, both from the perspective from the apprehensive powers of the sensitive part (of the soul) and that of its appetitive powers, there is something that belongs to the sensitive soul *in accord with its own nature* but also something *inasmuch as it has some slight participation in reason, coming into contact in its highest activity with reason's lowest activity*—as [Pseudo-]Dionysius says in *De divinis nominibus*, c. 7, Divine Wisdom joins the ends of first things with the beginnings of ones in a second rank.

---

[20] [Tr. note: Such remarks represent Fr. Garrigou-Lagrange's attempt to rescue the language of this tradition from some of the implied flawed cosmology. Above all, it is most important to note the implication in his remarks concerning the way that sensation requires a communication of form to form (as opposed to the communication of form to a material substrate that would then assimilate the form as its own). Yves Simon rightly noted the great deal of work that is necessary in explicating this position. However, it remains central for distinguishing knowers from non-knowers, and a failure to do so risks ending in a form of implicit materialism or, at best, dualism when one reaches the level of intellection.]

Thus, the imaginative power belongs to the sensitive soul in accord with its own nature, for forms received through sense are stored in it. However, the *estimative power*, through which the animal grasps intentions that are not received through sense, *such as friendliness and hostility*, exists in the sense soul *inasmuch as it participates in something of reason*. Whence, on account of this estimation, animals are said to have a kind of prudence, as is obvious in the words at the beginning of the *Metaphysics*. For example, the *sheep flees from the wolf, whose hostility nobody senses*. The case is similar from the perspective of the soul's appetitive powers.[21]

Also, *ST* I, q. 78, a. 4:

The sheep, upon seeing the wolf that is approaching it, flees, not because of the unbecomingness of its color or figure but *as if it were a natural enemy*. Similarly, the bird does not collect straw because this delights its senses but, instead, because it is useful for building a nest. . . . Now, the *estimative sense* is ordered to the grasping of intentions that are not received through the [external] senses, and the *memorative power* is ordered to the preservation of them.

Again, *ST* I, q. 78, a. 4, ad 1:

(Brute) animals perceive such intentions (i.e. friendship and hostility) *only through a kind of natural instinct*. Man, however, perceives them through a kind of gathering activity. Therefore, that which is called the *estimative sense* in other animals is called the *cogitative power* in man, which devises [*adinvenit*][22]

---

[21] [Tr. note: Fr. Garrigou-Lagrange ends with *et similiter ex parte sensitivae*. Consultation with the Leonine Edition (Leon.22/3.733:183–184) shows that the text actually is *et similiter ex parte appetitivae*. St. Thomas is continuing the discussion with which he opened this selection.]

[22] [Tr. note: The language of *adinvenit* is used by Aquinas to describe second intentions. For some of the ambiguities involved in such a term see Schmidt, *Domain of Logic*

such intentions by means of a kind of gathering.[23]

Again, *ST* I, q. 78, a. 4, ad 4:

Although the intellect's activity arises from the senses, none-theless in the thing apprehended through sense, the intellect knows many things that the senses cannot perceive. Something similar holds for the estimative sense, though in a lower manner.

In the thing grasped by the senses, sight grasps *color*, but it cannot grasp what the intellect knows: *being, substance, life, finality, efficiency*—in other words, the *raisons d'être* of that which this thing contains or produces.

There is an abyss, indeed an immeasurable distance (*immensa*), separating the most elevated sense knowledge and the lowest of intel-

---

According to Saint Thomas Aquinas (The Hague: Martinus Nijhoff, 1966), 168–174. M.-D. Philippe, "Originalité de 'l'*ens rationis*' dans la philosophie de Saint Thomas," *Angelicum* 52, no. 1 (1975): 94–95n6. There are interesting similarities between esti-mative / cogitative intentions and logical second intentions, both of which are not pure fabrications but which also depend upon the knower for their very possibility.]

[23] [Tr. note: On this point, it is necessary to be careful not to underestimate the role of experience in higher animals' estimations. Some preliminary remarks can be found in the text by Deely cited above in note 8. Also, see John Deely, *What Distinguishes Human Understanding* (South Bend, IN: St. Augustine's Press, 2002).

Also, one should note that St. Thomas does not hold that the estimative and cogi-tative powers are distinct powers in the human person. The cogitative power is more perfect than is the estimative sense of brute animals because of the many important roles that it plays in speculative and practical cognition. See *ST* I, q. 78, a. 4, ad 5. A reader interested in researching these matters would benefit from consulting Daniel D. De Haan, "Moral Perception and the Function of the Vis Cogitativa in Thomas Aquinas's Doctrine of Antecedent and Consequent Passions," *Documenti e studi sulla traditione filosofica medievale* 25 (2014): 289–330; "Perception and the *Vis Cogitativa*: A Thomistic Analysis of Aspectual, Actional, and Affectional Percepts," *American Catholic Philosophical Quarterly* 88, no. 3 (2014): 397–437. In addition, there are many relevant matters noted on this important topic in the clear texts of Fr. Austin Woodbury S.M., a student of Fr. Garrigou-Lagrange. See Austin Woodbury, *Natural Philosophy, Treatise Three: Psychology*, undated course text, The John N. Deely and Anthony Russell Collection, St. Vincent College, Latrobe, Pennsylvania, 639–649. Finally, the classic, albeit dated, historical study on these matters remains George Klubertanz, *The Discursive Power: Sources and Doctrine of the* Vis cogitativa *According to St. Thomas Aquinas* (St. Louis: The Modern Schoolman, 1952).]

lectual knowledge. Nonetheless, the former participates in the latter in some manner (*secundum quid, non simpliciter*). Thus, the estimative sense (or, animal instinct) is like a distant reflection of the intellect, a reflection that leads us to conclude that there must be an intellect that orders all things, that is, that God must exist as the Author of the universe. Here, we find ourselves ultimately faced with the mystery of the creation and preservation of all things by God.

We find a similar mystery when we elevate ourselves to the superior order of intellectual knowledge, above all if we consider its relations with sense knowledge.

The Mystery of Our Intellectual Knowledge and Its Twofold Relationship with Sense Knowledge

Here too we find a most striking chiaroscuro. What is clear is the *universality and absolute necessity of the first principles as laws* not only of the intellect but also *of reality*. It is utterly obvious that a square circle is not only something unthinkable but, moreover, is *unrealizable in itself* outside of the mind. Likewise, it is utterly obvious that one thing cannot, at one and the same time, be and not be. This is not only inconceivable for us; it is *really impossible* in itself. If, from the outset of our intellectual life the "thing in itself" is not accessible, at least as regards this fact, it will never be accessible.

Likewise, this universality and absolute necessity of the first principles quite clearly *absolutely surpasses* sense knowledge (no matter how perfect it may become in its own order), for sense knowledge grasps only that which is contingent and singular, which exists *here and now* and not *that which necessarily must be the case* always and everywhere. This universality and absolute necessity of the [first] principles, known by our intellect and by it alone, provide the foundation for the proof of the soul's spirituality and immortality.

What is obscure here is the intimate manner in which we form for ourselves the universal ideas that are presupposed by the first principles (or, laws) of being whose absolute necessity and universality are so obvious.

Ontologists think they see these first principles (or, primordial laws) of reality in a kind of vague (or, confused) knowledge of God. Innatists believe they grasp them through innate ideas after a manner that is somewhat similar to that of the angels. St. Augustine thought that our intellect perceives them under a Divine illumination which enlightens the intelligible in the sensible, as the sun makes colors visible.

According to Aristotle and St. Thomas, every indication suggests, as much *a posteriori* as *a priori*,[24] that our universal ideas (even the first notions of being, unity, etc.) are *abstracted* from sensible things by an intellectual light called the *agent intellect* which, with the concurrence of God (the first mover of spirits and bodies), draws into the light the intelligible found in the sensible and makes us see the *raisons d'être* of things, as well as the *raisons d'être* of their elements, activities, and effects, thereby making them intelligible for us. As the sensible light of the sun makes *colors* visible, the intellectual light of the agent intellect makes *the raisons d'être of things* intelligible. In this way, the sense of sight grasps *color* (or, the colored) and our intellect knows *being* (or, reality and the *raisons d'être* of things). An immeasurable distance separates the intellect from the senses (whether internal or external). The imagination could forever be perfected in its own order so as to represent sensible phenomena better and better, but it would never grasp *their raison d'être*, which makes them intelligible. Here, we are faced with the immeasurable distance separating the idea from the corresponding image: only the *idea*[25] expresses the *raison d'être* that makes the sensible phenomena represented in the image intelligible (at least vaguely so).[26] This is why the idea is *universal* and expresses what always and everywhere *necessarily* must be the case, without which the properties of a thing would no longer be conceived—for example, the properties of a

---

[24] [Tr. note: See note 1 in the second chapter of the first part of this book.]

[25] [Tr. note: Regarding the use of "idea" here, see the remarks above note 5.]

[26] In this way, the dog can have an image of the clock and the parrot can even say, "The clock chimes," but neither of them can know the *raison d'être* for the clock's movement, nor define *what a clock is*: "A machine for indicating the solar hour," nor know what is necessarily required *always and everywhere* in order that a machine may indicate this kind of time.

mineral, of a plant, of man,[27] or the properties of a triangle or a circle.

Despite the immeasurable distance separating the intelligible from the sensible, everything leads us to think that our intellect, by its natural light, abstracts the intelligible from the sensible and that our ideas therefore come from the senses. In the conjunction of these two very distant orders, we are faced with a very certain fact whose intimate mode [of interaction] cannot be fully grasped by us.

The obscurity of this mode [of interaction] does not remove the certitude of the fact: we see *a posteriori*[28] that, as St. Thomas says in *ST* I, q. 84, aa. 3 and 6, "if a given sense fails, one cannot have knowledge of things known by it. For example, the man born blind cannot have any idea of colors. This would not be the case if our intellect had innate ideas of all intelligible things" or if it saw them in God, vaguely known.

It is still a fact that we do not naturally know God and purely spiritual realities like our soul except by their likeness with sensible things, *in speculo sensibilium*. Indeed, we attribute to God and to created spirits that which they have *analogically in common* with sensible things (e.g. being, unity, goodness, action, etc.). However, it is only *in a negative and relative manner* that our intellect naturally knows what *properly pertains* to God and created spirit. Thus, we negatively conceive of spirituality as immateriality and we speak relatively of the light of the intellect in comparison with sensible light.[29] We do not naturally have

---

[27] Of all sensible beings, man is the one for which we know best the specific difference, *rationality*, whereas we cannot have a distinct idea of the specific difference of the lion or the deer, or that of the rose or the lily. Why? Because the specific differences of these inferior beings express forms that are in some way buried in matter and intrinsically dependent on it. By contrast, rationality expresses a spiritual form that is intrinsically independent from matter, namely, the rational soul whose intellect *is essentially relative to being*, the first intelligible object which enlightens all others.

This is why, after coming to know distinctly man's specific difference, we can *deduce* that he must be free, moral, sociable, religious, and that he must have the power of laughing as well as that of speaking with intelligence. Of all sensible beings, man is thus the only one for which the specific difference is the object of philosophical consideration. The philosophy that treats of the human soul can only treat of the soul of the lion or of the eagle from the perspective of their genera (i.e., of vegetative life and sensitive life).

[28] [Tr. note: See the remarks above in note 1.]

[29] Cf. *ST* I, q. 88, aa. 1–3.

a proper idea of God or of pure spirit which would come immediately from them without the concurrence of the senses and the imagination.

Every one of our acts of intellectual knowledge is naturally accompanied by a concurrent act of the imagination, and every idea is accompanied by an image, at least a verbal one.

Thus, *a posteriori,* everything leads us to think that, as St. Thomas says, the proper object of our intellect is the intelligible being of sensible things, which by way of analogy enables us to know the intelligible being of spiritual things. See his remarks in *ST* I, q. 87, a. 3, ad 1:[30]

> The object of the intellect is something common, namely *being* and *the true* under which is likewise contained the very act of understanding. Whence, the intellect can know its own act but not as its first and primary object [*primo*], for in this current state [i.e. of union with the body], the first object of our intellect is not any being whatsoever or any truth whatsoever but, rather, *being* and *the true considered in material things, as was said above in ST I, q. 84, a. 7, from which it arrives at knowledge of all other things.*

Also, see *ST* I, q. 87, a. 1:

> Our intellect understands itself inasmuch as it comes to be in act through *species* abstracted from sensible things.

This is strongly confirmed if we consider, so to speak, *a priori,* the very nature of our intellect as the faculty of a spiritual soul, naturally united to a body.

Indeed, why is our intellect *united to the senses* if not on account of its very nature as the *least of all intellects,* which has for its proper (or, proportionate) object *the least of all intelligibles,* namely, the intelligible being of sensible things which is known through the intermediary of the senses, enabling us to know, at least analogically, the intelligible

---

[30] [Tr. note: This is the correct text location. Fr. Garrigou-Lagrange cites it as *ST* I, q. 87, a. 4.]

being of spiritual things and that of God? As the Thomists say, "The proportionate object of the lowest intellect is the lowest intelligible in the shadow of sensible things." In this way, we can explain how the body exists *for* the soul, how the body is useful for the soul's intellectual knowledge, and how the human soul of its very nature needs the body,[31] although, accidentally speaking, it is weighed down by it. As St. Thomas says in *ST* I, q. 76, a. 5:

> Is the intellective soul suitably united to such a body?

> I answer that *since form is not for the sake of matter but, rather, matter is for the sake of form,* it is necessary that we take the reason why the matter exists in a given way from the form and not vice-versa. Now, as we discussed earlier in *ST* I, q. 55, a. 2, according to the order of nature, *the intellective soul holds the lowest grade among intellectual substances* inasmuch as it does not of its nature [*naturaliter*] have the notion of truth given to it, as is the case with the angels. Instead, it must collect it from divisible things by way of the senses, as [Pseudo] Dionysius says in *De divinis nominibus* c. 7. However, nature does not fail in necessary things. *Whence, it was necessary that the intellective soul* not only have the power of understanding but also *the power of sensing.* However, the action of sense is not performed without a bodily instrument. Therefore, it was necessary that the intellective soul be united to a body that could be a fitting organ for sense.

Therefore, the mystery of our intellectual knowledge is found first in the passage from the sensible image to the idea, despite the immeasurable distance separating these two orders. In the image, which is found in the imagination, *the intelligible* exists only *in potency,* somewhat like the oak in the acorn.

In order to have the *intelligible in act,* there must be, as Aristotle

---

[31] Consequently, as soon as it is separated from the body by death, it will be immobilized either in good or in evil. Cf. *SCG*, IV, chs. 91ff.

says, a spiritual (or, immaterial) *analogue* to what physical light does in rendering colors to be *actually visible*. Without this cause, called the agent intellect, we would not be able to pass beyond the empiricism of the nominalist and would not be able to explain why our intellect grasps not only color or sound but, instead, the *raisons d'être* of things, which make the things intelligible. Without the agent intellect, we would not be able to explain the *universality* of our first notions, nor would we be able to explain the *absolute necessity* of the first principles of reason and of reality—principles whose value resists every negative critique, like gold which resists the action of every acid, principles whose universality and absolute necessity are inaccessible to the senses and to the most perfect imagination that one can try to conceive.

Therefore, as St. Thomas says in *ST* I, q. 79, aa. 3 and 4, we must admit the existence of the natural light of the agent intellect, which along with the concurrence of God (who is the First Intellect, a point that St. Augustine's thought recalls), enlightens from on high the images of the imagination in order to place *the intelligible* in relief (i.e., in order to actualize it). To put it another way, it enables us to know the *raisons d'être* of things.

The mystery remains regarding the way that we are to determine the intimate nature and mode of influence of this intellectual light called the "agent intellect." It is not surprising that this remains mysterious for us since, as we have seen, we know purely spiritual realities only in their relation with sensible things, *secundum habitudinem ad sensibilia*. Thus, we say that this intellectual light is a *cause* that actualizes the intelligible as physical light renders colors to be actually visible. However, we know what *properly* pertains to this intellectual light only *negatively* (thus speaking of its *immateriality*) and *relatively* (thus saying things like, "It is a light which is very superior to physical light since it is of the vital order of suprasensible knowledge").

However, what is the intimate mode of the influence of this light, this intellectual faculty, which does not know but, instead, enables us to know the intelligible? This remains quite hidden inasmuch as our intellect, united to the body, is turned toward sensible things and knows itself only in the mirror of these latter, *in speculo sensibilium*. Consider St. Thomas's remarks in *ST* I, q. 88, a. 1:

According to the words of Aristotle, which experience cor-
roborates, our intellect in the state of this present life [i.e.
united to the body] has a natural relationship with the natures
of material things. Whence, it understands nothing except by
turning itself to the phantasms.

One could consider also *ST* I, q. 84, a. 7, ad 3; q. 88, a. 2, ad 1 and ad 2.
Similarly, consider St. Thomas's words in *ST* I, q. 87, a. 1:

> Since it is connatural to our intellect as it exists in this present
> life to turn its gaze toward material and sensible things, as we
> said earlier, it follows that *it thus understands itself inasmuch as
> it is in act through species abstracted from sensible things* by the
> light of the agent intellect, which gives actuality to these intelli-
> gibles [*est actus ipsorum intelligibilium*], and by their mediation
> the possible intellect understands. Therefore, our intellect
> does not know itself through its essence but, rather, through its
> act. This happens in two manners. On the one hand, it occurs
> *in a particular manner*, as when Socrates or Plato perceives
> himself to have an intellective soul on the basis of the fact that
> *he perceives that he understands*. On the other hand, it occurs *in
> a universal manner*, as when we consider *the nature of the human
> mind* on the basis of knowledge of the intellect's act.

Moreover, it is appropriate here to recall that the last among intellects is *much less intelligible in itself* than is the Supreme Intellect, which
is Light Itself, Thought of Thought, *ipsum intelligere subsistens*. Aristotle
noted this many times: "Divine things are more intelligible *in themselves* than all the others, although *relative to us* they are more difficult
to know, for they are more distant from the senses."[32]

Thus, although the Divine Intellect, which is identical with Eternal
Intellection of the Plenitude of Being, is sovereignly simple and
immutable, the last of intellects (i.e., ours) cannot reach this eminent
simplicity in an utterly evident manner. In our case, we must distin-

---

[32] Aristotle, *Metaphysics*, 1.2.

guish between the agent intellect, which by its light illuminates the intelligible being of sensible things, from the possible intellect, which knows this intelligible [reality]. As the Dionysian principle often cited by St. Thomas runs: "Those things that are divided in lower things are united in superior ones." At the lower limits of the world of the intellect and of the intelligible, we therefore must not be astonished to find division, a deficiency with regard to unity, and thus, an obscurity that is not found at the summit of this spiritual world.

Therefore, it is not surprising that the passage from the image to the idea is mysterious, like the passage from any given order to another, immensely distant one. Despite all of this, there is a kind of continuity. In order specify the meaning of the principle, we can say "*Supremum infimi secundum quid seu quodammodo attingit infimum supremae, quamvis simpliciter ab eo immense distet.*" ["The highest things of a lower order attains the lowest of the higher in a qualified manner (or, in some way), although speaking without qualification [*simpliciter*] it is immensely distant from it."]

It is no more astonishing that the same mystery is found, in an opposite sense, when our intellect descends from knowledge of the universal to that of the material singular. How can a faculty that knows the intelligible know *the material singular*, not like God whose knowledge is the cause of things, nor like the angel by infused ideas but, instead *by abstraction from the matter* that individualizes sensible things? The material singular thus seems to be below the lowly limits of the naturally knowable intelligible, just as the intimate life of God (i.e., the Deity itself) is above its superior limits. *Individuum est ineffabile*, the material individual in its idiosyncrasy is ineffable, although in a way that is opposite to how God is ineffable.

Nonetheless, there can be no doubt that our intellect knows material singulars and that it reasons in this way: "Of his nature, man is mortal. Now, Peter is a man. Therefore, Peter is mortal."

How does it come to know this singular which, properly speaking, is the object of the senses? St. Thomas responds: it knows it *indirectly, as by reflection*, for its ideas, abstracted from sensible, singular things, are relative to these things; these singular things, first being like the point of departure of the process of intellectual knowledge, are then like the terminus toward which it descends again, expressing the intelligible by the images from which it was drawn. As St. Thomas says in *ST* I, q. 86, a. 1:

> Our intellect *cannot know the singular* in material things *directly and primarily*. This is so because the principle of individu-atation [*singularitatis*] in material things is individual matter. As we said above in *ST* I, q. 85, a. 1, our intellect knows by abstracting the intelligible *species* from this kind of matter. However, what is abstracted from individual matter is univer-sal. Whence, our intellect only directly knows universals.

> *However, indirectly and by a kind of reflection it can know the singular.* This is so because (as was said in *ST* I, q. 84, a. 7) even after it has abstracted the intelligible species, it cannot under-stand them in act except by turning itself back to the phantasms in which it understands the intelligible species that it knows, as is said in *De anima* 3.7. Therefore, it directly understands the universal itself through the intelligible species; however, *indi-rectly*, it understands the singulars that are represented by the phantasms. In this way, it knows this proposition: "Socrates is a man."

Whether it is a question of elevating ourselves from the sensible to the intelligible or of descending from the intelligible to the sensible (from the universal to the singular), we therefore find the chiaroscuro that is forever encountered in the transition from one order to another. Error here denies the clear on account of the obscure, thus replacing mystery with absurdity, whether it be the absurdity of materialism which denies knowledge by reducing it to matter or the absurdity of subjectivist idealism which denies that knowledge can grasp reality. As Étienne Gilson quite rightly remarks, "Idealism must hold that what-ever is outside of thought is unthinkable. This is not only the perfect expression of idealism; it is also its condemnation."[33]

---

[33] See Gilson, "Le réalisme méthodique," 751.

* * *

Therefore, let us conclude: Thomistic realism is not only a naïve common-sense realism; it is a *methodical realism* and even is *critical*—not in the abusive sense of the term, but in its exact sense. Indeed, it is founded on the examination of the value of knowledge inasmuch as the intellect, reflecting on itself, not only knows its act but sufficiently knows the nature of its act and its own nature so as to grasp its proper, essential finality, which is to be conformed to reality: "*in cuius natura est ut rebus conformetur.*"[34] Why can the intellect know its own, proper finality, its *raison d'être*? It can do so because it has for its object being and the *raisons d'être* of things. By contrast, the sense of sight, having for its object not being but the colored, does not know its own finality, its *raison d'être*. Truth does exist in it, but it does not know that it possesses truth. In contrast, the intellect knows the truth and is aware of the fact that it knows it.

Nonetheless, as we have seen, if we consider not only the fact and nature of our knowledge but also the intimate mode according to which exterior things influence our senses (and, through our senses, our intellect), we find ourselves here faced with a double mystery that is found again in an opposite manner in our intellectual knowledge of the material singular (i.e., our intellectual knowledge of concrete material things).

Here, we have three facts that are certain. It is very certain that external things influence our senses (and by them, our intellect). It is also very certain that our intellect knows concrete external things. Likewise, it is very certain that it knows its own proper finality *ut rebus conformetur*, that it be conformed to things. Moreover, these three facts have explanations in accord with the requirements of the principles of contradiction, of efficient causality, and of finality, as well as the principle of the mutual relation of causes (i.e., of their inter-influence, *causae ad invicem sunt causae, sed in diverso genere*). Thus, we avoid every kind of vicious circle. However, the intimate mode of these facts—of the influence of external things upon our senses, of the influence of these

---

[34] Aquinas, *De veritate*, q. 1, a. 9.

upon our intellect, and of the intellectual knowledge of material singulars—cannot be fully grasped, and they remain obscure to some degree.[35] The works of God are more beautiful than we can express in words. We cannot come to know them in their intimate depths, inasmuch as they are knowable and inasmuch as the Creator knows them. Let us keep guard over the sense of mystery, which gives us a sense for the grandeur of the Divine Intelligence, and let us admire the chiaroscuros that the Divine Intelligence has placed in all things: where there is a transition from one order to another, the highest degree of the inferior order attains in a way (*secundum quid*) to the lowest degree of the superior order, from which, of its nature (*simpliciter*), it nevertheless remains immensely distant. Mystery is found precisely in the reconciliation of these technical terms of the scholastics: *secundum quid* (i.e., from a certain perspective) there is a conjunction, but *simpliciter* (i.e., purely and simply speaking) they are separated by an immeasurable distance.

Due to the relative obscurity that we find here, let us not deny what is clear (as does idealism), namely: 1° the primordial and indestructible evidence of the principle of contradiction as a law not only of the mind but of reality itself (i.e., a being at one and the same time both existing and not existing, from the same perspective, is not only *inconceivable for us* but, moreover, *is unrealizable in itself*); 2° the evidence of sensations of touch, sight, etc. In this latter case, we have physical certitude concerning the existence of the earth that carries us, concerning the persons with whom we speak, and concerning our own body as well as of our eyes. Idealists themselves are certain of the existence of bodies since they hold that our brain is an intermediary that separates the sensation from things and prevents it from reaching them. As the English neo-realists respond to them: at the moment when one perceives the external world, either the cerebral phenomenon is real without being

---

[35] Likewise, we experience that a given food is good without needing to undertake a chemical analysis. We see that a horse runs well without having anatomical knowledge concerning the disposition of its muscles. We see that an automobile drives well without verifying the details of its mechanism. We realize that our eye indeed perceives the color of objects without needing to verify whether all the rods of our retina are in a good state.

perceived (contrary to the principle of idealism, *esse est percipi*) or this cerebral phenomenon, not being perceived, is not real and thus it no longer prevents immediate, external perception.

Idealists do not understand that the two elements of the chiaroscuro we are here discussing mutually buttress one another and that to deny the first on account of the second is to condemn oneself to absurdity and to complete nihilism.[36]

Thomist realism does not deny what is obscure in the intimate mode [of the activity] of knowledge. It even says that *the knowledge of the least of intellects,* united to the senses, is quite removed from having the eminent simplicity of the knowledge had by pure spirits, above all the Divine Knowledge, and consequently is much *less intelligible* (or,

---

[36] Idealism suppresses the mystery of things by making the *idea* or the *representation* into a *materialist* conception; it conceives of it as though it were a painting upon the wall, as a terminus beyond which there is nothing. Instead, the representation is essentially relative (*intentionalis*) to what is represented, and the idea of being is relative to the extramental being (which is utterly different from *beings of reason*, which can exist only by being *conceived* and cannot be *realized*). See St. Thomas, *ST* I, q. 85, a. 2: "What is first known is the thing, whose likeness is the intelligible *species*." Also, *ST* I, q. 85, a. 2., ad 1, 2, and 3. (Also, see Cajetan on this article.) SCG II, ch. 75, no. 5. *De veritate*, q. 10, a. 9. *De spiritualibus creaturis*, a. 9, ad 6. *Quodlibet* 8, q. 2, a. 2. In III *De anima* (ed. Pirotta), lect. 8, nos. 717 and 718.

Properly speaking, *that which* is known is not the mental word but, rather, the *intelligible thing* that it expresses, as when one says, "Do you understand my words," meaning, "Do you understand what they express?" See *ST* I, q. 34, a. 1. Properly speaking, *the mental word* is not *id quod intelligitur* (that which is known) but *id in quo res concepta intelligitur* (that in which the conceived thing is known). Therefore, when discussing this problem, one that requires complete propriety in the terms being used, we cannot use the expression "*species quod*" [as though the *species* were the very *terminus* that (*quod*) is known].

Idealism, which, like Descartes, would like to make everything clear, has not noted that in the painted chiaroscuro, the color of the objects does not appear [as what is most important and most fully obvious], but only their form; and likewise here, in the case of the philosophical chiaroscuro of which we are speaking, one sees concerning the realities in question that they are (*an sit*) and not what they are intimately (*quid sit intime*). Only purely intuitive knowledge, which God and the angels have, grasps it.

[Tr. note: Fr. Garrigou-Lagrange has above "Quodl. 8 a. 4." The text to which he refers is almost certainly Quodl. 8, q. 2, a. 2. The contents of that article are relevant to the discussion here. Also, it is the fourth overall article in the Quodlibet. A similar kind of numeration of this particular quodlibet can be found in L.-M. Régis, *Epistemology*, trans. Imelda Choquette Byrne (New York: Macmillan, 1964), 503n94, 504n110.]

less luminous) *in itself,* although it is more comprehensible for us who experience it.

However, despite the obscurity that remains concerning how our intellect enters into contact with things, the primordial evidence of our intellectual life remains the same, and nothing can obscure it: a being that at one and the same time exists and does not exist is not only *inconceivable for us* but is *unrealizable in itself.* The principle of contradiction and the principles that are necessarily subordinated to it, which are denied only by falling into absurdity, are *laws of reality in itself* and not only laws of our intellect (that is, of reality in us or conceived by us).

From the first dawning of our intellectual life, we are already *absolutely certain* that, if God exists, however powerful He may be, He cannot make square circles, mountains without valleys, and [*pace* Descartes] there is no evil genius who can deceive us in this matter.

This primordial certitude is formally founded (*resolvitur formaliter*) *on the intellectual evidence* of the necessity, universality, and real value of this first principle. That is, it is founded on evident, intelligible being. It is materially founded (*resolvitur materialiter*) on the *sensible evidence* of the material thing from which our intellect has abstracted the notion of being. The value of this material foundation (*resolutio materialis*) is itself formally judged in the superior light of the intellectual evidence of the principles that show the impossibility of a sensation without something sensed,[37] a sensation without an objective cause and without finality. According to the principle of the mutual relation of causes (i.e., of their interaction) the senses furnish the *matter* for intellectual knowledge and their value is *formally* judged by this superior knowledge.

Therefore, the primordial affirmation that the principle of contradiction is the *law of reality in itself* is not only an affirmation of common sense. It is an affirmation of a methodical and critical realism. Moreover, it holds true not only for the principle of contradiction but also for the principles that are necessarily subordinated to it (inasmuch as the

---

37 [Tr. note: In order to understand this point as being more than a naïve remark, the reader should consult the works cited at the end of footnote 37 in the first chapter of this section.]

denial of them leads one to absurdity or inasmuch as doubt regarding them leads one to doubt the value of the principle of contradiction). *A contingent being that is not caused is absurd and obviously impossible.* So too is it absurd to speak of *a determinate tendency that does not tend toward any determinate end.*[38]

Without the affirmation of the real value and the necessity of these universal principles, there cannot be, as Gilson recognizes as well, any philosophy that is viable or conformed to the first evidences of natural reason as well as to those of experience. To express it another way, in opposition to subjectivist idealism, which denies or places in doubt the real value of these principles, and also in opposition to nominalist empiricism, which denies their necessity, traditional realism, such as it was formulated by Aristotle and St. Thomas, enables us to reach a true intellectual knowledge of reality, a knowledge that is true and knows that it is true—*veritas (scilicet conformitas cum re) est in intellectu sicut consequens actum intellectus et sicut cognita per intellectum;* truth (namely, conformity with reality) is in the intellect as following upon the act of understanding and as known by the intellect.[39] The human intellect can know not only the existence of its act but also the latter's nature as well as its own nature, *cuius natura est ut rebus conformetur.* In other words, *it can know its own, proper finality,* just as it knows the finality of the wings of the bird, the finality of the ear, or the finality of the living eye that is made for seeing.

---

[38] In registering a criticism against the demonstration by *reductio ad absurdum* that we made elsewhere concerning the principles of causality and finality (cf. *God,* vol. 1, 181ff, 199ff; vol. 2 360ff), Fr. Picard (cf. *Le Problème critique fundamental,* 61) thought that we wished to "deduce or draw out these principles from the principle of non-contradiction." It is a question only of showing that *their denial* leads one to deny the principle of contradiction. This is an entirely different affair.

Demonstration through *reductio ad absurdum* is *indirect* and does not give intrinsic evidence like direct and ostensive demonstration which gives a middle term. Here, one cannot place a *middle term* between an *immediately connected* subject and predicate. However, *vi absurdi illati* [by the strength of the absurdity inferred], demonstration by *reductio ad absurdum* prevents denial.

All the scholastics in all the schools, except for certain extremely radical nominalists like Nicholas of Autrecourt, have admitted that an *uncaused contingent being* is absurd and impossible. Without this being true, the proofs for the existence of God are no longer necessary, nor are they certain.

[39] Aquinas, *De veritate,* q. 1, a. 9.

"What greater absurdity," says realism, "Could there be than to claim that the intellect cannot know its own, proper finality, that it cannot know why it was made and cannot see in its very self its living relation to intelligible being!"[40] This is what one can call the realism of the principle of finality united to the principle of contradiction. Later on below, we will see the exigencies of this realism in relation to the will and to the existence of God, the Sovereign Good.

---

[40] On this subject, see the article of Régis Jolivet, "L'intuition intellectuelle," *Revue Thomiste* 15 (Jan. 1932): 52–71. In this article, Jolivet shows that most often, it is in opposition to the discursive operation of reason that St. Thomas defines intellectual intuition and that, although it has sometimes been contested, he assigns a rather large role to the latter. Also, see L. Noël, "La méthode du réalisme," *Revue Neo-scholastique* 33 (Nov. 1931), 433–447; in the latter article, the position of Étienne Gilson of which we have spoken is examined.

Chapter Three

THE FIRST DATUM OF OUR INTELLECT AND THE MARCH FROM THE KNOWN TO THE UNKNOWN

In order to better understand of the nature of our intellect's finality, it is important to state more precisely what is the first object that it knows and how it then passes from the known to the unknown.

In recent years, there has been a great deal of discussion, following the language of Henri Bergson,[1] about the immediate datum of consciousness. However, people give much less consideration to a matter of no less import, namely the first datum of the intellect, something that has been a concern of traditional philosophy since the time of Plato and Aristotle, a first datum variously interpreted by the great scholastics, Spinoza, and the ontologists, a datum which is nothing other than *being*.

Following Aristotle and Avicenna, St. Thomas often says, "That which the intellect conceives as, so to speak, most known and into which it resolves all its conceptions is being."[2] Likewise, "Being is that which first falls into the conception of the intellect, for inasmuch as something is in act, so too is that knowable. Whence, being is the first

---

[1] [Tr. note: In particular, he is referring to Bergson's *Time and Free Will: An Essay on the Immediate Data of Consciousness*, reprint ed., tran. F.L. Pogson (Mineola, NY: Dover, 2001).]

[2] Aquinas, *De veritate*, q. 1, a. 1: "Illud quod primo intellectus concipit quasi notissimum, et in quo omnes conceptiones resolvit est ens."

object of the intellect and thus is the first intelligible, just as what is first perceived by sight is color, by hearing, sound,"[3] and what is perceived by consciousness are the facts of internal experience.

Indeed, intellectual knowledge begins with a very imperfect act which reaches reality only in a very vague manner by considering what is most general in it.[4] Gradually, the intellect distinguishes different realities and their various aspects, and each idea, which at first is vague, progressively becomes distinct and tends toward being expressed in a precise definition. At the terminus of this progress, all intellectual notions, whether vulgar or erudite, necessarily contain an utterly universal notion, namely, that of *being*, just as in every judgment the verb is a nuance of the verb *to be*, and just as all reasoning claims to assign the *raison d'être*, the reason for the *being* of the thing affirmed (or at least the reason for the affirmation of this thing[5]). Likewise, in the end, every conclusion rests upon principles and, in the final analysis, upon the supreme principle, which enunciates that which is first and foremost fitting with regard to *being*, namely, its opposition to non-being: something cannot at one and the same time both be and not be in the same respect.

Whatever reality we try to conceive, it cannot be found *outside of being*. Otherwise, it would be nothing and would in no way be conceivable. It cannot belong to any determinate genus, neither to the mineral kingdom, nor to the plant kingdom, nor to the animal kingdom, nor to humanity. It can be found equally in all these categories and exceeds them all (e.g., the beautiful, order, and perfection), but this will always be at least a modality of being. As traditional philosophy never tires in proclaiming: "Just as the formal object of vision is the colored, the formal and adequate object of the intellect is *being*." In the order of discovery, the first object known by the intellect of the child, adds St. Thomas (with Aristotle) is *the being of sensible things*. At this first awakening of the intellectual faculty, the child does not yet distinguish things into genera and determinate species, and he does not know their

---

[3]   *ST* I, q. 5, a. 2.

[4]   See *ST* I, q. 85, a. 3.

[5]   [Tr. note: In the case of a *quia* demonstration.]

cause. However, he will soon seek out this cause and ask, "Why?"

Thereafter, philosophical reason deepens our grasp of what the adequate object of the natural intellect is. It seeks to determine the meaning of *being*, not only inasmuch as it is substance or accident, bodily or spiritual, created or divine—but, rather, *inasmuch as it is being*. And if the philosopher commits the least error concerning this fundamental notion, all his thought will be invalidated and will form the most unlikely and senseless of theories, *a small error at the beginning becomes great by the end*.[6] To be mistaken, even in a minor way, about the different ways that being pertains to different realities is an error not only regarding a contingent fact but also regarding a foundational necessity that is at the very principle of all things. One is thus necessarily led either to *pantheism*, which identifies God's being with that of the stone, plant, animal, and man, or to *agnosticism*, which holds that God's being is absolutely unknowable, in such a way that we cannot say whether God is an immanent or transcendent cause, whether He is intelligence, providence, justice, and goodness, or whether He is absolutely indifferent to good and to evil.

From this perspective, it is not useless to compare the Thomistic doctrine of being with modern systems that are opposed to it and to each other. In light of this comparison, the thought of St. Thomas, which in the eyes of some represents only a naïve common-sense realism, stands forth in all of its profundity and elevation, wholly different from eclecticism, which seeks out a [*mediocre*] *midpoint* between extreme errors but remains *midway* between these wanderings and the culminating point of truth. The surety of the Thomist doctrine arises above all from the fact that it has formed an exact determination of the fundamental truths of the order of discovery (i.e., the analytic or ascending order) and the supreme truth of the synthetic or descending order that assigns the highest reasons for things.[7]

---

6 Aquinas, *De ente et essentia*, introduction.

7 Cf. *ST* I, q. 79, a. 9: "According to the way of discovery, we arrive at knowledge of eternal things by means of temporal ones, but, in the order of judgment, by eternal things that are now known, we judge concerning temporal things." [Tr. note: One can consult with profit Reginald Garrigou-Lagrange, "On the Twofold *Via inventionis* and the Twofold *Via iudicii* According to St. Thomas," *Philosophizing in Faith: Essays on*

In this chapter, we would like to do the following, from the perspective of Thomistic metaphysics. First, we intend to indicate how the principal forms of modern pantheism and agnosticism are opposed to each other and, also, what notion of being each of them forms for themselves. Second, we intend to show that the Thomist doctrine of the analogy of being is elevated like a golden mean and a summit above these opposed conceptions concerning the fundamental character of reality.

Obviously, this question concerning our intellect's first datum is the crux of the great metaphysical problems. To it are connected the problem of being and becoming, that of the ontological value of the principle of contradiction or identity, that of universals [i.e., the nature of universality], that of the distinction of God and the world, that of the distinction of essence and existence in creatures—fundamental problems whose scope is incalculable. This chapter's goal is to briefly indicate these connections and to show their necessity.

The Notion of Being Held by the Opposed Forms of Modern Pantheism and Agnosticism

From the perspective of traditional metaphysics, it is clear enough that modern pantheism has passed from an ontological form to an evolutionist form (i.e., from a philosophy of *being* to that of *becoming*) by the intermediary of agnosticism under its double empirical and idealistic form.

1) *Spinoza*, following in this the ways of the Eleatics, affirmed that *substantial being is not only univocal*[8] *but, instead, is unique.* According to him, if there were two substances, they would either have or not have the same attributes. In the first case, they would not be distinct, and in

---

the Beginning and End of Wisdom, trans. Matthew K. Minerd (Providence, RI: Cluny Media, 2019), 11–20.]

[8] That is, absolutely alike in all substances.

the second, they would not even resemble each other as substances.[9] In other words, as Parmenides already thought, *being* cannot be diversified by itself but only by something *other* than it. Now, outside of being there is nothing. Therefore, being is one and unique.[10] The multiplicity of substances is an illusory appearance. Instead of sense experience, we must prefer the first principle of reason: "Being is, non-being is not. There is no way to part from this idea."[11]

According to Spinoza, the first object known by our intellect is the Unique and Divine Being, and it is by means of this being that everything becomes intelligible for us, both in the bodily order and in the spiritual. What can our *universal* notions of extension and thought be if not notions of the two fixed and eternal attributes of being (or, of the Unique Substance)?[12] Therefore, in metaphysics we can make use of *the mathematical method, which abstracts from efficient and final causality.* Thus, we can deduce *more geometrico* from the Divine Nature all the necessary truths, the objects[13] of the various sciences. The very existence of God does not need to be proven *a posteriori*. It is the object of the natural intuition of our intellect, which first perceives substantial being and then sees all things in it. We can call this doctrine "pantheistic ontologism." It represents a form of *absolute realism* holding that the universal (e.g., universal being) exists formally with its universality as we conceive it: "Understanding [*intellectus*] involves certitude; that is, it knows the thing so to exist formally speaking [*formaliter*] as it is encountered objectively in it."[14]

And as action follows upon being, if there is only one singular

---

[9] Spinoza, *Ethics*, I, prop. 6.

[10] Concerning Parmenides, see Aristotle, *Metaphysics*, 1.5. Also, see St. Thomas's Commentary, lect. 9.

[11] See the first chapter of this book above.

[12] Benedict de Spinoza, *De emendatione intellectus*, ed. J. van Vloten, vol. 1, p. 31. [Tr. note: The edition is not noted; van Vloten's edition was published in two volumes in 1882–1883, three volumes in 1895, and four volumes in 1914.]

[13] [Tr. note: French reads singular *objet*.]

[14] Spinoza, *De emendatione intellectus*, 32. [Tr. note: One should read the sense of "formally" and "objectively" in a similar manner to what is found in Descartes's *Meditations*. These are denatured uses of the scholastic notion of *esse obiectivum*, and the Suarezian treatment of the distinction between the formal and the objective concept.]

substantial being, there will be only one singular action, one singular activity. Our thought and our willing will only be finite modes of the Divine Intellection and Divine Love. This confusion of Divine causality and created causality is found in Malebranche's occasionalism, just as there is a vestige of pantheistic ontologism in his own ontologism.

Therefore, this form of pantheism is, properly speaking, ontological. It is founded on a certain notion—better yet, on an alleged intuition—of the Unique, Substantial Being. However, in thus starting off from the consideration of God, this pantheism does not succeed at deducing the true world with its finite and imperfect modalities. When one denies the existence of finite substances, their faculties, and their proper activities, this represents, so to speak, the denial of the world itself or the absorption of it into God.

According to this ontologist tendency, Malebranche believed that we see all things in God and thought that God alone acts, as though God alone existed, and as though we needed to take quite literally the words of Meister Eckhart: "All creatures are one pure nothing; I do not say that they are something ordinary or anything, but that they are one pure nothing."[15] According to the same tendency, it would be necessary to hold the Rosminian proposition, "There is no finite reality, but God causes it to exist by adding limitation to infinite reality."[16] Following the logic to its ultimate end, it would even be necessary to return to the pure monism of Parmenides and say, "There is only one single, immutable being. Multiplicity and becoming are a pure illusion. We must prefer the principle of contradiction (or, identity) to experience."

2) Turning now to our second consideration, let us consider how

---

[15] Denzinger, no. 976 (John XXII, *In agro dominico*, no. 26).

[16] Denzinger, no. 3212 (Decree of the Holy Office, *Post obitum*, no. 12.) [Tr. note: Bl. Antonio Rosmini-Serbati (1797–1855) had his work *Delle Cinque Piaghe della Santa Chiesa* placed on the index during his lifetime. After his death, forty propositions taken from his works were condemned. He was later rehabilitated and beatified for his heroic virtue in 2007. Details on his rehabilitation should be interpreted in light of the 2001 decree by then-Cardinal Ratzinger, "Note on the Force of the Doctrinal Decrees concerning the Thought and Work of Fr Antonio Rosmini Serbati," promulgated July 1, 2001. *Rosmini* was rehabilitated, not the conclusions that might be drawn from his works by those who are not careful.]

this ontological form of pantheism is radically opposed by *agnosticism, whether empiricist or idealist.*

Spinoza and the ontologists think that they have by their natural powers an intellectual intuition of the Divine Being and that they see everything in God. As often happens, this obvious exaggeration aroused a reaction that was no less excessive. Agnostics deny every intellectual intuition, even the very imperfect one that is united to abstraction, which St. Thomas calls the simple intellectual apprehension of the being of sensible things—i.e., intellection (*intus legere,* [reading, or seeing, into the depths of being])—immediately followed by the intuition of the first principles of being.[17]

The empirical agnosticism of Hume, John Stuart Mill, and the positivists reduces the idea of *being* to an utterly vague image accompanied by the name "being." Consequently, the first principles of reason and of being are reduced to empirical associations that are often renewed and confirmed by hereditary custom. Without a doubt, these principles are necessary for reasoning and discourse, like laws of grammar; however, they in no way surpass the phenomenal order that is an object of sense experience. For example, the notion of *substance* expresses only a collection of phenomena. Outside these phenomena, substantial being is only a word, a *flatus vocis,* a verbal entity. Likewise, *causality* designates only the succession of phenomena, and the principle of causality therefore cannot enable us to demonstrate the existence of God, the First Transcendent Cause. Moreover, the *syllogism* in general is only a verbal inference without probative force, for its demonstrative value presupposes a major premise that is truly universal. Now, *induction* cannot reach a truly universal principle but only a collection of particular cases, which is verbally designated as something universal. Such is the *absolute nominalism* that is radically opposed to realism or to pantheistic ontologism. Thus, we see the intellectual bent of empiricists or positivists.

The *idealist agnosticism* of Kant and his disciples wishes to recon-

---

[17] See Aquinas, *In III De anima,* ch. 6, lect. 11; *ST* I, q. 85, a. 1; q. 79, a. 8; II-II, q. 8, a. 1. Also, *De veritate,* q. 15, a. 1c and ad 7: "The gaze [*intuitus*] of our intellect is first fixed upon the natures of material things."

cile empiricism and idealism by avoiding the excesses committed by ontologism. Therefore, it reduces the idea of being (or, of reality) to a wholly subjective, though necessary, *mental category*. Thanks to this category and to those of substance, cause, possibility, necessity, etc., we can order the phenomena of external and internal experience and thus come to constitute a subjectively necessary science from these phenomena. Such is *subjectivist conceptualism*: the object of the intellect is no longer extramental being but, instead, is a subjective conception. Consequently, speculative reason cannot demonstrate the existence of God. Spinoza and the ontologists say, "The existence of God doesn't need to be demonstrated; it is the object of intuition." Kant and the positivists deny the very possibility of the demonstration.

3° This agnosticism led, in fact, to an *evolutionist form of pantheism* opposed to the first form of ontologism. By means of the critique of knowledge, modern thought passed from being to becoming.

The transition was brought about above all in the system of Fichte through a critique of Kantianism. According to Fichte, the Kantian doctrine contains an insoluble difficulty in itself: the application of the subjective categories to the external phenomena remains arbitrary and irrational [*sans motif*]. Why apply to a given group of phenomena the category of causality instead of the category of substance? If one responds, "Our intellect perceives in these external phenomena a relation to causality and not to substance," we thus find ourselves returning to the first intellectual apprehension admitted by the scholastics. In order to preserve the principles of subjectivism and to avoid the arbitrary application of the categories, Fichte concluded that we must say that *the phenomena themselves arise from the knowing subject*.

Unconsciously, the knowing subject produces or posits the correlative object, the non-self. This can be understood if one means by "reason," not the intellect of this or that individual but, instead, that of all humanity. This universal reason, according to Fichte, is essentially practical. Progressively, it conceives and realizes the moral order. Gradually, it constitutes the natural law, the civil law, penal law, the sciences, philosophy, and religions. The real and living God is humanity in evolution: "I have a horror of every religious conception that personifies

God," says Fichte,[18] "and I consider it unworthy of a rational being."

Evolutionist pantheism thus proceeds from agnosticism, for the principle for explaining phenomena no longer can be sought in a transcendent order. We must find it in ourselves, in our consciousness or subconscious, which progressively passes from spontaneous and vague knowledge to complex and distinct knowledge as well as to increasingly extensive moral and social activity. This "creative evolution" is its own self-justifying reason and has no need for a superior cause.

This evolutionist pantheism was given precision by Hegel, who held that the progress of mind [esprit] and of ideas is the exemplar and Cause of all things according to the axiom: "All that is real is rational." At the principle of all things, we must admit that there is the *ideal and universal* (or, indefinite) being that constitutes, by determining itself, the whole of things into which genera, species, and individuals are distinguished. This represents the last form of pantheism condemned by Vatican I.[19] In it, the world becomes God according to an ascending evolution, while in immanentism[20] and according to Spinoza, God is the one who becomes the world in manifesting Himself.

Pantheistic evolutionism is often proposed today in an empiricist form. Henri Bergson, in his *Creative Evolution*, writes, "*God* has nothing of the ready-made; he is incessant life, action, and freedom. . . . Vital activity *is a reality that makes itself* through that which unmakes itself."[21] God is evolution that is self-creative, a claim that is proven by renewing Heraclitus's arguments,[22] just as Spinoza similarly renewed those of Parmenides.

---

18 [Tr. note: This citation is unmarked in Fr. Garrigou-Lagrange's text. It may have been taken second-hand from a history of philosophy by Alfred Fouillée. This same text was cited by another Dominican in the late 19th century in A. Villard, "Nature du premier principe," *Revue Thomiste* 3 (1895): 372–395 (see 384). See Alfred Fouillée, *Histoire de la philosophie*, 9th ed. (Paris: Delagrave, 1901), 441–442. Fr. Garrigou-Lagrange engages with Fichte's thought at greater length in *God: His Existence and His Nature* and *De revelatione*. The latter text is to be published by Emmaus Academic in the near future.]

19 See Denzinger, no. 3024 (*Dei Filius* canon 1.4.)

20 [Tr. note: The text reads "emanentism," though its sense is that of *immanentism*.]

21 Henri Bergson, Évolution créatrice, 2nd ed., 270 and 269.

22 See ibid., 341–342. Also, see the third chapter of the first part of this book above.

The ontological form of pantheism that is based on the consideration of the perfect being (or, God) tends to deny the world. On the contrary, the evolutionist form of pantheism, basing itself on the consideration of the world or upon our consciousness, tends toward atheism or to the absorption of God into the world. If the whole of reality is ascending evolution, "God does not exist . . . yet," as Renan said.

Already, in this opposition of forms of pantheism, the absurdity of the pantheistic confusion is clear. This identification of God and the world is not conceivable. It is either the denial of the world or the denial of God. It passes from the first form to the second by way of the intermediary of agnosticism, as the history of modern philosophy shows us. These three conceptions, set in opposition to each other, already mutually refute each other. However, let us see more precisely what each one holds as its fundamental notion of being, which amounts to looking into what is, from the perpective of traditional metaphysics, the foundation—or, if one wishes, the radical vice—of these conceptions.

* * *

Generally, extreme errors that are opposed to one another arise from the same misunderstanding or from the denial of the same truth. In the case at hand, we are confronted with systems that misunderstand the analogy of being.

1) As discussed earlier, the foundation of *ontological pantheism* is *absolute realism*: universal substantial being exists formally with its universality, just as it is conceived. Spinoza affirmed this very clearly when he spoke of the clear idea of substance and of the distinct ideas of thought and extension that (according to him) immediately express the fixed and eternal attributes of God and are universal truths for our knowledge.[23]

---

[23] Spinoza, *De intellectus emendatione*, 31–32: "Understanding [*intellectus*] involves certitude; that is, it knows the thing so to exist formally speaking [*formaliter*] as it is encountered objectively in it." He speaks thus not of confused ideas but of clear and distinct ideas, which, according to him, represent something of the fixed and eternal: "These fixed and eternal things, although they are singular things, neverthe-

From this absolute realism, it necessarily follows that *not only is being univocal; it is unique*, as whiteness would be unique if the universal *whiteness* were to exist formally with its universality (i.e., as it is conceived). In this doctrine, the principle of contradiction (or, identity) not only has an ontological value but also excludes the multiplicity of beings. They become an empty appearance, as Parmenides said.

And it is not astonishing that from this absolute realism in relation to substantial being Spinoza would conclude that nominalism holds for the notions of genera and species. According to absolute realism, only one substance, God's substance, can in fact exist. Other substances— those of stones, animals, and men—can thenceforth be only vague images and names (verbal entities) that express collections of phenomena.[24] Likewise, the faculties of the soul are only a *flatus vocis*. There is only a single, solitary substance with multiple and variable modes.

2) Turning now to our second general category, what is the foundation of *empiricist agnosticism* as well as that of *idealist agnosticism*? Obviously, on the one hand it is a form of *nominalism* and, on the other hand, a form of *subjectivist conceptualism* inasmuch as the notion of being is reduced either to a very vague image accompanied by a common name or to a subjective category. Consequently, empiricist agnosticism reduces the principle of contradiction to a *grammatical convention* needed for language. Contradiction is only opposed to our customary manner of speaking, though it can perhaps exist in things [in their extramental reality]. This is what John Stuart Mill precisely affirmed,[25] as did

---

less, on account of their ubiquitous presence and most extensive power, will be to us as universals, or genera of definitions of mutable singular things, and first causes of all things."

24 See Spinoza, *Ethics*, pt. 2, prop. 40, schol. 1; prop. 49, schol.

25 John Stuart Mill, *A System of Logic Ratiocinative and Inductive, Being a Connected View of the Principles of Evidence and the Methods of Scientific Investigation (Books I–III)*, *The Collected Works of John Stuart Mill*, vol. 7, ed. John M. Robson (Toronto: University of Toronto Press, London: Routledge and Kegan Paul, 1974), bk. 3, ch. 5, §3 (p. 334–335): "In most cases of causation a distinction is commonly drawn between something which acts, and some other thing which is acted upon; between an agent and a patient. Both of these, it would be universally allowed, are conditions of the phenomenon; but it would be thought *absurd* to call the latter the cause, that title being reserved for the former. The distinction, however, vanishes on examination, *or rather is found to be only verbal*; arising from an incident of mere expression, namely,

Édouard Le Roy after him.[26] For idealist agnosticism, the principle of contradiction is only a *logical law*, or at the very least, its ontological value remains in doubt.

From this nominalism or subjective conceptualism, it follows that *being is equivocal*, at least for us, for besides phenomenon-level likenesses we know only verbal or purely conceptual likeness, not real ones. For example, making abstraction from phenomena, substance is a verbal entity or a purely subjective category. Consequently, two substances—again making abstraction from their phenomena—cannot have a real likeness (whether specific, generic, or analogical). They can only have a verbal likeness or, as the scholastics say, an equivocal likeness. Therefore, the notion of being does not designate anything really similar in the different beings any more than does the name "dog" when attributed to the domestic animal as well as to the "dog star" in the constellation *canis major*.

Once this position is accepted, God is unknowable, and His existence cannot be demonstrated. If a First, Infinitely Perfect Cause does exist, Its Being and that of finite beings are *equivocal*. The meaning of the word "being" is *totally* different in the two cases. In our knowledge of God, whether it be natural or founded on revelation, insoluble antinomies inevitably arise. This knowledge can be only symbolic, i.e., metaphoric, just as much when we say that God is just as when we say that He is annoyed [*irrité*].[27]

---

that the object said to be *acted upon*, and which is considered as the scene in which the effect takes place, is commonly included in the phrase by which the effect is spoken of, so that if it were also reckoned as part of the cause, the seeming incongruity would arise of its being supposed to cause itself."

26 Édouard Le Roy, "Sur la logique de l'invention," *Revue de métaphysique et morale* 13 (1905): 200 and 204: "The principle of non-contradiction [*sic*] is not as universal and necessary as it is believed to be. It has its domain of application and has its restricted, limited meaning. *As the ultimate law of discourse and not of thought in general, it holds only for the static*, the fragmented, the immobile—in brief, it holds for things endowed with an *identity. However, there is contradiction in the world*, as there is identity. It is made up of fleeting mobilities—becoming, duration, life—which by themselves are not discursive and are transformed by discourse in order to grasp them in contradictory schemata."

27 In the Middle Ages Maimonides (Rabbi Moses) spoke along these lines, wishing not to say, "God is being; God is good," but only, "God is the cause of the being [*l'en-*

3) What becomes of the notion of being in *evolutionist pantheism*, above all such as we find it in Hegel?

In a sense, Hegel agrees with the ancient *nominalism* of Heraclitus—and he says so himself. He does so by denying the real value of the notion of being opposed to that of non-being as well as the ontological value of the principle of contradiction (or, identity). Like the nominalists, he says that this principle is only a grammatical law necessary for language and a law of the inferior sort of logic (i.e., of discursive reasoning). It is not a principle of the superior sort of logic. Nor is it a law of reality, for reality is never identical with itself. It perpetually evolves, as Heraclitus says.

This comes down to saying that being, in opposition to nothingness, is only an equivocal term, a *flatus vocis*. In other words, according to Hegel, being and non-being are only verbally opposed to each other and are really identical in universal becoming, which is self-justifying. Consequently, there is no absolute truth but only relative truths, according to the current state of science. What the learned consider today as being true will be rejected tomorrow. Every thesis is followed by an antithesis. Together, they contribute to a superior synthesis. . . . and so on in the evolution of art, religion, and science. Thus, as the modernists said, that which is true for faith can be false for science.

Having accepted this universal becoming, all individuals can be only moments in the general flux of evolution. Thus, we once again have a form of *absolute realism* through the denial of individual substances, as though different men were only modes or transitory manifestations of universal humanity in perpetual evolution.

Thus, the opposed forms of pantheism touch each other as the extremes meet. Spinoza bases himself on the absolute realism of substantial being and is led to nominalism for the vague notions of genera and species. By contrast, Hegel in a sense bases himself on a form of nominalism in relation to being's opposition to non-being and is led to evolutionist realism for genera and species in evolution. If this still represents an abso-

---

tité] and goodness of things." See Aquinas *ST* I, q. 13, a. 2 and *De potentia*, q. 7, a. 7: "Certain people said that nothing is predicated analogically of God and creatures but, instead that everything is predicated of Him in a *purely equivocal manner*. Rabbi Moses was of this opinion, as is obvious in his own words."

lute realism of the intellect, becoming is substituted for being.

Therefore, these three opposed systems—ontologist pantheism, evolutionist pantheism, and agnosticism—proceed from a given notion of universal being.

According to ontologist pantheism, universal substantial being exists formally with its universality outside of the mind. Consequently, it is *univocal and, even, unique.*—According to evolutionist pantheism and agnosticism, universal being set in opposition to non-being is only an *equivocal* term or concept without real value. One must substitute for it a becoming which is its own self-justifying reason.

These extreme positions, themselves opposed to each other, all proceed from the same misunderstanding: they misunderstand the true notion of universal being. According to St. Thomas, this notion is expressed thus: the universal exists *formally* as a universal only in the intellect but has its foundation in the realities whose *real likenesses* it expresses; the notion of being expresses a real likeness, though it is only *analogical* in character. This is the thesis of moderate realism as it is applied to the fundamental notion of being and to the principle of contradiction (or, identity), set at equal distance from nominalism and subjectivist conceptualism, on the one hand, and from the excesses of absolute realism, which necessarily confuses the human intellect with that of God, on the other.

The Foundations of the Thomist Doctrine of the Analogy of Being, along with Its Relations with Opposed Systems

This doctrine, already formulated by Aristotle, is not constituted in an arbitrary manner like an eclectic *mélanges* made up of two extremes to be avoided. Rather, it stands forth like a summit above these extremes, founded on the principle of contradiction and the most certain facts of experience. In other words, it rests on the first truths of the order of discovery.

Indeed, if we consider, in the light of the principle of contradiction (or, identity), the multiplicity of beings that are the objects of experience, it is quite clear that being is neither equivocal nor univocal but, instead, is analogous.

1. The Principle of Contradiction (or, Identity) Excludes the Equivocity of Being

This principle is formulated by Aristotle from the logical perspective: "One cannot affirm and deny at one and the same time the same predicate of the same subject from the same perspective." Ontologically, this principle is expressed: "It is impossible that one and the same thing both be and not be at one and the same time." More briefly: "Being is not non-being"; or, in an affirmative form, "Being is being; non-being is non-being; they cannot be confused." Spiritual authors say the same, "Good is good; evil is evil; flesh is flesh; spirit is spirit; let us not confuse them."—Our Savior said, "*Est est, non non.* [Let your yes be your yes and your no be your no.]"

In the fourth book of the *Metaphysics*, Aristotle defends the real value of this principle against the Sophists ([who indeed are] nominalists and conceptualists) and against the absolute evolutionism of Heraclitus, which came to be renewed much later by Hegel.

Despite all the efforts of sophistical reasoning, this first intellectual evidence abides: that which is *obviously absurd* (like a square-circle) is not only *inconceivable* but also is *unrealizable*, even for the Infinite Omnipotence. This intellectual evidence, which exceeds [sense] experience, produces an absolute certitude in our intellect, one that is firmer and more dazzling than the hardness and brilliance of a diamond. Descartes thoughtlessly said, "Perhaps God can make a square circle." However, this doubt was not in Descartes's intellect as an intimate persuasion; it was only a sophistical play of images and words.—If thousands of people came to us to say that they have seen square-circles or that perhaps they exist in unknown nebulae, our intellect would respond with the most absolute certitude: "That is not only inconceivable for us. It is really impossible in itself."

Thus, the principle of contradiction stands before us with the greatest evidence not only as a grammatical convention or as a logical and subjective law of reason, or as a law of real phenomena but, instead, as an ontological and most universal law of reality, whatever it may be. It expresses a real, fundamental impossibility.

This indemonstrable principle is first, and according to Aristotle,[28] all the others are founded upon it, at least in the sense that one can demonstrate them indirectly by way of absurdity. Thus, against the claims raised by skeptics, we can defend the principles of *raison d'être*, of efficient causality, finality, substance, and change.

This foremost intellectual evidence of the real value of the principle of contradiction presupposes that *the notion of being is not equivocal* but, instead, that it has an objective value and represents *something positive and really similar* in different beings and *is opposed to non-being*. Indeed, the principle of contradiction is founded on the notion of being viewed in its opposition to non-being. If the word "being" were equivocal and signified a purely verbal or conceptual *non-real likeness,* the principle of contradiction thus founded would not self-evidently be a law of reality but would only be a law of reason and language. In other words, if the most universal term *being* were equivocally attributed to different realities akin to how that of "dog" is applied to a domestic animal and to the star Sirius in the constellation *Canis major* (i.e., the "dog star"), there would be no real likeness between different beings, not even that of opposition to non-being, and consequently some being could be identical to pure and simple nothingness. Something could be true according to faith and false according to science, as the Averroists said and, after them, the modernists—something which is, however, absurdity itself.

Therefore, being most certainly is not equivocal, for without any doubt we must affirm the ontological value of the principle of non-contradiction, against the assertions of empiricist or idealist agnosticism, as well as against evolutionist pantheism. Most firmly, we must say with Parmenides, "Being is being; non-being is non-being; they must not be confused; *est est, non non.*" This absolutely primary intellectual evidence has an infinite extension according to the full latitude of being, whether actual or possible. Expressing itself with metaphysical evidence, it absolutely surpasses experience, although it arises from it materially by the

---

[28] Aristotle, *Metaphysics*, 4.3.

abstraction of the notions of being and identity. Therefore, the principle of contradiction excludes the equivocity of being.

2. Experience Itself Is What Forbids Us from Affirming That Being Is Univocal

Indeed, we cannot join Parmenides in denying the value of experience in order to safeguard the principle of contradiction (or, identity). We cannot proclaim that the change and multiplicity that we experience in beings are illusory.

Moreover, far from being contrary to experience, the principle of contradiction clarifies it from on high. Under the light of this first principle of reason, the multiplicity and mutability of beings manifestly excludes the univocity of being.

Stones, plants, animals, men, as well as variable phenomena in them, all certainly exist. This multiplicity and this mutability would be impossible *if being were univocal* (i.e., *if it signified one, absolutely similar formality in all things*). Indeed, if this were truly the case, being would be diversified like a genus by *extrinsic* differences, as animality has rationality as an extrinsic difference. Now, it is inconceivable for there to be a difference that is extrinsic to being, for outside of being there is only nothing, as Parmenides justly said. *Therefore, if being were univocal* (like a genus), *it would, at the same time, be unique.* And, Spinoza, in virtue of his absolute realism, should have concluded like Parmenides: all multiplicity (not only substantial multiplicity but also accidental or modal multiplicity) and all change are an empty illusion. As St. Thomas profoundly noted, "Parmenides was deceived in this because he used being as though it were *a single notion and a single nature*, as is the nature of a genus. This is impossible, for being is not a genus but, instead, *is said in many ways about different things.*"[29]

Hence, it follows that the principle of contradiction excludes an

---

[29] Aquinas, *In I Meta.* ch. 5, lect. 9: "In hoc decipiebatur Parmenides, quia utebatur ente quasi *una ratione* et *una natura*, sicut est natura generis. Hoc est enim impossibile. Ens enim non est genus, set *multipliciter dicitur de diversis.*"

equivocal notion of being, and experience excludes a univocal notion of it.[30]

3. Finally, the Analogy of Being Imposes Itself as the Only Middle Way between These Extremes

In the end, the analogy of being imposes itself as the only conceivable middle between equivocation and univocation, which are both equally impossible. Aristotle[31] and St. Thomas[32] often teach it: being is said of different realities *analogically*. In all of them, it designates *something real and proportionally similar*. Thus, the term *knowledge* signifies in sensation and intellection something real and proportionally similar: what sensation is to the sensible, intellection is to the intelligible. Both of them are called knowledge in *a proper*, and not merely metaphorical, sense without it being the case that knowledge is *one* after the manner of a genus but, instead, is one in virtue of a real *proportional likeness*. Despite the generic diversity of the sensible and the intelligible, the term *knowledge* is applied in the two cases in a proper sense.

---

[30] The scholastic generally says "*univocitas*," though we would say in English "*univocation*," the character of that which is univocal (i.e., of that which designates numerous distinct objects, though of the same kind). This is opposed to *an equivocal term*, which has two different senses.

[31] See Aristotle, *Categories*, ch. 1; *Posterior Analytics*, 2.13–14; *Metaphysics*, 3.3, 4.1, 10.1, and 12.4; *Nicomachean Ethics*, 1.6.

[32] Aquinas, *ST* I, q. 13, a. 5; *De potentia*, q. 7, a. 7; *De veritate*, q. 2, a. 11; q. 3, a.1, ad 7; q. 23, a. 7, ad 9. Also, see Tommaso de Vio Cajetan, *The Analogy of Names, and the Concept of Being*, trans. Edward A. Bushinski and Henry J. Koren (Eugene, OR: Wipf and Stock, 2009), esp. c.4 and 6, as well as *The Concept of* Being. John of St. Thomas, *The Material Logic of John of St. Thomas*, trans. Yves R. Simon, John J. Glanville, G. Donald Hollenhorst (Chicago: University of Chicago, 1955), q.13, a.5 (p. 167–183). Also, we have treated this question of the analogy of being at length in Reginald Garrigou-Lagrange, *God: His Existence and His Nature*, vol. 2, 203–267. Also, see the excellent work of M. T.-L. Penido, *Le role de l'analogie en théologie dogmatique*, Bibliothèque thomist, vol.15 (Paris: Vrin, 1931), ch. 1.
  [Tr. note: Fr. Garrigou-Lagrange also cites "Quodlibet 10, 17, 1". The most likely candidate seems to be *Quod.* I, q.10, a.2, ad 1. Cf. George P. Klubertanz, *St. Thomas Aquinas on Analogy: A Textual Analysis and Systematic Synthesis*, 268–270. Note that Klubertanz himself has Quod. I q.10 a.22 ad 1. Also, note more generally that Klubertanz's systematic position differs from Fr. Garrigou-Lagrange.]

Likewise, the term *being properly* but *diversely* signifies contingent beings and their *accidents*: e.g., man is a being; his color is also a reality; however, man exists in himself, and color exists in him. Substance has *its being* in itself. Proportionally, an accident has *its own being*, though in a subject to which it belongs. Therefore, the term *being* designates in it a formality that is not purely and simply the same or similar but, instead, is proportionally the same—*ens significat in substantia et accidente rationem non simpliciter sed proportionaliter eamdem*. [In substance and accident, *being* signifies a meaning that is not *simpliciter* the same but, instead, is *proportionally* so.]

Contingent beings, which are generated and then succumb to corruption, cannot have their existence by means of themselves; in them, existence is an attribute that is not essential but, instead, contingent. Consequently, according to the principle of causality, which rests on that of contradiction (or, identity), contingent beings depend upon Necessary Being, which *is* Its own existence instead of *having* existence and in whom the principle of identity is verified in the purest manner. It is absolute simplicity and immutability: "I am He Who Is" (Exod 3:14).

This is why created beings are separated from the Uncreated One by an infinite distance. As St. Thomas says in *ST* I, q. 13, a. 5: "Every effect that is not equal to the power of the efficient cause receives the likeness of the agent *not according to the same notion [ratione]* but in a lesser manner." Being designates in God and in the creature a perfection that is not purely and simply the same but, instead, is proportionally the same (*non simpliciter eadem, sed proportionaliter eadem*). The Holy Doctor makes this point clear in *De veritate* q. 2, a. 11: "Between God and creatures there is a similitude of two proportions . . . as sight is said of bodily sight and of the intellect, meaning that sight is to the eye what understanding is to the intellect." Likewise, in *De veritate* q. 23, a. 7, ad 9, he says, "Although the finite and the Infinite cannot be proportioned (*proportionata*), they can however be proportional (*proportionabilia*) . . ., for God is to His attributes as the creature is to its attributes." For example, the Necessary Being has Its own Uncaused Existence just as the contingent being has its own caused existence. In the two cases, *being* is taken according to its *proper*, and not solely metaphorical, sense; however, it signifies something proportionally similar in God and in the creature. Thus, we say that intellection and sensation are *properly* called knowledge inasmuch as the first pertains to the intelligible and the second to the sensible. Knowledge is not a genus (purely and simply the same) of which intellection and sensation would be species. Being is not a genus which would have the necessary and the contingent as extrinsic differences differentiating it into species. Nothing is extrinsic to being.[33]

Such is the authentic doctrine of St. Thomas concerning the analogy of proportionality. We have shown elsewhere how it differs from that of Scotus and that of Suarez.[34]

Therefore, being is analogous and designates, according to its *proper* sense, something *real* and *proportionally similar* in Necessary

---

[33] Cf. *ST* I, q. 3, a. 5.

[34] See Reginald Garrigou-Lagrange, *God: His Existence and His Nature*, 246–267. For Suarez, analogates should be defined, "Those things having a common name, though the meaning [*ratio*] signified by the name is *simpliciter* the same and *secundum quid* diverse." By contrast, the Thomists say, "*secundum quid* the same and *simpliciter* diverse." Hence, for Suarez as for Scotus, being inasmuch as it is being is not essentially varied, designating in God and in the creature a perfection that is *simplicter* the same, thus leading one to hold that there no longer is a real distinction between essence and existence in the creature, something that is also the case in God. As we have shown in the work cited above, this Suarezian conception of analogy runs into the difficulties encountered by the univocity of being. If being inasmuch as it is being is *simpliciter unum*, it can only be diversified by differences that are *extrinsic* to it. However, nothing is extrinsic to being. Thus, we find it necessary to return to the position of Parmenides and deny the existence of the many. This can be seen in the first sixteen condemned Rosminian propositions. See Denzinger, no. 3201. (Decree of the Holy Office, *Post obitum*, no. 1.)

Already, *animality*, which is a *univocal* notion, is *simpliciter the same* and *secundum quid* diverse in man and the earthworm. In both cases, it designates the presence of sense life. It is clear that much more profound dissimilitude is encountered between the existence of the Necessary Being and the existence of a contingent being.

Furthermore, one cannot avoid rendering a judgment between Suarez and St. Thomas by avoiding the use of the word *simpliciter* and, instead, saying "*secundum quid* the same and *secundum quid* diverse." Here, one would have only a nominal definition which would not make the *essence* of analogy known. This would be like trying to distinguish a venial sin from an imperfect good act by wishing to avoid saying that venial sin is *simpliciter* evil. It would not be enough to affirm that it is an evil from one point of view (i.e., *secundum quid*). See J. M. Ramírez, "De analogia secundum doctrinam Aristotelico-Thomisticam," *La ciencia tomista* 24 (1921): 20–40, 195–214, 337–357; 25 (1922): 17–38.

Being, contingent being, and in the accidents of the latter.

In this way, we are able to rule out *pantheism*, for the transcendence of the Necessary Being is thus maintained. As the Fourth Lateran Council held, "Between Creator and creature no similitude can be expressed without implying a greater dissimilitude."[35] God is sovereignly simple and immutable Self-subsistent Existence distinct from the composite and changing world and from every being that has existence without being existence itself.[36]

Agnosticism is ruled out by the same doctrine of analogy: God is knowable not only in a metaphorical or symbolic way but, rather, according to the *proper* sense of the terms that express absolute (*simpliciter simplices*) perfections, in virtue of the proper proportionality that exists between the Uncreated Being and created being, between Divine Wisdom and human wisdom, just as the proper proportionality that exists between our intellection and our sensation enables us to call both of them *forms of knowledge* [*connaissances*] in a proper sense. Yes, we speak metaphorically when we say that God is *irritated*, since anger is a passion of the sensibility. However, this does not mean that

---

[35] Denzinger, no. 806: "Inter Creatorem et creaturam non potest tanta similitude notari quin inter eos maior sit dissimilitudo notanda." It is difficult to reconcile the Suarezian definition of analogy with this conciliar declaration, for the former holds that the analogous perfection is *simpliciter* the same and *secundum quid* diverse in God and in creatures. In this case, the similitude would be greater than the dissimilitude.

[36] Recently, it has been said that if God personally united Himself to the individual nature of different men, as the Word assumed the human nature of Christ, then some form of pantheism would be realized, analogous to Spinozism and which was not refuted by St. Thomas. See the article on pantheism in column 1326 of the *Dictionnaire Apologétique de la Foi catholique*.

It is clear that the hypothesis of which one has spoken has not been realized, for men would thus be incapable of sin whereas, in fact, they are sinners. However, even if this were the case, this would in no way be a form of pantheism, for on this hypothesis, individual human natures would, without any *confusion* with the Divine Nature, be freely created and freely assumed by God as was the human nature of Christ. Moreover, this hypothesis differs absolutely from Spinozism, which holds that God necessarily creates or produces His finite modes, a point that St. Thomas refuted in advance on many occasions. See *ST* I, q. 3, aa. 6 and 8; q. 9, a. 1; q. 19, aa. 3 and 4, etc.

Whatever the same article may say (cf. col. 1327), it is clear that Hegel (precisely because he denies the existence of the Self-Subsistent Being, always absolutely *identical* to itself, and posits in its place a *becoming* that is its own self-sufficient reason) came to deny the ontological value of the principle of contradiction (or, identity).

we speak in metaphor when we say that He is Wisdom Itself, for in this case we are faced with an absolute perfection which implies no imperfection.

These two consequences of the analogy of being contrary to pantheism and agnosticism are founded, like analogy itself, upon the principle of contradiction (or, identity) and upon the most certain experience that assures us of the many and of becoming. Therefore, they rest upon fundamental truths of the order of discovery. At first, these initial truths seem to be opposed to each other. How can we reconcile the many and becoming affirmed by experience with the identity affirmed by reason in its first principle? This represents the great metaphysical problem posed from the time of Parmenides and Heraclitus.

The doctrine of analogy, combined with the distinction of potency and act, resolves the question. It reconciles the initial truths of philosophy and leads to the ultimate truth of the natural order: "God alone is His own existence; in Him alone are essence and existence identical." *Ego sum qui sum.*

This truth is fundamental, no longer in the order of discovery, which is analytical and ascending, but, as St. Thomas says, *in via iudicii,*[37] in the synthetic and descending order that assigns the supreme reasons for doctrinal judgment concerning all things. It represents the response to philosophy's last question concerning God and the world: "Why is there only one Uncreated Being that is Immutable, Infinite, Absolutely Perfect, Sovereignly Good, Omniscient, Freely Creating (etc.)? Why must all other beings receive from Him everything that they are and why must they await to receive from Him everything that they must be?" This is because God is Self-Subsistent Existence and because in Him alone are essence, existence, and act identical.

Such is the purest and loftiest verification of the principle of contradiction (or, identity), the first law of our thought, which appears to us no longer as a grammatical convention, nor as a simply logical law or

---

[37] See *ST* I, q. 79, a. 9. Cf. Norbert del Prado, *De veritate fundamentali philosophiae christianae* (Fribourg: 1911), xliv: "Although it is not first *in the way of discovery,* nevertheless once this is known, the particular truths of Christian Philosophy spring up and flow forth; hereafter, the first truth *in the way of judging,* thus among the higher causes of scientific cognition, it appears as holding the highest place."

phenomenal and experiential law, but as the absolutely necessary and ontological law of all reality—indeed, much more, as the most universal and supreme law of being. This is why he who profoundly understands all the virtuality (or, scope) of this principle would see, immediately under its light, in the mirror of sensible things, the existence of God, Who is absolutely simple and immutable and, therefore, really and essentially distinct from the composite and changing world. Indeed, it is clear that created beings in their multiplicity and variability do not exist by way of themselves. Therefore, their existence requires a cause and, in the last analysis, an absolutely simple and immutable Cause: Being Itself, infinitely superior to that which is multiple, composite, and changing in the bodily and spiritual order.

In other words, if the principle of contradiction (or, identity) is the most universal and fundamental law of all reality, the essence, existence, and all the attributes of the supreme reality must be purely and absolutely identical. The First Being necessarily must be Being Itself, Truth, Goodness, Wisdom, and Love. It must always be absolutely *identical* to Itself, at the antipode from *becoming* or the creative evolution dreamed of by absolute evolutionism. "In God, everything *is* one where there is no opposition of relationship."[38] In God there is no real distinction except between the mutually-opposed Trinitarian relations, which we can only know through Revelation. By this, pantheism and agnosticism are defeated at one and the same time, both of which misunderstand (in opposite ways) the true notion of the analogy of being.

Thus understood, this Thomist doctrine of analogical being, founded on the principle of contradiction and on experience, stands forth like a metaphysical summit above these mutually opposed extreme errors, a summit also above eclecticism, which juxtaposes, for better or worse, the various aspects of reality without reconciling them. This lofty doctrine is thus like the keystone of general metaphysics and, through it, we can see why and how in traditional philosophy the supreme truth of the synthetic order corresponds to the fundamental

---

[38] Council of Florence, *Cantate domino* (Denzinger, no. 1330): "These three Persons are one God, not three gods, because there is one substance of the three, one essence, one nature, one Godhead, one immensity, one eternity, and everything <in them> *is* one where there is no opposition of relationship."

truth of the analytic order (or, the way of discovery), namely, to the principle of identity.

In this way, we have a kind of verification of Leo XIII's words in the encyclical *Aeterni patris*:

> The Angelic Doctor pushed his philosophic inquiry into the reasons and principles of things, which because they are most comprehensive and contain in their bosom, so to say, the seeds of almost infinite truths, were to be unfolded in good time by later masters and with a goodly yield.[39]

This is why Pius X added in his Motu proprio *Doctoris Angelici*:

> Those points that are capital theses in St. Thomas's philosophy ought not to be held as being in the general category of opinions concerning which one may dispute about either side of the matter but, instead, are to be held as being the foundations upon which all knowledge [*scientia*] of natural and Divine things is based.

Among these foundations, we obviously must count the metaphysical conception of being in general and the doctrine of analogy, according to which it is attributed to God and to creatures.

In this way, we grasp better the finality of our intellect and how it passes from the known to the unknown, how it rises upward from the principle of contradiction (or, identity), the first truth of the order of discovery, to that Ultimate Truth: God alone is Being Itself, *Ego sum qui sum*.

---

[39] Leo XIII, *Aeterni patris*, no. 18. [Tr. note: Text taken from official Vatican translation.]

Chapter Four

The Proper Order for Teaching the Philosophical Sciences

The question of our intellect's finality, as well as the first object that it knows, leads us to speak about the fitting order for proposing the various parts of philosophy (or, better yet, the different philosophical sciences) in order that we may be faithful to the doctrine and method of Aristotle and St. Thomas. Above all, the question is posed in order that we may know where to situate general metaphysics. Should it be placed before or after natural philosophy? We also must ask this question regarding the place for logic and the critique of knowledge.

As is well known, up to the 18th century (more precisely, up to Christian Wolff)[1] all scholastics[2] distinguished natural philosophy and metaphysics as being two sciences, natural philosophy having *ens mobile* as its object (according to the first degree of abstraction) and metaphysics having *ens in quantum ens* as its object (according to the third degree of abstraction).[3] And all the disciples of Aristotle, like their master, right after logic, exposited general natural philosophy (i.e., the Aristotelian *Physics*), then the specific branches of natural philosophy that are found in the treatises *On the Heavens and Earth, On Generation and Corruption,* and *On the Soul,* the last of which is devoted to a study of the soul united to a body. At the end of the studies undertaken in psychology (i.e., *On the Soul*), the study of νοῦς (i.e., of the intellect), having being as its object, served for

---

[1] [Tr. note: Christian Wolff (1679–1754) was an influential German scholastic, playing an important pedagogical role in the development of philosophical thought during the time between Gottfried Wilhelm Leibniz (1646–1716) and Immanuel Kant (1724–1804). Along with other German scholastics such as Baumgarten, Knutzen, Mendelssohn, and others, Wolff's systematic scholasticism played an incredibly important role in forming the thought of Kant, whose philosophy is only partially understood unless one understands his own place as a thinker in the tradition of this German scholasticism. There were many aspects of the Wolffian curriculum that insinuated themselves into Catholic thinkers, whether Suarezian or Thomist. Indeed, even in Fr. Garrigou-Lagrange's *language,* we can at times find resonances of the older curriculum that would call natural philosophy by the name "cosmology." Likewise, the distinction between "general ontology / metaphysics" and "special ontology / metaphysics" shows the background vocabulary involved. It is unfair, however, to follow thinkers like Gilson in accusing Garrigou-Lagrange of a covert Wolffianism. On this topic, see Ralph McInerny, *Praeambula Fidei: Thomism and the God of the Philosophers* (Washington, DC: Catholic University of America Press, 2006), 121–125. Also, see Matthew Levering, *Proofs of God: Classical Arguments from Tertullian to Barth* (Grand Rapids, MI: Baker Academic, 2016), 182n202. Finally see the texts cited above in note 5 of pt. 1, ch. 2 above.]

[2] [Tr. note: This likely overstates the historical facts. Even as early as the 14th century, one can find Dominicans like Hervaeus Natalis (c.1250/60–1323) fighting thinkers whose positions would risk reducing all of philosophy to metaphysics.]

[3] [Tr. note: The theory of the degrees of abstraction has sometimes been pilloried as being a kind of nominalist accretion to Thomism. However, as Maritain well shows throughout many of his works (above all *Degrees of Knowledge*), the distinction merely derives from the three generic divisions that one finds between the changing as such, the quantified as such, and being as such. A lucid précis of these points can be found in Jacques Maritain, *The Philosophy of Nature,* trans. Imelda C. Byrne (New York: The Philosophical Library, 1951), 12–31.]

providing a transition to the *Metaphysics*, the supreme science (or, indeed, wisdom).

Only then, after the study of sensible being, did one address what pertains to being inasmuch as it is being. Metaphysics first discussed its *cognoscibility*, providing the critique of knowledge (above all, the critique of intellectual knowledge) and the defense of the real (i.e., ontological) value of the first rational principles, notably that of contradiction, as is set forth in the fourth book of Aristotle's *Metaphysics*.

As can be seen in the very order of this same work, the study of being inasmuch as it is being would come next, considering being in itself and its divisions into substance and accident, as well as into potency and act.

From there, one would rise to God, through the proof of His existence and His principal attributes, which are discussed by Aristotle in the twelfth book of the *Metaphysics*.

Finally, one would address matters pertaining to practical philosophy, which included ethics, economics [i.e., household governance], and politics.

Such was the order according to which the different parts of philosophy were proposed and it was held that logic, natural philosophy, mathematics, metaphysics, and ethics are distinct sciences, having their distinction founded upon their formal object *quo* and *quod*.[4]

---

4   [Tr. note: To understand this distinction, which plays an important role in many philosophical and theological domains, a brief statement from Fr. Garrigou-Lagrange's student Austin Woodbury will suffice here. See Austin Woodbury, *Natural Philosophy—Psychology*, The John N. Deely and Anthony Russell Collection, St. Vincent College, Latrobe, PA, 756 (n.902): "That which is the OBJECT of some cognoscitive power may be considered AS IT IS A THING in itself absolutely: and then is had the MATERIAL OBJECT. Or it may be considered relatively, or AS IT IS AN OBJECT OF, the cognoscitive power, i.e., AS IT IS AN OBJECTED THING. But then it may be considered either AS IT IS OBJECTED, or according to that form which is the reason why it be manifested to the power: and this is the FORMAL REASON WHEREUNDER (or formal object whereby, i.e., *quo*). Or, it can be considered AS IT IS A THING, or according to what of it is manifested to the power by the 'formal reason whereunder' or in virtue of the order of the power towards this: and then is had the FORMAL REASON WHICH or the FORMAL OBJECT WHICH (*quod*)." He goes on to discriminate in the formal object *quod* the immediate, mediate, and extensive formal objects as well as the proportionate and adequate object.]

Up until the 18th century, the scholastics of all various nuances, who, after Albert the Great and St. Thomas, followed Aristotle, preserved this order, which he himself had given. One could merely cite here Scholastics such as Paul Soncinas, Chrysostom Javelli, John of St. Thomas, Antoine Goudin, Jacques-Casimir Guérinois, Salvatore Roselli, and Sylvester Maurus.[5]

It is only in the 18th century (and above all under the influence of Wolff, as was shown some years ago by Paul Gény[6]) that a new order began to prevail. One must not forget that Christian Wolff, the disciple of Leibniz, was a mathematician like him. Thus, he was inclined in the same manner to prefer the *a priori* method [that is used in mathematical reasoning]. In giving a scholastic form to Leibniz's philosophy, the new order that he had proposed had as its end the provision of a better refutation, on the one hand, of English empiricism and, on the other hand, of Spinozism. Likewise, he had the goal of distinguishing philosophy from experimental physics [*sic*] and mathematical physics, which were tending to set themselves up as being distinct sciences.

From the outset, Wolff separated himself from empiricism inasmuch as he placed general metaphysics (or ontology) immediately after logic, conceiving ontology as being *a priori* and wholly connected to the principles of identity and sufficient reason [*raison suffisante*]. By this very fact, he followed Spinoza upon his own terrain and attempted to refute him by means of his own *a priori* method, that is, by proceeding *more geometrico*, in the *a priori* manner used in geometrical proofs. His refutation was to remain weak, on account of the moral necessity of the creative act, which Wolff was led to affirm, like Leibniz, on account of this *a priori* rationalism.—After ontology came psychology, cosmology, and rational theology, all conceived as being three specific branches of metaphysics.

This seemed very clear and, at first sight, to be very convenient in teach-

---

[5] [Tr. note: The theologians cited are all Dominicans. One should keep this in mind when reading Fr. Garrigou-Lagrange's claims.]

[6] [Tr. note: Perhaps he is citing texts such as Paul Gény, *Questions d'enseignement de philosophie scolastique* (Paris: Beauchesne, 1913), 15, 37n1, 48n1. This text is cited in Étienne Gilson, *Being and Some Philosophers*, 2nd ed. (Toronto: PIMS, 2005), 113.]

ing. However, this apparent clarity perhaps came from a lack of profundity and also from forgetfulness regarding particular insights of Aristotle concerning the division of the sciences. Natural philosophy was no longer, as the Stagirite had thought, a science distinct from metaphysics because of their formal objects. Instead, it became a branch of metaphysics, like rational theology.

This Leibnizian-Wolffian metaphysics dominated the German schools up to the appearance of Kantianism. Kant himself—a disciple of Wolff before being his adversary—preserved this order on the whole in the Transcendental Dialectic in his *Critique of Pure Reason* where he undertakes his critique of the different parts of so-called "traditional" metaphysics.

Gradually, a number of scholastics followed along with the current and began to present Aristotelian and Thomistic philosophy according to this *a priori* order. In this cursus of studies, they would begin, after logic, with the consideration of being inasmuch as it is being, at the highest degree of abstraction. It was traditional Peripateticism dressed up, in a way, with the garments of Wolff's new manner of proceeding. Indeed, one could just as much say that it was dressed up after the manner of Spinoza, given that Wolff was imprudently inspired by Spinoza's method, as though it provided a means for better combatting Spinoza's own thought!

Today, it is asked whether this Wolffian fashion of dress—if not, indeed, this Spinozist fashion of dress—without completely being a straightjacket, does not in the end, interfere with the natural movements of Thomistic Peripateticism's arms, so to speak. Many scholastics think that it does, even among those who (practically speaking) must follow the new order, which came to prevail among many of the manuals and has been adopted by many seminaries and universities. Some masters have, indeed, reacted by returning in their works and lectures to the classical order commonly followed up until the 18th century. This classical procedure is followed by his eminence

Cardinal Mercier,[7] Fr. Gredt,[8] Fr. Hugon,[9] and Jacques Maritain,[10] as well

---

[7] [Tr. note: Désiré-Joseph Cardinal Mercier was incredibly influential through his involvement at the Catholic University of Louvain at the turn of the 20th century. He founded the *Institut supérieur de philosophie* at the same university and also founded the *Revue Néoscholastique* (now the *Revue philosophique de Louvain*). His *Manual of Modern Scholastic Philosophy* was influential in its English translations. It generally follows the aforementioned Peripatetic framework of disciplines, though it does accord a place to logic coming after natural theology. Louvain Thomism of that period was never quite isomorphic with the tradition in which we find Fr. Garrigou-Lagrange. However, Fr. Garrigou-Lagrange shows his generosity in recognizing the eminent Thomist of Louvain.]

[8] [Tr. note: Fr. Joseph Gredt's famed manual is *Elementa philosophiae Aristotelico-Thomisticae*. It was a digest of John of St. Thomas, attempting to bring it up to date with regard to the history of science and philosophy. As Maritain said, it is like an aerolite fallen from heaven. The doctrine is correct, but the tone is not helpful for a beginner, nor does it always work through the topics in a philosophical voice. In the manual, one is presented with a rather complete doctrine without really having the sense of the centuries (indeed millennia) of debate that gave rise to this kind of crystallization within the Thomist school. In any case, though, Gredt's work is to be commended indeed. See *Elementa philosophiae Aristotelico-Thomisticae*, 13th ed., vols. 1 and 2, ed. Eucharius Zenzen (Barcelona: Herder, 1961). Late in life, Maritain noted it as a work of excellence, though qualifying, saying in Jacques Maritain, *The Peasant of the Garonne: An Old Layman Questions Himself About the Present Time*, trans. Michael Cuddihy and Elizabeth Hughes (New York: Holt, Rinehart, and Winston, 1968), 137: "It is a precious repository of information, which we have only to consult should we want to know what St. Thomas thought on some given point. But how it was ever possible to have worked out such a conclusion, that's another story. We have in our hands an aerolite which has fallen from the sky, with everything we need to know written on it."]

[9] [Tr. note: Fr. Hugon was a confrere of Fr. Garrigou-Lagrange, slightly older than him. His Latin manuals are at times simpler than Gredt, though contain a great deal wisdom. They are in the process of being translated by Editiones Scholasticae. Hugon was also the author of a series of theology manuals as well. For the recently translated edition of his treatment of natural philosophy, see Edouard Hugon, *Cosmology*, trans. Francisco J. Romero Carrasquillo (Heusenstamm, Germany: Editiones Scholasticae, 2013). Also, see his recently-translated, *Mary, Full of Grace*, trans. John G. Brungardt (Providence, RI: Cluny Media, 2019).]

[10] [Tr. note: Maritain had been contracted to publish a complete series in philosophy, though he never finished the work. We only have his Introduction and his Formal Logic text. Notes for his Material Logic can be found in his French collected works. The outlines of his thought on moral philosophy can be found in his historical study of the topic as well as his lectures on the natural law and the basic concepts of moral philosophy. His *Preface to Metaphysics* provides a summary of his views concerning metaphysics. We do not have a full treatment of philosophical psychology, though important aspects of this are found in chapter 3 and appendix 1 of *The Degrees of Knowledge*.]

as all those who give themselves over to the direct study of Aristotle and St. Thomas's commentaries on him. The new laws regulating to doctorates in theology and philosophy promulgated by the Holy See in 1931[11] also enumerate the parts of philosophy in the following order: logic, cosmology, psychology, critique, ontology, natural theology, ethics, and natural law [*jus naturale*].

In what follows, we would like to propose three principal reasons for returning to the traditional order:

1. The authority of St. Thomas and Aristotle
2. The very nature of our intellect
3. The principle of the Aristotelian division of the sciences

I. Justification Based on the Authority of St. Thomas and Aristotle

First of all, we must not neglect here *the very authority of Aristotle and St. Thomas*. In order to exposit their philosophical doctrine, it is fitting that we preserve the same order that they chose as being the best—and not an order that is Platonic, or one that is Spinozist, or Wolffian. To take up such other orders would, in some way, lead us to do violence to the natural movement of their thought.

Now, Aristotle raised himself upward, passing from natural philosophy to metaphysics, and this is the order that he proposed for these two sciences. At the beginning of his *Physics*, in the very first chapter of the first book, he tells us that a good methodology ought to proceed from what is more known to what is less known. Now, as regards what is most known (if not in itself, i.e., *quoad se*, at least from our perspective, i.e., *quoad nos*), these are the sensible things with which natural philosophy is concerned; they are not purely intelligible objects, existing outside of all matter, or conceived by abstraction from all matter. First philosophy is concerned with these latter.[12] Aristotle speaks simi-

---

[11] [Tr. note: See the apostolic constitution of Pius XI, *Deus scientiarum dominus*.]

[12] [Tr. note: The immediate concern of the metaphysician is not with notions pertain-

larly in many places, notably at the beginning of his *Metaphysics*, in the second chapter of the first book, where he shows that metaphysics is the supreme science, more divine than human, a science to which man elevates himself only with great difficulty. Likewise, in the first chapter of the ninth book [i.e., book Θ] of the *Metaphysics*, Aristotle says that he will treat of potency and act not only in relation to *becoming*, as he already had done in natural philosophy [in the *Physics*], but in relation to *being inasmuch as it is being*, discussing them now according to their

---

ing to positively immaterial beings such as the angels and God. It is better to say that metaphysics is concerned with notions that are *not limited* to materiality. This is a kind of immateriality that could be termed "negative"—not material. Much has been made of this point by contemporary scholars of Aquinas. Just as an example, see the extensive work of Msgr. John Wippel. John F. Wippel, "Metaphysics and *Separatio* According to Thomas Aquinas," *The Review of Metaphysics* 31 (1978), 431–470. John F. Wippel, "Thomas Aquinas and Avicenna on the Relationship between First Philosophy and the Other Theoretical Sciences: A Note on Thomas's *Commentary on Boethius's De Trinitate*, Q. 5, art. 1, ad 9," in *The Thomist* 37 (1973), 133–154. Similar concerns (though for different reasons) animated the so-called River Forest tradition of Thomism. It is also represented in an older set of concerns regarding the proper subject of metaphysics, a topic that received much ink among Thomists of various inflections and persuasions. For some recent work on this, see See Phillip-Neri Reese, "Dominic of Flanders, O.P. (d. 1479) on the Nature of the Science of Metaphysics" (Ph.L. Thesis, The Catholic University of America, 2015).

These same points were not missed in Garrigou-Lagrange's day and, arguably, not by him if one reads the words in the narrative of his text carefully. As a confirmation, see the remarks of his disciple on many matters (especially metaphysical), Jacques Maritain. See Maritain, *Degrees*, 233n19, 453. Jacques Maritain, *Existence and the Existent*, trans. Gerald B. Phelan and Lewis Galantiere (New York: Pantheon, 1948), 32n15.

There are some of the school of Gilson (but others too, including those following the work of Msgr. Wippel) who may react poorly to Fr. Garrigou-Lagrange stating that it is "abstract." However, Fr. Garrigou-Lagrange is not referring here directly to the first operation of the intellect, whose psychological activity is rightly called abstraction, leading to conceptualization of the quiddities of things. Indeed, Fr. Garrigou-Lagrange's position regarding the centrality of proper proportionality among the types of analogy *requires* him to include *all three* acts of the intellect to explain how we come to know being in its full analogical scope. This will become more evident as we progress through this text. Thus being is "abstract" in a logical sense insofar as it *imperfectly abstracts* from its analogates in order to establish some unity for the notion, a unity that ultimately is imperfect and non-generic. For a defense of the claim that metaphysics can deal with being taken in the abstract (without thereby falling into some kind of conceptualism or essentialism), see John C. Cahalan, "The Problem of Thing and Object in Maritain," *The Thomist* 59, no. 1 (Jan. 1995): 31–36.]

full universality.

As St. Thomas writes in *In Boetium de trinitae*, q. 5, a. 1, speaking of first philosophy:

> It is called metaphysics—that is, *transphysica*, or beyond physics—because it comes to be taught to us after physics, for it is suitable that we proceed from sensible things to those that are not sensible.

> (Likewise, in ad 9:) Although the divine science is the first of all sciences, it is the case, however, that FROM OUR PERSPECTIVE (i.e., *quoad nos*) other sciences are prior. Whence, as Avicenna says at the beginning of his *Metaphysics*, "The order of this science is that it be taught after the natural sciences in which we determine many things that are used by this science, such as generation and corruption, motion, and other such things."

Likewise, St. Thomas speaks similarly in *Contra gentes* 1.3, where he opposes the philosophical method that raises itself from the sensible to the intelligible to that of theology, which has God Himself as its first object, known by revelation, descending from God thus known to creatures (the works of God) in order to end by considering the return of creatures to God, who is the ultimate end.

This contrast between the methodology used in a philosophical treatise and that used in a theological treatise is particularly salient if one compares, on the one hand, natural philosophy, which is brought to completion (according to Aristotle) by the proof of the existence of the First Mover, to, on the other hand, the cosmological part of the *Summa theologiae*, which begins in *ST* I, qq. 44 and 45 with a study of creation. Likewise, one will find the same difference between, on the one hand, the *De anima* of Aristotle, commented on by St. Thomas, and on the other, the Treatise on Man in the *Summa theologiae*. Following a method that ascends step-by-step, the *De anima* considers the vegetative soul, then the sensitive soul, then at last, the rational soul and the great problems that emerge in its regard. However, from the first question of the Treatise on Man in the *Summa theologiae*, we are faced with the problem of the immortality of the rational soul, the image of God, and the problem of its specific distinction from the angels (which have already been discussed by the theologian in accord with his descending methodology). The order to follow in psychology, at least in a work of Peripatetic philosophy, is obviously that of the *De anima* and not that of the theological treatise *De homine*.[13] Granted, it is easy to write a manual of philosophy by transcribing the parts of the *Summa theologiae* that are related to being, truth, the sensible world, the soul, God, and moral thought. However, a philosophical treatise should be something more than such a juxtaposition of texts.

Therefore, the first motive that we have for beginning (after logic) with natural philosophy is the very authority of Aristotle and St. Thomas, according to whom a good method is based on what is more known by us, namely sensible things.

Without a doubt, to make these things intelligible, we must have the first rational principles, which are more known *in themselves* than are sensible things. However, it suffices at the beginning to have a relatively vague knowledge of them and to consider them inasmuch as they are verified in the order of sensible things, without yet considering them distinctly in all their universality and their transcendent scope, as Aristotle does in the fourth book of his *Metaphysics*.

Now, we can add precision to this first reason by considering the very nature of our intellect.

---

[13] [Tr. note: This is an important point to remember, for it is tempting to think that the order of the *De homine* is close to that of the philosophical order that ought to be followed, at least in parts of it. However, in philosophy, we must always (and methodically) proceed from what is experientially known more to us (i.e., sensible realities) to more purely intelligible realities (e.g., from a careful study of the immanent action of sensation to intelligible knowledge). To see a somewhat dissenting opinion regarding the *De homine* (at least as regards the presentation of qq. 84–89), see Lawrence Dewan, "Jacques Maritain, St. Thomas, and the Philosophy of Religion" in *Wisdom, Law, and Virtue: Essays in Thomistic Ethics* (New York: Fordham, 2008), 353 and 598n20–21.]

II. Justification Based on the Very Nature of Our Intellect

It is not only factually the case that our intellectual knowledge is first concerned with sensible things and then rises upward to purely intelligible and spiritual things. It is moreover the case that this fact corresponds to *the very nature of our human intellect*, which, according to Aristotle and St. Thomas, far from being accidentally united to the senses, is connected to them by wholly natural bonds: "From the body and soul there is made something that is *per se* (i.e., essentially) one as from matter and form or from potency and act."[14]

Far from being, in itself, an obstacle to our intellectual life, the body and the senses are needed for us to live our intellectual life. Why is this the case? It is so because (as St. Thomas says in *ST* I, q. 76, a. 5): "Form is not for matter but, rather, matter is for form. . . . Now, the human intellect is *the least of all the [kinds of] intellects*" to which corresponds *the least of intelligible things*, namely that which is found in the shadows of sensible things. Given that the first datum of our human intellect is the being of sensible things, it is neither God[15] nor the soul itself.[16] "*The first thing that is known by us, at least as matters stand in this present state of life,*[17] *is the quiddity of material things, such quiddities being the object of our intellect, as we have repeated many times in earlier articles.*"[18] And

---

[14] [Tr. note: The maxim is cited without reference. It may well be derived from the work *De pluritate formarum*, attributed at one time to St. Thomas, though now, perhaps, to Thomas of Sutton, which reads, "Unde philosophus dicit in 2 de anima, quod ex corpore et anima fit unum tamquam ex potentia et actu."]

[15] See *ST* I, q. 88, a. 3: "If we are speaking without qualification, it must be said that God is not the first thing that is known by us. Instead, we come to knowledge of God by way of creatures, as is said by the Apostle in Romans 1:20: 'The invisible God is clearly seen through those things that have been made.'"

[16] See *ST* I, q. 87, aa. 1–4. [Tr. note: Though not in utter agreement with Fr. Garrigou-Lagrange, this matter has received detailed and excellent treatment in Therese Scarpelli-Cory, *Aquinas on Human Self-Knowledge* (Cambridge, UK: University of Cambridge Press, 2015). For Fr. Garrigou-Lagrange's own position in detail, see Reginald Garrigou-Lagrange, "Whether the Mind Knows Itself Through its Essence or Through Some Species," in *Philosophizing in Faith*, trans. Matthew K. Minerd (Providence, RI: Cluny Media, 2019), 79–100.

[17] [Tr. note: As opposed to the preternatural state of non-union with the body as a separated soul.]

[18] *ST* I, q. 88, a. 3. Also, see q. 84, a. 7; q. 85, a. 8; q. 87, a. 2, ad 2.

as our intellect passes from potency to act (and from the vague[19] to the distinct), as we have seen, what it first of all attains in these sensible things is that which is most general in them, namely *their very being,* which every other kind of knowledge presupposes.[20]

To speak in accord with Cajetan's terminology: "The first thing known by our intellect, as pertains to *actual, vague [confusa] cognition, is concrete being according to its sensible quiddity.*"[21] The first datum of intellect is the being of sensible things, abstracted from the sensible individual in which it is found but not yet abstract from the generic and specific predicates of this individual.

If this is indeed the case, it obviously is fitting to begin philosophy by studying sensible things in light of the first rational principles (though, known only in a vague manner). Thus, Aristotle begins his *Physics* by studying the change found in bodily substances, as well as the various movements of bodies. In this way, he discovers the distinction between potency and act in order to resolve the objections of Parmenides against becoming without denying, along with Heraclitus, the principle of contradiction (or, identity). In the same way, it is in natural philosophy that he discovers the fourfold division of causes. Only later on, in metaphysics, does he generalize these divisions, which were first discovered in order to explain becoming. Likewise, it is only in metaphysics that he applies them to all composed and caused beings by considering them in relation to being inasmuch as it is being. From these applications, he was able to rise upward to metaphysical knowledge of the existence of God, the First Being and Pure Act, from Whom one can then descend in order to have a superior understanding of the universe. Thus, the methodology is *analytico-synthetic,* first ascending and then descending.

If, on the contrary, our intellect's first datum (the *primum cognitum ab intellectu nostro*) were God (the *primum ontologicum*), then one would need to proceed in a purely *a priori,* synthetic, and deductive manner, like Parmenides, Plato (to a degree), and most especially Spinoza,

---

[19] [Tr. note: As has been noted above, this could also be translated "confused."]
[20] See *ST* I, q. 85, a. 3.
[21] Cajetan, *In De ente et essentia,* introduction.

who strove to deduce from God (known first as the unique substantial being) not only the infinite divine attributes but also the world, considered as an ensemble of finite modes following one after another *ab aeterno*. This is no longer a form of ontology but, rather, is ontologism, indeed, a pantheistic ontologism, which exists in the writings of Malebranche and his disciples: God alone acts, for God alone is, and we know all things in Him. Being in general is thereby confused with the Divine Being, as the good in general is confused with the Divine Good. Consequently, our intellect is no longer imagined as being only *a faculty of being* but, instead, seems to be *a faculty of the Divine*. It thus ought to be infallible like God's intellect or, at the very least, like infused faith. Likewise, from such a perspective, our will would no longer be specified by the universal good but, rather, would be *immediately* specified by God Himself, like infused charity. Henceforth, it would be incapable of sin [*impeccable*]. St. Thomas would say: This purely *a priori* metaphysical method can be only that of God Himself, who alone sees all things in Himself, i.e., in His creative causality.[22]

There is yet another possibility. If, on the contrary, our intellect's first datum, the *primum cognitum*, were ourselves (whether our own thought, the *cogito*, or the interior force of which Leibniz speaks or the exertion spoken of by Maine de Biran), then we would need to begin with psychology. St. Thomas would say: This process of knowledge is that which is proper to the natural intelligence of the angels, who know their own spiritual nature first and foremost.[23]

---

[22] Cf. *ST* I, q. 14, a. 5: "God sees Himself in Himself, because He sees Himself through His Essence. However, He does not see beings that are other than Him in themselves but, rather, sees them in Himself, inasmuch as His Essence contains a likeness of those beings that are other than Him." He knows possible beings inasmuch as He can create them and existing beings inasmuch as He has freely created them. [Tr. note: Another parallel case of such a methodology could be made as regards the Thomistic approach to so-called ontological arguments for the existence of God. God's necessity is known only by Himself in a direct manner. Even the angels have a quasi-inferential knowledge of God, knowing Him through the mirror of their own, created natures. Thus, if (*per impossibile*) God were to prove His own existence, He alone could do so in a purely *a priori* way, for by nature only He has Himself (i.e., the Deity in itself) as the formal object of His Knowledge.]

[23] Cf. *ST* I, q. 56, a. 1. [Tr. note: Thus, Maritain subtitled his Descartes section in the somewhat-pugilistic *Three Reformers*, "The Incarnation of the Angel." See Jacques

This is not the case for us, who begin first and foremost with sensible things. Therefore, we first must consider what external experience manifests to us without, however, neglecting internal experience (as sometimes happens among scholastic authors) and certainly without claiming like empiricism to formally resolve the metaphysical certitude of the first rational principles into the value of sensation, which is only presupposed in the inferior order of material causality, or better expressed, *ut materia causae* (i.e., as the matter of the cause).[24]

This second reason that we have provided is confirmed by a grave disadvantage of the opposed method.

Were we to place ontology immediately after logic, we would risk *not perceiving* the profound meaning of the fundamental theses of Aristotelian and Thomistic metaphysics, above all the *meaning and value of the division of being into potency and act.* Indeed, it is utterly important make clear the origin of this distinction, following the method of discovery used by Aristotle when, wishing *to explain* THE BECOMING denied by Parmenides and Zeno without following Heraclitus in *rejecting* THE PRINCIPLE OF CONTRADICTION (OR, IDENTITY), he

---

Maritain, *Three Reformers: Luther, Descartes, Rousseau* (New York: Charles Scribner's Sons, 1950), 53–89. Again, regarding Leibniz, he writes in Jacques Maritain, *Existence and the Existent*, trans. Lewis Galantiere and Gerald B. Phelan (New York: Pantheon, 1948), 137: "The monadism of Leibnitz[*sic*] is a metaphysical transposition of [Aquinas's] treatise on the Angels." Lest one think that such remarks are mere scholastic insults or insinuations, consider the explicit (and wrong, from a Thomist perspective) remarks in W. Leibniz, "Primary Truths" in *Philosophical Essays*, ed. and trans. Roger Ariew and Daniel Garber (Indianapolis: Hackett, 1989), 42: "What Saint Thomas asserts on these points about angels or intelligences (that here every individual is a lowest species) is true of all substances."]

[24] Cf. *ST* I, q. 84, a. 6: "It cannot be said that sensible cognition is the total and perfect cause of intellectual cognition; rather, it is in a way the mater of the cause [lit. *materia causae*]." In addition, the natural light of the intellect, called the *intellectus agens*, is needed. (See the same text on this point too.)

[Tr. note: Fr. Garrigou-Lagrange's qualification is due to the fact that the phantasm functions as an objective instrument, providing in potency the specification needed for the intellect. Strictly speaking, the intellect is *not* the formal cause in relation to the phantasm as matter. Rather, the latter is the objective instrument of the former. The depths of these matters are indicated in the profound pages found in Simon, *Introduction to the Metaphysics of Knowledge*, 113–127. Also, a similarly excellent and lucid presentation can be found in John Frederick Peifer, *The Concept in Thomism* (New York: Bookman Associates, 1952), 119–131.]

reconciled them with each other—being and becoming, the one and the multiple—not only by the vague sort of *non-being* spoken of by Plato but, instead, by POTENCY clearly distinguished from the *possible* and from *privation* and from the kind of *imperfect act* with which it was confused later on by certain scholastics and Leibniz. Indeed, behold now what Wolff did not see! He did not see this very profound distinction of potency and act by which one can explain hylomorphism, the division of the four causes, the solution of the objections of Zeno against the continuum and movement, as well as the doctrine of the *De anima* concerning the human composite, the relation of the faculty of knowledge to its object, and human freedom. The doctrine of act and potency is also the principle of the classical proofs of God's existence and the foundation of the *Nicomachean Ethics*: a power is spoken of in relation to its act, and its act with respect to its object;[25] accordingly, man, as a rational animal, must act rationally, according to a fitting end. In brief, the distinction of act and potency is the foundation of the whole of Aristotelian thought. Therefore, it is sovereignly important to show how Aristotle reached this utterly fertile distinction and to show how the existence of real potency (really distinct from act, no matter how perfect it may be) is for him the only way to reconcile the principle of contradiction (or, identity) with the existence of the profound becoming which reaches down to the very substance of corruptible beings.[26]

To present this doctrine concerning potency and act in another, *a priori* manner, as happens in many manuals, is to suggest that it has merely fallen from the sky or that it is only a simple, pseudo-philosophical translation of common language, whose worth still must be established, as has been said by Henri Bergson. In such an undertaking, there is no longer any profundity in analyzing matters. One is content

---

[25] [Tr. note: See "Actus specificantur ab obiecto formali. De universalitate huiusce principii" in *Acta Pont. Acad. Rom. S. Thom. Aq. Et Rel. Cath* 1 N.S. (1934): 139–153. This article is included in Reginald Garrigou-Lagrange, *Grace*, trans. Dominican Sisters of Corpus Christi Monastery (St. Louis: B. Herder, 1952), 467–480.]

[26] [Tr. note: See Reginald Garrigou-Lagrange, "Applicationes tum physicae tum metaphysicae doctrinae de actu et potentiae secundum S. Thomam," Acta primi Congr. Thomistici. Intern. Romae, 1925 habiti in: Acad. Rom. S. Thom. Aq. (Rome: 1925), 33–52. This article is included in Reginald Garrigou-Lagrange, *Reality: A Synthesis of Thomistic Thought*, trans. Patrick Cummins (original, St. Louis: B. Herder, 1950).]

with some quasi-nominal definitions of potency and act, and it is no longer clear how and why potency differs from the simply possible being, from privation, as well as from imperfect act or from the Leibnizian force / virtuality, which is only an impeded form of act.[27] Likewise, one can limit oneself merely to enunciating the relations of potency and act in the axioms proposed as commonly received in the School [i.e., the Thomist school, Suarezian school, etc.] without seeing their true value on which, nevertheless, everything depends. We must admit this fact: this fundamental chapter of metaphysics, i.e., regarding act and potency, remains in a state of great intellectual poverty in many manuals when we compare them to the first two books of Aristotle's *Physics* and to the commentary that St. Thomas left us concerning it. The method of discovery has been too neglected in philosophy, a method which is founded on the very nature of our intellect, the very least among created intellects.

III. Justification Based on the Aristotelian Division of the Sciences

Finally, let us consider the third point that invites us to return to the traditional order [of the philosophical sciences], namely the *principle of the Aristotelian division of the sciences*. According to this principle, the speculative sciences of natural philosophy, mathematics, and metaphysics are distinct on account of their formal objects as well as the specific perspective under which they consider it.

In the first chapter of the sixth book of the *Metaphysics*, Aristotle himself shows this by discussing the different ways of defining found in these three sciences. St. Thomas established this point at greater length in *In Boetium de Trinitate*, q. 5, a. 1. Natural philosophy has for its object *ens mobile according to the first degree of abstraction* (i.e., it abstracts only from individual matter, though not from common sensible matter). In addition, it considers the substantial change of sensible beings (i.e.,

---

[27] [Tr. note: The reader must distinguish the aforementioned Leibnizian *conatus / nisus* from motion, which properly speaking is an imperfect act.]

generation and corruption), as well as the sensible alterations that precede it, namely the movement of growth and local movement, as well as time, which is the measure of such motion.[28]

Mathematics has for its object *ens quantum*, quantity, whether it be continuous or discrete, *according to the second degree of abstraction*. That is, it abstracts from common sensible matter (from sensible qualities) in order to consider only quantity.[29] Because of this, it abstracts also from substance, efficient causality, and final causality, and it would be fitting in this regard to maintain its traditional place in the philosophy of mathematics.

Finally, metaphysics considers *being inasmuch as it is being, according to the third degree of abstraction*. That is, it makes abstraction from all matter so as to consider only the pure intelligible, whether it is realized (like being and substance) in material things without including matter in its formal notion or whether it exists completely outside of the material order, as is the case for spirit and also God Himself.

From this perspective, it is therefore false to say that *natural philosophy* and *psychology*, which discusses vegetative and sensitive life, should be *specific branches of metaphysics*—though, metaphysics does indeed consider sensible things as well, though only inasmuch as they are beings. Thus, in the seventh book of the *Metaphysics*, issues concerning matter and form are considered, no longer in relation to becoming (as in the *Physics*) but, instead, in their relation to being inasmuch as it is being.

---

[28] Natural philosophy is not content, however, with explaining *phenomena through mathematically-expressed experimental laws*. Instead, it explains *through the four causes in the physical order*, through matter, substantial form, the end, and through the efficient causality of various physical agents subordinated to the *First Mover*. (See book eight of Aristotle's *Physics*.) However, it is not elevated so as to consider being inasmuch as it is the being of sensible things, nor does it consider God as the Creative Cause of their very being. This pertains to metaphysics.

[29] [Tr. note: For an overview of different Thomistic opinions regarding mathematics, see Armand Maurer, "Thomists and Thomas Aquinas on the Foundation of Mathematics," *The Review of Metaphysics* 47, no. 1 (Sept., 1993), 43–61. Also, for particular views, see Yves R. Simon, "Nature and the Process of Mathematical Abstraction" in *Philosopher at Work*, ed. Anthony O. Simon (Lanham, MD: Rowman and Littlefield Publishers, 1999), 113–133; Vincent E. Smith, *St. Thomas on the Object of Geometry* (Milwaukee: Marquette University Press, 1954).]

It goes without saying that natural philosophy, conceived after the manner of Aristotle and St. Thomas, does not treat of creation (i.e., the production *ex nihilo* of the being inasmuch as it is the being of sensible things). This topic pertains to Metaphysics, and it discusses it in an appropriate manner after having proven God's existence by then discussing His relations with the world. In many scholastic manuals written after the 18th century, creation is instead discussed at the beginning of cosmology, before even having proven the existence of God in rational theology. This represents another disadvantage of the order adopted from the time of Wolff.[30]

Thus, we can find among numerous scholastics of the past two centuries a tendency to forget what St. Thomas (following Aristotle) said, namely, that there are *many distinct philosophical sciences*. Some have wished to unify philosophy to an excess and, by contrast, have often misunderstood the unity of theological science. Contrary to St. Thomas, some have wished to make various, distinct sciences out of apologetics, dogmatics, moral theology, asceticism, and mysticism.[31]

It is utterly important not to blur the formal objects of the philosophical sciences, for by so doing, one is thus habituated to blur them everywhere else, and this would lead to universal confusion. *It is a great sin in philosophy and theology to confuse the formal objects of superior habitus with the formal objects of inferior ones, whether it is a question of sciences or of the acquired and infused virtues.* This would lead one to

---

[30] One thus sees again that this order is inspired far too much by Spinoza, for it is in him that we see the idea that it is appropriate to make cosmology into a special metaphysics and to speak of the origin of the world immediately after ontology, for according to him, ontology is identified absolutely, in virtue of his pantheistic ontologism, with rational theology. Given that God, the sole and unique substance, is, according to Spinoza, the first object known by our intellect, it is necessary then to *deduce the world* from Him, thus explaining its origin.

[31] In *ST* I, q. 1, a. 3, ad 2, St. Thomas very clearly says, "Nothing prohibits inferior powers or *habitus* from being diversified according these matters that commonly fall under a single superior power or *habitus*, for the superior power or *habitus* considers an object under a more universal formal notion. . . . Whence, . . . those things that are treated *in various philosophical sciences* can be considered in this one, single sacred theology [*sacra doctrina*] from the perspective of one formal notion [*sub una ratione*], namely inasmuch as they are included in Divine revelation. In this way, sacred theology [*sacra doctrina*] is like, as it were, an impression of the Divine knowledge, which is a unified, simple knowledge of all things."

confuse the intelligible with the sensible (thus leading one to sensualism / empiricism) and, also, to confuse the order of supernatural truths with that of natural truths (thus leading one to naturalism).

Perhaps someone will object that natural philosophy and the other philosophical sciences *depend* on first philosophy or metaphysics and that, consequently, metaphysics should be proposed first.

This would be true if the philosophical sciences were *properly subalternated* to metaphysics, as optics is subalternated to geometry. However, in this case, there is only *subalternation in an improper sense.*[32] While, indeed, optics does proceed from conclusions reached in geometry and not from its own proper principles, natural philosophy has its own self-evident, *per se nota*, principles. For example, with regard to physical motion, there are the principles, "Every change requires a subject," and, "Everything that is moved is moved by another." However, these principles of natural philosophy can be considered from a superior and more universal perspective, so that they are applied to change taken in its complete universality and even to movements of the spirit, the movements of the intellect and the will.[33] Also, these principles are defended in the last analysis by metaphysics (according to a resolution made to loftier notions and more universal principles), at least by reducing other positions to absurdity.

---

[32] See St. Thomas's comments on the first book of the *Posterior Analytics*, lect. 25 and 41. Also, *ST* I, q. 1, a. 2, and Gredt, *Elementa philosphiae*, vol. 1, 206–208. [Tr. note: The reader will benefit from the clarity found also in John of St. Thomas, *Material Logic*, q. 26, a. 2 (p. 510–518).]

[33] [Tr. note: Clearly, Fr. Garrigou-Lagrange does not hold that one immediately applies movement (an imperfect act) to the other cases. Instead, a properly proportional set of analogates is established, and we see the similarity and dissimilarity between each of the analogates to which the notion is applied. The same could be said for our notion of time, which gives birth to the analogical notion of duration (applicable to time, the immediacy of sensation, aeviternity, eternity, etc.); likewise, one could say the same regarding life, which is first understood in terms of the self-motion of ensouled wholly material beings, though it also applies to motionless self-actualization of humans and (especially) the angels, as well as to God. On these topics, the reader would benefit much from reflecting on Yves R. Simon, "On Order in Analogical Sets" in *Philosopher at Work*, ed. Anthony O. Simon (Lanham: Roman & Littlefield, 1999), 135–171. Yves Simon, "The Philosophy of Change" and "Time" in *The Great Dialogue of Nature and Space*, ed. Gerald J. Dalcourt (Albany, NY: Magi Books, 1970), 59–86, 129–137.]

Metaphysics thus has a *priority of dignity and certitude* over the other philosophical sciences whose principles it defends. However, it does not, by the same token, have a *priority of time*, as geometry does over optics. For natural-philosophical investigations, it suffices that one have the implicit metaphysics of common sense, which represents a rudimentary kind of ontology, since it attains (at least in vague outlines) the first laws of being which are also the first rational principles.[34]

There is no vicious circle here. Instead, as St. Thomas says, "We elevate ourselves from sensible effects to knowledge of causes, which teach us the reason for these effects."[35]

Some will grant everything we have said, if we are speaking of the order of discovery or investigation, but not if it is a question of the *order of doctrine* or teaching, which they believe should be the opposite of the preceding order.

We believe that we must respond to such a claim as follows. The order of teaching, *the via doctrinae*, is opposite to that of discovery only if it is purely synthetic or deductive, as it perhaps is in mathematics. However, in philosophy, the order of teaching cannot be purely synthetic or deductive, for the reasons that we have already given. It is analytico-synthetic. Given the nature of our intellect, which first knows the nature of sensible things, philosophy—even when it is taught—should begin by the analytico-synthetic study of sensible beings, so

---

[34] Cf. *ST* I, q. 79, a. 8: "Human reasoning, according to the paths we take in acquiring knowledge (i.e., the *via inventionis*, or way of discovery) proceeds from certain simply understood things, which are the first principles. And, again, it returns in the way of judgment making a resolution to first principles, in light of which it examines what it has discovered."

[35] St. Thomas, *In Boetium de Trinitate*, q. 5, a. 1, ad 9: "Nor, however, is it necessary that there be a vicious circle [in this argument] because [first philosophy] presupposes those things that are proven in other sciences, while first philosophy itself proves the principles of the other sciences. This is so because the principles that another science, namely, natural philosophy, accepts from first philosophy do not prove that which the first philosopher accepts from the natural philosopher; instead they are proven through other *per se nota* principles . . . and thus there is not a vicious circle. Besides, *the sensible effects* from which natural demonstrations proceed are *more known to us* at the beginning; however, when we arrive by them unto knowledge of the first causes, those first causes manifest to us the reason [*propter quid*] for those effects. . . . For this reason, Boethius places the divine science last, for it is last from our perspective [*quoad nos*]."

that it may at last arrive at knowledge of being inasmuch as it is being, the principle of the synthesis proposed by general metaphysics. Finally, it should then raise itself to God, the supreme principle of the universal synthesis: "According to the *way of discovery*, through temporal things we arrive at knowledge of eternal things. . . . *In the way of judgment*, through eternal things now known, we judge concerning temporal ones, and according to eternal reasons we order temporal ones."[36]

In this, the analytico-synthetic method of philosophy differs from the synthetic method of theology, which descends from God, known by revelation, in order to return to Him (according to the very plan of the *Summa theologiae*). This was precisely the error of Spinoza and, to a degree, Wolff, namely that they applied to philosophy the purely synthetic and deductive method of mathematics, a method that helped lead the author of the *Ethics* to deny the existence of the two causes that mathematics does not take into consideration: efficient causality properly so called (i.e., as an extrinsic cause), as well as final causality. At the same time, this led him to deny creation, the Divine Freedom, and Providence.

Thus, we have the three principal reasons that lead us to return to the classical order of the various philosophical sciences: (1) the authority of the traditional Masters, (2) the nature of our intellect, and (3) the principle of the Aristotelian division of the sciences.

---

[36] *ST* I, q. 79, a. 9. The *via iudicii* is that of doctrinal judgment founded on the supreme reasons of things, that of the Wisdom that judges all things by the First Cause and Final End. It is the synthetic order which follows an extensive analysis and gives an overall view of all things. There is also another *via iudicii* noted by St. Thomas in *ST* I, q. 19, a. 8, that of critical reflection which traces back conclusions to the first rational principles: *resolvendo redit ad prima principia, ad quae inventa examinat*. [Tr. note: See Reginald Garrigou-Lagrange, "On the Twofold Via inventionis and the Twofold Via iudicii According to St. Thomas," in *Philosophizing in Faith*, 11–20. An extensive textual study of this and related topics can be found in S. Edmund Dolan, "Resolution and Composition in Speculative and Practical Discourse," *Laval théologique et philosophique* 6, no. 1 (1950): 9–62.]

Final Remarks (Especially as Regards Logic)

From this perspective, the critique of knowledge is to be moved to where Aristotle placed it in the fourth book of the *Metaphysics*. That is, it should be moved to the beginning of general metaphysics, following the psychological study of sensation and intellection contained in the *De anima*. Before asking oneself about the ontological value of the intellect, we must know *what the intellect in fact is* from the psychological perspective. We must know what its proper object is as something distinct from the proper object of the internal and external senses.[37] Only then can we, if not directly demonstrate that the intellect is capable of attaining *being*, at least show that it is so capable by explaining our terms and by refuting agnostic objections that claim to establish that the knower cannot pass beyond subjective phenomena. The metaphysical study of the phenomena or appearances[38] shows that it does not hold and that a "natural illusion" is a kind of nonsense, not a principle of explanation. The critique of intellectual knowledge thus stands forth as being a part of metaphysics. It represents a *metaphysical critique* distinct from logic, for it is concerned already with *being inasmuch as it is extramental being*, if not in itself, at least inasmuch as it is *knowable* or accessible to our intellect.

Logic, which, by contrast, is concerned with *ens rationis*[39] (i.e., with

---

[37] Before coming to the critique of the value of knowledge, we must psychologically know *what the knower is—operari sequitur esse et modus operandi modum essendi*. We must know that the knower differs from the non-knower on account of the former's *immateriality* which enables such a being not only to *become other* but, instead, *to become other beings* in a kind of immaterial manner, *fieri aliud a se*. Cf. *ST* I, q. 14, a. 1. We have explained this point at greater length in Reginald Garrigou-Lagrange, "Cognoscens quodammodo fit vel est aliud a se (On the Nature of Knowledge as Union with the Other as Other)," in *Philosophizing in Faith: Essays on the Beginning and End of Wisdom*, trans. Matthew K. Minerd (Providence, RI: Cluny Media, 2019), 63–78.

[38] [Tr. note: Presumably in the Kantian sense, at least as Kant is interpreted by Fr. Garrigou-Lagrange.]

[39] [Tr. note: I am translating cases of *être de raison* and *ens rationis* directly as *ens rationis* to avoid the many difficulties involved in this expression. Although Fr. Schmidt's expression "rationate being" has benefits, I have found that it does not always add the requisite clarity needed for understanding *ens rationis* as a very unique domain of "being." Regarding Fr. Schmidt's opinion, see Robert W. Schmidt, "The Translation

the order to place in our concepts subjectively),[40] should be exposited at the beginning [of philosophical study] as Aristotle did in his *Organon*. This should be done for the reason given by St. Thomas:

> We do not seek to know the things with which logic is concerned so that we may know them for their own sakes. Instead, they

---

of Terms Like *Ens rationis*," *Modern Schoolman* 41 (1963): 73–75.]

[40] [Tr. note: Fr. Garrigou-Lagrange is a bit loose here. Technically, the traditional Thomistic position is that logic is a science of a particular kind of *ens rationis*, namely the *relationes rationis* that are called second intentions. These are the *relationes rationis* formed among objects of knowledge *inasmuch as they are objects*. The order in question is not the order found in the subjective qualities found in the intellect of the knower. If one is not careful on this score, he or she will fall into a Suarezian conception of logic. On this topic, one can read to much benefit the first two questions of John of St. Thomas's *Material Logic*. See the lengthy textual study, Robert Schmidt, *Domain of Logic According to Saint Thomas Aquinas* (The Hague: Martinus Nijhoff, 1966). Also, see Matthew Minerd, "Thomism and the Formal Object of Logic," *American Catholic Philosophical Quarterly* 93, no. 3 (2019): 411–444.]

The points pertinent here are well summarized by Fr. Garrigou-Lagrange's student and disciple, Fr. Austin Woodbury. See Austin M. Woodbury, *Logic*, The John N. Deely and Anthony F. Russell Collection, St. Vincent College Library, Latrobe, PA, 3–4: "No one denies that logic deals with mental relations, that is, relations that can exist in the intellect only, between Predicate and Subject, and between the diverse propositions of reasoning. But, the question is: Whether the primary and essential reference of logic is to these relations? For, since logic is the art directive of reason itself to the attainment of the true, the question formally concerns the artificial order necessary to attain the true, to wit: Whether this order consists in the acts of the mind inasmuch as they are directible; or, in other words, in something real? Or whether this order consists in the very ordination of concepts by way of subject and predicate, and of middle term; or, in other words, in some mental relation. Against SUAREZ, who holds the former opinion, to wit, that the object of logic is the acts as directable, or in other words, real being, it must be said, with St. Thomas and Thomists, that the formal object of logic is the MENTAL RELATION (*relatio rationis*) resulting from the ordering of concepts by way of subject and predicate and middle term . . ..

Hence, logic can be defined essentially (a) either from its adequate formal object [as being] *the speculative science of mental being [ens rationis] of second intention*; or (b) from its object of attribution [as being] *the speculative science of reasoning* (note that the object of attribution of a science is that whereunto everything which is treated in a given science is attributed or ordered; as for example, moveable body in natural philosophy, and substance in metaphysics; or (c) from its principle object [as being] *the speculative science of demonstration* (note that the principal object of a science is that which is more principally and principally [sic] intended by a given science, so that everything which is treated in that science is treated intentionally on account of it, [e.g.] Pure Act in metaphysics."]

are sought as providing a kind of tool for the other sciences. Therefore, logic is not contained under speculative philosophy as a kind of principle part but, rather, is in a way reduced to speculative philosophy inasmuch as it serves as the instrument for speculation, such instruments being things like syllogisms, definitions, and other such things of this sort, which we need for the speculative sciences. Whence, also, one can understand Boethius's remark in his commentary on Porphyry, namely, that logic is not as much as science as it is *the instrument of science*.[41]

In order to take a position in logic that is opposed to nominalist empiricism, which denies the existence of our knowledge of the *universal* (and, consequently, induction's foundation as well as the value of the syllogism, which [for nominalist empiricism] is thus reduced to a tautology), it suffices that one have some preliminary treatment of the three operations of the intellect, namely apprehension, judgment, and reasoning. These preliminaries will be justified much later, first in philosophical psychology and second in metaphysics's critique of knowledge.

Here again in logic it is fitting to return to Aristotle's own order, founded precisely on the distinction of the three operations of the intellect, as we see in the order of the *Organon*, namely: *the Categories, On Interpretation*, the *Prior Analytics*, and the *Posterior Analytics*.[42]

---

[41] Aquinas, *De Trinitate*, q. 5, a. 1, ad 2.

[42] It is particularly important to retain the distinction between the *Prior* and the *Posterior Analytics* (and even the *Topics*), which consider in sequence: (1) *the formal syllogism inasmuch as it is a valid consequence*, making abstraction from the truth of the conclusion, (2) *the syllogism in scientific matters*, or, *demonstration*, and (3) *the syllogism in probable matter* and in *sophisms*.—The *ontological* value of scientific demonstration is not definitively examined except in metaphysical critique. See the fourth book of the *Metaphysics*.

[Tr. note: Technically, sophistical syllogisms are treated in the *Sophistical Refutations* of Aristotle. This text and the *Topics*, which deals with dialectical syllogisms, round out the logical corpus in very important ways. On the latter, one can consult the insightful work of Garrigou-Lagrange's teacher, Ambroise Gardeil, *La certitude probable* (Paris: Gabalda, 1911) and *La notion du lieu théologique* (Paris: Gabalda, 1908). Also, see L.-M. Regis, *L'opinion selon Aristote* (Paris: Vin, 1935). Finally, from the Thomistic perspective, one should consider the *Rhetoric* and *Poetics*, though, historically, these texts are not equally included in the *Organon* by all Aristotelians. See

Above all, it is fitting to carefully heed the sections of the second book of the *Posterior Analytics*[43] pertaining to everything concerning our methodical research for definitions: *verus modus venandi quod quid est*, the hunt for the *quod quid est* [that which is, or, essence] which is defined by the genus and specific difference, in other words, the passage from the abstract, vague idea (*quid nominis*) that directs this *venatio* (or hunt) to the distinct idea, expressed in the good definition (*quid rei*), which is itself the foundation for the demonstration of its properties.[44] Many of the definitions currently in use by contemporary thinkers stand in need of revision in light of the procedures found in this Aristotelian text.—Thus, we already have at the end of logic a kind of defense of the value of natural reason and its first principles, while awaiting the deeper critique that can only be undertaken at the beginning of metaphysics.

To our eyes, this seems to be the fitting order for proposing the various philosophical sciences in order that we may truly be faithful to the principles of Thomistic Peripateticism concerning the genesis of our knowledge and concerning the relations between the twofold way spoken of by St. Thomas: the *via inventionis* and the *via iudicii*, the analytic order of discovery and the synthetic order of the overall view that can only be attained at the end of one's research, at the culminating point of philosophical thought.

Thus, we now have a better idea about the intellect's finality and how it passes from the known to the unknown. It knows its own, proper finality: to judge in conformity with the nature and existence of things and to raise itself up to their First Cause and Final End.

Deborah Black, Logic and Aristotle's Rhetoric and Poetics in Medieval Arabic Philosophy (Leiden: Brill, 1990).]

[43] See Aquinas, *In II Post. An.*, lect. 14–17. [Tr. note: See Reginald Garrigou-Lagrange, "On the Search for Definitions According to Aristotle and St. Thomas," in *Philosophizing in Faith*, 21–34.]

[44] Thus, we will see better how *general logic* has its value in itself, independent of any particular method for a given specific science. It is fitting, however, to speak of the particular methods of the different sciences, as Aristotle himself does in the fourth book of the *Metaphysics* in distinguishing the three degrees of abstraction, but in metaphysics this can be only an application of the principles of general logic which ought to be first considered in themselves. It is also fitting to give a place for *logistique* [Tr. note: what we would call, at least roughly speaking, symbolic logic] by showing its relations with general logic.

Chapter Five

THE FINALITY AND REALISM OF THE WILL: DOES THE NATURAL DESIRE FOR HAPPINESS PROVE GOD'S EXISTENCE?

We have seen the intimate relations that metaphysical realism (or, the realism of the intellect) has with the principle of finality. There are relations that are no less intimate between this principle and the will's own particular form of realism.

In the fourth way in *ST* I, q. 2, a. 3, St. Thomas shows how our mind elevates itself by considering the degrees of perfection that we see around us: degrees of truth, of nobility, and of beauty and goodness that lead us to the Supreme Truth, Supreme Beauty, and Supreme Goodness. According to him, the principle that enables us to elevate ourselves to that height is this one: "The more and the less perfect are said of different beings inasmuch as they more or less approach the Being that is this perfection itself." The Holy Doctor helps us to understand better the meaning and the value of this principle in the words that he provides as an explanation in *De potentia* q. 3, a. 5:

> If some *one* thing is found in common *in many things*, it must be caused in them *by some*[1] *one cause*, for it cannot be that said common thing would belong *to each one by reason of itself* since each one, with regard to what it itself is, is distinguished from

---

[1] [Tr. note: Reading *alia* as *aliqua*, following the 1951 edition of *De potentia*.]

the others; and diversity of causes produces diverse effects . . .

(Moreover) since *something* is found to exist in several things *by participation in varied degrees*, it must be bestowed upon *all those things in which it is more imperfectly found* by *that one* in which it is found most perfectly. . . . For if it were to belong to each one of them *by reason of itself*, there would be no reason why it would be found more perfectly in one than in another.

In other words, as he says in *ST* I, q. 3, a. 7, "Those things that of themselves are *diverse* do not agree *in some one thing* except through some cause uniting them." *The multiplicity of beings*, resembling each other with regard to *one and the same perfection* (e.g., goodness), does not suffice to account for this unity of likeness found among them. As Plato said, the multiple cannot explain the one. And moreover, *none* of the beings that possess this perfection in an *imperfect degree* suffices to account for it, for each is a composite of this perfection and of the restricted capacity that limits it. Like every composite, it requires a cause: "Those things that of themselves are diverse do not agree in some one thing except through some cause uniting them." This composite *participates* in this perfection. It receives it and, indeed, can only receive it from Him who is this very perfection, the notion of which implies no imperfection.

From the moral perspective, this doctrine becomes singularly lively by reminding us that *the more that we see our limits* (i.e., those of our wisdom and of our goodness), the more we come to think of Him who is Wisdom Itself and Goodness Itself. The multiple is only explained by the one, the different [*diverse*] only by the same, the composite only by the simple, the imperfect mingled with imperfection only by the Perfect that is free of all imperfection.

This proof of God's existence implicitly contains within itself another one that St. Thomas develops elsewhere in *ST* I-II, q. 2, a. 8 by showing that the beatitude (or, true happiness), which man naturally desires, cannot be found in any limited or restricted good but only in God known in at least a natural way and efficaciously loved above all else. He shows that man's beatitude can be found neither in riches, nor in honors, nor in glory, nor in power, nor in any bodily good, nor in a good of the soul like virtue, nor in any limited good whatsoever. The demonstration that he gives for this last point is due to the very nature of our intellect and our will:

> It is impossible for man's beatitude to be found in any created good, for beatitude is a perfect good that completely brings the appetite to rest. Otherwise, it would not be the final end if something still remained to be desired. Now, the object of the will, which is the human appetite, is the good in its universality [universale bonum], just as the object of the intellect is the true in its universality [universale verum]. Hence, it is clear that only the universal good can bring man's will to rest; and the universal good is not found in any created thing but, rather, is found in God alone because every creature only has goodness by participation. Whence, only God can satisfy man's will. . . . Therefore, man's beatitude is fixed solely in God.

Do we not find here, in man's *natural desire* for happiness, a proof for the existence of God, who is the Sovereign Good? Do we not find a proof that is implicitly contained in St. Thomas's fourth way which we just spoke about, though here explained by the *principle of finality*, "Every agent acts for an end; a natural desire cannot be in vain"? Could the metaphysical value of this principle be less certain than that of the principle of efficient causality? Also, is it not certain before even having proven God's existence, for without finality there can be neither efficiency, nor even desire?

Many who have written recently on this subject do not seem to have noted well enough that, while we cannot admit the *absolute realism of the ontologists*, who transform this argument into a supposed intellectual intuition of God, we must also avoid falling into *nominalism*, which, denying the metaphysical value of the principle of finality, does not recognize the cogency of this argument (unless it is transformed into the religious experience spoken of by modernists). However, between these two extreme errors (and, indeed, above them), there is the *moderate realism* of Aristotle and St. Thomas, which shows the ontological and absolutely universal value of the principle of finality, before even having proven God's existence, as well as its value for leading us to God.[2]

Therefore, let us see: 1° what is the fact on which this proof is based; 2° what is the principle on which it rests; 3° what is the terminus

---

[2] This proof for God's existence by natural desire was profoundly set forth in the work of Fr. Ambroise Gardeil, "Les exigences objectives de 'l'action'," *Revue Thomiste* 6 (1898): 125–138, 269–294; "L'action: ses ressources subjectives," 7 (1899): 23–39. These articles would have merited being united in a single volume.

We have also explained this matter in a less-developed form in Reginald Garrigou-Lagrange, *God: His Existence and His Nature*, vol. 1, 332–337. There, we showed that the character of one's answer to this question completely depends on whether or not one admits or does not admit the ontological and absolutely universal value of the principle of finality on which it rests. When one does not admit the principle, the proof leads to an objectively insufficient certitude, and it is presented in this form by modernists and those who hold the philosophy of action. [Tr. note: The last comment being a thinly veiled comment aimed at the philosophy of Maurice Blondel.]

More recently, Fr. Roland-Gosselin has defended the same proof well in M. Roland-Gosselin, "Le désir du bonheur et l'existence de Dieu," *Revue des sciences philosophiques et théologiques* 13 (1924): 162–172. In order to respond to the objections of Fr. Manser against a particular formulation of this proof given by Fr. Gredt (a formulation that is notably different from our own), Fr. Roland-Gosselin rightly insists on this point: although truth is formally in the intellect that judges in conformity with things, *the good is in things*, and a natural desire pertains to a real good.

[Tr. note: Several remarks are necessary regarding the articles by Gardeil. Although Fr. Garrigou-Lagrange refers here only to the aforementioned articles, the series continues by Gardeil for some time. The texts at least go so far as the following in *Revue Thomiste*: "Les ressources de vouloir" 7 (1899): 447–461; "Les ressources de la raison practique: *Utrum beatitudo sit operatio intellectus practici* (1)" 8 (1900): 377–399; "Ce qu'il y a vrai dans le néo-scotisme" 8 (1900): 531–550, 648–665; 9 (1901): 407–443." Despite possible appearance to the contrary, the last set of articles is explicitly linked to "Les ressources de la raison practique" by Gardeil. The final article of the series "Ce qu'il y a vrai dans le néo-scotisme" indicates more is to follow. It is not clear where it is taken up, though the article is cited several times later in his career. In a posthumous remembrance of Gardeil, Garrigou-Lagrange links the concerns with contents that would later be taken up in *Le Donné révélé et la Théologie*. In Gardeil's bibliography, one does sense a shift in focus after 1901 as he begins to study the topics pertaining to the nature of theological knowledge for which he is perhaps best known. See H.-D. Gardeil, "Le Père Ambroise Gardeil (1859–1931)," *Bulletin Thomiste* (Notes et communications, October, 1931): 69–92. Reginald Garrigou-Lagrange, "In memoriam: Le Père A. Gardeil," *Revue Thomiste* 39 (1931): 797–808. In this last-cited article, Garrigou-Lagrange does include "Les ressources de la raison practique" among the articles that should be gathered together. He still emphasizes the first series, however. Also, he places "Ce qu'il y a vrai dans le néo-scotisme" in relation to several other articles by Gardeil.]

to which it leads, and what it does and does not demand.

1. The Factual Point of Departure for This Proof

We can rise to the Supreme Good, the source of a perfect and unalloyed happiness, either on the basis of *imperfect, subordinate goods* or on the basis of *the natural desire* which cannot be satisfied by these goods.

If we take as our starting point the finite and limited goods which man is naturally inclined to desire, we will quickly see their imperfection. When it is a question of health, bodily pleasure, riches, honors, power, glory, and scientific knowledge, we indeed must recognize that we are here confronted with *goods that pass away*, goods that are quite *imperfect and limited*. Now, as we have said, the imperfect thing (or, *the good mingled with imperfection*) is only a *good that is participated in* by a restricting capacity that receives it. It is a good that presupposes the pure Good, without mixture with its contrary, as wisdom mixed with ignorance and error is only a participated wisdom that presupposes Wisdom Itself. This is the metaphysical aspect of the argument. It is the intellectual dialectic by way of causality considered at once as exemplary and efficient.

However, the proof of which we are speaking becomes livelier, more convincing, and more engaging if we base our point of departure *on our natural desire for happiness* which all of us feel so strongly within ourselves. This is the psychological and moral aspect of the argument. It is the dialectic of love, founded on that of the intellect, which proceeds either by way of efficient causality (productive or ordinative causality)[3] or by way of final causality.[4] These are the two extrinsic causes, each one as necessary as the other, and indeed, the end is the first of the causes. In *Metaphysics* 12.7, Aristotle was more aware of God's final causality than

---

[3] [Tr. note: That is, the efficient causality involved in man qua agent through art and prudence.]

[4] Cf. *ST* I-II, q. 1, a. 4 ("Whether there is some ultimate end of human life"): "*Speaking essentially [per se loquendo], it is impossible to proceed to infinity with regard to ends from any perspective.... If there were not an ultimate end, nothing would be desired,* nor would any action be terminated, nor would the intention of an agent come to rest."

of His efficient causality (whether productive or ordinative).[5]

In *ST* I-II, q. 2, aa. 7 and 8, St. Thomas, following Aristotle and St. Augustine, insists on the fact that *man naturally desires to be happy*, and given that his intellect (which is far superior to the senses and imagination of animals) knows not only *a given, particular good* but, instead, *the good in general (universale in praedicando)*, i.e., that which constitutes the good as such and the desirable whatever it may be, this means that man, tending as he does toward *the real good that is in things* and not toward the *abstract idea of the good*, cannot find his *true beatitude* in *any finite or limited good* but only in the *Sovereign Good (bonum universale in essendo et in causando)*.[6]

It is impossible for man to find true happiness, which he naturally desires, in any limited good, for his intellect, *immediately noting THE LIMITATION [of this good]*, then conceives a superior good, and the will naturally desires it.

Here we see a fact profoundly noted by St. Augustine in *Confessions* 1.1 where he says, "*Irrequietum est cor nostrum, donec requescat in te, Domine.* Lord, our heart is restless until it rests in thee."

Who among us has not noticed this fact in the depths of his or her life? If we are sick, we naturally desire health as a great good. Then, upon being healed, however overjoyed we may be because of this healing, we are aware that health does not suffice for our happiness and does not give peace to our soul. One can have perfect health and still be overwhelmed with distress. Such is also the case for pleasures of the senses. Far from sufficing to give us happiness, they throw those who abuse them into distress and disgust, for our intellect, which conceives

---

[5] If instead of considering only *the end* of this natural desire, one were to consider *its ordination* to this end (an ordination that requires *an efficient ordaining Cause, ordinans vel imperans movet ut agens non ut finis*), then the argument would be connected to St. Thomas's fifth way, taken *from the order of the world (omnis ordination praesupponit ordinatorem)*. In this sense, the passive ordination of our will to the fitting good, to the moral good, superior to the pleasing good and to the useful good, presupposes a Supreme Orderer; or, moral obligation, manifested by the remorse or peace concerning an accomplished [(or unaccomplished)] duty, presupposes a supreme Legislator. We showed the foundation of this proof above, at the end of the fifth chapter of the first part of this text.

[6] See Cajetan's commentary on *ST* I-II, q. 2, a. 7.

of the universal and limitless good, immediately says to us, "Now that you have attained this sensible delight, which just a moment ago was attractive to you, you can now see that it is poverty itself and incapable of satisfying the profound void found in your heart, something incapable of responding to your desire for happiness."

The same is true for riches and honors, which are often so very desired. As soon as we have them, we see that the satisfactions that they give us are horribly transient and superficial. They too are unable to fill the void in our heart. Our intellect says to us, "All these riches and honors are again nothing but a poor, finite good, smoke that is dispelled by the slightest breeze."

We must say the same thing about power and glory, for the man who is raised up on the wheel of fortune begins to fall downward again scarcely after he has arrived at its highest point. He must make room for others; he will soon be a star whose light has burned out. And even if the most fortunate keep power and glory for some time, they cannot find *true happiness* in it. Instead, they often find so much anxiety and boredom in it that they yearn to withdraw from everything.

Yet again, we must say the same regarding *scientific knowledge*. Here we are faced with a very limited good. *Truth*, even if it is complete and unmixed with error, is the good of the intellect *but not the good of the whole man*. Besides the intellect, the heart and the will also have their profound spiritual needs, and if they are not satisfied, we will have no true happiness.

Do we find happiness in *a very pure and very lofty friendship*? Certainly, it will bring us great joys, indeed, sometimes very intimate ones; however, we have an intellect that conceives the universal, limitless good and here too it does not delay in seeing that this very pure and very lofty friendship is, yet again, only a finite good. Recall the words of St. Catherine of Sienna: "If you wish to be able to drink for a long time from this cup of a true friendship, leave it under the source of living water, otherwise you will quickly come to empty it, and it will no longer be able to respond to your thirst." If it does respond to it, this is because the beloved person becomes *better*, and in order to become better, the beloved needs to receive an increase in goodness from a higher source.

Even if we were able to see an angel, indeed gazing on him in all of his supra-sensible, purely spiritual beauty, we would at first be filled with wonder but then, our intellect, which conceives the universal and limitless good, would not delay in saying to us: "Here again is only a finite good. Precisely because of this finitude, it is a good that is very poor in comparison with the limitless Good Itself, which is unmixed with imperfection."

2. The Principle on Which the Proof Rests

Is it the case that this natural desire for happiness that each of us carries within ourselves cannot be satisfied?

Can it be the case that a NATURAL desire would be vain, chimerical, senseless, and without any real scope?

We understand that a desire born of an imaginative fantasy or an error of reason, such as the desire to fly, is chimerical. However, can a desire immediately founded on nature without the intermediary of any conditional judgment be chimerical? The desire for happiness is not a simple, conditional velleity. It is innate, that is, immediately founded on our nature, which is something stable and firm, being found in all men of all countries and of all times. Moreover, it is the very nature of our will which, before every act, is an appetitive faculty desiring the good in its universality.

The nature of our will, just as much as the nature of our intellect, cannot be the result of chance, of a fortuitous meeting, for our will (as also our intellect) is a wholly simple principle of operation. In no way is it composed of diverse elements that chance could have assembled.

Can this will's natural desire be chimerical?

Already, the *natural* desire of beings inferior to us is not in vain, as is noted from the naturalist's experimental perspective. The natural desire of the herbivore is to find grass, and it finds it. The natural desire of the carnivore is to find flesh to eat, and it finds it. The natural desire of man is to be happy, and true happiness in fact is not found in any limited good, nor can it be found there. Is this true happiness incapable of being discovered? Would man's natural desire thus be deceived and without finality, whereas the natural desire of inferior beings would not be in vain?

However, concerning this matter there is not only the naturalist's argument, founded on experience and the analogy of our natural desire with the natural desires of inferior beings. In addition, there is a metaphysical argument founded on the metaphysical certitude of the necessity and ontological value of the principle of finality.

Is it not the case that the consideration of this principle and of our natural desire presents us with what is contained within this profound remark made by St. Thomas in *ST* I, q. 2, a. 1, ad 1:

> We naturally know, in a general and vague kind of way, that God exists, namely inasmuch as God is man's beatitude, *for man naturally desires beatitude*, and that which is naturally desired by man is naturally known by him. However, this is not the same thing as knowing, without qualification [*simpliciter*], that *God exists*, just as to know that someone is approaching does not mean that one knows Peter (even though it is Peter who is approaching in this way), for many think that man's perfect good (i.e., *beatitude*) is riches, while others think it to be pleasures, and others hold it to be something else.

However, now, in this proof, we will set aside such errors by considering this natural desire and its finality, as well as by considering the insufficiency of goods that pass away.

If the natural desire for true happiness is chimerical, this means that all human activity inspired by this desire is without finality, without a *raison d'être*, all in contradiction to this evident and necessary principle: *Every agent acts for an end.* In order to understand the truth of this principle, formulated thus by Aristotle, we merely need to understand its terms: Every agent (whatever it may be, whether capable of knowledge or not) *tends* to some *determinate* thing that is fitting for it. Now, the end is precisely the determinate good to which the agent's action tends (or to which the movement of something that is mobile tends).

This principle is self-evident for those who understand the meaning of the words *agent* and *end*. It is demonstrated by a *reductio ad absurdum*, for otherwise (as St. Thomas says in *ST* I-II, q. 1, a. 2), "The agent would have *no reason for acting* rather than for not acting; likewise, it would have no reason for ACTING THUS rather than acting in some other way," of *desiring this given thing* rather than some other.[7]

If there were no natural finality, if every natural agent did not act for an end, there would be no reason for the eye to see instead of hearing or tasting, no reason for the wings of the bird to enable flight instead of enabling walking or swimming, no reason for the intellect to know rather than for it to will. Then, everything would come to lack a *raison d'être* and would be unintelligible. There would be no reason for the stone to fall instead of rising, no reason for bodies to be attracted to each other instead of repelling each other and being dispersed, thus destroying the entire harmony of the universe.

The principle of finality has a necessity and an ontological value that are no less certain than is the necessity and value of the principle of efficient causality: "everything that happens and every contingent being demands an efficient cause," and in the last analysis everything that happens requires an efficient cause that is not caused, which is its own acting, its action, and therefore which is its very own existence since action follows upon being and the mode of action upon the mode of being.

These two principles of efficient causality and of finality are *equally certain*, having a certitude that is not only physical but metaphysical.

---

[7] Fr. Picard has critiqued this demonstration of the principle of finality (as well as the principle of efficient causality) by way of *reductio ad absurdum*. In so doing, he has not understood *that it is not a question of* "deducing or drawing out these principles from the principle of non-contradiction." Instead, it is a question of showing that their denial leads one to *deny* the principle of non-contradiction. This is a wholly different matter than deducing or drawing out said principles. Demonstration by *reductio ad absurdum* is *indirect* and does not give intrinsic evidence as does direct and ostensive demonstration that furnishes a middle term. Demonstration by *reductio ad absurdum* or by way of reduction to an impossibility only prevents one from denying *vi absurdi illati*, by the force of the absurd inference to which such a denial would lead. Regarding Fr. Picard's position, see Gabriel Picard, *Le Problème critique fundamental*, 61. On this question, also see Reginald Garrigou-Lagrange, *God: His Existence and His Nature*, vol. 1, 181ff, 199ff; vol. 2, 360ff.

Must not Fr. Picard himself also admit that an *uncaused, contingent being* is something that is impossible (or, *absurd*) and so too is a desire or tendency without finality? If this is denied, one would arrive at an absolute sort of nominalism. The entire school following St. Thomas affirms that first principles cannot be denied without denying the principle of non-contradiction. Cf. *ST* II-II, q. 1, a. 7.

They have this certitude before we come to demonstrate the existence of God. Indeed, efficient causality itself cannot be conceived of without finality, for as we have seen, without finality, it would lack a *raison d'être* and, therefore, would be unintelligible.

The Terminus to Which the Proof Leads

Therefore, our natural desire for happiness has a finality; it tends toward a *good*. Would this be only toward an unreal good, or rather, toward a real but inaccessible good?

First of all, this good toward which our natural desire tends is not only an *idea* formed by our mind, for (as Aristotle said many times) although truth is formally found in the intellect that judges, the good is formally in things. When we desire nourishment, an idea of it does not suffice. What nourishes is not the idea of bread but, rather, bread itself. Therefore, the will's natural desire (founded not upon the imagination or upon an aberration of reason but, instead, upon the very nature of the intellect and of the will) does not tend toward an idea of the good but, instead, toward a real good. Otherwise, this is no longer a desire (and above all, a natural desire).

Perhaps, it will be said that the universal idea of the good leads us to seek after happiness in the *collection* or *succession* of all the finite goods that attract us: health, bodily pleasure, riches, honors, as well as the joy of scientific knowledge, art, and friendship. Those who, wildly racing onward, wish to enjoy all finite goods (either simultaneously or, at least, successively) seem to think for a time that true happiness is found here.

However, experience and reason disabuse us of such a thought. The heart's emptiness always remains, manifested by our boredom, and the intellect tells us that even if we simultaneously possessed the collection of all these finite goods which are mingled with imperfection, such a collection can no more constitute the Good Itself which we conceive of and desire than an innumerable multitude of fools would have the worth of a man of genius.

Here, quantity does not matter; instead, it is a question of *the quality of the good*. Even if we were to multiply all finite goods to infinity, they would not constitute the pure, unalloyed Good that our intellect conceives and that our will consequently desires. Here, we are faced with the profound reason for the boredom that the worldly experience, dragging it along with themselves on all the beaches of the world. They go from one created being to the next, and so forth, without ever being truly satisfied or *truly happy*.

* * *

But then, if our intellect can conceive the universal, limitless good, then our will, which is illuminated by it, also has a *limitless amplitude and depth*. Can its natural desire, which calls out for a real good, and not for an idea of it, be *vain and chimerical*?

This natural desire, founded on our nature and not our imagination, is firm and immutable like our nature. It cannot be vainer than the herbivore's desire or the carnivore's desire. It cannot be vainer than the natural ordering of the eye to vision, of the ear to hearing, and of the intellect to knowledge. And thus, if this natural desire for happiness cannot be *vain* and if it cannot find satisfaction in any finite good, nor in the collection of finite goods, we must say, with all necessity, that an unalloyed, Pure Good, the Good Itself (or, the Sovereign Good) exists, one that alone is able to respond to our aspiration. *Otherwise, our will's universal amplitude would represent a form of psychological absurdity*, something radically unintelligible and without *raison d'être*.

The Form and Force of the Proof

Therefore, this proof of the existence of God, the Sovereign Good, by the desire for happiness comes down to the following proof, which first requires the enunciation of the principle that is its major premise.

A natural desire (not one founded on the imagination or on an aberration of reason), *cannot be vain or chimerical* and cannot tend to an unreal or inaccessible good. Were it to have such a tendency, it would at once tend toward something and toward nothing, contrary to the principle of finality: "Every agent acts for an end." This principle would no longer have any certain, metaphysical value before having proven the existence of God. In reality, its necessity and its metaphysical certitude are equal to the necessity and metaphysical certitude of the principle of efficient causality; moreover, efficiency cannot itself be conceived of without finality, for otherwise it would not have any determinate direction and would not tend toward anything, thus producing nothing.

Finally, the principle of finality is not only true for tendencies and desires that we *see* fulfilled. It is also true of *natural* desires whose *realization we have not yet seen*, for the principle of finality is not only a merely empirical law (e.g., "heat expands iron") but, rather, is a metaphysical law that enunciates both that which is and *that which must be the case* under pain of lapsing into absurdity: the tendency that, properly speaking, is natural and immediately founded upon the nature of a thing (especially the nature of our mind [*esprit*]) cannot be vain or chimerical. Otherwise, our intellect's tendency to know the truth would equally be deceitful and illusory; likewise, our intellect could not be assured of the truth of its judgment by reflection upon the nature of its act and upon its nature, *which is made for being conformed to reality*, as St. Thomas says.[8] The intellect sees its own essential finality in its very nature—a capital point in epistemology—and it also sees, in the nature of the will, the will's own finality.

Now (and this is the proof's minor premise), *every man naturally desires to be happy*. Indeed, experience, like reason, shows that *true happiness is not found in any limited or finite good*, for the natural amplitude of our will, illuminated as it is by our intellect, which conceives of the universal and limitless good, is itself without limit.

Moreover, here, we are not concerned with an inefficacious and conditional desire like our natural desire for the Beatific Vision, founded on

---

[8] See Aquinas, *De veritate*, q. 1, a. 9: "Truth is known by the intellect inasmuch as the intellect reflects back upon its act, not only inasmuch as it knows its act, but also inasmuch as it knows its *proportion* (or conformity) *to reality*. Now, indeed, the intellect can know this proportion only if it knows the nature of its act; and it can know the nature of its act only if *the nature of its active principle* (i.e., the intellect, *to whose nature it belongs to be conformed to reality*) is known." It is the essential finality of the intellect.

this conditional judgment: "This vision would be perfect beatitude for me, if it were possible that I could be elevated to it and if God would wish to elevate me to it."[9] Here, we are concerned with an *innate* natural

---

[9] We have explained this point at length elsewhere in Garrigou-Lagrange, *De revelatione*, ch. 12 (in the recently-published, two-volume edition). There, we have shown, with the majority of Thomists, that this *natural velleity* to see God *sicuti est* (as He is) gives a very strong *argument from fittingness* on behalf of the *possibility* of our supernatural elevation to the Beatific Vision. However, it does not rigorously demonstrate it. Solely by its own powers, reason can demonstrate neither the existence nor the possibility of mysteries that are supernatural *quoad substantiam vel essentiam* (i.e., essentially supernatural mysteries), for they are likewise supernatural *quoad cognoscibilitatem* (i.e., with regard to their knowability). Without a doubt, we can show that nobody can prove the impossibility of the Beatific Vision; however, we can no more rigorously demonstrate its possibility than we can demonstrate the possibility of sanctifying grace, the light of glory, the Trinity, or the Incarnation. See Billuart, *Summa sancti Thomae, De Deo uno*, d. 4, a. 3. That which is supernatural *quoad substantiam vel essentiam* is supernatural *quoad cognosibilitatem, quia verum et ens convertuntur*, [i.e., because of the convertability of truth and being]. In this, supernatural mysteries differ from the miracle that is only supernatural *quoad modum productionis suae* (with regard to its mode of production). If one were to demonstrate the intrinsic possibility of the Trinity, one would demonstrate Its existence, for in the order of necessary things, existence immediately follows from possibility.

With regard to the possibility of our elevation to the order of grace, this question is not only concerned with the possibility of something that is *wholly contingent* but also is something essentially supernatural and, therefore, indemonstrable. This is why we cannot accept what was recently written on this subject in A. Fernandez, "Naturale desiderium videndi Divinam Essentiam apud D. Thomam eiusque scholam," *Divus Thomas* (Piacenza) 33 (Sept.-Dec. 1930), 512. [Tr. note: Fr. Garrigou-Lagrange only cited the periodical, month, year, and page. As I have done for numerous other citations, I have filled out the details. This citation, however, was particularly under-informative in details. His reticence to cite the name does show modesty in his engagement in polemics. The article is written in two parts, both published in 1930 in *Divus Thomas* on pages 5–28 and 503–527.]

In recent days, many people have written articles (in most opposed senses) concerning the natural desire to see God and obediential potency. We doubt that they seriously help to advance the question; many even confuse the question by misjudging the meaning and scope of the distinctions given by the greatest commentators on St. Thomas.

Some of these articles come down to saying, joining the Augustinians of the 18th century Noris and Berthi: the intuitive vision of God is our last natural end *quoad appetitionem* [with regard to desire], but it is our last *supernatural* end *quoad consecutionem et quoad media quibus obtinetur* [with regard to attainment and with regard to the means by which it is attained].

This way of seeing things, which is close to Baianism, can retain a certain distinction of the order of nature and the order of grace only by denying the principle of

desire which is not founded on a conditional judgment but, instead, finds its foundation immediately on the very nature of our will and its universal amplitude. There is no natural desire without a desirable good and without a good of the same amplitude as this natural desire.

Therefore, a limitless Good must exist, a Pure Good lacking any mixture with that which is not good or with imperfection, for in it alone do we *really* find the universal good that specifies our will. Without the existence of the Sovereign Good, our will's universal amplitude or depths, which can be filled by no finite good, would be a radical absurdity, an absolutely meaningless reality.

Here, we find ourselves faced with an impossibility that is inscribed in the very nature of our will, whose natural desire tends not toward the idea of the good but toward a *real good* (for the good is not in the intellect but in things), indeed toward an unrestricted, real good, which has the same amplitude as the natural desire that is carried toward it.[10]

---

finality: every agent acts for an end proportioned to it. Indeed, from this principle, it follows that God, the Author of our nature, cannot give us the *innate natural desire* for an end toward which He could not conduct us *ut auctor naturae* (as the Author of nature). The order of agents would no longer correspond to the order of ends.

After having read these articles, we maintain in the fourth edition of *De revelatione* (ch. 12) what we taught in the preceding editions.

[10] One sees that this way of formulating the proof, founding it on the principle of finality, differs quite significantly from the proof that has been proposed by Fr. Gredt who says in the fifth edition of his *Elementa philosophiae Aristotelico-Thomisticae*, vol. 2 (Freiburg: Herder, 1929), 194: "If the human will has a natural appetite for beatitude, specified by the infinite good as its object, this infinite good is not impossible; however, if the infinite good is not impossible, it exists in reality. Therefore . . ."— We do not deny this argument's value, but it is quite different from the one that we ourselves propose. Moreover, it requires a point of precision to be added to it.— St. Thomas says exactly in *ST* I-II, q. 2, a. 8: "The object of the will is *the universal good*, just as the object of the intellect is the universal true. Therefore, it is obvious that nothing can quiet man's will except for the *universal good, which is not found in any created thing* but only in God, for every creature has goodness by participation."

The specifying object of the will must be distinguished from its own last, natural end. This specifying object is neither God nor the Divine Good, which immediately specifies infused charity. The specifying object of the will is *the universal good*, which nonetheless is only found as a good that is at one and the same time real and universal in God (*bonum universal in essendo et in causando*), for in every other case, the good is limited. Cf. Cajetan's comments on *ST* I-II, q. 2, a. 7: "The object of the will is the universal good, i.e., not contracted to this or that good, but, instead, absolute. And if it is understood that there is a difference between the good and the true based on what is

St. Thomas proves also the immortality of the soul by means of a similar argument.[11]

Likewise, to explain the first lines of Aristotle's *Metaphysics* (before the question of God's existence is even raised), St. Thomas remarks, "In all men, there is a natural desire for knowing . . . (and) a natural desire cannot be in vain."[12]

Founded on this principle of finality, the proof which we are discussing should have a dazzling clarity for an angelic intellect. *If we begin with the existence of a human will that is specified* not by God (as infused charity is) but, rather, *by the universal good*, which *precisely as universal* is really found only in God, we can prove the existence of God, *either by way of efficient causality* (only an absolutely universal efficient cause was able to produce this will, which stands in need of a cause, for it is

---

said in *Meta.* IV, ch. 4, lect. 4 (namely, that *the true and the false are in the soul*, WHILE THE GOOD IS IN THINGS), it follows that our beatitude, which is the object of the human will, will exist *only in that thing in which the good is found absolutely.* And thus, it is in God alone." Thus, one passes legitimately from the universal good *in praedicando* to the universal good *in essendo.*

The same reality (*ut res est* [i.e., from the perspective of a thing as a thing]), namely God, is the object of natural knowledge *sub ratione entis et primis entis* [i.e., from the perspective of being and, indeed, the first being]; He is the object of faith *sub ratione Dei obscure revelati* [i.e., from the perspective of God, or the Deity, obscurely revealed]; He is the object of the Beatific Vision *sub ratione Dei clare visi* [i.e., from the perspective of God, or the Deity, clearly seen]; He is the object of natural love *sub ratione boni naturaliter cogniti* [i.e., from the perspective of the good, naturally known]; He is the object of infused charity *sub ratione boni divini per supernatulem revelationem cogniti* [i.e., from the perspective of the Divine Good known through supernatural revelation]. He is the same *res, ut res est* but not *ut obiectum est* [i.e., from the perspective of a thing considered as an object]; there are distinct formal objects.

Thus, one avoids the ontologism that blurs formal objects by confusing being in general with the Divine Being. It is not ontologism to say with Aristotle, St. Thomas, and Cajetan, "The good is in things and the universal good is not found without limit except in God." See *ST* I, q. 2, a. 1, ad 1: "We naturally know, in a general and vague kind of way, that God exists, namely inasmuch as God is man's beatitude, *for man naturally desires beatitude*, and that which is naturally desired by man is naturally known by him."

[11] See *ST* I, q. 75, a. 6: "The intellect apprehends being [*esse*] absolutely and according to all time; whence, everything that has an intellect *naturally desires* to exist forever. *However, a natural desire cannot be in vain.* Therefore, every intellectual substance is incorruptible."

[12] Aquinas, *In I Meta.* lect. 1.

not its own act of willing, nor the good itself) *or by way of final cau-sality* (if God, who alone has in Himself the universality of good, did not exist, the universal amplitude of this will and its natural desire are a meaningless reality; thus, the principle of finality is a empty verbal expression, a *flatus vocis*, and so too is the principle of efficient causal-ity, which cannot be conceived without finality; thus, meaning that one would find oneself faced with an absolute form of nominalism).

Is not this proof contained in these words that we cited from the beginning of *ST* I-II, q. 2, a. 8: "*It is impossible* that man's beatitude would be found in any created good. . . . Hence, it is clear that only the universal good can bring man's will to rest; and the universal good is not found in any created thing but *in God alone* because every creature only has goodness by participation."

* * *

In this way, we ascend from the effect to the cause and, indeed, to the Supreme Final Cause. St. Thomas says in *ST* I, q. 2, a. 2, "*On the basis of any given effect* we can demonstrate the existence of its *proper cause.*" Now, the natural desire for happiness is the effect of the attraction and pull of the Sovereign Good (and, indeed, of the true Sovereign Good, which can only be God). We ascend upward to this Sovereign Good no less by the way of finality than by that of efficient causality. St. Thomas is clear on this point, and we are surprised to see that many contemporary scholastics have forgotten this fact.[13] Nonetheless, we know that Aristotle much more explicitly affirmed (in *Metaphysics* XII, ch. 7) the attraction of Pure Act as the final cause of all beings than he affirmed Pure Act's effi-cient causality, for he never reached the explicit notion of creation, above all of creation that is sovereignly free and *not from eternity*.

---

[13] Above, we cited the capital text of *ST* I-II, q. 1, a. 4 ("Whether there is some ultimate end of human life"): "*Speaking essentially [per se loquendo], it is impossible to proceed to infinity with regard to ends* (just as in moving causes). . . . *If there were not a final end, nothing would be desired,* nor would any action be terminated, nor would the intention of an agent come to rest." And, further, in *ST* I-II, q. 2, a. 8, St. Thomas shows that the ultimate end (or true beatitude) cannot be found in any finite good but, instead, can only be found in God.

Therefore, the proof comes down to this:

An innate natural desire cannot tend toward an unreal good.

Now, by an innate natural desire, man desires true happiness, which is not found *de facto* in any limited good, nor can it be found in any limited good, nor even in the collection of these goods.

Therefore, there must be a Sovereign, Limitless Good, which we call God.[14]

3. What Is Not Demanded by the Natural Desire for Happiness

Does it follow that our natural desire for happiness *demands* that we arrive at the immediate vision of God, the Sovereign Good?

Not at all. This immediate vision of the Divine Essence is essentially supernatural and therefore is gratuitous, in no way owed to our nature, nor to angelic natures.

In this sense, St. Paul says to us, "'What no eye has seen, nor ear heard, nor the heart of man conceived, what God has prepared for those who love him,' God has revealed to us through the Spirit. For the Spirit searches everything, even the depths of God" (1 Cor 2:9–10, RSV).

However, far below the immediate vision of the Divine Essence and far below Christian faith [which itself is essentially supernatural], there is *the natural knowledge of God*, the Author of nature, which we arrive at through the proofs of His existence.

And if original sin had not weakened our moral powers, this natural knowledge of God would enable us to arrive at *an efficacious, natural*

---

[14] Pantheistic evolutionism will say, "The sovereign good toward which we tend does not yet exist; it is only the evermore elevated end toward which evolution marches onward." However, then, in this ascending evolution, without a creative or ordaining cause, without any real end that attracts it, *the more comes from the less* and the more perfect arises from the less perfect. No longer is there an ultimate end, no longer a true Sovereign Good, nor, consequently, secondary ends that motivate action and effort.

love of God, the Author of nature— a love of God, the Sovereign Good, naturally known.[15]

Now, if man had been created in a purely natural state, he would have found *true happiness* in this natural knowledge and natural and efficacious love of God—not in the form of absolutely perfect beatitude, which is supernatural beatitude (i.e., the immediate vision of God), but, nonetheless, *a solid and durable, true happiness*, for if this natural love of God is efficacious, it truly orients our life toward Him and allows us, in a true sense, to rest in Him, at least in the natural order, that is, in the order of that which is owed to our nature. This would have been the state of affairs for the immortal souls of the just, if man had been created in a purely natural state. And we have seen that St. Thomas, amidst the proofs of the immortality of the soul, noted that *every intellectual being*, conceiving being in an absolute manner, superior to every temporal limit, *naturally desires to exist* FOREVER and not only *here and now*. This natural desire cannot be in vain.[16] In a purely natural state, it would have been satisfied by a firm and error-free knowledge of God and by efficacious natural love for God that would have been possessed by the immortal souls of the just.

However, we have received much more *gratuitously*. We have received grace, which is the seed of glory, and along with it, supernatural faith and *supernatural love* of God, who is no longer only the Author of nature but also the Author of grace.

And then, for us Christians, *the proof* that we have discussed in this chapter finds a profound *confirmation* in the happiness (or, peace) that we find here below in our union with God.

Far above what philosophical reason can glimpse, without yet possessing the perfect beatitude that exists in heaven, we have found true happiness to the degree that we sincerely, efficaciously, and generously love the Sovereign Good above all else, more than ourselves and more than every other creature, to the degree that each day we order our

---

[15] [Tr. note: Regarding the aversion from our natural end included in our aversion from our supernatural end, see the text cited above in note 36 in the fifth chapter of part one.]

[16] See *ST* I, q. 75, a. 6.

entire life toward Him ever more profoundly.

Despite the sometimes-overwhelming sadness of the present life, we have found true happiness (or, peace), at least at the soul's summit, when we love God above all else, for peace is the tranquility of order, and we are thus united to the very principle of all order and of all life.

Thus, our proof finds an incredible confirmation in the profound experience of the Christian life wherein the Savior's word is realized: "Peace I leave with you; my peace I give to you; not as the world gives do I give to you" (John 14:27, RSV). The Savior has given us peace, not through the accumulation of pleasures, riches, honors, glory, or power, but, instead, through *union with God*. And He has thus given us this solid and durable peace, which he can (and indeed does) preserve for us, as He foretold us: "Blessed are the poor. . . . Blessed are those who hunger and thirst for righteousness. . . . Blessed are those who are persecuted for righteousness' sake, for theirs is the kingdom of heaven" (Matt 5:3–10, RSV). Already, the kingdom of heaven exists in them in the sense that in their union with God, they already have, through charity, eternal life as something that has already begun: *inchoatio vitae aeternae*.[17]

Epicurus boasted of being able to give happiness to his disciples by means of his doctrine, even in the bull of Phalaris, in the brazen bull that was red-hot and in which they would be burned to a crisp.[18] Only Jesus was able to realize such a thing in the martyrs by giving them peace and true happiness through their union with God, even in the midst of their torments.

To the degree that one possesses this union with God, the proof that we have been discussing thereby receives a very great confirmation through a profound spiritual experience, for God, through the Spirit's gift of wisdom, deigns thus to make Himself be felt by us as being the very life of our life: "It is the Spirit himself bearing witness with our spirit that we are children of God" (Rom 8:16, RSV). We thus come to have a quasi-experiential awareness of God as the principle of the filial love for Him which He inspires in us.

---

[17] See *ST* II-II, q. 24, a. 3, ad 2.

[18] [Tr. note: He is referring to a torture device used in the Graeco-Roman world.]

Here, we are certainly faced with a very precious confirmation, one that is more precious than the proof itself, for it is of a qualitatively superior order. However, the proof itself, founded on the principle of finality, has, like said principle, its own metaphysical rigor, which considerably surpasses the supposed religious experience spoken of by agnostics, who deny or place in doubt the ontological and transcendent value of the first rational principles of contradiction, efficient causality, and finality.

If we were to reject this metaphysical value of the first principles, the traditional proofs of God's existence would no longer have any [real] scope.[19] However, if we recognize the value of the principle of efficient causality, we must also recognize the value of the principle of finality, for there can be no efficiency, tendency, nor passion without finality.

If the proof of God's existence by the desire for happiness is trans-formed into a supposed intellectual intuition of God by the *absolute realism* of the ontologists, we must not fall into the opposite extreme of *nominalism*, which, denying the ontological and transcendent value of the principles of efficient causality and finality, does not recognize any significance in the proof unless one has the religious experience spoken of by the modernists. Between these two extreme errors, and elevated far above them, we have the *moderate realism* of Aristotle and St. Thomas, which starts with the existing facts and, by means of the metaphysical principles of efficient causality and finality, leads to God by legitimate paths.[20] Here, our intellect first conceives the abstract universal good (*universale in praedicando*). Then, it notices that the desired good does not exist the mind *sub statu abstractionis* [in a state of abstraction] but, instead, exists in things. Likewise, it notes that

---

[19] We have shown this at length elsewhere. See Garrigou-Lagrange, *God: His Existence and His Nature*, vol. 1, 111–205 ("The ontological value of first ideas and first principles") and 205–241 ("The transcendent validity of first ideas and first principles," that enable us to elevate ourselves to knowledge of God).

[20] In the proofs of God's existence, St. Thomas (in *ST* I, q. 2, a. 3) first states the *fact*, which is the contingent point of departure, *before the principle* (or, the major premise) of the argument. This is often his procedure in the *Summa theologiae*, where he also often states the *minor premise*, then elevates himself to the *major* in order to arrive at the conclusion.

the real good is found without limits only in God (*bonum universale in essendo et in causando*). If this sovereign Good did not exist, the universal amplitude of our will and of our natural desire would be without a *raison d'être* and could no longer exist.

Chapter 6

MORAL REALISM: FINALITY AND THE FORMATION OF CONSCIENCE

"Qualis unusquisque est, talis finis videtur ei."

Moral realism is no less connected to the principle of finality than is metaphysical realism.

We must number the moral question concerning the use of probability in the formation of our conscience among the most disputed problems that can be illuminated by the principle of finality.

A good number of theologians who have discussed the value of probabilism, equi-probabilism, and probabiliorism[1] for the past three

---

[1] [Tr. note: He is referring here to the debates concerning the binding obligation of conscience that is organized under the doctrinal headings of rigorism, tutiorism, probabiliorism, equiprobabilism, probabilism, and laxism. See Merkelbach, *Summa theologiae moralis*, vol. 2, 5th ed. (Paris: Desclée de Brouwer, 1947), n. 77 (p. 70–72). For recent studies of this era, without necessarily endorsing all the conclusions drawn by their authors, one can consult Stefania Tutino, *Uncertainty in Post-Reformation Catholicism: A History of Probabilism* (Oxford: Oxford University Press, 2017); Julia Fleming, *Defending Probabilism: The Moral Theology of Juan Caramuel* (Washington, DC: Georgetown University Press, 2006). From within the Thomist school, see the treatise on prudence in the aforementioned manual by Merkelbach as well as the text of Fr. Reginald Beaudouin cited below. Also, see H.-D. Noble, *Le discernement de la conscience* (Paris: Lethielliux, 1934); P. Richard, *Le probabilisme moral et philosophie* (Paris: Nouvelle Librairie Nationale, 1922); P. Mandonnet, "Le décret d'Innocent XI contre le probabilisme," *Revue Thomiste* 9 (1901): 460–481, 520–539, and 652–673; Mandonnet, "La position du probabilisme dans l'Eglise catholique," *Revue Thomiste* 10 (1902): 5–20; Mandonnet, "De la valeur des théories sur la probabilité morale,"

centuries do not seem to have sufficiently grasped the principles that for St. Thomas illuminate the nature of prudence and the *proper character of prudential certitude*. Now, conscience that is right and certain is nothing other than the *act of prudence*, which counsels, practically judges, and commands.[2]

Among the principles that most illuminate the problem concerning the formation of our consciences, we must above all include this corollary to the principle of finality, formulated by Aristotle: *Qualis unusquisque est, talis finis videtur ei.* According to the way that a man is well or poorly disposed (in his will and his sensibility), so does the end seem suitable or not suitable to him.

Each Person Practically Judges according to His Interior Dispositions. Therefore, They Must Be Rectified.

St. Thomas, speculatively considering the intimate nature of prudence (i.e., its formal object and its mutual relations with the other moral virtues), by the same token determined the nature of its acts and of right conscience in particular. Likewise and equally, he was able to resolve from on high the difficult questions of the treatise on conscience, questions that remain without a solution in the majority of modern writers.

The first of these difficulties is as follows: how can we arrive at a *certain judgment of conscience* despite the fact that we experience invincible ignorance concerning many of the circumstances of human acts, for example, when it is a question of future contingents of which we must have foreknowledge in order to take all the necessary precautions? Likewise, how can I determine with certitude, *here and now*, in matters that directly concern *me* (and not you) the *golden mean* to preserve in matters of temperance, meekness, humility, courage, patience—all

---

Revue Thomiste 10 (1902): 315–335; and Fr. Thomas Deman's article "Probabilisme" in the *Dictionnaire de théologie catholique*. All of these later texts are cited by Fr. Garrigou-Lagrange in other works.]

[2]   See *ST* II-II, q. 47, a. 7 and 8.

while this golden mean depends on many particular circumstances that are still known only in a vague manner (or, even at times are unknown), such circumstances including my temperament (be it high-strung, sanguine, or phlegmatic), my age, the season (be it summer or winter), my social status, etc. . . . etc.? To what must we have recourse in order to have this *practical certitude of conscience* in the presence of such a diversity of conditions that we can only vaguely grasp? Ought I to weigh probabilities for and against this or that action? They must be considered, but does this suffice, even when one adds to them certain reflex principles that are more or less certain: *a doubtful law does not oblige; the one in possession is in a better position?*[3] This investigation into probabilities sometimes may be lengthy. It even surpasses the capacity of many and often leads to nothing that is actually certain.

St. Thomas provides a more profound solution to this question. He does not disdain the consideration of probabilities for and against a course of action. Nor does he disdain commonly received reflexive principles. However, he insists before all else on a *formal principle* spoken of by few modern theologians even though it can be found even in Aristotle.[4] This principle can be expressed: "*The truth of the practical intellect* (or, prudence) *is found in conformity with right appetite,*" for, "*According to the way that a man is well or poorly disposed* (in his will and his sensibility), *so does the end appear suitable or not suitable to him.*" The truth of the practical intellect (i.e., of prudence) consists in *conformity to rectified appetite*, that is, to the *sense appetite* rectified by the virtues of temperance and courage and above all to the *rational appetite* rectified by the virtue of justice and the other virtues of the will. In other words, pratico-practical[5] truth consists in conformity with the habitually and

---

3   [Tr. note: This maxim represents one of a number of commonly received "reflex principles" said to be of use in trying to settle difficult cases of conscience. One can find such principles ubiquitously in texts that take into account the ramifications of the probabilist controversies in regard to the problem of conscience.]

4   See Aristotle, *Nicomachean Ethics* 3.4, 6.2.

5   [Tr. note: Like many of the chapters in this text, a version of this chapter originally was published in the *Revue Thomiste*. On this topic, see Reginald Garrigou-Lagrange, "Remarks Concerning the Metaphysical Character of St. Thomas's Moral Theology, in Particular as It Is Related to Prudence and Conscience," trans. Matthew K. Minerd, *Nova et Vetera* 17, no. 1 (2019): 266–270 ("Translator's Appendix 2: On the Specula-

actually *right intention* of the will, for as Aristotle says, "According to the way that a man is well or poorly disposed, so does the end appear suitable or not suitable to him." For example, he who is chaste, even if he does not know moral science, judges with rectitude (by way of the inclination of this virtue) concerning things relative to chastity. They appear to him as being good and obligatory.

St. Thomas explains this truth with great clarity in *ST* I-II, q. 57, a. 5, ad 3, as he does elsewhere throughout the treatise on prudence.[6]

---

tive, the Speculatively-Practical, and the Practically-Practical").]

[6] See *ST* II-II, qq. 47–57. As some have noted, the ever-present importance of this treatise on prudence would be quite clear to modern thinkers if only two words were added to its title: "Concerning prudence and the connected moral virtues, in relation to the formation of conscience." Prudence, which directs all the moral virtues, is so fundamental that no human act is good without also being prudent. And despite this fact, numerous modern manuals of moral theology, which do devote a large place to the treatise on conscience, quickly and silently pass over this virtue, the principal cardinal virtue. They sometimes dedicate only eight or ten pages to it and seem to forget that right and certain conscience is an act of prudence, whose formal object must be determined, as well as its proper nature and connection with the other virtues.

[Tr. note: On this topic, Fr. Garrigou-Lagrange stands on the side of Fr. Merkelbach in holding that the appropriate place for treating the details of conscience are in the treatise on prudence, so that one can thereby have knowledge concerning the conditions needed for right and certain judgments of conscience, which he ascribes to prudence. Here, however, there is a difference in terminology among Thomists, one that to be honest is not all that clear in Aquinas's own texts.

For some, including Frs. Garrigou-Lagrange and Merkelbach, we should consider the judgment of prudence to be one form of conscience-judgment (namely, right and true conscience). And, indeed, in *De beatitudine*, Fr. Garrigou-Lagrange seems to say that casuistry itself should be assigned to prudence in the end, although the comment is made in passing. However, certain texts in Aquinas assign conscience to the level of "moral science," that is, the speculatively-practical knowledge that we can have about human actions. Thus, such "judgments of conscience," would be moral-philosophical and moral-theological judgments of particular cases of moral actions without them being fully existentialized as applied *to us* or to any agent, ever lacking all the details of a completely concrete action.

Thomists are divided on this matter, as one can see readily in several excellent treatments of the topic in the following works: Reginald Doherty, *The Judgments of Conscience and Prudence* (River Forest, IL: The Aquinas Library, 1961); Cajetan Cuddy, "St. Thomas Aquinas on Conscience" in *Christianity and the Laws of Conscience: An Introduction,* ed. Helen M. Alvaré and Jeffrey B. Hammond, (Cambridge: Cambridge University Press, 2020); P. M. Noonan, Auriga et Genetrix: Le rôle de la prudence dans le jugement de la conscience 114 (2014): 355–377; 531–568.

For Fr. Merkelbach's own position, see Benedict Merkelbach, "Note: Quelle place assigner au traité de la conscience," *Revue des Sciences philosophiques et théologiques*

Indeed, in the aforementioned text he says:

> The truth of the practical intellect (i.e., the practico-practi-
> cal intellect or prudence) is understood in another, different
> sense than is the truth of the speculative intellect, as is said in
> *Nicomachean Ethics* 6.2. This is so because *the truth of the specu-
> lative intellect* is understood in terms of *conformity to the known
> reality [per conformitatem ad rem]*. Now, because the intellect
> cannot have infallible conformity in contingent matters (espe-
> cially future things to be prudently foreseen) but can have such
> conformity only in necessary matters, therefore no speculative
> *habitus*[7] concerning contingent matters is an intellectual virtue;
> only those *habitus* that concerned with necessary matters are
> intellectual virtues. *However, the truth of the practical intellect*
> (i.e., the practico-practical intellect or prudence) is understood
> in terms of *conformity with right appetite*. This sort of conform-
> ity has no place in the order of the necessary matters that do
> not depend upon our will, but it does with regard to contingent
> things that depend upon us, as is the case with human acts.

Thus, we can have PRACTICAL CERTITUDE concerning the
morality of the act that we will perform, even though it may well be
accompanied by *invincible ignorance* or an involuntary speculative error.
Such is the case for a faithful Catholic who, following an invincible (i.e.,
absolutely involuntary) error, believes that a consecrated host is placed
before him and judges, "I must adore this host." This judgment is practically true (i.e., has practico-practical truth) in conformity with right
intention, while it is speculatively false and, hence, is not conformed to

---

12, no. 2 (1923): 170–183; this text can be found in English as "Where Should we
place the Treatise on Conscience in Moral Theology?" a text to be published in translation by *Nova et Vetera* in 2020.]

7   [Tr. note: With good reason, one should refrain from referring to the virtues as habits,
which could lead the reader to think that they are mere subjective dispositions and
not ones that give objective capacity with regard to choice. Accepting the conclusions
of Simon's lifelong reflection, I am choosing to leave *habitus* untranslated; see Yves
Simon, *The Definition of Moral Virtue*, ed. Vukan Kuic (New York: Fordham University Press, 1986), 47–68.]

the thing itself: the host was not really consecrated.

The danger of subjectivism is removed if one limits this kind of certitude *by way of conformity to right appetite* to the order of contingences and if one recalls that the *right intention* of the moral ends of the different virtues itself has a rectitude that is immediately founded on the order of the *necessary* and the universal, *per conformitatem ad rem*, for the truth of the first moral principles (grasped by synderesis[8]) and the truth of the moral science[9] derived from them is indeed in conformity with the *object*.

However, this speculative rectitude of the first moral principles, as well as that of the necessary and universal conclusions of moral science, cannot descend or reason all the way to our human act in its *unique contingency*. In this matter, they can only determine the golden mean by way of the intermediary of *rectified appetite*, the rectitude of the will and the sensibility, a rectitude that is assured by the moral virtues. This is a point of capital importance.

Thus, we can understand that it is never legitimate to act with a conscience that is *practically probable*, for that which is probable can be *false*, and if the judgment were practically false, the human act directed by it would not be prudent but, instead, would be imprudent.

One also understands why each person, in the formation of his conscience, can pass from speculative probability to *practical certitude* concerning the moral fittingness of the act to be performed, even when he does not know the reflex principles enumerated in works of moral theology. These reflex principles, which are sometimes useful for theologians, are hardly known by most Christians, who nevertheless must form their consciences and do not always have time to take counsel before acting.

Even without resorting to these reflex principles, most Christians can form their consciences with the ordinary diligence that is possible to everyone and pass from probabilities for and against a course of action to the *practical certitude* of the prudential judgment *in conformity with right intention*.

---

[8] [Tr. note: Though, see the text from Merkelbach cited in note 31 above in pt. 1, ch. 35.]

[9] [Tr. note: That is, the knowledge of conclusions (*scientia*) drawn in light of the first moral principles.]

* * *

Certainly, it often happens that modern theologians, in treating the formation of right and certain conscience, present their readers with an edifying statement: "In order to form your conscience, virtue is required and even the practice of the virtues." However, they do not explain well enough *why* virtue is thus required, and they do not see well enough that this element concerning *the conformity of the practical judgment to rectified appetite* enters as a *formal* element into the *practical certitude* of the prudential judgment. In order to better determine the necessity of this element, one must have recourse to a metaphysical study of the nature of prudence and of its relations with the moral virtues. Indeed, prudence presupposes the *habitual* rectification of appetite by the moral virtues, and the prudential judgment presupposes the *actual* rectification of the intention of the end. This right intention must persist so that prudence can determine what are the best means in view of the end that is willed, so that it can direct *here and now*, as it must, the particular and passing acts of the moral virtues by determining the *golden mean* that pertains to each person according to his temperament, age, circumstances—all of which admit infinite variation.

To try to pass in silence over this metaphysical study of the virtues—even while citing St. Thomas's *Summa*—would be like merely preserving the setting of a ring without keeping the very diamond contained therein. By contrast, it is the role of the great commentators to show precisely where the most beautiful jewels are in St. Thomas's work, just as great art critics make known the beauties of Raphael and Michelangelo. So too, the work of someone like Cajetan or John of St. Thomas begins where superficial commentators stop, commentators who barely exceed the letter of St. Thomas. Sometimes, these commentators respond saying, "if you wish to understand Cajetan, read St. Thomas." However, without the help of the great interpreter, few would be able to resolve certain objections raised by Scotus. It is very easy to neglect them, but one sometimes is content with juxtaposing conclusions without seeing how they are rigorously deduced from the principles that give the doctrine of St. Thomas the true spirit that animates its letter.

Cajetan excels in placing these principles in relief. In particular, one should consult his remarks concerning the matter occupying us here in *ST* I-II, q. 57, a. 5, and q. 58, aa. 3 and 5, and in the treatise on prudence in *ST* II-II, qq. 47–57. He shows that the good or bad disposition of our appetite (i.e., of our sensibility and will) gives rise to a *relation of conformity* or of non-conformity with the object or end of a given virtue, an end which consequently appears to the intellect as being something desirable or not. Cajetan insists on this Aristotelian and Thomistic doctrine, noting that Scotus did not understand it. Indeed, this is an astonishing fact, for Scotus, who generally is a voluntarist, becomes, in the treatise on prudence, an intellectualist to excess, for he places prudence solely in the intellect as though (like *synderesis* and moral science) it did not presuppose the rectification of appetite. This is why, as Cajetan notes (in his comments on *ST* I-II, q. 57, a. 5, ad 3), Scotus cannot explain the fact that the judgment made by prudence concerning every particular action to be performed is not only true in most cases, but instead, is *always true*. This is why prudence has a value surpassing probable opinion, which is not an intellectual virtue, for in order to be a virtue, an intellectual virtue must *always* incline reason to the truth, *never* to falsity. Indeed, the prudential judgment *cannot ever* be practically false, for at the same stroke it would be imprudent (or, not prudent).

Therefore, as a result of its conformity to right appetite (that is, to right intention [rectified by the other moral and theological virtues]), prudence succeeds at attaining practical certitude in the direction of particular and contingent acts in the midst of the most varying of circumstances. Thus, it is *superior to opinion* and deserves to be called an intellectual virtue. However, it is *inferior to synderesis and moral science*, which have necessary and universal principles as their objects and which do not presuppose rectification of the appetite, though they contribute to constituting it in the virtuous person or establish only the advertence in sin in the person who is not virtuous.[10]

Therefore, St. Thomas profoundly understood, much better than Scotus, as well as many modern thinkers, the double axiom of Aristot-

---

[10] [Tr. note: Reading "pécheur" for "péché."]

le's *Nicomachean Ethics*: "As each is well or badly disposed in his will, so does a given end appear good or bad to him"—"The truth of the practical intellect (i.e., of prudence) consists in conformity to rectified appetite" (or, right intention).

This conformity to rectified appetite is not something artificial or quasi-mechanical, like the comparison of probabilities for or against some action, or like various reflex principles that are more or less certain. Rather, it is something *vital* and *excellent*. It is the virtuous life itself, which contributes to forming the rectitude of prudential judgment on the condition—it goes without saying—of presupposing knowledge of the first moral principles (i.e., *synderesis*[11]) and ordinary diligence in examining the circumstances, something that is possible for everyone.

Given that a particular man is truly humble, that which pertains to true humility (and not to false humility) pertains also to him. He has a *sensitivity* that enables him to discover what precisely must be done in this difficult matter. That which *here and now* for him is the golden mean between pusillanimity and vainglory has a profound *relation of suitability* to the virtuous inclination found in him, with his humility of heart. Thus, the virtuous man has this judgment by inclination or sympathy (*iudicium per modum inclinationis*) precisely where the universal and necessary syllogism cannot descend, namely into the domain of individual, ever-variable contingencies, where one must, nonetheless, act without going astray, without confusing true with false humility, magnanimity with vainglory, firmness with inflexibility, indulgence with softness, or true charity with that form of liberalism which is only a lack of intellectual and moral rigor. Here, one must have the sensitivity given by virtue, indeed great virtue, sanctity that does not deceive in these matters.

Therefore, every virtuous man, above all when he is aided by the counsel of others, can generally succeed at forming a right and certain conscience without recourse to a meticulous comparison of probabilities for and against an action, and likewise without needing to consider

---

[11] [Tr. note: Though, see the text from Merkelbach cited in note 31 above in pt. 1, ch. 5.]

the reflex principles known only by theologians. Thus, we here have a principle that is at once vital, dynamic, organic, and virtuous, a principle of rectitude and of prudential certitude loftier than an empirical knowledge that is more or less artificial and that would not generally surpass the level of probability. This is something we can indeed call moral realism.

Thus, St. Thomas clearly determined the specific character of the certitude proper to prudence, as he likewise showed concerning the certitude of faith[12] and the certitude of hope.[13] He was able to succeed in doing so only because he undertook a metaphysical study of these great questions and because he clearly determined the formal object and specific finality of the judgment of conscience and the relation of prudence (from which it proceeds) to the other virtues.

The End to Be Attained Sometimes Renders the Use of Probabilities to Be Illicit

The principle of finality illuminates no less another difficulty that touches closely on the preceding one, namely: *In the formation of one's conscience, why is the use of probability sometimes permitted and sometimes not?* From the time of the condemnation of laxism, all theologians have agreed in recognizing that *the use of probability is not permitted when there is a danger of an evil that one must absolutely avoid and that is independent of the formation of one's conscience.* For example, this is so in the administration of the sacraments, if one is concerned about their validity (unless there is a grave necessity). Likewise, if one is concerned with things that are necessary for salvation, with a necessity of means, one must choose the course that is more certain: *tutior pars elegenda*

---

[12] See *ST* II-II, q. 4, a. 8: "Faith is, without qualification (*simpliciter*) more certain than the intellectual virtues, namely than wisdom, insight into first principles, and science."

[13] See *ST* II-II, q. 18, a. 4: "Certitude . . . *essentially* is found in a cognoscitive power; however, it is found participatively in everything that is *infallibly* moved to its end by a cognoscitive power." [Tr. note: These remarks are well compared with Garrigou-Lagrange, *The Sense of Mystery*, 40–46.]

est (the safer way must be chosen). One cannot make use of a probable judgment that would be contrary. This also holds when there is a question of some right of a third party, as well as a grave danger of spiritual or temporal harm to oneself or to others, something that must absolutely be ruled out. In all of these cases, recourse to probability in favor of freedom is illicit. However, in other cases, it is permitted, and the matter is explained differently depending on whether one holds to probabiliorism, equiprobabilism, or probabilism.

It would be truly useful to relate this common teaching of Catholic theologians to a superior principle. For this, we must consider what is opposed to *the end to be obtained* in these cases. As Fr. Reginald Beaudouin, O.P. rightly showed in his *Treatise on Conscience* (wherein he reconciles the teaching of St. Alphonsus with that of St. Thomas),[14] such a relation to a superior principle can be established by means of St. Thomas's distinction between the *medium rationis tantum* [the mean of reason alone] and the *medium rei* [the mean of the thing].[15] Before St. Thomas, Aristotle himself had already said that the equitable mean of justice is the *medium rei* (that is, the just measure or just price established according to the very thing that one buys), while the golden mean of temperance (e.g., the quantity of food to eat) or of courage (as well as that of the virtues annexed to these) is the *medium rationis tantum, non rei* (i.e., the just measure constituted in the interior dispositions of the subject who acts, dispositions that vary according to age, temperament, circumstances of time and place, and so forth).[16]

In this way, we can easily see that the use of probability is *illicit* when the measure of the action to be performed is the *medium rei* (i.e., the golden mean established according to the exterior thing that one absolutely must do or avoid whatever may be our age or the circumstances in which we find ourselves). Such is the case when one is faced with a question of justice in matters pertaining to sales and purchases, when one is concerned about the validity of sacraments to be adminis-

---

[14] See Reginald Beaudouin, *Tractatus de conscientia*, ed. Ambroise Gardeil (Tournai, BE: Desclée, 1911), 84–87.

[15] St. Thomas explains this matter in the treatise on virtues in general (*ST* I-II, q. 60, a. 2; q. 64, a. 2) and in the treatise on prudence (*ST* II-II, q. 47, a. 7).

[16] See Aristotle, *Nicomachean Ethics*, 2.5.

tered, and always when there is a danger of evil that one absolutely must avoid and that is *independent* from the formation of one's conscience. *In all such cases, the end to be obtained excludes the use of probability.*

On the other hand, the use of probability is *licit* when the measure of the action to be performed is a *medium rationis tantum*, meaning the golden mean constituted not by the exterior thing that one should do or avoid, but rather according to the interior dispositions of the subject who acts, as in a matter pertaining to temperance or courage (as well as the virtues annexed to them). Indeed, when the golden mean of one's action is only a *medium rationis*, practical reason itself (i.e., prudence) must *determine* by itself what this mean is, according to the probabilities in play in accord with its conformity with rectified appetite. However, in the other case (namely, when the golden mean of the action is a *medium rei*), prudence must only *direct the execution* of the action, the measure of the action already being determined in accord with an external thing or to a given right of the other party in question. In that case, prudence cannot respond to a given obligation by commanding a doubtful or only probable satisfaction of the matter at hand, but must without doubt render that which is without a doubt owed.

And thus, this other difficulty—that concerning recourse to probabilities (a recourse that sometimes is licit and sometimes is not)—is resolved by St. Thomas's principles concerning the intimate nature of human acts and of the virtues, especially through a consideration of the end to be obtained and the golden mean to be observed.

* * *

What then should we conclude? In the moral domain, we do not at all need to leave aside abstract speculation in order to determine here and now what one must do in a given concrete case. Were one to do this, one would disregard the universal and necessary principles that are the rule of particular and contingent actions. Even in moral science, one must first, in light of nominal definitions, raise oneself upward by means of abstraction from concrete facts both to *real definitions* and to universal and necessary *principles*, as is done by the intellect in its purely speculative use [lit. *comme le fait l'intellect spéculatif*]. Second, one must *descend*, as is done by the intellect in its practico-practical use (i.e., by prudence), from abstract, universal, and necessary principles to particular and contingent concrete acts in order to direct oneself well toward the proper ends of the virtues and toward the final end. Without this outlook, nearly all of moral theology would be reduced to its inferior application (i.e., to casuistry). Moreover, casuistry itself would be abolished, since it cannot apply principles to concrete practical cases unless these principles of morality are in themselves known in advance.

This is why, although the metaphysical study of the virtues at first seems useless to many people, it is in fact very useful, *more than useful*—indeed, supra-useful. It is a befitting good (i.e., something that is good in itself). If we say with Aristotle that "metaphysics is useless," we must understand this adjective "useless" as meaning that it is above usefulness, not below it—like the befitting good, which is good in itself independent of every delightful or useful consequence.[17]

Such is the moral theology conceived of by St. Thomas. It is not specifically distinct from dogmatic theology. It has a distinctly metaphysical character in the supernatural order. And if it truly remains at this loftiness, it will then proceed not only to *casuistry* but, by way of its superior applications, to *asceticism* and *mysticism*, the latter opening the way to contemplation of the mysteries of salvation. Thus the circle of sacred theology is brought to perfection, proceeding from faith in supernatural mysteries, then directing the human person toward contemplation of these mysteries, a contemplation that is, here below, along with charity, the normal disposition to the Beatific Vision in heaven.

It is above all in moral theology conceived in this manner that we grasp all the realism of the principle of finality, as well as the realism of this corollary: *qualis unusquisque est, talis finis videtur ei conveniens*—as our will and our sensibility are well or poorly disposed, the true final end appears to us as being sovereignly befitting or not. This principle explains not only the certitude of the prudential judgment or of conscience, but also explains the Spirit's *gift of wisdom* which makes us judge concerning Divine things by means of a connaturality or sym-

---

[17] [Tr. note: Quite obviously, Fr. Garrigou-Lagrange is noting that this sort of study is a *bonum honestum*, in contrast to a *bonum utile* or a *bonum delectabile*.]

pathy founded on the love of God. He who loves God with all of his strength is increasingly led to judge that God is truly the Sovereign Good for him. See *ST* II-II, q. 45, a. 2: "Inasmuch as it is a gift of the Holy Spirit, it belongs to wisdom to have a right judgment concerning Divine things *according to a kind of connaturality with them*."

Chapter Seven

REALISM AND OUR KNOWLEDGE
OF THE SUPERNATURAL

As we have seen, metaphysical realism and moral realism are intimately connected to the principle of finality. This is also true regarding the realism that we can call "supernatural," namely, the realism of our knowledge of the supernatural and its different forms.

If there is an oft-debated problem in apologetics which can be truly illuminated by the principle of finality, it is the problem of the relations between the grace of faith and the miracles that confirm revelation.

Are miracles naturally knowable? If they are, what kind of knowledge absolutely requires the supernatural light of infused faith? How do we pass from the loftiest natural knowledge to that of the order of grace?

This problem is only one particular case of the mysterious transition from one order of reality to another. Already, when it is a question of rising from the domain of brute matter to that of vegetative life, then to that of the senses and the passions, and finally, to that of the intellect and the will, our reason encounters a mystery: the admirable union of two things whose intimate reconciliation escapes our reason—the union of soul and of body, of the imagination and the intellect, of the physical order and the moral order. Indeed, on one hand, we see a kind of continuity in nature: *natura non facit saltum*, nature does not jump from one order to another. The summit of the lower order in a sense touches the lowest degree of the immediately superior order, *supremum infimi attingit infimum supremi*. This is why, once upon a time, it was possible to believe that the sponge was only a plant. Nonetheless, on the other hand, when our reason wishes *to define* the various classes of beings methodically and philosophically, it must admit that specific differences exist between the mineral kingdom, the plant kingdom, and the animal kingdom and that such differences are not only accidental but, instead, are essential, indeed, generic differences and not merely specific ones. For all the more reason is there an abyss, an infinite distance, between the senses (whether external or internal), which know only the individual (i.e., the singular being which is sensible through its qualities), and the human intellect, which reaches the universal, the essence of sensible things, their *raison d'être*, and from there rises to natural knowledge of God.

The intimate nature of the harmony (or, union) of these profoundly distinct orders forever remains a mystery for us, and those who wish to suppress every form of mystery either reduce the superior order to the inferior (as materialists or mechanistic philosophers do) or wish to see in the inferior only a projection or attenuation of the superior order, as is asserted by various forms of idealism, whether subjective or objective. In order to avoid mystery, these extreme positions are condemned to contradiction. Clearly, the truth is found between the two—not as the mediocre is found between good and bad but, instead, as perfection rises above the vices opposed to each other through excess and defect. Philosophical truth is not the mediocrity obtained through a kind of effacement of ideas (as is often intended by eclecticism or opportunism). Instead, it is the culminating point, the peak, dominating the wanderings and perpetual fluctuations of error. Nevertheless, as Aristotle saw, these fluctuations of error, however extravagant they may be, can help us in discovering the truth, somewhat like how the sides of a triangle's base enable us to determine the summit of the triangle. Indeed, the partial truths contained in errors that are opposed to each other converge toward the summit. We merely need to meditate on the *Metaphysics* and the *Physics* of Aristotle so that we might see that his doctrine is constituted in this way. Whence, we can find two interpretations offered for Aristotelianism and even for Thomism: one drawing them toward an inferior middle, the *media via* that satisfies eclectic thinkers and another one which sees them in their true place, raised above mechanism and dynamism, above empiricism and idealism, above pantheism and dualism, and above the other fluctuations of error.[1]

This is also the case in theology, in particular when it is a question of explaining the passage from our highest natural knowledge to the essentially supernatural knowledge of infused faith.

The distance between these two orders is absolutely infinite. We are inclined to forget that infused faith, by its elevation, so surpasses every form of rational demonstration (whether philosophic or apologetic) and even every natural intuition of the angels, that it is more distant from these inferior forms of knowledge than it is from the Beatific Vision. It is of the same *essentially supernatural order* as the Vision experienced by the blessed in heaven and as the knowledge that God

---

[1] In the eyes of Thomists of tradition, this is what distinguishes their position (expressed in the 24 theses proposed by the Sacred Congregation of Studies under Pius X) from the *media via* followed by those who deviate from these theses. In the judgment of the former, this [latter] *media via* is found, not between two tendencies to be avoided, but instead halfway between the true doctrine of St. Thomas and the errors condemned by the Church. The Very Reverend Fr. Wlodimir Ledochowski, S.J. [1866–1942, Superior General of the Jesuits from 1915 to 1942] recognized this also, in a sense, in his letter *De doctrina S. Thomae magis magisque in societate fovenda*: "I would not, however, direct these words against those who believe themselves to be following the Angelic Doctor in the strictest manner since we are convinced that this plan [*propositum*] is also most useful for the Church. But this rule is not common; however, it is clear that the Society accommodates itself to the more common manner, although more accurately defined for certain teachings, and hence that it goes forth by a kind of middle way from disputes that have occurred heretofore [*ex hucusque disputatis*]." Earlier in the same text, on p. 32, after having explained the formal statute by which the Society of Jesus is connected to St. Thomas, he wrote, "From those things that were set forth above, it is obvious that we do not make use of that same freedom of following whatever school is received in the Church, a freedom that is used by others."

M. J. Rivière notes on this subject in *Revue du Clergé français*, July 1918, 61: "By bringing these two complementary passages together, one obtains a diagram of the main theological tendencies accredited in the Church, among which the Society of Jesus holds, indeed, the *golden mean* [*juste milieu*]. If parliamentarian language were not too profane or inadequate in these matters, one could nearly speak of a right, a left, and a center."

[Tr. note: Ledochowski's letter can be found in Wlodimir Ledóchowski, "Epistola A. R. P. Wlodimiri Ledóchowski: Praepositi Generalis Societatis Jesu: De Doctrina S. Thomae magis magisque in Societate fovenda," *Zeitschrift für katholische Theologie* 42, no. 2 (1918): 205–253. The selections above are found on pages 240 and 230. Fr. Garrigou-Lagrange cites pages 44 and 32 of some other edition.]

has of Himself and of His intimate life. *Fides est sperandarum substantia rerum.* Faith is the substance of things hoped for.[2] Infused faith, the gift of God, is incomparably superior to the loftiest philosophy and even to theology, which proceeds from it by deducing its conclusions.[3] This is what enables us to say with St. Paul, "If . . . an angel from heaven, should preach to you a gospel contrary to that which we preached to you, let him be accursed!"[4]

Hence, when we seek to see how *rational* knowledge of the credibility of the mysteries of faith disposes us *to the essentially supernatural act of faith,* we must not be surprised to find ourselves confronted with obscurities analogous to the aforementioned philosophical mysteries. And, as is expected, we here encounter two erroneous and heretical explanations that are radically opposed to each other. On the one hand, there is the Pelagian or semi-Pelagian *naturalism* that disregards the necessity of grace and the supernaturality of faith or of the *initium fidei,* the beginning of faith. On the other hand, there is the *pseudo-supernaturalism* of the first Protestants, the Jansenists, and the fideists, a pseudo-supernaturalism that diminishes the powers and rights of reason.

While avoiding these condemned, extreme theses, certain theologians do not seem to rise high enough above them and seem to yield more or less to one or the other of these two temptations: either they tend to reduce the supernatural act of faith to a rational, discursive form of knowledge (of the Gospel and of miracles), a knowledge that is plated with a *supernatural modality,* which calls to mind the gold plate applied to copper in order to make a replica, or on the contrary, they tend to reduce the rational knowledge of credibility to the supernatural

---

[2] Heb 11:1. See the commentary of St. Thomas on this text in the letter to the Hebrews.

[3] [Tr. note: Note, however, that theology has other tasks as well, for it is a form of wisdom which must reflect upon its principles, something that Fr. Garrigou-Lagrange himself affirms elsewhere. On this topic, see Reginald Garrigou-Lagrange, "Remarks Concerning the Metaphysical Character of St. Thomas's Moral Theology, in Particular as It Is Related to Prudence and Conscience," trans. Matthew K. Minerd, *Nova et Vetera* 17, no. 1 (2019): 261–266 ("Translator's Appendix 1: Concerning the Formal Object of Acquired Theology"); also, Matthew K. Minerd, "Wisdom be Attentive: The Noetic Structure of Sapiential Knowledge," *Nova et Vetera* (2020).]

[4] Gal 1:8 (RSV).

act of faith and, in certain respects, call to mind a kind of fideism.

These two opposed tendencies manifest themselves in two theories.

The first of these theories teaches that the infused light of faith is not necessary for knowing and adhering to the *formal motive* of this theological virtue. Reason by its own powers can attain unto it. Grace is not necessary for producing the very substance of the act of faith but only for believing with the *supernatural modality* necessary for salvation—*ut oportet ad salutem*. This theory, as we will see, is that of Molina and of numerous Jesuit theologians. For several centuries, the Thomists have argued that it compromises the *essential* supernaturality of infused faith, whose elevation (as we have already said) is closer to the Beatific Vision than to the natural knowledge of the angels.

A radically contrary theory has been proposed in the very same the Society of Jesus, thanks to the eclecticism that it professes, by Frs. Pierre Rousselot[5] and Joseph Huby,[6] and was recently taken up in a work composed by a young Italian philosopher. According to these latter thinkers, not only is the light of grace needed for producing the very substance of the act of theological faith and attaining its formal object, but moreover, they say that one cannot discern with certitude the reality of a miracle without faith: "The light of grace is necessary for knowing miracles."[7] One could ask oneself whether or not this thesis unduly diminishes the powers of reason and compromises the rational evidence of credibility, as well as the probative force of miracles; like-

---

[5] Pierre Rousselot, "Les yeux de la foi," *Recherches de science religieuse* 1 nos. 3 and 5 (1910): 241–259, 444–475. Pierre Rousselot, "Remarques sur l'histoire de la notion de foi naturelle," *Recherches de sciences religieuse* 4 (1913): 1–36. Pierre Rousselot, "Réponse à deux attaques," *Recherches de sciences religieuse* 5 (1914): 57–69.

[Tr. note: Fr. Garrigou-Lagrange cites the 1910 and 1913 articles in this note, though he only mentions the title "Les yeux de la foi." The 1914 article was included in the English translation of the 1910 articles. See Pierre Rousselot, *The Eyes of Faith: With Rousselot's Answer to Two Attacks*, trans. Joseph Donceel (New York: Fordham University Press, 1990). The 1913 article can be found in English translation in Pierre Rousselot, *Essays on Love & Knowledge*, ed. Andrew Tallon, Pol Vandevelde, trans. Andrew Tallon, Pol Vandevelde, and Alan Vincelette (Milwaukee: Marquette Unviersity Press, 2008), 183–224.]

[6] Joseph Huby, "Miracle et lumière de la grâce," *Recherches de science religieuse* 9 (1918): 36–77.

[7] Huby, "Miracle et lumière de la grâce," 55.

wise, we wonder if it also provides a sufficiently lofty enough idea of the essential supernaturality of faith.

Naturally, each of these two opposed theories cites St. Thomas, but upon reading these citations, we can see how they have been chosen: the Master has been consulted, though without studying his articles one by one and without giving sufficient consideration to the subordination of the principles that provide their foundation.

Here, as in all the great problems, the Thomist doctrine is placed between two extremes, not by oscillating from one to the other, but by rising above them through a loftier, more metaphysical and theological view of the principles at hand and through a more profound comprehension of the facts. From this apex, we can see that the systems opposed to Thomism and opposed to one another are generally true in what they affirm and false in what they deny, as Leibniz once said. St. Thomas seeks reconciliation not, "in the effacement of ideas and forgetting what separates," but by taking into account everything that is true in the opposed systems, going "all the way to the summit of his thoughts and those of others"[8] and by manifesting a superior principle equally disregarded by the opponents in the battle. Instead of superficially looking on everything as though they were on the same level, St. Thomas sees from on high and in depth. In this way, he grasps the admirable harmony of the most different of orders.

Here, to our eyes, the two opposed theories arise from an equal misunderstanding of the profound distinction that exists between the *supernaturality of the mysteries and invisible grace*, and *that of the sensible miracle*. They are separated from each other according to whether or not one admits the *natural* knowability of the supernatural [order] on the basis of sensible miraculous facts. However, neither of these two theories has a lofty enough idea of the superior, intimate, and invisible supernatural [order] of grace and of the object of faith.

This is what we intend to show by examining, one after another,

---

[8] We borrow these expressions from one of the most beautiful pages of Léon Ollé-Laprune, *Le prix de la vie*, 3rd ed. (Paris: Belin frères, 1896), 456ff. We believe that they apply to St. Thomas more than to any other thinker.

  [Tr. note: Fr. Garrigou-Lagrange does not cite the edition. The expression appears to come from remarks on p. 460.]

these two opposed theories as well as their relations to St. Thomas's teaching. We would not have written anew concerning this subject if we had not been attacked by those holding these two opposed theses, which, curiously enough, focus their attack on the position that wishes to reconcile them by considering things from a loftier perspective.

And, since the criticisms that have been addressed to us arise from the fact that they isolate our conclusions from the principle that founds them (i.e., that which at the very least makes them unique), we find ourselves faced with the particular obligation of insisting upon this principle. We will do so with the greatest calm, avoiding every personal animus. Indeed, we would even like to be able to speak without naming the contemporary authors to whom we will be responding, as did the masters of the Middle Ages, *"aliqui dicunt..., alii vero tenent . . ."* However, the discussion would become unclear if we wrote like this.

The First Theory: The Grace of Faith Is Not Absolutely Necessary for Adhering to the Formal Motive of This Theological Virtue

We will only briefly consider this first theory, which we have examined at greater length in a Latin work to which we will refer throughout this chapter.[9]

This thesis is that of Scotus, Durandus of St. Pourçain, the Nominalists, Molina, Juan Martínez de Ripalda, Giles de Coninck, Juan de Lugo and of numerous contemporary theologians such as Billot, Lahousse, Mendive, Palmieri, and Schiffini, as the Very Reverend Fr. Ledochowski, the Master General of the Jesuits, remarks in his letter concerning the doctrine of St. Thomas. This letter does not, however, present this doctrine as conforming to the teaching of St. Thomas but rather as an innovation of Molina that was at first vigorously combatted

---

[9]   See Reginald Garrigou-Lagrange, *De revelatione per Ecclesiam Catholicam proposita* (Paris: P. Lethielleux, 1926). Also, see Reginald Garrigou-Lagrange, "La surnaturalité de la foi," *Revue Thomiste* 22 (1914): 17–39. [Tr. note: A translation of the fifth edition of *De revelatione* is planned by Emmaus Academic in the near future.]

but was then accepted by many.[10]

According to this theory, given that man's natural understanding (and, *a fortiori*, that of the demons) can, by its own powers, know that God is the Truth Itself and that He has confirmed, by visible signs, the revelation contained in the Gospel, can likewise *without grace* believe in the revealed mysteries, indeed believing in them on the basis of the same formal motive as that of infused faith.

Thus, acquired faith (which is called "natural" because it does not proceed from a supernatural interior light, that is, from an infused *habitus*) would have the same formal motive as theological faith.

We have shown at greater length elsewhere[11] that this thesis is contrary to the teaching of St. Thomas, according to whom virtues and acts are specified by their formal objects—"the species of any *habitus* depends on the formal character of its object, without which, the species of the *habitus* cannot remain"—*species cuiuslibet habitus dependet ex formali ratione obiecti: qua sublata, species habitus remanere non potest.* St. Thomas presents this in *ST* II-II, q. 5, a. 3, in relation to the

---

[10] See Ledochowski, *Epistola de doctrina*: "For it can easily happen in controverted questions, especially in speculative matters, that either of two opinions be safe or even probable; nay rather, it sometimes happens that an opinion which first seems to be less pleasing afterwards ends up being common and is approved. . . . The same thing happened in that chief point of doctrine, upon which not a small number of other things depend, [i.e., the point of doctrine] that is *concerned with the identity of the formal object in natural and supernatural actions.* For the opinion (for some time now more common) teaches that supernatural acts do not differ by necessity from natural ones on account of their formal object; and Lugo, Ripalda, the Wirceburgenses (i.e., the Würzburg Jesuits), His Eminence Cardinal Billot, Lahousse, Mendive, Palmieri, and Schiffini hold this opinion—which doctrine, however, is among those in Molina's *Concordia*, which not few people said ought to be condemned."

However, let us note that if Cardinal Billot, in this thesis, follows Scotus, the nominalist Gabriel [likely Biel], Durandus, Molina, and de Lugo, as he expressly declares, he nonetheless separates himself from de Lugo by distinguishing *scientific* (or, discursive) *faith*, which like that of the demons rests above all upon the evidence of miracles, from the *faith of authority* that rests on the Authority of God revealing. On his express agreement with Scotus et al., see Ludovico Billot, *De virtutibus infusis: commentarius in secundam partem S. Thomae* (Romae: Ex Typographia Iuvenum Opificum a S. Ioseph, 1905), 71–74. Regarding the latter distinction, see pp. 291ff.

[Tr. note: The selection from Ledochowski can be found on page 237 in the edition cited in note 1 above. Fr. Garrigou-Lagrange cites pages 40ff in some other edition.]

[11] Garrigou-Lagrange, *De revelatione*, 3rd ed., 469–481, 498–514.

formal heretic, who cannot pertinaciously deny one dogma without rejecting the formal motive of faith and, consequently, can no longer believe in other dogmas with this same motive, even though he may hold that they are revealed in the Gospel by the sovereignly true God and confirmed by miracles. Indeed, the formal motive of faith is not the visible miracle, nor is it the philosophical truth of the infallibility and absolute truthfulness of God, the Author of nature and of miracles. The motive of faith is the revelation of God the Author of grace, a revelation proposed by His infallible Church: "The formal object of faith is the First Truth as manifested in the Sacred Scriptures and the teaching [*doctrina*] of the Church, which proceeds from the First Truth."[12] Moreover, the faith of the faithful is supernatural by its essence and not by a super-added modality: "Since man is elevated above his nature when he assents to those things that are of faith, this must belong to him by means of a supernatural principle that interiorly moves him; this principle is God."[13]

Therefore, we need not be astonished that the Thomists, from the time of Capreolus to our own days, rejected the thesis of Scotus, the nominalists, and of Molina. The criticism that they make against this thesis always remains the same in its foundation and is only given precision in its form, as we have shown elsewhere by setting forth the texts of St. Thomas's great commentators.[14]

In particular, Tomás de Lemos (1555–1629) said in substance at the Congregation *De auxiliis*, "This theory overturns the whole of philosophy by denying the principle of the specification of *habitus* and acts by their formal objects, and it overturns the whole of theology by reducing faith, hope, and charity to a form of merely *plated supernatural*."[15] This criticism was recently made in the same terms by Fr.

---

[12] *ST* II-II, q. 5, a. 3.

[13] *ST* II-II, q. 6, a. 1.

[14] See Garrigou-Lagrange, *De revelatione*, 3rd ed., I, 481–498.

[15] See Jacques-Hyacinthe Serry, *Historia congregationem de auxiliis* (Louvain: 1699), bk. 3, chs. 35 and 36. Also, Tomas de Lemos, *Panoplia gratiae*, bk. 4 n. 25 and 26. We have reported these texts of Thomas de Lemos in Garrigou-Lagrange, *De revelatione*, 3rd ed., I 491ff.

Rousselot, S.J.,[16] who did not need to read it in Lemos.

Moreover, here Suarez is nearly in agreement with the Thomists and separates himself from Molina. Indeed, he almost sounds like Lemos:

> To hold that grace is only necessary in order for the act of faith to be more perfect in its entity (but not on account of the formal object of this act) is to bring oneself much closer to Pelagius, who said that grace is only necessary in order to believe more easily. And this would seem to be a loophole invented in order not to contradict conciliar texts.[17]

In fact, were one to follow this direction, one would well seem to travel down the pathways of Pelagianism in opposition to fideism. Suarez adds, "Also, this represents the overturning of the principle of the distinction of faculties, *habitus*, and acts by their formal objects, as well as the entire philosophy that rests upon this principle."[18]

We are happy to see Fr. J. Huby, S.J., following Fr. P. Rousselot, writing:

> The principle that dominates everything is that of the specification of faculties by their formal object: *species cuiuslibet habitus dependet ex formali ratione obiecti, qua sublata, species habitus remanere non potest* (*ST* II-II, q. 5, a. 3). When it is a question of knowledge, this comes down to saying that it must have a kind of "connaturality" for it, a kind of natural correspondence between the subject and the object, between the knowing faculty and the known object. . . . And (in faith) this supernatural principle is not the simple motion and elevation of the will. It presupposes the elevation and supernaturalization of the intellect. Indeed, it is "a kind of light . . . divinely infused into the human mind" (*In*

---

[16] Pierre Rousselot, "Remarques sur l'histoire de la notion de foi naturelle," 33.

[17] See Suarez, *De gratia*, bk. 2, c. 9 n. 11–13, 17, 21–27. We have reported these texts in Garrigou-Lagrange, *De revelatione*, 3rd ed., I p. 491. [Tr. note: I am following Fr. Garrigou-Lagrange's French here.]

[18] Suarez, *De gratia*, bk. 2, c. 9 n. 11–13, 17, 21–27.

Boetium de Trinitate, q. 3, a. 1, ad 4).[19]

After having insisted greatly for many years on this principle's scope, it is not without satisfaction that we see Fr. Huby and several others recognize its truth and importance. However, we now come to the new theory that he believes must be deduced from it.

The Second Theory: The Light of Grace Is Absolutely Necessary, Not Only in Order to Adhere to the Formal Motive of Infused Faith, but Also in Order to Discern Miracles

See how Fr. Huby, following Fr. Rousselot in this, exposited this thesis in 1918, one that has been taken up by others since then:

Thomist theologians—except Cardinal Billot—are generally in agreement with each other and with Suarez on this principle (i.e., of the specification of *habitus* and acts by their formal object), but we can ask ourselves whether they have deduced all of its consequences. There is one that appears to be logically imposed and which, nonetheless, does not seem to have been explicitly proposed by the theologians or by modern apologists (or, if some seem to have caught a glimpse of it or to have begun to express it, I do not believe that they have explicitly developed it). It is summarized in this simple proposition: *the thesis of the specification of the faculty by its formal object must be applied not only to our knowledge of the articles of faith, properly speaking, but also to the perception of the very signs of credibility.* These signs are supernatural signs or, as St. Thomas says, supernatural effects. Therefore, in order that they may be known under *their formal aspect [raison] of supernatural being,* they require a corresponding faculty, one that is "attuned" and of the same order, namely, a supernatural faculty. If we con-

---

[19] Huby, "Miracle et lumière de la grâce," 54.

sider the most dazzling of these signs, namely miracles, we will say that *the light of grace is necessary for knowing miracles.* This proposition can seem surprising. Nonetheless, it is *the logical consequence of the thesis enunciated above,* and as we hope to show, it is perfectly in harmony with the details furnished by St. Thomas concerning the psychology of faith.[20]

Does this not, we say, come down to exaggerating the extension of the Thomist principle rather than applying it to the case of miracles, consequently, diminishing its comprehension and elevation, and at last approaching unconsciously the Molinist thesis that one combats?[21]

Certainly, we admit quite willingly that the light of grace *ordinarily aids* those who are undergoing conversion, helping them to to discern the signs of revelation and their probative force,[22] and that apologetics carried out done *sub directione fidei.*[23] We go as far as to say that this light of faith *is sometimes necessary* in order to arrive at a certain *judgment of credibility,* either on account of an insufficient presentation of the motives of credibility or on account of the prejudices and other defective dispositions of the person who examines them.[24] We even say, in separating ourselves from Molina, that an intrinsically efficacious Divine motion of the natural order (called "grace" in a broad and improper sense of the word) is needed for the accomplishment of every natural good act. Finally, we add that the *ultimate* practico-practical *judgment* of *credentity* is supernatural in its essence (*quoad substantiam*) and *never* can be made without grace, properly speaking.

---

[20] Huby, "Miracle et lumière de la grâce," 54, 55. The emphases are not in the original.

[21] We will see this at the end of this chapter when we speak of the demon's faith.

[22] See Garrigou-Lagrange, *De revelatione,* 3rd ed., vol. 1, 523–527, 535ff, 548.

[23] See Garrigou-Lagrange, *De revelatione,* 3rd ed., vol. 1, 43. [Tr. note: For a brief summary of Fr. Garrigou-Lagrange's thought on these matters, the reader can profitably consult Jacques Maritain, *An Essay on Christian Philosophy,* trans. Edward H. Flannery (New York: Philosophical Library, 1955), 55–61. Also, see the work of Fr. Garrigou-Lagrange's student, Fr. Joseph C. Fenton, *Laying the Foundation: A Handbook of Catholic Apologetics and Fundamental Theology* (Steubenville, OH: Emmaus Road, 2016).]

[24] See Garrigou-Lagrange, *De revelatione,* vol. 1, 535 nota 1. In this case, the judgment is only modally supernatural (*quoad modum tantum*).

It is formulated thus: the mysteries of the Gospel, confirmed by miracles, not only are rationally believable, but moreover, it is obligatory and good for me *hic et nunc* to believe them. This judgment of credentity (with which Fr. Huby, like Fr. Rousselot, wishes to identify that of credibility) immediately rules the *pius credulitatis affectus* spoken of by the Council of Orange[25] and is supernatural like it. We have discussed this point more extensively in *De revelatione*,[26] and Fr. Gardeil has spoken of it at great length in the second edition of his *La crédibilité et l'apologétique*, in speaking about the intention of faith.[27] Thus, we can easily explain the facts related to conversions insisted on by this second theory.

However, to hold that grace is *necessary* for knowing miracles, let us say, "the proposition can seem surprising," as Fr. Huby himself acknowledged. And, for our part, the surprise remains when we compare this thesis with the teaching of Scripture and of the Church, with the common teaching of the theologians, with the teaching of St. Thomas and of his school, and, moreover, with the very principle invoked by this new theory.

* * *

It seems that many questions remain without a satisfying response.

According to this thesis, the Pharisees, precisely because they resisted the interior light of grace, were unable, not only to know that Jesus was the Son of God,[28] but also to discern the divine origin of the

---

[25] See Denzinger, no. 375.

[26] See Garrigou-Lagrange, *De revelatione*, vol. 1, 540ff.

[27] See Ambroise Gardeil, *La crédibilité et l'apologétique* (Paris: J. Gabalda et Fils, 1928), 11–32.

[28] On this point, their blindness is explained, and in this sense St. Peter says, "[You] killed the Author of life, whom God raised from the dead. . . . And now, brethren, I know that you acted in ignorance, as did also your rulers. . . . Repent therefore, and turn again" (Acts 3:15–19, RSV).

The ignorance spoken of by St. Peter is certainly not the ignorance that suppresses culpability; he wishes to say that by committing the crime of deicide, the Jews did not see the enormity of it. In this sense, Our Lord said, "Father, forgive them; for they know not what they do" (Luke 23:34, RSV), words that do not suppress what we will cite.

most brilliant of His miracles. How would our Lord have said, "If I had not done among them the works which no one else did, they would not have sin; but now they have seen and hated both me and my Father" (John 15:24, RSV)? Did the chief priests, who "planned to put Lazarus also to death" (John 12:10, RSV) in order to prevent people from speaking about his resurrection, themselves doubt the divine origin of this resurrection? After having interrogated at length the man born blind after his miraculous healing, could the Pharisees still doubt that it was the work of God (John 9)? And what do we read in the *Acts of the Apostles* concerning the members of the Sanhedrin when they began to deliberate as a result of St. Peter's miracle? They said, "What shall we do with these men? For that a notable sign has been performed through them is manifest to all the inhabitants of Jerusalem, and we cannot deny it. But in order that it may spread no further among the people, let us warn them to speak no more to anyone in this name" (Acts 4:16–17, RSV). Finally, must we not say that the sin against the Holy Spirit committed by the Pharisees went so far as to attribute to a demon the miracles that *clearly* to their eyes came from God?

If we absolutely need the light of grace in order to discern miracles with certitude, why does the [First] Vatican Council say on the subject of miracles, "As they *manifestly* display the omnipotence and infinite knowledge[29] of God, they are the *most certain signs* of the divine revelation, *adapted to the intelligence of all men*,"[30] and, "If anyone says . . .[31] miracles can never be *recognized with certainty* and that the divine origin of the Christian religion cannot be *legitimately proved* by them, let him be anathema."[32] If no intellect, even that of the demons, can certainly, by its natural powers alone, discern miracles, why are such miracles called, "most certain signs *adapted to the intelligence of all men*"? The Antimodernist Oath likewise says, "*Maxime accommodata*." And what can be a *true proof* (*rite probari*) of the Divine origin of the Christian religion whose probative force would be inaccessible to the

---

[29] [Tr. note: Fr. Garrigou-Lagrange does not have *et infinitam scientiam* in his text.]

[30] [First] Vatican Council, *Dei filius*, c. 3 (Denzinger, no. 3009).

[31] [Tr. note: Fr. Garrigou-Lagrange considers only part of this canon. The first half is concerned with those who say that miracles are not possible at all.]

[32] [First] Vatican Council, *Dei filius*, 3.4 (Denzinger, no. 3034).

natural understanding of the greatest philosophers and theologians, and even to the natural intelligence of the angels?

Why do the Comments to the pre-conciliar schema for the [First] Vatican Council state the following?

> Nor are there others lacking who would teach that such super-natural facts (i.e., miracles) cannot be understood as a motive of credibility unless faith is already presupposed, and for this reason that the very fact of revelation cannot be *demonstrated* to a man who has not yet received faith, and that, hence, *there cannot be a certain, prior persuasion concerning the truth of the fact of revelation or concerning the existence of revelation directed toward the reception of Christian faith*; but [instead, they hold that], without persuasion of this sort, faith is produced through divine grace such that this would be a spontaneous and immediate act of reason. However, the Holy See has already frequently considered it necessary to proscribe errors of this sort.[33]

Why too are they followed by citations of a proposition condemned by Innocent XI (Denzinger, no. 2121), the condemnation of fideism (Denzinger, nos. 2751–2757), and Pope Pius IX's Encyclical *Qui pluribus* against the followers of Georg Hermes:

> Indeed, human reason, lest it be deceived and err in a matter of so great importance, ought to investigate diligently the fact of divine revelation so that it can know with certainty that God has spoken. . . . And so, human reason, knowing clearly and distinctly from these most splendid and equally most strong proofs that God is the author of this faith, can proceed no farther but . . . must render all obedience to this faith.[34]

---

[33] See Jean-Michel-Alfred Vacant, *Études théologiques sur les constitutions du Concile du Vatican d'après les actes du concile*, vol.1 (Paris: Delhomme et Briguet, 1895), 593 (*Schema constitutionis dogmaticae de doctrina catholica contra multiplices errores ex rationalismo derivatos partum examin propositum*, adnotationes, XVI).

[34] Pius IX, *Qui pluribus* (Denzinger, nos. 2778 and 2780).

We are content to pose these questions here. Certainly, those who hold the theory that we are discussing have examined all these texts and believe that they can preserve their obvious meaning. The matter is not so clear to our eyes. We say with John of St. Thomas, "It still indeed remains the case that someone can judge evidently concerning the credibility of a miracle that has been seen and, nevertheless, not wish to believe on account of one's perversity."[35]

One goes so far as to say:

To consider only the physical circumstances, it is *impossible to judge* concerning the transcendence of a phenomenon. However brilliant one may suppose a miracle to be, even be it the resurrection of a dead man, one cannot affirm that a demon would be incapable of imitating a miracle's external appearances and phenomenal representation. Hence, how are we *to discern true miracles if not by the consideration of the moral and religious circumstances*, principally of the end? *It is impossible to render a judgment* concerning, for example, the resurrection of Christ, considered not only as a historical fact whose cause could not be predetermined, but also as a *properly Divine work*, without examining the end of this mystery, i.e., the glorification of Jesus and of His mission. Hence, given that the end of the miracle is a supernatural intention, *ad manifestandum aliquid supernaturale* [for the sake of manifesting something supernatural] (as St. Thomas says in *ST* II-II, q. 178, a. 1, ad 3), we are brought back to our general principle: that knowledge of a supernatural formal object presupposes a supernaturalized intellect.[36]

Yes, indeed, the demon can seek to imitate all miracles, but can one not distinguish the simulacrum from reality by an examination of the fact and of the physical circumstances first, as one differentiates the

---

[35] John of St. Thomas, *Cursus theologicus, De fide*, disp.3 , a. 2, n. 10. Such an assertion is common among theologians.

[36] See Joseph Huby, "Miracle et lumière de la grâce," 69. We have emphasized several passages in the text.

hallucination from a sensation? Can the demon, for a lengthy time, give a corpse such a perfect appearance of the acts of vegetative, sensitive, and intellectual life that the most attentive observer could not make the distinction? If reason by its own powers can know the resurrection of Christ only as a *historical fact whose cause it cannot predetermine*, reason cannot say whether there had indeed historically been a true resurrection or a simulacrum of one, for God alone can resurrect the dead. The demon can only imperfectly imitate this miracle. And then, it is no longer clear how one can avoid the modernist proposition, "The Resurrection of the Savior is not properly a fact of the historical order. It is a fact of merely the supernatural order (neither demonstrated nor demonstrable) that Christian consciousness gradually derived from other facts."[37] As St. Thomas teaches on this matter: "Through given *evident signs*, Christ showed Himself truly to have been resurrected."[38]

And if, in addition, it is fitting to examine the moral circumstances of miracles, must we say that without such an examination we *can never have any certitude* and that they are *always*, not only a confirmation, but indeed, the decisive criterion without which the others are absolutely insufficient?[39]

---

[37] Decree of the Holy Office (under Pius X), *Lamentabili*, no. 36 (Denzinger, no. 3436).

[38] *ST* III, q. 55, aa. 5 and 6. We have explained this point in Garrigou-Lagrange, *De revelatione*, 3rd ed., vol. 2, 349ff. There, we show that St. Thomas means by the *fides oculata* of the Apostles that it grasps the fact of the resurrection as a miracle and as a mystery attested to by Jesus, the angels, and the prophets and manifested by *evident* sensible signs.

[39] We have provided a lengthy exposition on this point of doctrine of St. Thomas in Garrigou-Lagrange, *De revelatione*, 3rd ed., vol. 2, 63–106: "*De discernibilitate miraculi ex natura operis et ex circumstantiis physicis et moralibus.*"

As we state on page 99 of that text, we admit that doctrine and miracles mutually confirm one another, in virtue of the axiom "causae sunt invicem causae *in diverso genere.*" However, we insist more than Fr. Huby on this axiom's closing words, which alone enable one to avoid contradiction. In the revealed doctrine and miracles, there are signs accessible to reason confirming it solely by its own powers: if the doctrine is obviously immoral and impious, the miracle performed in confirmation of it is false; if on the contrary, the doctrine is obviously worthy of God and of such a nature as to give peace to men, this is a new sign, helping us to see that such a wonder [*prodige*], which manifestly exceeds the powers of sensible nature and of human nature, does not come from a demon.

Finally, we recognize that grace is sometimes necessary for avoiding illusion, in the case of exceptional and numerous diabolical wonders [*prestiges*] like those that are

Finally, is it absolutely *necessary* that one have the light of grace in order to judge concerning these moral circumstances? Is reason *always* incapable of seeing that there is nothing immoral and perverse in these circumstances but, instead, that they are in perfect harmony with the moral ideal of natural intelligence? Do not many of the rationalists recognize that Jesus's life, doctrine, and influence are admirable on all points and have never been equaled? The *end of the miracle* is manifested to reason alone through the announcement of the wonder-worker, who declares that He does this prodigy to confirm a given revelation; it is then manifested through the moral effects, whose excellence is so clear that even a non-believer can write that in all the ages when society has wished to dispense with Christianity, "It became an evil and cut-throat place."[40]

Therefore, we believe that the new theory diminishes the powers of reason, as well as the elevation of grace, for it requires the elevation of grace as being indispensable in an inferior order that is not necessarily its own and fails to recognize the sublimity of the order of invisible and essentially supernatural mysteries, which it does not distinguish well enough from that of sensible miracles.

Like the preceding theory, we believe, it does not consider things in a lofty enough manner.

We do not ignore the fact that Fr. Rousselot has written to show what separates his thesis from the traditionalist fideism of Bautain.[41] Granted, in order to fortify reason in its impotence, Bautain appealed to primitive tradition and to humanity's common faith, not to the interior

---

announced for the end of time: "False Christs . . . will arise and show great signs and wonders, so as to lead astray, if possible, even the elect" (Matt 24:24, RSV). However, this should not lead us to say that Christ's miracles were not perfectly accommodated (*maxime accomodata*) to the natural understanding of all men. Even though certain hallucinations can be distinguished from real miracles only with difficulty, we must not say that sensation is always doubtful; and even though death is sometimes uncertain in the case of lethargy, one must not have doubt of death when the heart has been pierced [*lorsque le cœur est ouvert*].

[40] Hippolyte Taine, *Origines de la France contemporaine: Le régime moderne*, vol. 2, 118–119.

[41] Pierre Rousselot, "La vraie pensée de Bautain," *Recherches de science religieuse* 5, no. 4 (1914): 453–458.

illumination of souls. However, we cannot admit, with Fr. Rousselot, that "only supernatural faith, considered as a perfection of the subject, gives natural reason its firm footing and knowledge of any object whatsoever its full legitimacy."[42] We think that, without this supernatural illumination, Aristotle gave us a theory of the four causes as well as proofs of the existence of God that are perfectly legitimate. Nor do we believe that the light of grace is indispensable for grasping the demonstration given by the greatest theologians concerning the discernibility of miracles.[43]

Fr. Huby recognizes that, "Most modern theologians pronounce against the theoretical necessity of the gratuitous light, the *lumen gratuitum*, for perceiving the credibility of religion."[44] Therefore, one would need to have quite solid reasons for affirming that they are mistaken.

At the very least, one must admit that the demon's intellect can, without grace, by its natural perspicacity, discern miracles: a true resurrection from a false one, from a diabolical wonder. St. Thomas says:

> Faith is found among the demons, inasmuch as, *on the basis of natural knowledge itself,* as well as from miracles (which they see to be above nature much more subtly than we do), they are compelled to believe those things that exceed their natural cognition.[45]

> The faith that is found in the demons is not a gift of grace, but rather they are compelled to believe by *the natural perspicacity of the intellect. . . .* And this very fact displeases the

---

[42] Fr. Rousselot, "Intellectualisme," *Dictionnaire apologétique de la foi catholique*, II, 2, ed. A. d'Alès (Paris, 1914), col. 1074.

[43] We have exposited this demonstration at length in Garrigou-Lagrange, *De revelatione*, vol. 2, 63–106. Also, in the work of Fr. Joseph de Tonquéc, S.J., the reader can find a proof whose value is certainly graspable by natural reason. See Joseph de Tonquédec, *Introduction a l'étude du merveilleux et du miracle*, 2nd ed. (Paris: Beauchesne, 1916), 230ff.

[44] Joseph Huby, "Miracle et lumière de la grâce," 50.—"No difficulty from the perspective of the learned [*Nulla difficultas quoad doctos*]," says Camillus Mazzella, *De virtutibus infusis*, 3rd ed. (Rome: 1884), 794.

[45] Aquinas, *In III Sent.*, d. 23, q. 3, a. 3.

demons, [namely] that *the signs of faith are so evident* that they are compelled to believe; and therefore, their malice is in no way diminished by the fact that they believe.[46]

Finally, how would the impossibility of having natural knowledge of miracles be the logical consequence of the Thomist principle of the specification of acts by their formal objects?

It would be surprising that this consequence would not have been deduced by St. Thomas, nor by the great theologians of his school, who for seven centuries have studied this question in its various aspects, doing so with a profundity, a metaphysical penetration, a supernatural elevation, a reverential sense for tradition, a spirit of continuity, and finally, a measure all surpassing so many essays of our own days—hasty systematizations formed around an idea that momentarily strikes one's mind and seems to respond to current needs and to address current prejudices. The Thomist theologians have studied this problem in itself, in light of the principles of theology, which are not current or past experience but, rather, are the immutable truths of the faith (as well as the metaphysical analysis of the notions that it implies) in conformity with experience. And we will see that their teaching is scarcely in agreement with the newly proposed thesis.

The Third Theory, the Thomist Doctrine: The Finality of Naturally Knowable Miracles and the Much-Superior Finality of Grace and of Faith

After many years of having studied closely the texts of St. Thomas and his greatest commentators concerning this question, and having classed them according to their chronological order, which bears witness to growing terminological precision, we believe it necessary to formulate the Thomist doctrine as we did in *De revelatione*:[47]

---

[46] *ST* II-II, q. 5, a. 2, ad 2 and 3.
[47] See Reginald Garrigou-Lagrange, *De revelatione*, 3rd ed., vol. 1, 498.

1. Inasmuch as Divine Revelation is essentially supernatural (i.e., *quoad substantiam*), and proceeding from *God the Author of grace* and constituting the formal motive of infused faith, it can only be known by this faith which it specifies ("est id *quo* et *quod* supernaturaliter creditur," it is that *by which* and that *which* one supernaturally believes).

2. Nonetheless, inasmuch as the fact of revelation is supernatural *quoad modum* in its cause and confirmed by miracles, it can be known naturally, as one naturally knows the veracity of *God, the Author of nature*.[48]

In this way, we can see the finality of miracle as well as that superior good of the grace of faith; we can also see the application of the principles that we formulated above concerning the subordination of ends.

We devoted a hundred pages of the aforementioned work[49] to the history of this doctrine, to its theoretical proof, and to the resolution of the objections that have been raised against it. With texts from different works by St. Thomas, we have collected in the aforementioned work texts from Capreolus, Cajetan, Cano, Bañez, Lemos (the decision of the Congregation *De auxiliis*), Alvarez, Reginald, John of St. Thomas, the Salmanticenses, Goudin, Gonet, Billuart, Gotti, Lepidi, Zigliara, de Groot, Gardeil, del Prado, de Poulpiquet, Schaezler, and Scheeben. According to all these Thomists, the thesis is the same; it is only given precision as regards its terminology, which achieves its full clarity with the Salmanticenses in their refutation of Scotus, the

---

[48] From this inferior and external perspective, the fact of revelation is considered, not as an essentially supernatural *mystery*, but instead, as a *miraculous intervention* by God in the prophet's mind, itself confirmed by a sensible miracle. This miraculous intervention would have existed even if God was content to reveal to us the sum of *the natural* truths of religion without making us know anything about supernatural mysteries like the Trinity.—Therefore, *the end* of the miracle, which is the evident credibility of the revealed truths, is naturally knowable (cf. *De revelatione*, vol. 1, 527).—Thus, the Church is *visible* through her notes, but the *intimate life* of the Church is a mystery only accessible to faith. So too, St. Thomas says of the Apostle St. Thomas, "*He saw the man and the wounds and from this* believed in *the divinity* of the resurrected one." Aquinas, *In XX Ioann.*, 29, lect. 6, fine. Also see *ST* II-II, q. 1, a. 4.

[49] Garrigou-Lagrange, *De revelatione*, vol. 1, 458–515, 548ff; vol. 2, 63–106.

Nominalists, Molina, and De Lugo.[50]

Here, we can only recall some of St. Thomas's texts and insist on the principle of the thesis in question.

The principal texts, which express the two parts of the thesis, were cited above in our criticism of the first two theories.

There can be no doubt that for St. Thomas the infused light of faith is necessary in order for us to adhere to the formal motive of this theological virtue since, according to him, *habitus* are specified by their formal objects.[51] Thus, infused faith is supernatural by its very essence and by its essential finality.

According to him, it is no less certain that, without grace, the demons discern with certitude miracles and their probative force.[52] And, St. Thomas likewise thinks that the Pharisees who resisted the grace of faith had no doubt interiorly concerning the Divine origin of Jesus's miracles, from which comes their sin against the Holy Spirit.[53]

---

[50] Salmanticenses, *Cursus theologicus, De gratia*, tr. 14, disp. 3, dub. 2 and 3, nos. 28, 37, 40, 45, 48, 49, 52, 58, 60, 61. These texts are cited in Garrigou-Lagrange, *De revelatione*, 3rd ed., vol. 1, 494ff.

[51] *ST* II-II, q. 5, a. 3: "the species of any *habitus* depends upon the formal character of [its] object, without which, the species of the *habitus* cannot remain."—q. 6, a. 1: "Since man, in assenting to those things that are of faith, is elevated above his nature, he must have this by means of a supernatural principle that interiorly moves him; and this is God."—q. 5, a. 3, ad 1: "The heretic does not hold the other articles of faith, about which he does not err, in the same way as a faithful person holds them, namely *by adhering, without qualification [simpliciter], to the First Truth, for which man needs to be aided by the habitus of faith.*"—q. 5, a. 1: "In the object of faith, there is something quasi-*formal*, namely *the First Truth surpassing all natural knowledge of a creature*, and something material, namely that to which we assent when adhering to the First Truth."

See the other texts of St. Thomas cited in Garrigou-Lagrange, *De revelatione*, 3rd ed., vol. 1, 469–481.

[52] See *ST* II-II, q. 5, a. 2, ad 2 and 3. We have reported these texts in the selections associated with note 46 above.

[53] See St. Thomas, *In V Ioannem*, lect. 6, no. 9: "God testifies to something in two ways, namely sensibly and intelligibly. He does so *sensibly* as through a sensible voice. . . . However, He testifies *intelligibly* by inspiring in the hearts of those who believe what they ought to believe and hold. . . . Therefore, you (i.e., the unbelieving Jews to whom Jesus was speaking) were able to receive the first kind of testimony, and no wonder, for it was from God only *effectively* (i.e., according to supernaturality pertaining to efficient causality), as was said—those words and sights [*species*] (or, miracles). However, you did not understand these words—*neque vocem eius umquam audistis,*

Therefore, according to St. Thomas, miracles are naturally knowable. They are signs whose finality is to confirm to the eyes of reason the Divine origin of Revelation or the holiness of the servants of God.[54]

What is the principle of this thesis? It is completely found in the distinction between *the supernaturality of the mysteries and of invisible grace* and *the supernaturality of sensible miracles*. In other words, it is wholly found in the classical distinction between that which is intrinsically and entitatively supernatural (i.e., *supernatural quoad substantiam*) and that which is extrinsically and effectively supernatural (i.e., *quoad modum*), a distinction omitted by Fr. Huby who fails to recognize its importance, and this led him to believe that the new doctrine that he proposes is necessarily derived from the Thomist axiom concerning the specification of acts by their formal object.

However, without overturning the whole of theology, one cannot deny this distinction between the *essential supernaturality* [*surnaturel essentiel*, sic] of the mysteries, which surpasses our natural knowledge, and the *modal supernaturality of efficient causality* [*surnaturel modal d'efficience*], which surpasses, not our natural faculties of knowledge but only all created (and creatable) *productive* powers. No creature can, like the Principal Cause, *perform* a miracle, but it does not follow that a creature cannot naturally *know* one when God does produce it.

One example suffices for manifesting this distinction: the miracle of the resurrection of a dead person does not give a corpse a *supernatural life*; instead, such a resurrection *supernaturally* gives it a *natural life* that is vegetative and sensitive. By contrast, sanctifying grace is an essentially supernatural life, like the mysteries of the intimate life of God.

---

etc.—that is, you were not among those partaking in them. . . . In other words, you did not have that intelligible testimony, . . . That is, you did not have the interiorly inspired word. And the reason for this is *that you do not believe in Him whom He*, the Father, *has sent."*

This text is cited by the Salmanticenses as containing a particularly clear formula of the theses that we defend alongside them.

54 See *ST* II-II, q. 5, a. 2: "If some prophet were to foretell in a word from God some future thing and were to bring forth a sign by resurrecting a dead man, the intellect of a witness would be convinced by this sign so that it would know *manifestly that this is said by God*, who does not deceive; however, that future thing thus foretold would not be evident in itself." Also, see *SCG*, 3.155 [sic]. See these texts in Garrigou-Lagrange, *De revelatione*, vol. 2, 102.

The essential supernatural (*quoad substantiam*) is precisely that of the intimate life of God and of the mysterious participations in this life. We can very well naturally know and demonstrate the existence and attributes of *God, the Author of nature* but not attain the intimate life of God. To do this, we would need to know Him not only according to the common notion of *being* or of *cause* but, instead, according to the absolutely proper and eminent notion of the *Deity*.[55] God alone naturally knows Himself in this way, for nothing in the natural order (even in the angelic order) is a participation in the Deity as such, and, consequently, nothing of this order enables us to know the *intimate life of God*. Likewise, *grace* and the mysteries of salvation are *essentially* supernatural; grace, along with the infused virtues that derive from it, is an *intrinsically* supernatural life, a formal and physical participation in the *Deity*.

As the Author and Master of nature, God can very well perform a miracle (e.g., by resurrecting a dead person), but *as Author and Master of nature, He cannot produce sanctifying grace* in the soul of a sinner, nor even the actual grace that disposes one to conversion. This would be contrary to the principle of finality, which is the object of this work: it would no longer be true to say that the order of agents corresponds to the order of ends. The essential supernaturality of grace and of the infused virtues immensely exceeds that of the miracle. This is at once an elementary and capital truth in theology.

Therefore, this essential supernaturality (*quoad substantiam*) is taken (as is said by the Thomists, Suarez, and the majority of theologians[56]) from the *intrinsic cause*, the formal cause, i.e., the formal constitutive of the reality which is said to be supernatural. And as truth follows being (*verum et ens convertuntur*), this essentially (*entitative, formaliter*) supernatural reality is a supernatural *object* exceeding every form of natural knowledge, even that which the angels can have. There-

---

[55] This is how the Thomists distinguish the formal subject of supernatural Theology from that of natural Theology. The former is *Deus sub ratione Deitatis* (God according to the formal *ratio* of His Deity); the second is *Deus sub rationis entis* (God according to the formal *ratio* of being). Thus, natural theology is part of metaphysics (or, the science of *being inasmuch as it is being*). See Garrigou-Lagrange, *De revelatione*, 3rd ed., vol. 1, 8ff.

[56] We have reported their texts in Garrigou-Lagrange, *De revelatione*, 3rd ed., vol. 1, 204ff.

fore, this supernatural *quoad substantiam* is, as the Thomists commonly say, supernatural *quoad cognoscibilitatem*[57] and can only be known by a supernaturalized intellect in virtue of the principle of the specification of acts by their formal objects.

By contrast, the *miracle* (or, miraculous effect) is not *intrinsically* supernatural by its essence; it is only supernatural by its *mode of production* (*quoad modum, seu effective, non formaliter*): as we said above, the resurrection of a dead person does not give supernatural life to a corpse; instead, it supernaturally gives it natural vegetative and sensitive life. Also, the theologians commonly say that the miraculous, sensible effect is not supernatural by its intrinsic formal cause (like invisible grace) but, instead, by its efficient cause, which is, like the end, an *extrinsic* cause.[58] This metaphysical consideration of the four causes is far from being useless in the problem that occupies us. We have made this point this elsewhere.[59]

It follows that, given that it does not contain a participation in the intimate life of God, the sensible miracle, as opposed to invisible sanctifying grace and the mysteries of salvation, can be known naturally as an *effect of the very Author and Master of nature*, whose existence can be demonstrated by natural reason and philosophy. God does not here

---

[57] Cf. Zigliara, *Propaedeutica ad sacram theologiam*, p. 10 (*supernaturale in ordine cognoscibilitatis et in ordine efficientiae*). [Tr. note: Fr. Garrigou-Lagrange does not cite the edition in question. The basic point can be found on page 10 of T.-M. Zigliara, *Propaedeutica ad sacram theologiam in usum scholarum seu tractatus de ordine supernaturali*, 5th ed. (Rome: 1903).]

[58] Thus, St. Thomas always distinguished miracles as *supernatural effects* from the *supernatural truths* that it confirms; he never said that the existence or probative force of a miracle is a supernatural truth that exceeds reason: "Just as man, led by natural reason, can arrive at some knowledge of God through natural effects, so by certain *supernatural effects*, which are called miracles, is man led to a particular [*aliquam*] *supernatural knowledge* of things of faith" (*ST* II-II, q. 178, a. 1).

In note 53 above, we have cited St. Thomas's commentary on John 5 in which he says that the Pharisees could indeed know Jesus's miracles: "And, no wonder, for it was from God only *effectively*...those words and sights [lit. *species*] (or, miracles)."

[59] See Reginald Garrigou-Lagrange, "Le surnaturel essentiel et le surnaturel modal selon les thomistes," *Revue Thomiste* 21 (1913): 316–327. [Tr. note: Fr. Garrigou-Lagrange cites 313ff.] Also, Garrigou-Lagrange, *De revelatione*, 3rd ed., 191–217. [Tr. note: See also the fourth chapter of the second part of Emmaus Academic's forthcoming translation of Fr. Garrigou-Lagrange's *Le sens du mystère*.]

intervene according to the mystery of His intimate life, as when He communicates a mysterious participation in it to the sinner by justifying him.

Therefore, an infinite distance separates the inferior supernaturality of the miracle and that of grace or of the mysteries.[60] This explains why the infused light of faith, which is needed so that we might know the latter, is not absolutely necessary for discerning the former with certitude.

* * *

We cannot here examine the different objections that have been formulated against the Thomist thesis. We have done so in the work to which we have often referred in this chapter.[61]

It suffices to note that this distinction between the supernaturality of miracles and that of the mysteries and of grace alone enables us to show the harmony between the order of reason and that of faith, the *rationabile obsequium fidei* [the reasonable service of faith] with the essential supernaturality of the three theological virtues. We showed this at length in the work cited above.[62] Finally, only this distinction enables us to reconcile what is true in the two theories previously examined, which, according to us, are true in what they affirm and false in what they deny.

However, it is insisted: "Where do we see this distinction being taught to the faithful and expressed in the formulas of the act of faith?"[63]

It is easy to respond that the catechism is not the place for teaching the solutions for the most difficult problems of theology. Moreover, in

---

[60] Thus, St. Thomas shows that sanctifying grace is a gift that is much higher than graces *gratis datae*, especially higher than certain such graces—ST I-II, q. 111, a. 5: "Gratia gratum faciens est multo excellentior quam gratia gratis data."

[61] See Garrigou-Lagrange, *De revelatione*, 3rd ed., vol. 1, 504–511, 545–549. Reginald Garrigou-Lagrange, "La grâce de la foi et le miracle. Trois theories. A propos de travaux récents," *Revue Thomiste* 23 (1918): 289–320. [Tr. note: Fr. Garrigou-Lagrange cites 309–320.]

[62] See Reginald Garrigou-Lagrange, *De revelatione*, 3rd ed., vol. 1, 498–514, 516–517, 527.

[63] Huby, "Miracle et lumière de la grâce," 66.

the formulas concerning the act of faith, it is clear that it is a question of God, the Author of grace, since this is always how the Christian religion considers our Heavenly Father. However, if unbelievers claim that the testimony of God the Author of grace is indiscernible, we have recourse to signs that manifestly can be produced only by God, the Author and Master of nature, whose existence must be admitted by every honest man and every philosopher of good faith. Thus God, the Author of nature (and then also of the sensible miracle) provides our reason with a sensible confirmation of His essentially supernatural testimony, which introduces us into the sublime mystery of His intimate life.

But then, we are told, "The infused supernatural does not fall under direct experience, if one admits the possibility of a natural, acquired faith, which cannot be distinguished from infused faith."[64] The faithful will not be able to determine whether he has the latter or only the former.

To this difficulty, we must respond that the soul of good will, believing *without restriction, propter auctoritatem Dei revelantis* [on account of the authority of God, who reveals], makes the act of supernatural faith such as it is required for salvation: *facienti quod in se est Deus non denegat gratiam*; [God does not deny the grace to him who does what lies within his power]. We believe that the natural faith spoken of in the objection is extremely rare among men, if it indeed even exists.[65] None-

---

[64] Huby, "Miracle et lumière de la grâce," 53.

[65] What is sometimes found in men who are unenlightened and who do not pray, is a natural faith that, rather, is an *opinion* concerning the truth of Christianity, founded on the human testimony of parents, pastors, and wise men, not on the testimony of God the Author of nature.

With regard to the certitude that the believer can have concerning the existence of his infused faith, an inexact presentation is given for our position expressed in "La surnaturalité de la foi," *Revue Thomiste* N.S. 14 (1914): 27 and 33. We refer the reader to our own words. Also, see the end of John of St. Thomas, *Cursus theologicus, De fide*, disp. 5, a. 2: The believer by reflection is aware that his act of faith is *certain* and *infallible*, as St. Thomas teaches in *ST* I-II, q. 112, a. 5, ad 2; and by signs and conjectures, we also know that this act is supernatural. Also see Bañez on *ST* II-II, q. 6, a. 2 (dub. 2). Indeed, in order to have lost the infused faith received at baptism, one would need to have committed not any mortal sin whatsoever but, instead, a grave fault against faith. He who is not aware of such a fault and adheres with absolute certitude to the Christian dogmas, does not doubt the essentially supernatural character of his own faith.

theless, it is found in the demons on account of their great perversity.

Moreover, the conscience of a convert sometimes manifests to him the moment when he passes from a judgment of certain credibility to supernatural faith. This fact was brilliantly discussed by Fr. Lacordaire in his seventeenth conference at Notre Dame.[66] And it also is just as clear in the letters left by Ernest Psichari concerning his conversion.[67]

In this, we can see the profound difference separating the infused faith of the faithful from the faith that remains in the demons (according to the testimony of Scripture): *credunt et contremiscunt*, they believe and shudder. The demon's *ultima resolutio fidei* is made into the natural evidence of the principles that manifest the divine origin of miracles and of revelation,[68] whereas for the faithful this *ultima resolutio fidei* is

---

[66] "He is such a learned man . . . (who would like to believe and cannot). He knows what the Catholic Church teaches. He admits the facts of this teaching. He feels its power. It is fitting that a man who was called Jesus Christ existed, living and dying in a prodigious manner. He is moved by the blood of the martyrs and by the constitution of the Church. He will readily say that it represents the greatest phenomenon that has traversed the world. He will nearly say, 'It is true!' However, he does not draw this conclusion. *He feels oppressed by the truth*, as one is in a dream in which one sees without seeing. However, one day, this learned man is brought to his knees. He feels the misery of the human condition. He lifts his hands to heaven and says, 'From the depths of my misery, Oh my God, I have cried to you!' At this moment, something happens in him. The scales fall from his eyes. A mystery is accomplished—he is changed! He is a man who is sweet and humble of heart. He can die; he has conquered the truth."

[Tr. note: Fr. Garrigou-Lagrange does not directly cite the edition. See H.-D. Lacordaire, *Conférences de Notre-Dame de Paris*, vol. 1 (Paris: Librairie Garnier Frères, 1921), 297–298.]

[67] See Henri Massis, *Le sacrifice* (Paris: Plon, 1917): "So he wrote, 'I did not believe anything. I lived like a pagan and, nevertheless, I felt the irresistible invasion of grace. I didn't have faith, but I knew that I would have it.' Another convert once said to us, 'After having seriously studied the Catholic religion and the proofs of its Divine origin, my difficulties disappeared. I wanted to believe but could not yet; however, on the day of my little girl's baptism, the Good God gave me the grace of faith.'"

[Tr. note: An account of Psichari's conversion can be found in Raïssa Maritain, *We Have Been Friends Together & Adventures in Grace: Memoirs* (South Bend, IN: St. Augustine's Press, 2016), 237–280.]

[68] St. Thomas said very clearly in *In III Sent* d. 23, q. 3, a. 3 (*Whether unformed [informis] faith is found in the demons*): "Reason leading to belief can be taken *either from something created*, as when through a given *sign* we are led to believe something either about God or about other things, *or it is taken from Uncreated Truth itself*, as when we believe something which is said to us divinely through ministers. . . . And *in the*

made into the supernatural revelation received under the infused light of faith, and here we are faced with *two very different ways of affirming the verb "to be" in a dogmatic formula.* Through infused faith, one thus *formally* attains the supernatural mysteries as such. Through acquired faith, they are attained only *materially.*[69]

---

first manner faith is found among the demons inasmuch as *through their own natural knowledge* as well as on the basis of miracles, which they see to be above nature much more subtly than we do, they are compelled to believe those things which exceed their natural cognition. *However, not in the second manner."* See the other similar texts cited in Garrigou-Lagrange, *De revelatione,* 3rd ed., vol. 1, 470ff. Also see 475 and 180, St. Thomas's commentary on 1 Cor 11:14 (DR): "But the sensual man perceiveth not these things that are of the Spirit of God; for it is foolishness to him, and he cannot understand." He attains only the *letter* of the Gospel and the *miracles* that confirm it.

[69] We have explained this point at length in Garrigou-Lagrange, *De revelatione,* 3rd ed., vol. 1 p. 181ff, note, and 505. Also, Leo XIII, in the Encyclical *Providentissimus Deus,* no. 15, says in the same sense, "The sense of Holy Scripture can nowhere be found incorrupt outside of the Church, and cannot be expected to be found in writers who, *being without the true faith, only gnaw the bark of the Sacred Scripture, and never attain its pith."*

See also St. Thomas, *In III Sent.,* d. 23, q. 3, a. 3, qc. 2: "Man can believe that which ought to be believed from a real estimation without an infused *habitus;* however, it is only on the basis of an infused *habitus* that he can be inclined to this and not to that with discretion—which is the discretion according to which *we do not believe in every spirit."* Also, *ST* II-II, q. 1, a. 4, ad 3; q. 2, a. 3, ad 2.

To understand this point well, it is necessary to recall the principle of Aristotle often cited by St. Thomas: "Utterances [*voces*] are signs of understandings [*intellectuum*] and understandings [*intellectus*] are likenesses of things." Cf. *ST* I, q. 13, a. 1.

Therefore, formally speaking, a reader only understands the entire meaning of the words of a proposition if these signs awaken in him the same ideas and the same judgment (as well as the same modality of judgment) as that of their author. Now, the judgment of the inspired author (above all when it is a question of supernatural mysteries) could only be formed under an infused light which, according to St. Thomas, ordered the images and concepts to the representation of a supernatural object (cf. *ST* II-II, q. 173, a. 2, ad 3). The mental word in which the judgment of the sacred author is expressed is illuminated by this superior light. See Garrigou-Lagrange, *De revelatione,* vol. 1, 510.

And, therefore, the reader lacking infused faith, unable to judge in the same interior light as the inspired author, cannot *formally* understand *the full meaning* of the words and the propositions of the divine book. [Tr. note: At this point, Fr. Garrigou-Lagrange inserts a footnote into this already-lengthy footnote. I have placed its contents at the end of this note.]

What will escape him? "It is," as remarks a good Thomist, "an element irreducible to analysis and which one is therefore entitled to call synthetic. We might call it the *spirit* of the concepts and the words, hearing in 'spirit' something mysterious, imperceptible to the senses and to the intellect that analyzes, intangible like spirit, floating around things like their double, the principle of life par excellence, without which words are only skeletons and bones."—P.-B. Lacome, *Questions de Principes concernant l'exégèse catholique contemporaine* (Paris: Bureaux de la Revue Thomiste, 1904), 152.

What a difference exists between a reading of an Epistle of St. Paul performed by the most educated but unbelieving philologist, and a reading performed by a saint who truly finds the supernatural thought of St. Paul beneath the letter of his writing. Indeed, to hear the *meaning of this Letter*, it does not suffice to know by means of grammar and a lexicon *the most exact grammatical meaning of each word* (as for appreciating a symphony, it does not suffice to hear each note). In one's reading, one must place the accent on what is principal in St. Paul's thought and not on that which is accessory. Otherwise, as modern thinkers say, one thus reverses the scale of values. One can confuse piety with pietism and holy sorrow with pessimism. While preserving *the grammatical meaning of the letter* of this Epistle, one can even completely disfigure the spirit of the text—the *spirit*, which is the soul of the *literal sense*, for the latter is distinct from the material configuration of the *letter* (even the very-scientifically known letter of the text). In the ninth chapter of the letter to the Romans, in relation to the question of Predestination, one can read the words either in the Catholic sense and with the Catholic accent or, in contrast, with a Calvinistic tone: "But the sensual man [*animalis homo*] (the natural man) perceiveth not these things that are of the Spirit of God; for it is foolishness to him, and he cannot understand."

In his Commentary on this text, St. Thomas says, "One is called a sensual [*animalis*] man on account of the apprehensive power, because he *judges concerning God* in terms of *bodily images* [*phantasiam*], *the letter of the law*, or *philosophical reason*, all of which are grasped according to sense powers. . . . Such a man cannot perceive those things that are of the Spirit of God. . . . For the things concerning which *the Holy Spirit illuminates the mind* transcend the senses and human reason . . . and therefore cannot be grasped by him who relies on sense knowledge alone." In the same place, St. Thomas adds, "In another way, one is called a sensual [*animalis*] man on account of the appetitive power, which is attracted only to those things that appeal to the sense appetite." On this point, see Garrigou-Lagrange, *De revelatione*, 3rd ed., vol. 1, 180ff.

[Tr. note: Here begins the aforementioned footnote within the main footnote.]

See Tabulum oper. S. Thomae: *Significatio*—3. Nomen non significat nisi mediante conceptione intellectus. 4. Modus significandi sequitur modum intelligendi. 7. Nomen totius non significat partes nisi materialiter. 8. Plus est in significatione nominis compositi quam in significationibus componentium. Significatio est essentialis enuntiationi. Significatio orationis relata ad rem significatam est simplex, in quantum significat unum, scil. compositionem: licet relata ad partes orationis videatur composita, tamen significationes earum sunt ut dispositio materialis ad significationem totius.

[3. A term (*nomen*) signifies only by mediation of a conception of the intellect. 4. The modes of signifying follow on the modes of understanding. 7. The term for a whole only signifies the parts materially. 8. There is more in the signification of a composite term than in the signification of the components. Signification is essential to an enunciation (i.e., formed by the second operation of the intellect). The signification of an expression (*orationis*) in relation to the thing signified is simple,

Certainly, this distinction is not new. St. Thomas presents it even for distinguishing the different ways by which prophecy and infused faith attain a supernatural mystery,[70] and the Thomists commonly make use of it.[71]

What we have just said does not prevent us from admitting that miracles confirm doctrine and are confirmed by it. However, in what sense is this true? If doctrine, to the eyes of simple reason, is evidently worthy of God, if it elevates souls and responds to their aspirations, if its mysteries (despite their obscurity) seem sublime rather than absurd and incoherent, if it contains, moreover, all the natural truths of religion, more perfectly expressed than they are expressed anywhere else, it is a new sign and helps us see that such a prodigy, which manifestly surpasses sensible and human powers, cannot come from a demon. These considerations provide evident credibility prior to faith. Certainly, the sublimity of Christ's doctrine is clear above all to the believer who attains the intimate mystery of said doctrine, but do not many rationalists say like the envoys of the Pharisees, "No man has spoken as this man has?"[72] Jesus's holiness was as externally *visible* by its effects as is the holiness of the Church.

In conclusion, we can only insist upon the profound distinction between the supernaturality of naturally knowable *miracles* and the supernaturality of the *mysteries of grace* which exceeds natural knowledge. This distinction is of sovereign importance, and we have noted[73]

---

inasmuch as it signifies one thing, namely a composition; although, in relation to the parts of the expression (*orationis*) it may seem to be composite, nonetheless, their significations exist as a material disposition to the signification of the whole.]

[70] Aquinas, *In III Sent.*, dist. 24, q. 1, a. 1, ad 3: "Although prophecy and faith are concerned with the same thing, for example the Passion of Christ, they are not, however, the same, for *faith formally considers* the Passion from the perspective of that by which it is a basis for expressing *something eternal*, namely, inasmuch as God died, and it considers *materially* that which is *temporal*; however, prophecy considers matters vice-versa."

[71] See John of St. Thomas, *Cursus theologicus, De gratia,* disp. 20, a. 1, solv. obj. 5. Also, see Lemos in his explanations to the Congregation *De auxiliis* concerning the subject that occupies us now. See the texts reported in Garrigou-Lagrange, *De revelatione*, 3rd ed., vol. 1, 503 and 491ff.

[72] See Garrigou-Lagrange, *De revelatione*, 3rd ed., vol. 2, 267ff.

[73] See Garrigou-Lagrange, *De revelatione*, 3rd ed., vol. 1, 511–514 and 210.

elsewhere its principal consequences pertaining to apologetics, theology (properly speaking), Church history, as well as questions relative to faith, hope, charity, and the Gifts of the Holy Spirit. As we have shown,[74] as did Fr. Arintero, O.P.,[75] it illuminates a great number of problems in mystical theology by enabling one to better discern what is of the order of the sanctifying grace of the virtues and the Gifts (which reach their full development in the mystical state) and what pertains to the much less elevated order of graces *gratis datae*.[76]

All that we have just discussed makes clear *the finality* of miracles and that of infused faith: if miracles, as signs of revelation, were not naturally knowable, they would not be, as the Church says: "a sign that is well adapted to the understanding of all ages and of all men, even those of the present time."[77] In other words, they would lose their finality.—On the other hand, if the formal object of infused faith could be attained without infused faith, it would be *useless*. So too would infused hope and infused charity be useless if their formal objects were accessible (as the Pelagians thought) to the *natural good will* of the man who historically knows the Gospel and the miracles that confirm it.

Thus, the principle of finality shows us the essential finality and realism of faith and of the other theological virtues, as it showed us the essential finality and realism of the intellect and of the will in our earlier discussions above.

---

[74] See Garrigou-Lagrange, *Christian Perfection and Contemplation*, trans. Sr. Timothea M. Doyle (St. Louis: B. Herder, 1958), 48–80.

[75] J.G. Arintero, *Cuestiones misticas* (Salamanca: 1916), 447ff.

[76] *ST* I-II, q. 111, a. 5: "Gratia gratum faciens est multo excellentior quam gratia gratis data."

[77] Pius X, *Sacrorum antistitum* (Denzinger, no. 3539). [Tr. note: Fr. Garrigou-Lagrange has a slightly truncated and reordered form of this selection from the Antimodernist Oath. It is rendered above in accord with the official text.]

Chapter Eight

THE PRINCIPLE OF RECIPROCAL INFLUENCE OF THE CAUSES AND THE MAIN APPLICATIONS OF THIS PRINCIPLE

"Causae ad invicem sunt causae"

Among the principles subordinated to the principle of finality, we mentioned above[1] that of the interdependence (or, reciprocal influence) of causes: *causae sunt invicem causae, sed in diverso genere*. It is important that we here insist on its true meaning and scope and also note its principal applications.

Many problems, according to the Thomists, are illuminated by this principle, as we can easily see in what they have written concerning sensation and intellection, as well as concerning the relations between the intellect and the will in free choice, as well as in theology concerning the relations between actual grace and the will at the moment of conversion, and also concerning the relations between the Incarnation and the Redemption. Far too few people are aware of this aspect of Thomism. It is even the case that the initial difficulty that is illuminated and resolved by the principle with which we are now concerned is itself sometimes forgotten.

---

[1]   See ch. 5 of the first part.

The Initial Difficulty to Be Resolved

It is not rare that those who are inspired by Henri Bergson's *Creative Evolution* say to us, "The abstract intellectualism of Aristotle and St. Thomas wishes to find in reality itself distinctions that are only logical in character (or, distinctions of reason). Consequently, this abstract intellectualism believes that we even have within ourselves *distinct realities* that are extrinsic to one another, such as matter and form, the body and the soul, and really distinct faculties. This position leads to the destruction of life's unity, as well as the unity of universal evolution, which seems wholly absurd in the eyes of this 'extrinsicism.' Indeed, if there is a real distinction between matter and form, as well as between agent and end, there would thus be four *immobile principles*, from which (as Henri Bergson says) movement cannot arise. The end, according to Aristotle, attracts like an immobile perfection. Likewise, the agent only moves if it is *already in act*. When it tends toward its act, it does not yet move. A body, we are told, only warms if it is already hot. On the other hand, matter cannot move itself. Finally, the form is a specific, immutable principle. Becoming cannot arise from these four immutable causes, and above all, an ascending form of evolution is absurd from the Aristotelian point of view. But, moreover, the distinction of the four causes does away with the profound *unity* of reality and of life." With various inflections in their voices, many of Henri Bergson's disciples speak with words such as these.

* * *

To this, the Thomists respond that the distinction of the four causes is derived immediately from the division of reality (or, of being) into *potency and act*, and that this division is absolutely necessary for us to reconcile the principle of contradiction or, identity ("Being is being, non-being is non-being," or, "being is not non-being") with becoming.

Indeed, nothing can arise *from an already determined being*. We cannot make a statue from a statue, for it already exists. *Ex ente iam determinato non fit ens, quia iam est ens.* On the other hand, becoming cannot proceed from pure nothingness—*ex nihilo nihil fit*. Therefore, becoming presupposes a *middle* between nothingness and actual, determined being. This middle is called *potency* (or, being in potency).

Thus, the statue is made from the wood that *can* be sculpted, the plant arises from the seed, and all bodies arise from *matter*. However, nothing is reduced from potency to act except by a being that is already in act, called the *agent*. Thus, the sculptor makes the statue, and man begets man. Matter is thus determined by the form, which is *the end* of generation or of becoming, the end toward which the action of the agent tends, as does the passion of the patient (or, of that which is mobile). In this, we have a summary of the first two books of Aristotle's *Physics*.

In this way, becoming can be rendered *intelligible*, for it is thus linked to *being*, which is the first intelligible object, as the colored is the first object perceived by sight. Becoming can only be conceived in relation to being if being is divided into potency and act, and the distinction of the four causes proceeds immediately from this division.

Does this distinction destroy the unity of reality and of life, as the evolutionists say? Certainly, it does away with the unity of monism whose formula is found in the first proposition condemned in Pius IX's *Syllabus of Errors*: "God is produced in man and in the world, and all things are God and have the very substance of God, and God is one and the same thing with the world, and, therefore, spirit with matter, necessity with freedom, good with evil, justice with injustice."[2] This pantheistic evolutionism is excluded by the principle of non-contradiction in virtue of which God *is* God (and nothing else), spirit *is* spirit (and not matter), etc.

It is clear that the unity of monism is denied by the theory of the four causes, according to which God is conceived as the efficient and final extrinsic Cause of the world.[3]

However, must we say that the distinction of the four causes does away with the unity of life in every living thing, the unity of the human composite, the unity of action in the man who has the spirit of continu-

---

[2] [Tr. note: I have followed Fr. Garrigou-Lagrange's text, which slightly differs from Denzinger, no. 2901.]

[3] See *ST* I, q. 3, a. 8.

ity and ever perseveres in the same direction?

On the contrary, this unity, in its various aspects, is truly safeguarded by the Aristotelian principle of the reciprocal influence of causes: "*causae ad invicem sunt causae, sed in diverso genere*—καὶ αλλήλων αἴτια."[4] Thus, moderate labor is the efficient cause of the health that it maintains, and health is the end for the sake of which one engages in this work.

The True Sense of the Principle of the Reciprocal Influence of Causes

St. Thomas thus explains this principle[5] in his Commentary on *Metaphysics* 5.2:[6]

> Now, it is impossible that something be both cause and caused in one and the same genus of cause. . . . However, it must be kept in mind that as there are four causes given above, two of them correspond to each other, and similarly do the other two correspond to each other. In fact, the efficient and final causes are correlative, for the efficient cause is the principle of the motion, while the end is the terminus of the motion. Likewise, matter and form are correlative, for form gives existence [*esse*], while matter receives it. (For example, the form of the

---

4 Aristotle, *Metaphysics*, 5 (Δ).2 (1013b9).

5 We translate this Aristotelian principle as "the reciprocal influence of causes," although one rarely speaks of the "influence" of the material cause but only of the influence of the efficient, final, and formal causes. This expression, "influence," is here extended *analogically*, as causality is attributed analogically or proportionally to the four causes. A *cause* is *that upon which something depends* in some manner [for its being], whether this dependence be *efficient, final, formal, material*. Thus, the statue depends on the sculptor, on the end that he had in view, on the matter he used, and on the form which he gave to it.

Therefore, the principle we are discussing can just as well be called the principle of the mutual dependence (or, that of the interdependence) of causes.

6 [Tr. note: In the original, this is translated by Fr. Garrigou-Lagrange. I have translated from the Latin, though I have kept a close eye to French, occasionally nuancing in a way similar to Fr. Garrigou-Lagrange, and otherwise noting where he slightly departs from the sense of the passage.]

lion gives it being of a given, determinate species, and matter receives this determination.)

Therefore, the efficient cause is the cause of the end, while the end is the cause of the efficient cause (from different perspectives). The efficient cause is the cause of the end inasmuch as it makes it exist, for by causing motion, the efficient cause *brings about* the final cause; however, the final cause is the cause of the efficient cause, not as making it exist, but inasmuch as it is the *reason for the causality* (its *raison d'être*). For the efficient cause is a cause inasmuch as it acts; however, it does not act except on account of the final cause. Whence, the efficient cause has its causality from its end.

However, form and matter are causes of one another with regard to their very being. Indeed, form makes matter exist in act;[7] however, matter is the cause of form inasmuch as it sustains[8] it. (Without the substantial form, matter would not exist.)[9]

The end was the first of the causes; this principle concerning the reciprocal influence of causes thus appears as being a corollary of the principle of finality.

Therefore, the *two extrinsic causes*, i.e., the agent and the end, are correlative. So too are the *two intrinsic causes*, i.e., matter and form. Here, we see a mutual dependence from different perspectives, according to different genera of causality and, therefore, we must not hold there is any contradiction or any vicious circle here.

Thus, there is a very intimate union and, so to speak, interpenetration of causes. Form would not determine matter if it were not received and

---

7   [Tr. note: Here, Fr. Garrigou-Lagrange has, "Form gives to matter that it be actually determined, that it be in act."]

8   [Tr. note: Fr. Garrigou-Lagrange has "receives."]

9   [Tr. note: This last remark is not in parentheses in Fr. Garrigou-Lagrange's French. However, it is not exactly the point that Aquinas makes in the selection. He goes on to discuss how both form and matter are causes of being in their own ways.]

limited by it; however, matter would not receive and limit form if it were not determined by it. Moreover, matter cannot exist without some form.

Likewise, the agent would not act, nor would it tend toward any end, if it were not attracted by said end; however, *the end would not actually attract the agent, if the latter did not actually tend toward it.* For example, a given good would not actually attract our will, if our will did not already tend toward it, at least by way of an initial desire. Nonetheless, it remains the case that the end is the first of the causes.

Therefore, the causes exhibit a very intimate union, with mutual priority, without contradiction.

What would be contradictory would be to say, "In the same kind of efficient causality, the subordinate cause [*cause seconde*] depends upon the primary cause [*cause première*], and the latter depends upon the former." This is impossible, for the subordinate cause [*cause seconde*] acts only as it is premoved by the primary cause [*cause première*], and therefore, the action of the subordinate cause [*cause seconde*] can in no way move the primary cause [*cause première*] to cooperate with the effect to be produced. This would be to invert the subordination of causes, which is a subordination not only in the order of being, but also in the order of acting. For the same reason, Providential decrees *determine* what is real and good in everything that happens, even in that which happens freely. Otherwise, God would be *determined* (or, *passive*) in His foreknowledge regarding the merits of men, of whom He would be the Spectator rather than the Author. However, He intends and makes it be the case that our act happens freely at the terminus of our deliberation; the Divine motion extends all the way to the *free mode* of this act, a mode that is still too a mode of *being*, thus falling under the adequate object of the Divine causality.[10]

The principle of the reciprocal influence of causes does not contain any contradiction or vicious circle and, moreover, *it is quite clearly applied everywhere where the four causes are involved.* Innumerable difficulties find solutions in light of this principle, difficulties which we would, at first glance, believe to contain a vicious circle or a begging of the question [*pétition de principe*]. Often, Thomists resolve these

---

[10] See *ST* I, q. 19, a. 8.

difficulties simply by recalling the aforementioned principle, which can look like a *deus ex machina* to the eyes of certain novice readers, whereas in reality it expresses the most foundational interrelations at play in the causes of all becoming.

We will note the principal applications of this principle, elevating ourselves from the physical order, to that of knowledge, then to the moral order, and finally to the supernatural order.

The first of these applications was indicated by Aristotle himself.

Applications in the Physical Order

Not only do matter and form depend on one another inasmuch as form determines or actuates matter and is received and limited by the latter but, moreover, at the terminus of substantial generation (e.g., the generation of an animal), *the ultimate disposition* to the form and *the form itself* are correlative and interdependent from different perspectives.

St. Thomas says this clearly in *In IV Sent*. d. 17, q. 1, a. 4, qc. 2:

Similarly, this holds in natural generation (for example of the lamb), which is the terminus of alteration. For *in the same instant* is the alteration terminated at the necessary *disposition* and at the generation to the *form*; and, nevertheless, according to the order of nature, each is prior to the other in a different manner: for *the necessary disposition precedes the form according to the order of material causality*, whereas, *the form is prior according to the order of formal causality*. And in this way, the quality that is brought about is also the formal effect of the substantial form.[11]

Likewise, a bit earlier, St. Thomas said in *In IV Sent*. d. 17, q. 1, a. 4, qc. 1:

---

[11] [Tr. note: In this passage and the next, I have followed the Latin, adding emphasis from Fr. Garrigou-Lagrange's French. The parenthetical remark is added by him.]

And because the form and end and agent coincide in the same thing with regard to number or species,[12] therefore also *in the order of efficient cause, the introduction of the form is prior*: because the form, before having been introduced, is the likeness of the agent's form through which the agent acts; *and, similarly, in the order of final cause*, for nature principally intends the introduction of form and orders to this the expulsion of everything that cannot remain with the introduction of the [new] form.

At first, this doctrine can seem complicated but, in fact, it is a simple application of the principle of the reciprocal influence of causes. *The substantial form* (e.g., of the begotten lamb) *depends on its concomitant accidents, as dispositions* that appropriate the matter to it and which then preserve it in this matter that has been thus adapted. However, on the other hand, *these concomitant accidents depend on the substantial form as upon their radical principle*. Indeed, they are the properties that derive from the substantial form in the order of formal causality.

In this way, *the ultimate disposition*, which, in the order of material causality, precedes the form, follows it as a *property* and preserves it in the matter. Thus, according to the ancients, the animal's heartbeat is at one and the same time the ultimate disposition to the form and the property whose disappearance would lead to its death.

This law is verified even in man's generation. The final disposition that requires the creation of a given human soul and the union of this spiritual soul to a given portion of matter precedes the soul itself in the order of material causality, though only in this order.[13]

---

[12] The form, end, and agent all *numerically* coincide with each other when the animal nourishes itself. They coincide *specifically* only when the animal begets that which is like unto itself.

[13] Cf. *ST* I, q. 118, a. 2, ad 4: "Man [*homo*] generates one similar to himself inasmuch as through the power of his semen matter *is disposed to the reception of such a form*." See also Cajetan's commentary on this article, no. 7. Likewise, see Aquinas, *De potentia*, q. 3, a. 9, ad 2 and ad 6.

[Tr. note: Thomas's treatment of the moment of the infusion of the spiritual soul is a controverted topic in Thomism. Maritain defends Aquinas in "Toward a Thomist Idea of Evolution" in *Untrammeled Approaches*, trans. Bernard Doering (Notre

In the same way, St. Thomas gives a profound explanation of the adage, "A healthy mind in a healthy body." He admits that there is a kind of *inequality among human souls*, despite their specific identity. For example, the soul of St. John is superior to the soul of this or that other man. From what does this inequality arise? St. Thomas explains it from the perspective of material causality, by saying, "When, by way of generation, the body is better disposed, the soul is better."[14] However, the

---

Dame, IN: University of Notre Dame Press, 2007), 85–131 (esp. 96–110). A critical appraisal of Maritain can be found in James Hanink, "Jacques Maritain and the Embryo: A Master's Muddles" in *Life and Learning*, XVIII, ed. Joseph W. Koterski (Bronx, NY: University Faculty for Life, 2011), 249–262. Thoughtful reflections on these matters can be found in Elizabeth Anscombe, *Human Life, Action, and Ethics*, ed. Mary Geach and Luke Gormally (Exeter, UK: Imprint Academic, 2005), 39–73.]

[14] See *ST* I, q. 85, a. 7: "For it is obvious that *when the body is better disposed, so too is the soul allotted to it better*. This obviously is clear in the cases of those things which differ in species (e.g., the lion and the maggot). The reason for this is that act and form are received into matter according to the capacity of matter. Whence, because some men have a better-disposed body, they are allotted a soul of a greater power in intellection. Whence, it is said in *De anima* 2.9, that *we see that those who have soft flesh are of apt mind*. In another way, this happens with regard to the inferior powers of the soul of which the intellect has need for its operation; for, those in whom the imaginative, cogitative, and memorative powers are better disposed are themselves better disposed for intellection."

[Tr. note: Note that it is a matter of the *spiritual soul (as individual nature / form)* being differentiated. This same issue led Maritain to note the intimate differentiation that occurs in the case of sexual differentiation. See Jacques Maritain, "Let Us Make for Him a Helpmate Like to Himself" in *Untrammeled Approaches*, trans. Bernard Doering (South Bend, IN: University of Notre Dame Press, 1997), 151–164. Also, Fr. Garrigou-Lagrange's text is almost certainly at the basis of the remarks by his student Fr. Austin Woodbury in Austin Woodbury, *Natural Philosophy, Treatise Three: Psychology*, The John N. Deely and Anthony Russell Collection, St. Vincent College, Latrobe, PA, n.934Ab: "[There is a certain correspondence between the human intellect and the senses] in the order of entity (and of intellectivity), for, since the intellective soul, as will be shown hereunder, is created, *not only IN the body, but also ACCORDING TO the body*, there results to the intellective soul and to its intellect a more perfect entity and a more perfect intellective vigour from a more perfectly disposed organism, especially according as the organs of the internal senses, seated in the cortex, are the more perfectly disposed for the functions of sensitive lie. Wherefore: not only is the intellect the better furnished with the objects of its knowledge, but also *the intellect is of greater intellective vigour and penetrativeness IN ITSELF*" (italic emphasis added, uppercase in original). Fr. Woodbury cites Aquinas, *In II De Anima*, lect. 19. *ST* I, q. 79, a. 5; q. 85, a. 7. One may also consult Matthew Minerd, "Maritain and the Metaphysics of Sexual Differentiation," in *The Things That Matter: Essays Inspired by the Later Works of Jacques Maritain*, ed. Heidi M. Giebel (Washing-

holy Doctor also holds that, given that matter is for the sake of form, in the order of final and formal causality, *the body is better disposed* inasmuch as it is *ordered* from all eternity by Providence *to a more noble soul.*[15]

Likewise, again, in man, there is a similar correspondence between *individuation* by matter and the *personality* or subsistence that is of the spiritual order. They depend on one another, somewhat like how the body and soul depend on one another, but they are quite distinct, to such a point that in Christ, individuation is brought about (as in us) by matter, whereas His personality is uncreated, indeed, that of the Word made flesh. They are, in Christ, two extremes. Much could be said concerning this subject, which is very intimately linked to that of the

---

ton DC: The Catholic University of America Press, 2018), 150–167.]

[15] See *ST* I, q. 76, a. 5: "Form is not for the sake of matter but, rather, *matter is for the sake of form.*" Also, see Aquinas, *De veritate*, q. 12, a. 6, ad 4: "A form that is received follows the mode of the receiver inasmuch as it has existence in the subject . . . with regard to the requirements of the receiving subject. However, with regard to something *does the received form draw the receiver to its own mode of existing*, namely, insofar as *the excellences* that belong to the nature of the form *are communicated to the receiving subject*; . . . and in this way is the corruptible body made immortal through the glory of immortality."

Also, see *ST* I, q. 24, a. 8, ad 6: "That which is received into something can be considered both in relation to its existence [*esse*] and to its formal character [*ratio*]. In relation to its existence, it is in that in which it is received according to the mode of the receiver; however, *this very receiver is drawn to its formal character*"—as heat in water, light in air, the soul in the body, grace in the soul.

Thus, the spiritual soul, when separated from its body, remains *individuated* according to St. Thomas, by its transcendental relation to this body which it will one day regain. Given that a transcendental relation is identical with the very nature of the subject wherein it is found, it subsists even when the terminus no longer exists.

As Fr. Gredt says in his *Elementa*, vol. 1, n. 461: "One human soul differs from another in perfection *substantially* indeed, however not essentially but, instead, *accidentally.*" One soul is nobler than another by an *accidental substantial perfection*, which is an accident, not a predicament but a *predicable*, in the sense that it may or may not belong to the human species. It is the same with the relation of *this* soul to *this* particular body.

[Tr. note: Concerning transcendental relations, see the editor's appendix in Reginald Garrigou-Lagrange, "There Cannot Be Genuine Sensation Without a Real Sensed Thing," in *Philosophizing in Faith: Essays on the Beginning and End of Wisdom*, trans. Thomas DePauw and Edward M. Macierowski, ed. Matthew K. Minerd (Providence, RI: Cluny Media, 2019), 116–119.]

influence of the physical [order] upon the moral [order] and vice-versa.[16]

* * *

Another application: our principle is verified *in each movement*, as St. Thomas explains in *ST* I-II, q. 113, a. 8, ad 1:[17]

Every movement presupposes a point of departure and an

---

[16] We have studied this elsewhere in Garrigou-Lagrange, *Le sens commun*, pt. 3, chs. 2 and 3. *The principle of individuation* is that in virtue of which two beings of the same species, like two drops of water that are as similar as possible, nonetheless are *distinct* and two, not one. "The individual is indivisible in itself and distinguished from any other." Two drops of water are distinct from one another because the substantial (or, specific) form of water is received in two distinct portions of matter. Also, for St. Thomas, the principle of individuation is *matter* inasmuch as it is *ordered to a given quantity* and not to another (*materia quantitate signata*). This holds true in the case of man, even in Christ, namely that the principle of individuation, quite distinct from Christ's uncreated personality, is *matter apt for a given quantity* rather than some other (or by reason of which he was born in a given place and not some other, in a given age, in a given people, and so forth). The principle of individuation brings about a restriction and a limitation. By contrast, given that Christ's personality is Uncreated, it is really identical with the Divine Essence common to the three Persons of the Trinity.

[Tr. note: The topic concerning the distinction between personality and individuality has been the source of great contention in the Thomist world vis-à-vis debates aroused regarding Jacques Maritain, *The Person and the Common Good*, trans. John J. Fitzgerald (Notre Dame, IN: University of Notre Dame Press, 2009). This is not the place to negotiate that hotly contested debate. However, due to certain claims regarding this matter, it is fitting to cite a number of texts in which he deploys this distinction (drawn from Fr. Marie-Benoît Schwalm and utilized by Maritain as coming from Frs. Garrigou-Lagrange and Schwalm). Indeed, the distinction is deployed by Fr. Garrigou-Lagrange precisely in the contested political sense—even after he and Maritain fell out over certain political matters. See Reginald Garrigou-Lagrange, *Le sens commun*, 4th ed. (Paris: Desclée de Brouwer, 1936), 347–349; *The Trinity and God the Creator*, trans. Frederic C. Eckhoff (St. Louis: B. Herder, 1952), 155–156; *Christ: The Savior*, trans. Bede Rose (St. Louis: B. Herder, 1950), 119ff; *De beatitudine* (Turin: R. Berruti, 1951), 85–87 and 372; "La subordination de l'état à la perfection de la personne humaine selon S. Thomas," *Doctor Communis* 2–3 (1949): 146–159. In particular, the reader should note that the current translation of *De beatitudine* is a paraphrase, not a full textual translation.]

[17] [Tr. note: I have chosen to follow Fr. Garrigou-Lagrange's French, as it slightly paraphrases some content (without mangling the sense of the text). I have presented it as though it were in his own words, rather than as a direct quote from St. Thomas.]

opposite point [of arrival or completion]. However, we can consider it from two perspectives. From the perspective of the mobile thing, it is true to say that it moves away from the point of departure before arriving at the opposed point (or, if it is a question of qualitative motion and not local motion, water ceases to be cold before becoming hot). However, from the perspective of the agent, the *opposite* is the case, in the sense that it is by its form (and by producing something similar to it) that the agent removes the opposed form. Thus, *according to a priority (not of time but of nature) the sun illuminates the air before removing the darkness*, whereas *the air ceases to be dark before being illuminated*, even though this happens at the same instant.[18]

Therefore, our principle is applied wherever the four causes are involved.

It has many other applications in the physical order and in physiology, above all in organisms that are plants or animals, where so many parts and functions depend on one another. Thus, in us, the circulation of blood depends on the respiration that is needed for revitalizing the blood, and respiration depends on circulation.

In physiology, the term "synergy" is used for the influence of various organs on one another in the state of health. The applications of the principle of the reciprocal influence of causes shows us the nature of synergy in the metaphysical order wherever the four causes are involved, even where there is no longer any matter and where *material causality* is attributed *analogically* to every *subject*, even the spiritual subject, which receives a perfection, somewhat like how matter receives the form that determines it.

---

[18] [Tr. note: Because of the context and very slight changes made to the passage by Fr. Garrigou-Lagrange, I have translated with an eye to Fr. Garrigou-Lagrange's French.]

Applications in the Order of Knowledge

The principle of the interdependence of causes also illuminates the mystery of knowledge, whether it be sense knowledge or intellectual knowledge.

As we have already seen,[19] sense knowledge is mysterious in that our senses, which have a kind of spirituality,[20] can be *impressed* by an object that is purely bodily and inferior to them (e.g., a stone). How can the stone produce in our senses not only an organic or physical impression but also a *psychological impression,* a *representative,* "*intentionalis,*" likeness which has a kind of immateriality (as St. Thomas shows well in *ST* I, q. 14, a. 1)? It seems that the effect would be nobler than the cause.[21]

As we said above,[22] this difficulty would remain insoluble if sensation (as Descartes held) were the act of the *soul alone* and not of an *animated organ,* e.g., of the living eye. However, even if it is the act of the animated organ, the difficulty still remains inasmuch as sensation requires not only an organic, physical impression but also requires a psychological impression,[23] a representative likeness by which the knower can, in some way, become the thing that is other than itself, *fieri quodammodo aliud a se.*

Here, we forever find an obscurity in the intimate mode according to which sensation comes about. Nevertheless, we avoid contradiction by having recourse to our principle, which clearly must be applied here as it must be applied everywhere that the four causes are involved. According to this principle of the interdependence of causes, we must say, "The knowing faculty assimilates the object and, from another perspective, is assimilated to it."

As St. Thomas says in *ST* I, q. 79, a. 3, ad 1, "*The actually sensible object* exists outside the soul, and therefore we do not need to hold

---

[19] See chapter two in this section.

[20] Cf. *ST* I, q. 14, a. 1.

[21] [Tr. note: The reader would likely benefit from the lucid, though technical, discussions undertaken in Simon, *Introduction to the Metaphysics of Knowledge,* 85–112.]

[22] Again, see chapter two of this section.

[23] See *ST* I, q. 78, a. 3.

there is an 'agent sense' analogous to the agent intellect that renders objects as intelligible in act." Hence, it follows that, according to our principle, the sense of sight is *determined* by the actually sensible and colored object (i.e., is *assimilated to this object*), while, on the other hand, the likeness of color in us, inasmuch as it is vital and in some way is immaterial, *depends* on the visual faculty and is *assimilated* (or rendered similar) *to it*. Without contradiction, there is a double assimilation: the subject assimilates the object and is assimilated to it from different perspectives. In this way, we also have an explanation for another principle applied here: *quidquid recipitur ad modum recipientis recipitur*, whatever is received is received according to the mode of the receiver.

Even though the *colored* object (e.g., the stone) is, simply speaking, bodily, precisely because it has this determination, namely color, it is superior to the sense of sight that is not yet determined. Thus, it can give this determination to the sense of sight. On the other hand, the sense is nobler than the colored object inasmuch as it is a faculty that is vital and capable of knowledge [*cognoscitive*].

Here, we find correlative causes that depend upon one another, *causae invicem sunt causae*.

According to one order of causality, the sense is impressed by the external object (e.g., by the stone that is illuminated by the sun) and, according to another order of causality, the representative likeness of the stone is vital and psychological *in dependence* upon the visual faculty into which it is received.[24]

In this way, we avoid contradiction in expressing this natural mystery on the borders of the order of sense knowledge and the inferior order that is wholly material.

Thus, the sense receives the impression of the sensible object and then reacts by the very act of sensation.

---

[24] This principle here is involved in the form expressed by St. Thomas in *In IV Sent.* d. 17, q. 1, a. 5, qc. 3: "The ultimate disposition is the effect of the form from the perspective of formal causality; however, the ultimate disposition precedes the form from the perspective of material causality." The psychological impression received by the senses is the *ultimate disposition* to their immanent, vital, and assimilative action; it is the effect of that action in the order of formal, efficient, and final causality, although it precedes it in the order of material causality. See *In IV Sent.* d. 17, q. 1, a. 5, qc. 3: "Form, end, and agent fall into the same number or species."

* * *

The principle of the reciprocal influence of causes is also quite clearly applied in the relations that we find between intellectual knowledge and sense knowledge. Given that *our intellect*, united to the body, is (as we have seen) the least of all intellects, it *has for its proper object the least of all intelligible things*, i.e., the intelligible being of sensible things. This is why it needs to be united to the senses.[25] Hence, it follows that *our intellect materially depends upon the senses but formally it judges them.* In other words, it receives from them the *matter* of knowledge [*science*]; its light abstracts from sensible things the very notions of the first, universal and necessary principles. However, then, by means of these principles, *it formally judges* concerning the value of sensation. It sees in its superior light that there can be no sensation without a sensed object,[26] without an objective, efficient cause, and without finality.

Also, as St. Thomas says at the close of *ST* I, q. 84 a. 6: "It cannot be said that sensible cognition is the total and perfect cause of intellectual cognition; rather, it is in a way the matter of the cause [lit. *materia causae*]."[27] Sensation is not the total cause of intellection; rather, it provides the "matter of the cause" inasmuch as it furnishes the matter of knowledge under the natural light of the intellect, called the "agent intellect" by Aristotle and St. Thomas.

This mutual dependence of the intellect and the senses exists from the first judgment that we bring to bear upon bodies. Our intellect receives from the senses, under the light of the agent intellect, the idea of *being* and of substantial being (which is something sensible *per accidens* and intelligible *per se*). Then, it judges the value of the senses which furnish it with the matter of knowledge. *Causae ad invicem sunt causae in diverso genere.* There is a mutual dependence of causes without a vicious[28] circle, just like what we find between matter and form. Thus,

---

[25] See *ST* I, q. 76, a. 5.

[26] [Tr. note: See Reginald Garrigou-Lagrange, "There Cannot Be Genuine Sensation Without a Real Sensed Thing," in *Philosophizing in Faith*, 101–119.]

[27] [Tr. note: On this, see note 24 in chapter four in this section.]

[28] [Tr. note: Reading "vicieux" for "vivieux."]

as we have said, matter receives and limits the form by which it is actuated and determined.

Applications in the Moral Order

There are two applications that we should especially note, one related to the foundation of moral obligation and the other related to the mutual dependence of the intellect and the will on each other in choice (or, free election).

As St. Thomas remarks on the topic in *ST* I-II, q. 94, a. 2, *moral obligation* is founded upon the principle of finality, "Every agent must act for an end," and upon this corollary of the principle of finality, "The order or subordination of agents (or of those who rule [*dirigeants*]) *corresponds to the subordination of ends.*" The *rule* would not direct us and would not obligate us if there were no *end* to attain; and, on the other hand, there would be no end that ought to be attained if there were no *rule* directing us and obligating us. Thus, right reason is, in us, *the proximate rule* of the will[29] when it declares, not only by manifesting the good but also by commanding it, "*bonum est faciendum et malum vitandum;* the good must be done and evil avoided." What good must be done? *The fitting good,* superior to the useful and to the pleasing good—the fitting good to which our faculties are essentially ordered: to live according to right reason, to love truth and virtue, even if the agent must die for their sake.

Above right reason, the Eternal Law, which is in God, is the *ultimate rule* of the will, when it commands, "*The ultimate good must be loved above all else.*"[30] Thus, the proximate rule is subordinated to the ultimate rule inasmuch as the order of agents (or of rulers [*dirigeants*]) corresponds to the subordination of ends.[31]

In other words, man must tend to the end for which he was made by the Author of his nature. Thus, the foundation of obligation can be

---

[29] [Tr. note: See note 35 in the fourth chapter of the first section above.]

[30] See *ST* I-II, q. 19, aa. 3 and 4.

[31] See *ST* I-II, q. 109, a. 6.

considered either from the perspective of the end or from the perspective of the rule (and, indeed, the double rule, i.e., the proximate and ultimate rules).

For the same reason, because the subordination of agents corresponds to the subordination of ends, there must be *help from God*, the Supreme Agent, in order to tend efficaciously to the ultimate end, even the natural, ultimate end (i.e., God, Author of our nature, as naturally knowable). And for all the more reason is help needed in order to tend to the supernatural ultimate end (i.e., God, the Author of grace, seen face to face and loved above all things).[32]

* * *

Another application of our principle concerns the *relations between the intellect and the will,* at the terminus of deliberation, *in free election.* This is a problem posed not only in the case of man but also in the angel and, analogically, in God.

St. Thomas spoke often about the mutual influence of our two superior faculties on each other, inasmuch as the intellect moves the will *quoad specificationem,* i.e., with regard to the specification of its act by proposing to it the good from the perspective of the true (i.e., a true good), and the will reciprocally moves the intellect *quoad exercitium,* that is, with regard to the exercise of its act, inasmuch as the true (the object of the intellect) is a kind of *good* (the object of the will).[33]

From this it follows that at the end of deliberation, the *last practical judgment directs free election* (or, voluntary choice), but *the free will is what makes it be the case that a given practical judgment is the last,* instead of leading the intellect to prolong the investigation or deliberation. Indeed, the object proposed by this last judgment is a particular good, which is good from one given perspective while not from another, therefore consequently being unable to invincibly attract our choice.[34]

---

[32] See *ST* I-II, q. 109, a. 6.

[33] See *ST* I, q. 82, a. 4, ad 1. Also, see the entry no. 222 for the word *intellectus* in the *Tabula Aurea* of Peter of Bergamo.

[34] *ST* I-II, q. 10, a. 2.

This doctrine is found among the twenty-first of the twenty-four theses proposed under Pius X by the Sacred Congregation of Studies as the expression of St. Thomas's doctrine.

Many Thomists, like the Carmelites of Salamanca,[35] explain this mutual dependence of the intellect and the will in the following way: "The ultimate practical judgment, emitted at *the same instant* as the free election, *precedes it in the order of formal or directive causality,* but the judgment follows the election *in the order of efficient causality,*" at least inasmuch as the will *freely accepts this direction.* If the free will did not accept this direction, it would apply the intellect to form another judgment, and the judgment of which we were just speaking would not be the ultimate judgment. In the same text, the Carmelites of Salamanca add, "The efficient cause *is prior, simply speaking,* to the material and formal cause *in their act of causation.*"[36] Thus, in the present case, the free will, by choosing, makes it be the case that the ultimate practical judgment is the ultimate one and *actually directs* the will, which accepts this direction.[37]

As the artist by his will uses his *idea* to direct his will and action, so too does the free agent by his election use his last judgment to direct his election. *Causae ad invicem sunt causae, sed in diverso genere.* We are not faced here with a contradiction, nor with a vicious circle, but, rather, with the influence of the two superior faculties upon one another. In brief: the free will, beginning to choose, accepts the direction of the last practical judgment and thus makes it be the last judgment that actually directs the will.

Similarly, we are faced here with the mutual relation between the agent and the end. Indeed, our will would not act, nor would it actually tend toward a given good, if it were not attracted by it; and, on the

---

[35] [Tr. note: Fr. Garrigou-Lagrange cites Salmanticenses, *Cursus theologicus*, vol. 4, *De angelis*, disp. 10, dub. 3, 270. This does not appear to be correct. Instead, the text appears to be, disp. 10, dub. 8, no. 270 on p. 679–680 of 1877 edition of the text from which the next citation is taken. I have followed here Fr. Garrigou-Lagrange's French.]

[36] [Tr. note: Fr. Garrigou-Lagrange has slightly ellipsed the Latin (taking out a reference to the material cause that has been added).]

[37] We have explained this point of doctrine at much greater length in Reginald Garrigou-Lagrange, *God: His Existence and His Nature*, vol. 2, 268ff.

other hand, this good *would not actually attract it* if it *did not actually tend* toward it, at least by an initial desire, which inclines to the free election. Similarly, our will would not choose a given good if it did not attract its choice, and this good would not actually exercise this attraction upon choice if choice did not actually tend toward it.[38]

Applications in the Supernatural Order

First and foremost, our principle holds in different ways in the proposal of revealed mysteries, the objects of faith.

Indeed, we say *that the miracle confirms revealed doctrine and that it is confirmed by it*, without there being a vicious circle, for what is clear in one confirms what is obscure in the other (and vice-versa). Thus, the

---

[38] Thus, in free election, there are three causalities that mutually depend on one another: (1) *the attraction (allicientia)* of the end or of the particular good; (2) *the intellectual direction*; (3) *the efficiency (efficientia aut elicientia)* or the production of the election by the will. The Divine motion transcends these three causalities and actualizes them without violating freedom (*cum sola necessitate consequentiae, non vero consequentis*). These three causalities can be schematically presented under the Divine motion:

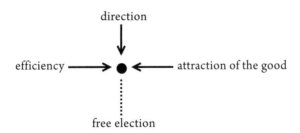

Divine motion

The end remains the first of the causes.

Also, as the Thomists show concerning this matter, it is impossible for the will to be necessitated by the divine motion so long as an indifferent judgment remains in force: *implicat voluntatem, stante iudicio indifferenti* (*circa obiectum non ex omni parte bonum*) *a motione divina necessitari*. [That involves the will being necessitated by the divine motion while an indifferent judgment remains (i.e., one concerning an object that is not good from every perspective).] Indeed, it is impossible that the will should will an object *in a different manner than* how it is proposed to it. See *ST* I-II, q. 10, a. 3, ad 3; also, Aquinas, *De veritate*, q. 22, a. 5. The Divine motion makes the will pass from the state of potential freedom to the state of actual freedom. See ST I, q. 19, a. 8.

Divine origin of revealed doctrine is confirmed by the miracles whose existence is physically certain for their witness and morally certain for those who know of them by way of history. However, on the other hand, the revealed doctrine of the Gospel—inasmuch as it is manifestly conformed to right reason, holy, and is a principle of harmony and peace (despite the obscurity of its dogmas)—confirms that which remains obscure in the miracle, e.g., in the miracle of Jesus' resurrection and in the different narratives in which it has been preserved. Thus, the manifest holiness of the evangelical doctrine is placed among the number of favorable moral circumstances that lead one to accept the narratives concerning Jesus' resurrection. On the contrary, an extraordinary sign performed in order to confirm a prideful and divisive doctrine appears like a false miracle. As the causes are dependent upon one another, the signs mutually confirm one another.

Another application: the intellect knows *the evident credibility* of the mysteries revealed through the external, Divine signs that confirm them. Then, it formally believes these mysteries because of the authority of God, who reveals, *propter auctoritatem Dei revelantis*, and this authority confirms their evident credibility from on high. We are no more faced with a vicious circle here than we are when we consider how the intellect receives from the senses the matter of its consideration and then formally judges the value of sensation in accord with the principles abstracted from sensible things.

Similarly, again, whatever certain Protestants may say about it, Catholics *believe*, without any vicious circle, that the Church is infallible because of the authority of God, who reveals, *propter auctoritatem Dei revelantis*, and on the other hand, *would not infallibly believe* that God has revealed this point of doctrine, *if this were not proposed by the Church*. Why are we not faced here with a vicious circle? Because in the first proposition, it is a question of the *formal motive of faith*, and in the second, it is a question of *its conditio sine qua non*. Now, this motive and this necessary condition depend on one another *from different perspectives*. *Causae ad invicem sunt causae, sed in diverso genere.*

When we say, "Catholics believe that the Church is infallible, *propter auctoritatem Dei revelantis,*" we thereby indicate the formal motive of faith. Then, when we say, "They would not believe infallibly that God has revealed this if it were not proposed by the Church," we then are no longer indicating the formal motive of faith but, instead, are indicating its *conditio sine qua non* from the perspective of the proposition of the object. Furthermore, the value of this infallible proposal, like revelation itself, is confirmed by miracles and other signs in the rational order of evident credibility, which is utterly inferior to the essentially supernatural order to which the act of infused faith belongs.

Thus, the supernatural certitude of faith is *formally* founded on the authority of God who reveals,[39] and *materially* on the evidence of miracles and other signs. Here, we are again faced with a case of the mutual dependence of causes: we believe the mysteries because of the authority of God who has revealed them, but we would not believe that God has revealed them if there were not certain signs of revelation. Moreover, these signs, which of themselves are evident and certain, are confirmed from on high by revelation when the Church, speaking in the name of God who reveals and not only in the name of history and of philosophy, defines:

> If anyone says that *no miracles are possible* and that, therefore, all accounts of them, even those contained in Holy Scripture, are to be dismissed as fables and myths; or *that miracles can never be recognized with certainty* and that the divine origin of the Christian religion cannot be *legitimately proved* by them, let him be anathema.[40]

The miraculous sign disposes reason to accept revelation by infused faith, which is essentially supernatural; then, revelation confirms from on high the probative force of the miracle already naturally known by reason.[41] This represents an application of the same principle which led

---

[39] See *ST* II-II, q. 2, a. 2. Here, St. Thomas shows that by one and the same act we believe in God who reveals and in God revealed. *Uno et eodem actu credimus Deo et Deum.* Likewise, see Cajetan's remarks on *ST* II-II, q. 1, a. 1, no. 11: "Divine revelation is that by which and that which we believe."

[40] [First] Vatican Council, *Dei filius*, canon 3.4 (Denzinger, no. 3034).

[41] Thus, the infused light of faith confirms the judgment of credibility from on high, a judgment that already is rationally certain. Quite ordinarily enough, an actual, preve-

us to say above: in the physical order, at the terminus of substantial generation of, for example, a lamb, the ultimate disposition for the specific
form of the lamb *precedes* this form in the order of material causality
and, at the same instant, *follows it* as a property in the orders of formal,
efficient, and final causality.

* * *

Our principle also explains the mutual relations between the
causes that concur in the *justification* or conversion of the sinner and,
conversely, in the causes that bring about *the loss of grace.*

Indeed, as St. Thomas says in *ST* I-II, q. 113, a. 8, ad 1:[42]

> According to a priority (not of time but of nature) the sun illu-
> minates the air before removing the darkness, whereas the air
> ceases to be dark before being illuminated, even though this
> happens at the same instant. It is the same with the infusion
> of grace and with the remission of sin. They are effects of God
> who justifies; likewise, *the infusion of grace precedes the remis-
> sion of sin* (again, according to a priority of nature but not of
> time). However, if one considers things from the perspective
> of man, the opposite is the case, for according to a priority of
> nature, *man is delivered from sin before receiving sanctifying grace,*
> even though this happens at the same instant.

This is obviously in agreement with the explanation that we have
given of the principle of the mutual dependence of causes (i.e., the
principle of their reciprocal priority from different perspectives). It
remains the case that *the infusion of grace,* being the work of God and

---

nient grace helps us to reach a judgment of certain credibility. However, this grace is
not absolutely necessary for reaching it, and there can even be, with a great resistance
to grace, full awareness of the obligation to believe, as in the sin against the Holy
Spirit.

[42] [Tr. note: As has occurred earlier in this chapter, Fr. Garrigou-Lagrange makes small
changes to Aquinas's text (presumably for the sake of clarity). In this passage, I have
chosen to follow his translation.]

not that of man, *purely and simply* precedes the remission of sin.

This principle, invoked by St. Thomas for explaining the conversion of the sinner, is applied in the opposite manner in the case of the *loss of sanctifying grace; eadem est ratio contrariorum*—contraries obey the same law in virtue of which a given quality like heat or light is here present and there absent. How does the principle of the mutual priority of causes apply in the *opposite* sense to the loss of grace? As the Council of Trent says, "*Deus non deserit iustificatos, nisi ab eis prius deseratur.*"[43] God does not abandon the just unless He is first abandoned by them. Why? Because, far from arising from God like justification, *sin as such comes from a deficient cause*; consequently, even in the first sin, *the virtually voluntary non-consideration of the duty* to be accomplished *purely and simply precedes the Divine refusal of efficacious grace* necessary for the accomplishment of the work, although this occurs at the same instant.[44] St. Thomas spoke of this voluntary non-consideration of duty [or, of the rule of morals] when discussing the Angel's sin.[45] Through this non-consideration, the created will abandons God before God abandons it by refusing His efficacious grace to it. This Divine refusal is a penalty that presupposes at least an initial fault. It is only the *Divine permission* that is the condition for sin's possibility, but it is in no way its cause, for it influences it neither directly nor indirectly. God can allow the failure of a creature that of itself is capable of failure. He is not *required* to prevent it from failing, and if He permits this failure, He does so in view of a superior good of which His infinite wisdom is

---

43 Trent, Decree on Justification, chap. 11 (Denzinger, no. 1537). [Tr. note: Fr. Garrigou-Lagrange incorrectly has Denzinger, no. 806. In his edition, it would have been no. 804. The quote is taken from Augustine, *De natura et gratia* 43, no. 50. The text from the Tridentine decree is slightly different, though the sense is the same. It reads, "*Deus namque sua gratia semel iustificatos 'non deserit, nisi ab eis prius deseratur.'"*]

44 [Tr. note: On this subject, the reader would benefit much from the reflections undertaken by Maritain on the topic. See Jacques Maritain, *God and the Permission of Evil*, trans. Joseph Evans (Milwaukee: Bruce, 1966). Written late in his life, this work mentions Fr. Garrigou-Lagrange's works (*Predestination* and *Providence*) on the problem of evil and predestination with warm praise.]

45 See *ST* I, q. 63, a. 1, ad 4. [Tr. note: On this topic, even if the reader does not agree with Maritain, much insight would be gained by pondering the matters explained in Jacques Maritain, *The Sin of the Angel*, trans. William L. Rossner (Westminster, MD: The Newman Press, 1959).]

the judge. In this way, we can see the difference that exists between the *Divine subtraction* of grace and the *simple permission* of sin. The Divine permission of the first sin is in no way a penalty, whereas the Divine subtraction of grace is a penalty presupposing at least an initial fault. Thus, it is true to say that God does not abandon the just by the subtraction of Divine grace unless He is abandoned by them. Thus, the loss of sanctifying grace always presupposes mortal sin.[46]

* * *

St. Thomas noted another application of our principle in connection with predestination:

> *Nothing prevents one effect of predestination from being the cause of or reason for another*; a later effect is the final cause of the preceding ones, and the preceding effects are the dispositive causes, as if we were to say, "God decided from all eternity *to give glory to a given man on account of his merits*," and, "He decided to give him grace in order that he merit glory."[47] However, one can also consider *the whole effect* of predestination, and it is impossible that the whole effect of predestination, considered in general, have a cause in us, for *everything that* orders man to salvation is understood as being entirely under the effect of predestination, even the preparation for grace, according to these words from *Lamentations* 5:21: "Convert us to You, O Lord, and we will be converted."[48]

---

[46] We have examined this point at greater length elsewhere. See Garrigou-Lagrange, *God: His Existence and His Nature*, vol. 2, 371–374.

[47] Thus, wishing to save the good thief rather than the other, God decided to give him at the last moment grace so as to make him merit, and then gave him glory on account of his merit. In this way the gratuity of predestination in the order of intention is safeguarded as well as, against the Protestants, the necessity of good works for adults in the order of execution.

[48] *ST* I, q. 23, a. 5. "*Quidquid est in homine ordinans ipsum ad salutem comprehenditur totum sub effectu praedestinationis.*" *Quidquid* (whatever), even the free determination of our salvific acts; God produces it in us and with us, for He produces everything, up to the *free mode* of our acts, up to their actual, dominating indifference,

Thus, as many theologians say, "God *freely wills* to give glory to His elect in the order of intention but does not will to *give it freely* to them in the order of execution." *Freely* has a different sense depending on whether it falls upon "wills" in the order of intention or the "to give" in the order of execution.

This application of our principle is suggested by Scripture itself. One reads in Zechariah, "Return to me, and I will return to you, says the LORD of hosts," when he exhorts the sinner to not resist prevenient grace and to thus dispose himself to habitual grace. On the other hand, Jeremiah says, as we have seen in Lamentations 5:21, "Convert us to You, O Lord, and we will be converted," for even the preparation for grace, as we just saw in St. Thomas's own words, is an effect of actual prevenient grace and an effect of predestination in the elect.

Let us note that, in virtue of the principle of finality, "Every agent acts for an end and only wills the means for the sake of the end," eternal predestination to glory must precede predestination to grace and to merits *in signo priori*.[49] Indeed, like every intelligent agent, God wills the end before the means. The end is first in the order of intention and last in the order of execution.[50]

Consequently, predestination to glory is gratuitous. This doctrine rests on the principle of predilection formulated by St. Paul: "What do you have that you have not received" (1 Cor 4:7, RSV). St. Thomas formulates this by explaining the reason for its truth: "Since the love of God is the cause of the goodness of things, one thing would not be *better* than another if God did not will a greater good to the one than to the other."[51] If one reflects on this principle, one will see that it virtually

---

which is still something in the domain of being. Far from thus destroying freedom in us, He actualizes it; He makes it pass from the state of potential freedom to the state of actual freedom. See *ST* I, q. 19, a. 8.

    [Tr. note: In the main selection from Aquinas, I have had an eye to Fr. Garrigou-Lagrange's rendering, which is faithful to the original.]

[49] Without a doubt, there are not two really distinct and successive acts in God and in the unique instant of immobile eternity. Instead, there is one and the same act that contains a virtual, ordered multiplicity. As St. Thomas says in *ST* I, q. 19, a. 5: "God wills this to be on account of that, but He does not will this on account of that."

[50] See *ST* I, q. 23, a. 4

[51] *ST* I, q. 20, a. 3.

contains[52] the entire treatise on grace and that on predestination. On the other hand, it is true that God never commands the impossible and renders salvation possible for all. The intimate reconciliation of these two principles is one of the most impenetrable mysteries. As certain as each is when taken by itself, so too is their intimate union mysterious. Indeed, it is one of revelation's most captivating *chiaroscuros*. Here, we must elevate ourselves above theological reasoning; there is no rest except by the simple act of contemplation, in the obscurity of faith. The principle of the mutual dependence of causes cannot give light here; it only enables us to avoid contradiction.

* * *

Finally, let us note one last application that touches on *the motive of the Incarnation* and *the predestination of Christ* prior to every other person. It represents the explanation of these words of the Creed relative to the Son of God, "For us men and for our salvation He came down from heaven, and was incarnate by the Holy Spirit."[53]

According to the doctrine exposited by St. Thomas in *ST* III, q. 1, a. 3c and ad 3, we must consider two things. On the one hand, "If sin had not existed, the Word would not have become incarnate," as he says in the body of the article. Thus, the motive of the Incarnation is formally a *motive of mercy*: God came to us in order to raise us from our misery. On the other hand, St. Thomas adds in ST III, q. 1, a. 3c, ad 3:

> Nothing prevents it from being the case that human nature could have been led to something greater after sin, for God only permits evils to happen *in order to draw a much greater good from them*. As St. Paul says in Romans 5:20: "Where sin increased, grace abounded all the more." So too do we sing during the blessing of the Paschal candle, "O happy fault, that

---

[52] [Tr. note: That is, implicitly contains all of the conclusions to be drawn in said treatise.]

[53] [Tr. note: I have taken this text directly from the approved English-language liturgical translation of the Nicene-Constantinopolitan Creed.]

merited so great and glorious a Redeemer!"[54]

As many Thomists—like Pedro de Godoy (1599–1677), the Salamanca Carmelites,[55] and Jean Baptiste Gonet (c. 1616–1681)—very justly say:

> By one and the same act, and at one and the same instant, God decreed the existence of the world, permitted the sin of the first man, and willed Christ as the Redeemer and as the *end* of all the Divine works. Thus is verified the principle *causae ad invicem sunt causae*, for although Christ depends on sin and on the redemption of humanity as the material to be perfected (*tanquam a causa materiali perficienda*) and although in this order of material causality sin precedes Christ, nonetheless, the redemption depends on Christ as its end and perfecting agent (*tanquam a fine et a perficiente*) and, in this order of final and perfective causality, Christ precedes the redemption; and it is for Christ (in view of this superior good of the redemptive incarnation) that original sin was permitted by God. Thus, sin and the Incarnation depend on one another from different perspectives.[56]

Do we not have here the most profound of explanations for the words of St. Paul, "Where sin increased, grace abounded all the more"? And why did God permit the fault if not so that grace may superabound? He could permit evil only for a greater good.

This explanation does not contain any vicious circle. It is immediately derived from the principle of the mutual dependence of causes. Christ is the first of the predestined, but He has been predestined by God as the Redeemer of the human race to be redeemed,[57] and He depends on it *only in the order of material causality*. Thus, the form

---

[54] Also, see *ST* III, q. 24 and q. 46, a.1, ad 3; *ST* I, q. 20, a. 4, ad 1.

[55] See Salmanticenses, *Cursus theologicus*, vol. 13, *De incarnatione*, disp. 2, no. 29 (p. 291–292).

[56] [Tr. note: I am following Fr. Garrigou-Lagrange's French text.]

[57] See *ST* III, q. 23, a. 4, ad 3.

is willed by God to actuate or determine its matter, and matter to be actuated by it; however, the form is, properly speaking, the end of the matter, whereas, if we are to speak truly, matter is not the end of the form—*materia est proprie propter formam; non vero forma est proprie propter materiam.*

God could not here and now create this human soul if there were not a body disposed by way of generation to receive it; however, *the body exists for the soul, more than the soul for the body.* Similarly, *God would not have willed the Incarnation* of His Son *if there had not been a human race to be saved,* but *men exist for Christ,* the first of the predestined, more than Christ exists for them. In the doctrine of St. Thomas concerning the relations of the Incarnation and the Redemption, the words of St. Paul thus remain perfectly true, *"For all things are yours . . .; and you are Christ's; and Christ is God's"* (1 Cor 3:21–23, RSV).

On the one hand, God only permitted original sin in view of a much greater good, and we see *post factum* that this much greater good is the Redemptive Incarnation. On the other hand, God willed Christ as the Redeemer, as the conqueror over sin, over the devil, and over death.[58]

All of this is a simple application of our principle concerning the mutual priority of causes. Thus, God, willing matter as actualizable and perfectible by form and form as actuating and determining the matter, the form has priority in its own genus of causality and matter in its, without there being any vicious circle.

Thus, the principle of the mutual dependence of causes, *causae ad invicem sunt causae,* is quite clearly applied everywhere where we find the four causes. It is subordinated to the principle of finality inasmuch as the end is the first of the causes. It represents one of its most beautiful and fruitful corollaries.

Everywhere the four causes are involved, the form determines the matter (or the subject) that receives and limits it, and the end attracts the agent that realizes or obtains it. Many difficulties that at first sight seem insoluble are resolved by this. This is a manifest sign that this

---

[58] It remains the case that our salvation is the reason for the Incarnation—in the sense that *ratio miserandi est miseria sublevanda,* as St. Thomas explains well in *ST* II-II, q. 30, a. 2. The misery to be relieved is the reason for mercy, which is the highest manifestation of God's goodness and omnipotence.

principle, and that of finality of which it is the corollary, express a foundational law, not only of the intellect but of reality, a law that radiates over every order from brute matter all the way up to the order of pure spirit and even to the order of grace. It is a law that sets before our consideration, in the harmony of these different orders, a reflection of the perfection of God, the First Cause and Last End. If *wisdom* (i.e., the highest of sciences) is knowledge of things through their loftiest cause, and if the end is the first cause, the principle of finality is indeed one of the loftiest principles of the loftiest of the sciences. We now more clearly see the virtualities that it contains and the immense regions of the intelligible world that it illuminates. They can all be embraced, by fixing our gaze upon its formula: *"Every being acts for an end,"* from the grain of sand, which tends to the center of the earth for the cohesion of the universe, all the way to God, Who does all that He does for the manifestation of His Goodness.

INDEX

Abstraction, 186, 189–190
    degrees of, 240–245
    subalternation and, 243
Agnosticism, 206–223
Allegory of the Cave, 23
Analogy,
    in relation to the question of realism, 210
    involving use of negative and relative knowledge, 187
    proper proportionality, 102
    summary and contrast with opposed, 214–224
Anaxagoras, 33
Anderson, James, 102n19
St. Anselm of Canterbury, 30n18
Antimodernist Oath, 65
a priori vs. *a posteriori*, 41n1
Arintero, Juan, 318
Aristotle, *passim*
    presents meaning of principle of [non-]contradiction as central to
        metaphysics, 77–78, 148ff
    noting limitations of Aristotle's metaphysics as regards notion of
        providence, 33
    on induction, 122n1
Atomism, 37
St. Augustine, 7, 67, 87, 186, 256
Avicenna, 201, 233

Báñez, Domingo, 313n65
Bautain, Louis-Eugene-Marie, 304

Histories of Philosophy, great and minor philosophical minds mixed
together in, 7, 162n31, 163n34
Hochschild, Joshua P., 102n19
Huby, Joseph, xxx, 287–319
Hugon, Édouard, 41n1, 230
Hume, David, 8, 207

Idealism, 149–157, 162–170, 179, 198, 207–208, 288
Individuality, distinct from personality, 328–329
Innocent XI, 301
Intellect
agent, 186
and knowledge of singulars, 192–193
mutual causality involved in activity, 333–334
proper object as intelligible being of sensible things, 30, 188–192, 333

James, William, 95, 147
Janet, Paul, 96, 98
Jansenism, 290
St. John of the Cross, xix
John of St. Thomas, 113n31, 127n17, 175n9, 178, 181, 243, 279, 302,
313n65, 317n71
St. John Paul II, xv
Jolivet, Régis, 199n40
Jouffroy, Simon, 97

Kant, Immanuel, 7, 8, 41n1, 83, 92, 118, 207, 229
Kantian subjectivism, 122, 146
Klubertanz, George P., 178n14, 184n23, 218
Knowledge
Cognoscens quodammodo fit vel est aliud a se, 246n37
involves union that is closer than that between mater and form, 173
phantasm as objective instrument, 238n24

Labourdette, Michel, xxii
Lachelier, Jules, 53n7, 97, 122